Establishing Religious Freedom

Establishing Religious Freedom

JEFFERSON'S STATUTE IN VIRGINIA

Thomas E. Buckley

UNIVERSITY OF VIRGINIA PRESS

Charlottesville & London

University of Virginia Press
© 2013 by the Rector and Visitors of the University of Virginia
All rights reserved
Printed in the United States of America on acid-free paper
First published 2013

1 3 5 7 9 8 6 4 2

Library of Congress Cataloging-in-Publication Data
Buckley, Thomas E., 1939–
Establishing religious freedom : Jefferson's statute in
Virginia / Thomas E. Buckley.
pages cm
Includes bibliographical references and index.
ISBN 978-0-8139-3503-4 (cloth : alk. paper) —
ISBN 978-0-8139-3504-1 (e-book)
1. Freedom of religion—Virginia—History. 2. Virginia.
Act for establishing religious freedom. I. Title.
KFV2812.R45B83 2013
342.75508'52—dc23
2013023502

Frontispiece: Portrait of Thomas Jefferson (1743–1826) by Mather Brown, 1786, the
year Jefferson's statute became law in Virginia. Oil on canvas, 90.8 x 72.4 cm.
Bequest of Charles Francis Adams. (National Portrait Gallery,
Smithsonian Institution/Art Resource, NY)

For Mike—my brother
three times over

Contents

Illustrations

Acknowledgments

This study began forty years ago in a graduate history seminar taught by Morton Borden at the University of California at Santa Barbara. For his wise direction and supportive friendship I remain deeply grateful. A seminar paper on the passage of Jefferson's statute developed into a doctoral dissertation and a first book. I then set to work trying to understand what the statute meant for Virginians and how they resolved their church-state issues. A succession of essays and talks followed with digressions to write a book on legislative divorce and to edit a volume of courtship letters, both of which were spin-offs from this project.

In one way or another, every scholarly effort is a shared enterprise. Over the years so many fellow historians and academic colleagues have offered suggestions and generously critiqued my work that I am afraid to mention names lest I leave someone out. Yet I want to acknowledge the assistance and friendship of Rick Beeman, Warren Billings, Ed Bond, Pat Bonomi, Bob Calhoun, Julie Campbell, Daniel Driesbach, Mel Ely, Sally Gordon, Mark Hall, Jim Hutson, Cindy Kierner, Anne Klejment, John Kneebone, Jon Kukla, Leonard Levy, Jeff Looney, Don Mathews, Mike McGiffert, Susan Miller, Bill Shade, Jewel Spangler, Jim Sweeney, Sandy Treadway, John Witte, Mark Valeri, and John Wilson. My faculty colleagues, first at Loyola Marymount University and later at the Jesuit School of Theology at Berkeley, gave me wise counsel on various essays and chapters as they were being developed, and I'm especially grateful to Joseph Tiedemann and Jerome Baggett. In their final stages Thad Tate carefully corrected the chapters dealing with the colonial and Revolutionary periods. From the outset of this enterprise decades ago, Brent Tarter has been a bulwark of support for me as he has been for so many students of Virginia history who beat a path to the Library of Virginia. Brent suggested avenues of exploration, dug out materials for my inspection, and read each chapter critically with liberal doses of solid advice and encouragement.

Many librarians and archivists have been of invaluable assistance, but among the fine staffs at all the archives and libraries where I have worked, I want to acknowledge in particular the help of Frances Pollard and Lee Shepard at the Virginia Historical Society, Barbara Batson, John Deal, Gregg Kimball, Minor Weisinger, and the late Sara Bearss at the Library of Virginia, Margaret Cook at the Swem Library at the College of William and Mary, Grace Zell at the Beth Ahabah Archives and Museum, Fred Anderson at the Virginia Baptist Historical Society, and Julie Randall at the Virginia Theological Seminary. For solid assistance in the book's final stages I want to thank Matthew Carroll, my research assistant in my concluding years at the Jesuit School of Theology of Santa Clara University, Caisen Mirassou, my current research assistant at Loyola Marymount University, and Susan Foard, for her meticulous copyediting.

In Richmond I have made my home away from home at St. Bridget's Parish where wonderful parishioners and a succession of fine pastors—Bill Sullivan, Tom Miller, and Bill Carr—have graciously welcomed me for many summers. In northern Virginia Peg and Steve O'Brien repeatedly opened their home to me, and I am grateful for their friendship. Most of all, for fifty-five years I have been enormously blessed with fine companions in the Society of Jesus who gently change the topic of conversation when I get on a Virginia roll.

Over the years Mellon Research Grants from the Virginia Historical Society and summer travel grants from Loyola Marymount University and the Graduate Theological Union supported my research, while a Lilly Faculty Fellowship for the year 1999–2000 from the Association of Theological Schools, the Bannon Chair at Santa Clara in 1995–96, and the Gasson Chair at Boston College in 2010–11 provided time for writing.

This study of Jefferson's statute has been a long time in coming, and I have drawn upon and in some cases corrected previous work published along the way. Ideas and parts of various chapters have appeared earlier in the following essays: "Evangelicals Triumphant: The Baptists' Assault on the Virginia Glebes, 1786–1801," *William and Mary Quarterly*, 3d ser., 45 (1988): 33–69; "After Disestablishment: Thomas Jefferson's Wall of Separation in Antebellum Virginia," *Journal of Southern History* 61 (1995): 445–80; "The Use and Abuse of Jefferson's Statute: Separating Church and State in Nineteenth Century Virginia," in *Religion and the Founding of the Republic*, ed. James H. Hutson (Lanham, MD, 1999), 41–64; "'A Great Religious Octopus': Church and State at Virginia's Constitutional Convention, 1901–1902," *Church History* 72 (2003): 333–60, Copyright © 2003 American Society of Church History, reprinted with the permission of Cambridge University Press; "Patrick Henry, Religious Liberty, and the Search for Civic Virtue," in *The Forgotten Founders on Religion and Public Life*, ed. Daniel L. Dreisbach, Mark David Hall, and Jeffrey H. Morrison (Notre Dame, IN, 2009), 125–44, Copyright © 2009 by University of Notre Dame, Notre Dame, IN 46556; "Placing Thomas Jefferson and Religion in Context, Then and Now," in *Seeing Jefferson Anew: In His Time and Ours*, ed. John B. Boles and Randal L. Hall (Charlottesville, 2010), 126–51; and "Establishing New Bases for Religious Authority," in *From Jamestown to Jefferson: The Evolution of Religious Freedom in Virginia*, ed. Paul B. Rasor and Richard Bond (Charlottesville, 2011), 138–65.

Throughout my life my brother Mike has been all one could wish for in a brother. As he celebrates his fiftieth year as a Jesuit priest, this book is for him.

Establishing Religious Freedom

INTRODUCTION

More than two hundred years ago Thomas Jefferson composed the most significant letter in the history of American church-state jurisprudence. Writing to the Danbury Baptist Association in Connecticut in 1802, the president stated that the First Amendment to the U.S. Constitution had created "a wall of separation between Church and State."[1] Jefferson's judgment bore added weight because during the Revolution he had crafted Virginia's "Statute for establishing religious freedom." That law offered the most sweeping guarantees of the rights of conscience approved by any state in the new nation. Its author was so proud of his composition that he ordered its title inscribed on his tombstone. Approved by the legislature early in 1786, Jefferson's statute resolved a decade-long dispute about the kind of support that state government might afford religion in the Old Dominion.[2]

The Church of England had been established by law in the Virginia colony almost from the outset of its settlement in 1607. The colonial government set up Anglican parishes with their lay vestries, ensured their financial support by taxes or tithes, required the inhabitants to attend Sunday worship on a regular basis, set fees for ministerial duties, and severely restricted the activities of dissenter or non-Anglican clergy and congregations. For over a century, first Quakers, then Presbyterians, and finally Baptists struggled to obtain some measure of religious toleration against the strongest church establishment in the British colonial world. Then the Revolution produced a language of political freedom founded on the rights of conscience that directly contradicted the very idea of an establishment of religion. Virginia's political independence eased the dissenters' position substantially, and Jefferson's statute seemingly ended governmental oversight and control by "establishing religious freedom." One kind of religious establishment had given way to another that appeared to be its opposite in law.[3]

Seizing upon the language in Jefferson's letter to the Danbury Baptists, Virginians later claimed that this new situation of religious freedom required the absolute separation of church and state. With Jefferson and James Madison looking over their shoulders, Virginia's leaders conscientiously set out to construct their "wall of separation." In this effort the Old Dominion's government possessed a level of authority no state holds today. Because the First Amendment's religion clause did not apply to the states until the 1940s, Virginia provided much greater scope for legislative activity and judicial interpretation in the church-state arena than the federal government. But dissolving the innumerable links between religion and government proved much more complicated than anyone had anticipated. Indeed, the two founders were still congratulating themselves over the benefits the law conferred on both state and church when Virginians began to demonstrate the formidable problems inherent in what Madison styled "total separation."[4] Ironically, their struggle to achieve separation curtailed the very religious freedom they sought to establish. Giving up state control over the churches and religion took more than a century. In the process the rigidity with which the statute was applied in the first half of the nineteenth century was mitigated as the lay elites who governed the state discovered that a consistent policy of absolute separation threatened another key value: their evangelical vision of Virginia as a Christian commonwealth. The history of their efforts to write religious freedom into law and the contest between separation and evangelicalism that followed upon the passage of Jefferson's statute provide the subject of this book. The principal focus is on the four major denominations of Anglicans/Episcopalians, Presbyterians, Baptists, and Methodists and the sometimes supportive, sometimes oppositional relationship they maintained with Virginia's political, judicial, and educational leadership.

It is a Virginia story, but with national import. Although, as John Wilson has recently reiterated, the state's experience in no way provided a blueprint for the nation, the statute's impact has been felt across America, chiefly because of the uses the U.S. Supreme Court has made of it.[5] In the court's initial interpretive foray into the First Amendment's religion clause, *Reynolds v. United States* (1878), Chief Justice Morrison Waite, urged on by his friend the historian George Bancroft, quoted approvingly from the documents of the Virginia contest surrounding the statute's passage and Jefferson's letter to the Danbury Baptists. But as Donald Drakeman has explained, Waite's decision was problematic on several counts. Relying on denominational historians of the Virginia event but ignoring the crucial roles they ascribed to the evangelical Baptists and Presbyterians, the chief justice credited the statute's passage exclusively to Madison and Jefferson. He also overlooked the varying perspectives on church and state within the broader context of the new republic where various states chose alternatives to the Virginia model.[6] Massachusetts and Connecticut, for example, opted for public tax support for the churches.[7] Waite's opinion linked the statute to the First Amendment approved by Congress a few years later but said nothing about the debates surrounding the latter's formulation and approval. Finally, the chief justice skipped other sources of judicial interpretation that clashed with his own viewpoint, including the treatises of earlier justices, most notably Joseph Story's *Commentaries on the Constitution*, which argued that Christianity was part of the common law.[8]

However flawed, Waite's judicial opinion in *Reynolds* plotted an interpretive course that subsequent courts followed. In the 1947 *Everson* case that nationalized the establishment clause, Justice Hugo Black returned to the story of the Virginia statute and Jefferson's language to the Danbury Baptists to declare: "The First Amendment has erected a wall between church and state. That wall must be kept high and impregnable." The dissenting opinions in that case reinforced Black's approach. "No provision of the Constitution," wrote Justice Wiley Rutledge, "is more closely tied to or given content by its generating history than the religious clause of the First Amendment." He also emphasized Virginia's experience and the writings of Jefferson and Madison as definitive.[9]

What all these justices ignored, however, was the complicated historical background to the passage of the statute and its subsequent interpretation and lived experience in Virginia. Quickly taking on the character of sacred writ, Jefferson's handiwork became by 1800 the sole authority in the Old Dominion for determining the proper church-state relationship even before its incorporation into the state constitution thirty years later.

The larger historical context is crucial. This book begins with an examination of the nature and extent of the church establishment the colony possessed practically from its foundation at Jamestown in 1607. A century and a half later, a series of revolutionary events transformed Virginia from a bulwark of the established Church of England with only a grudging and restrictive toleration for religious dissenters to a position of relatively complete religious freedom for all citizens in an independent state. The first four chapters examine this complicated politico-religious development and the turmoil that surrounded the passage of the statute shortly after the Revolution.

The final decades of the religious establishment also marked the emergence of the dissenters, mainly Baptists and Presbyterians, as important participants in the political arena. By the early years of the nineteenth century, their evangelical ranks swelled with the inclusion first of the Methodists, who had separated from the former Church of England in 1784, and in the early nineteenth century with the members of that church who by then styled themselves Episcopalians. Together with a few smaller denominations, these evangelicals strove to transform nineteenth-century Virginia into a fervently Protestant society that would be part of America's evangelical empire. Unlike the situation in other states, however, the churches in Virginia faced major obstacles that arose legally from Jefferson's statute and emotionally from a broad-based commitment to the separation of church and state.[10]

Chapters 5 through 8 explore the growth of the evangelical churches and the problems they encountered in their attempts to foster a culture supportive of their religious faith. Their difficulties revolved around such issues as the ownership of church property, the appointment of legislative chaplains, the protection of religious services, the legal status of the clergy, legislation in matters such as divorce, the incorporation of churches, church schools, and religious organizations, and the proper role for religion in public education. Conflicting perspectives pitted churches against one another, inflamed legislative and state constitutional debates, and engaged the state court system for more than a century and a half.

At the opening of the twentieth century, a constitutional convention debated neuralgic points within the church-state relationship and resolutely clung to the past. Then, for the next three decades Virginians argued about requiring Bible reading in the public schools, prohibiting alcoholic beverages, maintaining Sunday closing laws, and other measures designed to preserve and enhance a Christian commonwealth as they conceived it. Virginia's religious flavor was evangelical Protestant, and the electoral repudiation in 1928 of the Democratic candidate, Al Smith, a Catholic and a "wet," moved the state into the Republican column for the first time since Reconstruction. The last two chapters study the convention of 1901 and the Bible wars and moral reform efforts that followed it. Only the Great Depression that came on the heels of Smith's defeat turned Virginia's focus away from evangelical politics and back to economics. Finally the U.S. Supreme Court definitively assumed jurisdiction in the 1940s when its *Cantwell*[11] and *Everson* decisions nationalized the religious clause of the First Amendment, thus superseding the state constitution. Since then the ultimate authority on religious liberty and church-state issues is lodged in the federal courts and out of the hands of Virginia's jurists.

The sharply divergent opinions that surfaced periodically starting with the Great Awakening before the Revolution demonstrate the close relationship between legal-constitutional development and the socioreligious values of a society. They also anticipated the discussions about church and state in America today. The meaning of expansive ideas such as religious freedom, equality, and church-state separation can only be known within their historical contexts. A study of the statute from the colonial period into the twentieth century reminds us that its text was never fixed. Rather, through press and public debate, the formulation of laws, judicial decisions, and constitutional revision, Virginians drew upon Jefferson's work to construct politico-religious, church-state identities for their society, just as Americans do today with the First Amendment.[12] Defining and maintaining religious freedom remains a challenge in every generation, and the subject is deeply controversial.

Given the importance of that controversy, it is surprising that so few historians have chosen to investigate Virginia's long argument over the correct interpretation of the statute. For the Revolutionary era we have important studies, but few of them deal with the entire period from the Great Awakening to 1800. Denominational historians in the nineteenth century produced a bevy of works, some of which were more hagiography than history. At the beginning of the twentieth century, Hamilton James Eckenrode provided a study that remains helpful for the religious petitions he appended to his analysis.[13] Eighty years ago Sadie Bell mined the published materials for a massive dissertation subsequently published as *The Church, the State, and Education in Virginia*.[14] Though the analysis is dated, her study of education provides the best documentary source for that topic up to the First World War. It has been the only work that treats the effect of the statute for almost the entire period it governed the laws in Virginia.

My own legislative history of the statute's passage focused on the Revolutionary War years and their immediate aftermath. Rhys Isaac's social history, which begins with Virginia's Great Awakening, concludes in 1790, thus omitting the church property conflict of the next decade.[15] More recent studies either applaud the freedom of conscience that resulted from the statute as primarily the work of Jefferson and Madison or else give the dissenters the lion's share of the credit.[16] Contemporary examinations of the broader church-state landscape in America offer the requisite paeans to Virginia's leadership but ignore what happened in the state following the Revolutionary era. Steven Green, for example, has proposed as a church-state paradigm a progressive disestablishment that began with a political separation during and after the Revolution. The next phase involved a legal separation in the nineteenth century when the state removed the various props that gave religion a privileged place in society. The twentieth century brought a cultural separation of the churches from civil society. Green's work is deeply learned, but while his scheme may work elsewhere, it does not fit Virginia. He recognizes this implicitly because, like the modern U.S. Supreme Court, Green gives due attention to the Jefferson-Madison period in the Old Dominion but ends his analysis there. The next century and a half of Virginia's church-state dynamic does not fit his model.[17] Nor do the quarrels in the Old Dominion over religion in private as well as public education figure in his analysis of the school question in the nineteenth century.[18]

Philip Hamburger also focused on the nineteenth century in developing his thesis that anti-Catholicism was the driving force behind the separationist interpretation of the First Amendment.[19] That did not apply in Virginia, however, which paid scant attention to its few Catholics until the constitutional convention of 1901. Long before that assemblage met and well over a century before the U.S. Supreme Court justices began assembling their bricks and mortar, Virginians understood their statute in terms of a wall of separation. Thus, for example, they had no need to enact a Blaine Amendment forbidding public funding of church-related schools. Their statute took care of that issue. Embedded in state law and then in the state constitution, Jefferson's work set Virginia on a distinctive trajectory. This book explores that path.

1

Establishment

"True Churchmen for the Most Part"

The Reverend Patrick Henry was outraged. As rector of St. Paul's Church in Hanover County, Virginia, he had dealt with dissenters before—heedless, deluded men and women, generally drawn from the lower ranks in society, who refused to attend his parish services and instead gathered on Sundays to listen to one of their ranting itinerant preachers. He had complained earlier to the commissary, William Dawson, who represented the bishop of London for the Church of England in Virginia. Based in Williamsburg, Dawson had commiserated with Henry, but there was little that either clergyman could do. In increasing numbers people were drawn to "new light" preachers with their "peculiar" beliefs who were multiplying like rabbits throughout the colony, screwing up the common folk to "heights of religious Phrenzy," and then moving on to leave settled Anglican ministers like Henry to cope with the wreckage in their parishes. Now in June 1747 a new itinerant had turned up in Hanover County. Presbyterian minister Samuel Davies had been traveling about setting up preaching stations with "circular Letters and Advertisements" broadcasting his arrival and sermon dates. Lately Davies had even offered the Holy Communion in Hanover for "a great many Communicants." The distraught Anglican rector foresaw a dismal future. One "Enthusiast" after another would come through to siphon off his parishioners, empty out his Sunday services, and leave his parish in shreds.[1]

Henry had never envisioned such a prospect a decade earlier when he first preached at St. Paul's. Then the growing parish possessed two churches and held 1,299 tithables—men and women, whites and blacks, sixteen years of age and older who could be assessed for tax purposes. Because the people had responded well to his sermons, the vestry, which comprised a dozen laymen who managed parish affairs, had offered him the rector's position at the usual annual salary of 16,000 pounds of tobacco. For his glebe, the farmland that supplemented his income, they arranged to purchase a handsome tract of 388 acres called Mount Pleasant from his brother, John Henry. John had facilitated Patrick Henry's transfer to St. Paul's. The two brothers were on close terms, and the clergyman welcomed the opportunity to live near John and his family, which included his young namesake, Patrick Henry Jr. The vestry, which now included John Henry, was solicitous for their new minister's needs. During the next few years they built a barn and laid out a garden on the glebe. They also accepted their rector's plan to construct a brick glebe house, thirty-four feet by twenty-eight feet, at a cost of £220. As the number of Henry's parishioners increased and began to crowd the lower church on Sunday mornings, the vestry added a gallery to the back of the church. Only recently the men had decided to construct two vestry houses for their meetings, at the upper and lower churches respectively.[2]

Clearly the vestrymen took their duties seriously. They hired the minister and oversaw his support and the church buildings and other properties. They also had other responsibilities in the parish including the care of the poor and orphans and processing land boundaries. Together with the county court composed of a varying number of justices of the peace, the vestrymen ran local affairs. Often enough an individual might be a member of both. Historian John Nelson has suggested that colonial Virginia's local government can best be thought of as parish-county. A significant measure of the importance Virginians gave to their parish is that they taxed themselves more heavily for parish concerns than for any other purpose.[3]

The value Virginians placed on religion found expression, from the earliest days of the colony, in a formal religious establishment. They conceived of their society in organic terms. Just as all belonged to a single political entity—the English colony of Virginia governed from Williamsburg—so all should be members of the Church of England, each sitting in his or her proper place in the church on Sunday. Relationships were neatly ordered and hierarchical. Moreover, the church-state relationship was mutually beneficial. The church supported the state by its public worship and by teaching the Christian gospel, the moral law, and the obligations of good subjects of the Crown. The colonial government supported the church by favorable laws, public taxes, and benevolent oversight. Church and state worked together in friendly alliance for the well-being of the whole society.

This was the secure, comfortable world which Parson Henry embraced, and which the growth of religious heterodoxy threatened. Of course the authorities recognized the existence of religious "dissenters," principally Quakers, Presbyterians, and Baptists. But in Virginia before the 1740s, as in England, they comprised a tiny minority of the population, the exception rather than the rule, whose presence necessitated at best a limited toleration.

The Quakers

The Quakers, as members of the Society of Friends were called, formed the first recognizable group of dissenters to appear in the colony. Founded by George Fox in the aftermath of the English Civil Wars, the Quaker faith spread rapidly in England and its overseas colonies. In the vanguard to Virginia came Elizabeth Harris, a "messenger" or traveling Friend from London who arrived in 1655 just a few years after Fox had begun his witness to the Truth. An effective preacher of the Inner Light, Harris "convinced" a number of her hearers on the south side of the James River, and by 1660 there were five distinct groups or meetings of Quakers in the colony.[4]

The colonial government was not pleased. Quakers were no more welcome in seventeenth-century Virginia than in England. Harris left the colony voluntarily, but the authorities locked up Thomas Thruston and Josiah Cole as soon as they arrived in 1657 and quickly deported them to Maryland. Other Quakers, presumably Virginia residents who had joined the nascent sect, were ordered fined and whipped, and the following year the General Court made a concerted effort to suppress the Quakers throughout the colony.[5] But Quaker missionaries persisted in entering Virginia and immediately attracted followers. Today we think of Quakers at meeting as seated in silence, waiting for the Spirit to move one or another to speak. But the founding generation of this new faith was not quiet or reserved at prayer. Staid Virginians had never witnessed anything quite like their emotional worship services, which were marked by complete gender equality and were punctuated by ecstatic testimonies to the work of the Spirit. Moreover, Quaker belief and practice defied social conventions, religious practices, and the law. They refused to attend militia musters, to swear oaths or remove their hats in court, or to permit Anglican clergy to baptize their children and perform their marriages.[6] Yet while some Virginians found the Quakers outrageous, others were drawn to this new community. Women in particular flocked to Quaker meetings, and African Americans whether free or slave also found their services congenial. The result was an almost spontaneous growth in Quaker numbers that local magistrates in the late 1650s watched with impotent alarm. On the Eastern Shore, for example, the fining and imprisonment of leaders among the Friends only increased Quaker activity; and in York County on the peninsula between the James and York Rivers, the county justices found themselves unable to stop these "turbulent people" from meeting.[7] Clearly this was a matter for the colony's government in Jamestown.

Toward the end of the 1650s, the council moved against them, and then the colonial assembly passed an act to suppress this "unreasonable and turbulent sort of people." *Turbulent* was clearly a favorite descriptive. By their "teaching and publishing, lies, miracles, false visions, prophecies and doctrines," Quakers threatened "to destroy religion, lawes, comunities and all bonds of civil societie." Anyone bringing these people into Virginia, entertaining them in their homes, or hosting their meetings was liable to a fine of £100, and any Quakers coming into the colony would be immediately imprisoned and then deported. If they returned a second time, they would be "punished" and again deported. If they came a third time, they would be treated as "felons." But traveling Friends had already done their work, and Virginians continued to embrace the growing movement.[8]

After the restoration of Charles II to the English throne in 1660, Sir William Berkeley, Virginia's governor, encouraged even more stringent laws and their strict enforcement against what he called "this most pestelent Sect." Early in his administration the assembly imposed a stiff fine of £20 per month on Quakers and "other recusants" who failed to appear at parish services and another fine of 200 pounds of tobacco every time they attended a Quaker meeting.[9] In April 1662 the General Court, composed of the governor and his council, also moved against the Quakers; and when a new assembly convened the following December, the first statute it approved dealt entirely with the Quakers. Designed to forbid their "unlawfull assembling," this draconian piece of legislation spelled out the government's chief concern in the preamble: these people were "separating and dividing themselves from the rest of his majesties good and loyall subjects, and from the publique congregations and usuall places of divine service." Virginia's elite operated within a worldview in which religious uniformity was a given. In any state there could be room for only one church. The law prescribed progressively stiffer fines for those attending Quaker meetings with banishment for the third conviction. Ship captains who brought Quakers into the colony and those who permitted them "to teach or preach" in their homes would pay similar fines or have their property seized and sold. County justices of the peace were to enforce this act and pay half of the fine to the informer. The law concluded, however, with an inducement to "Quakers or other separatists." If, after their trials and conviction, they gave security, that is posted a bond, never again to attend these "unlawfull assemblies," their fines would be excused.[10]

That law worked, at least temporarily. By 1664 only two Quaker meetings remained: the first at Thomas Jordan's home at Chuckatuck in Nansemond County on the south side of the James River and another across Chesapeake Bay in Northampton County on the Eastern Shore.[11] Yet everything depended upon the vigilance of local magistrates. What if, as sometimes happened, their wives or other members of their families, friends, or they themselves became attracted to the Quaker faith? Then enforcement of the statutes lagged.[12] So lax had it become in Nansemond that by 1675 the governor was receiving reports that Quakers had "Severall Coventicles" there. Berkeley wanted them suppressed, but he had to depend upon local authorities. George Fox's visit to Virginia while on his North American tour had swelled Quaker numbers in the Old Dominion. In his journal he noted the warm reception he received in Nansemond in 1672 and the presence at his services of militia "officers and magistrates who were very much taken with the declaration of truth." Even more magistrates and county notables were present when he preached on a return visit.[13] So sympathetic were the Nansemond authorities that Thomas Jordan and his Chuckatuck Quakers even built a meetinghouse for themselves during that decade.[14] Thus in Virginia, as sometimes happened elsewhere, local noncompliance stymied the best intentions of a central government to ensure religious conformity, and a de facto toleration anticipated a change in the government's instructions from London.[15] Before Berkeley's replacement, Thomas Culpeper, Baron Culpeper of Thoresway, sailed for Virginia in 1680, the Board of Trade, anxious to encourage the settlement of the colony, instructed him "not to suffer any man to be molested or disquieted in the exercise of his religion" as long as "he be content with a quiet and peaceable enjoyment of it, not giving offense or scandal to the government." Those instructions remained in place except for Roman Catholics until the Revolution.[16] Though they did not have the force of statute law, they help to explain the general tolerance dissenters experienced at the hands of royal governors even in the face of a hostile colonial assembly. British imperial policy required expanding colonies and necessitated more settlers than England or even Britain could produce.

The English Toleration Act

Law eventually caught up with practice, at least in England, as a result of the Glorious Revolution in 1688. Nonconformity was already a fact of English church life, and pressure had been mounting there from different quarters for greater toleration of religious dissent. Within a few years of his accession to the throne in 1685, James II, a Roman Catholic, ignoring Parliament and the widespread English antipathy for anything even faintly papist, issued a Declaration of Indulgence permitting freedom of religion.[17] Anxious to advance the royal prerogative in the colony and to curry favor back in London, Virginia's governor Francis Howard, Baron Howard of Effingham, ordered it promulgated in Jamestown with drums beating and guns firing and "with all the joyfulness" the Old Dominion could muster. A few months later Effingham proposed that he and his council send "an humble Address" to the king, thanking him for his "most Gracious and tender Declaration" to which the council members "with one heart and Voice most Loyally and Dutifully Said Amen."[18]

A year later, shortly after Jamestown's celebration of the birth of the Prince of Wales, Effingham sailed back to England, leaving the president of the council, Nathaniel Bacon, temporarily in charge of affairs. In April 1689 Bacon and the council ordered the proclamation of William and Mary as king and queen. Again, out came the "Great Guns" along with "Trumpetts" and "Drums," but this time the rejoicing was genuine. Virginians had not been enthusiastic for James II's "indulgence," which they interpreted as an excuse to multiply papists across the land. The new monarchs would work with Parliament to secure Protestantism for England and its colonies. As it turned out, Effingham remained in England and a lieutenant governor, Francis Nicholson, was appointed to act in his name.[19]

England under William and Mary was prepared to legitimize religious dissent so long as it was not of the Catholic variety. In the first year of their joint reign, Parliament passed "An Act for Exempting Their Majesties' Protestant Subjects Dissenting from the Church of England from the penalties of Certain Laws." The act rendered null a number of previous statutes provided dissenters swore oaths of allegiance to the monarchs, rejected "any authority of the see of Rome," and professed faith in the Christian Trinity and the "divine inspiration" of the Hebrew and Christian Bible. In the required declaration of assent by clergymen and teachers to the Thirty-Nine Articles of Religion approved by Parliament in 1571, dissenters were granted exemptions from certain words in the twentieth article that dealt with the church's authority, the thirty-fourth article that defended church traditions, the thirty-fifth article that endorsed the Anglican Book of Homilies, and the thirty-sixth article that provided for the ordination of ministers and the consecration of bishops. The act also showed sensitivity to the opposition of Baptists to infant baptism and of Quakers to swearing oaths.[20]

Despite its limitations, this so-called Toleration Act offered Trinitarian Protestants in England, mainly Presbyterians, Baptists, Independents, and Quakers, freedom to worship as they wished. But what did it mean in Virginia where suddenly war threatened and pacifist Quakers formed the only significant body of dissenters? In 1690 as the first of a new series of conflicts broke out between England and France, Quaker dissent threatened not only civic unity but domestic security. Perched on the western frontiers of Virginia, the hostile French with their Indian allies threatened an invasion. To the north William Penn's newly established Quaker colony pledged to abstain from any war with the French and Indians. In fact, according to worrisome reports reaching Jamestown, the Pennsylvanians planned to furnish the Indians and even the French with supplies and a possible refuge if they attacked Virginia. To an anxious Nicholson and his council, Virginia Quakers appeared to be potential traitors. Friends from Pennsylvania and Maryland often attended Quaker meetings in Virginia, and from those gatherings they could then pass along information to the French and Indians. These Quaker services were being held in various places without the government's knowledge or the fulfillment of the conditions laid down by the new English statute. The Toleration Act, with Friends in mind, specified exemptions from oaths but mandated a "declaration of fidelity" to the monarchs. Dissenters had to notify county authorities of their meeting places, and they were forbidden to lock or bolt the doors during services. Nicholson and his council, albeit grudgingly, accepted the extension of this law to the colony, but they demanded that Quakers conform exactly to its licensing and other regulatory provisions. Local magistrates published the council's orders in the county courts. People who followed such "evill and Seditious practices" endangered the colony.[21]

Yet there was little the government could do if the Quakers obeyed the law. Meanwhile, Nicholson was challenged from another quarter as the century drew toward a close. On the last Saturday of April 1699, a Presbyterian clergyman, Francis Makemie, asked the governor to proclaim formally to the colony "the freedome and Liberty of Conscience" granted by the English Act of Toleration and to prohibit anyone from disturbing any congregation of dissenters "in the free and open Exercise of Religion." Born and educated in Scotland, the minister had been living in Accomack County on the Eastern Shore for a decade or more. There he had married the daughter of a wealthy landowner, William Anderson, and when the latter died in 1698, his will made Makemie, who already possessed land and slaves, a wealthy man. A newfound sense of importance in his local community may have encouraged Makemie to approach the governor and push the issue of dissenter rights. An unsympathetic Nicholson summoned the Presbyterian minister into the council's chamber and bluntly told him that religious dissenters could enjoy the freedom the law permitted them so long as they behaved "Civily and Quietly and doe not disturb the peace." If anyone bothered their meetings, they could complain to the proper authority, but Nicholson would do nothing further for them.[22]

The assembly had met for only two days when Makemie appeared. Its first act that spring was designed to squash a series of moral evils including violations of the Sabbath, but referring to the Act of Toleration in its conclusion, the Virginia law excused from church attendance anyone who worshipped with a "congregation" or at a "place of public worship" permitted under Parliament's act.[23] Yet evidently over the next month and a half the interview with Makemie rankled Nicholson. How many people did the Presbyterian represent? When the council reconvened in June, it ordered that all county courts "as soon as possible" were to report the following information: "what Publick or Private Meetings of any other Religion than the Church of England . . . are in their respective Counties; where they are kept, & how long they have been kept? how lycensed? how many and what persons resort thereto? what particular Religion they are of? how their Preachers are qualified? & whither any wandring Strangers come into their Counties as Preachers or upon any other pretence of Religion whatsoever?"[24] Later that year the council instructed the attorney general to draw up a "Proclamation to enjoyn a more due observance" of the colony's penal laws and "more especially" to order all colonial officials to "use their utmost endeavours" to ensure that the Act of Toleration "be duly observed." What that meant became clear when Nicholson issued his proclamation in December. All county and parish officials were "to use their utmost endeavours" to ensure exact conformity to the Act of Toleration and to punish "all Dissenters and others" who violated it. This did not end the business, however, and four years later the council repeated its directive to the county courts to inform the colonial government on the number and size of dissenting congregations within their respective jurisdictions and whether they conformed to the Toleration Act.[25]

By the beginning of the eighteenth century, Nicholson had reason to want such information. Along with Presbyterian congregations under Makemie's preaching in Accomack County and along the Elizabeth River, other religious communities were putting down roots in the colony. French Calvinists known as Huguenots arrived in 1700 after their expulsion from France by Louis XIV's revocation of the Edict of Nantes. The government permitted them to settle at Manakin Town with a separate parish created by the General Assembly.[26] A few English General Baptists also wandered into the colony. A Quaker missionary encountered one of their preachers holding forth in Yorktown.[27] In the first quarter of the new century, German Reformed and Lutheran immigrants arrived to work in the iron mines at a place named, appropriately, Germanna. From there they moved to establish congregations in Fauquier and Prince William counties in the Northern Neck where they were joined by Pennsylvania Germans. By midcentury they were spilling over the Blue Ridge Mountains into the Shenandoah Valley where German Mennonites had settled earlier.[28]

Meanwhile the Quakers discovered a level of peace and stability they had not known before in the colony. They had already moved up the socioeconomic ladder. Voters in Henrico County even elected John Pleasants, a wealthy Quaker slaveholder, to the House of Burgesses in 1692, though because he refused to swear the requisite oaths, he could not take his seat. Still, the Chuckatuck meeting reported to Friends in England in 1700 that their meetings were "Quiet and Peaceable at present and the Rulers, magistrates are very tender and loving to us."[29] A few years before, Thomas Story, a traveling Friend, noted the presence at the Chuckatuck Monthly Meeting of the county sheriff, "a Colonel," and some other prominent members of the local community. Anne Cary, wife of Miles Cary, a member of the governor's council, was now a Quaker. On his travels Story conducted a meeting for worship at the home of local justice, and later another magistrate lent him a boat to cross the river.[30] Quaker worship services had become much less exuberant by this time, and their evangelizing had lost its confrontational style. Youthful converts, however, might still cause disturbances. One Sunday in Isle of Wight County in 1712, a Quaker who had recently been baptized by an Anglican minister burst into Newport Parish Church with some Quaker companions and offered "a Scandalous prayer" attacking the Church of England's "doctrine & discipline." Most likely he was making amends to the Quaker communion for his lapse into Anglicanism, but the council ordered him to be prosecuted.[31] By this time Quakers had about twenty meetings and were busily constructing meetinghouses. Their church polity was now complete with monthly meetings for worship and business, quarterly meetings, and a Virginia Yearly Meeting that met each September in Isle of Wight.[32] A measure of their newfound respectability may be surmised from the welcome that Nicholson afforded Story during the latter's visit to Williamsburg in 1705. The governor was "kind beyond expectation" and "treated" the Quaker evangelist "with various Sorts of choice Wines and Fruits, and much Respect." Story found the whole experience "remarkable" given Nicholson's previous attitude toward Quakers.[33] Lieutenant Governor Alexander Spotswood, following instructions from London, formally repealed by proclamation in 1717 the act that had forbidden the "unlawful assembling of Quakers." By that time, of course, it was a dead letter. A few years later Commissary James Blair informed the new bishop of London, Edmund Gibson, that "the English toleration of Dissenters takes place here."[34]

Toleration, however, did not produce significant religious pluralism. As one careful Anglican clergyman observed in 1724, in contrast to most of the other colonies, "Virginia may be justly esteemed the happy retreat of true Britons and true churchmen for the most part."[35] Nor did toleration remove religious disabilities. For Virginia's Quakers three significant matters of conscience remained. A long-standing grievance was the "priest dues," that portion of the mandatory parish tithes devoted to clerical salaries. Quakers detested the very idea of a "hireling" clergy, but the Toleration Act specified no exemption from church tithes so they either paid or suffered accordingly. In the seventeenth century, for example, members of the Jordan family of Nansemond County were fined or had their property seized for refusing to pay these taxes voluntarily.[36] In his meeting with Nicholson, Story argued that a government which offered "liberty of Conscience in Matters of Religion" should liberate people from paying tithes to clergy whose services they did not use. Nicholson disagreed, of course, but Story noted afterward that the governor at least had listened to him "with Candour, and took no Offence."[37] In 1738 a group of prominent Quakers submitted a petition on behalf of their whole Society, asking the governor and assembly for an end to these "Annual Seizures and Distresses made upon our Goods and Persons, on Account of Parish Levies." They willingly paid all their other taxes including those for the "Public Poor," and they cared for their own poor without parish assistance. The government was unsympathetic, however, and in 1748 the assembly even stiffened the penalties. Until Virginia eliminated the tithe for dissenters in 1776, Quakers regularly had their property seized and occasionally faced imprisonment for refusing to pay these parish assessments.[38]

Members of the Jordan family also represented a second Quaker concern, the refusal to swear an oath on the grounds that it violated Christ's explicit command in Matthew's Gospel. Both the English and the Virginia governments had recognized this concern. In 1696 Parliament provided that Quakers could make a "solemn affirmation" instead of an oath, and Virginia in 1705 incorporated that provision into its own laws and prescribed the form for the affirmation.[39] Unfortunately at least some Quakers considered that the affirmation formula too closely resembled an oath. Parliament finally obliged the Friends in 1722 with a new formula for affirming. About this time Thomas Jordan's grandsons Robert and Joseph Jordan were summoned to testify in a court case. When they refused the "solemn Affirmation" prescribed by the Virginia law, the justices clapped them into jail. The Jordan brothers then petitioned the governor and council to be allowed to follow the new British formula, which the colonial administration apparently had not yet seen. The council turned them down until they could produce a copy of Parliament's new act.[40]

A third concern and probably the most significant for Quakers and non-Quaker pacifists alike involved military service and particularly the enforcement of the militia laws. This became especially troublesome during the wars between Britain and France that broke out periodically between 1690 and 1763. For Virginia the gravest threat came from the Indian allies of the French in Quebec. Military readiness was a constant necessity, but war and the preparation for war violated the Quaker peace witness. A group of Quakers petitioned the new Lieutenant Governor William Gooch and his council in 1727 for relief from the fines imposed on them for not attending militia musters, but Virginia's leaders summarily rejected the request. Had the colony been at war, the Quakers most likely would have been jailed.[41] By the 1740s they had company when the Mennonites joined them in petitioning for freedom from the muster laws.[42]

During the first half of the eighteenth century, Quaker growth slowed noticeably, perhaps because toleration lessened the group's appeal. In his somewhat dyspeptic report on the condition of his parish in Isle of Wight in 1724, Anglican clergyman Alexander Forbes took note of an increasing number of Quakers including "Proselytes" in neighboring Nansemond County, but that was the heart of their community. So many nominal Anglicans were "offended" by his church's "Ministry" that Forbes thought "a learned, talkative, and Subtle Quaker Preacher" would be able "to persuade a great number of them to Quakerism." But in fact that does not appear to have happened. A decade later the rector of St. James Parish in Goochland County reported that the Quakers, with the support of "high-minded men," presented "many difficulties," but he had baptized fifteen of them. Estimates place Quaker numbers in Virginia between one and two thousand by 1750, concentrated mainly in the southeast. Even though that figure quadrupled by the end of the Revolution, the Society of Friends remained a relatively insignificant religious minority.[43]

The Presbyterians

Another group of dissenters surfaced in the 1720s and within the next two decades emerged as an important religious presence in the colony. In 1724 a group of Presbyterians in the Northern Neck asked the Northumberland County Court for permission to erect a meetinghouse. Even at this late date, it quickly became clear that the colony had no established policy or procedures for dealing with dissenters' requests. The county justices, unsure of their authority, forwarded the request to Lieutenant Governor Hugh Drysdale, who turned to the colony's attorney general John Clayton for his opinion. The next spring a similar request came to the governor from the Richmond County justices. After Clayton consulted with John Holloway and John Randolph, two distinguished Williamsburg lawyers and politicians, he advised the justices that so long as the dissenters registered their place of worship with the county court and conformed to the stipulations in the Toleration Act, they might enjoy "the free exercise of their religion" at their place of worship.[44]

Such was the legal situation for dissenters when the great migration began in the 1730s into the Valley of Virginia. Those who came were mainly Presbyterians of Scotch-Irish background. Soon congregations began to form and build meetinghouses at places named Opecquon, Tinkling Spring, and Timber Ridge. Their clergymen arrived on the scene, and in 1738 the Presbyterian Synod of Philadelphia wrote Governor Gooch asking for "the liberty of their consciences" and freedom of worship. Delighted to have this new buffer against frontier attacks by the French and Indians, Gooch generously welcomed the western settlers and stipulated only that they should "conform" to the provisions of the Toleration Act and register their meetinghouses.[45] Their presence, like that of the German Lutherans and Reformed, supported British imperial policy,[46] and they faced no problems from the established church, perhaps because it was so sparsely represented in the western portion of the colony.

The conflict with the establishment came in Hanover County. There in the Virginia Piedmont a small group of the Reverend Patrick Henry's parishioners, dissatisfied with the dry quality of his sermons, began to withdraw from Sunday services at St. Paul's Church. They gathered instead at the home of Samuel Morris, a bricklayer, to read and discuss various books and sermons. Hungry for experiential religion and a heartwarming piety, they plunged into Martin Luther's *Table Talk* and his *Commentary on St. Paul's Epistle to the Galatians*, newer books by John Bunyan, and Thomas Boston's *Human Nature in Its Fourfold State, of Primitive Integrity, Entire Depravation, Begun Recovery, and Consummate Happiness or Misery*. According to Morris, this last book launched the religious revival. Eventually the reading group formally withdrew from St. Paul's Parish and built a meetinghouse. In the beginning it was unclear to which sect they belonged. Some considered them Lutherans, but no less a personage than the bishop of London pronounced them to be Methodists. When William Robinson, a minister from the Presbytery of New Castle, arrived on the scene in 1743, he organized them along Presbyterian lines, taught them hymns, and demonstrated the use of extemporaneous prayers.[47] Presbyterian polity centered on the presbytery, a group of ministers and lay elders in a specified region which certified its clerical members, ordained men for the ministry, and issued pastoral assignments in response to requests from local congregations. This body also served as a guardian for faith and order. A group of presbyteries formed a synod, and new presbyteries and new synods were established as needed.

Robinson was a "New Light" Presbyterian and had studied for the ministry in the Log College established by William Tennent in Neshaminy, Pennsylvania. By the time he preached in Virginia, what historians would later call the Great Awakening had begun in earnest. George Whitefield, the transatlantic Anglican revivalist who would be its heart and soul, had arrived in the colonies in 1739. During the next thirty years, he made six more voyages to America, preached thousands of sermons from Georgia to Maine, and was seen by more Americans than any other person before the Revolution. En route to Savannah that fall, he reached Williamsburg shortly before Christmas and in Bruton Parish Church delivered a sermon entitled "What Think Ye of Christ?" The *Virginia Gazette* reported that "most" of the crowded church responded favorably to his "extraordinary Manner of Preaching."[48] But not all were enamored by his emotional rhetorical style or the demonstrable reactions it produced in his congregations. His itinerancy also challenged the practice of a settled ministry preaching within the ordered hierarchical setting of a parish church. Whitefield's success produced a host of imitators and ultimately split the colonial religious world into opposing "New Light" and "Old Light" camps. A particularly bitter schism occurred in Presbyterian ranks in 1741 when the Scotch-Irish antirevival majority in control of the Synod of Philadelphia expelled the prorevival Log College preachers led by William and Gilbert Tennent. They then formed the rival Synod of New York, and American Presbyterianism remained divided for the next seventeen years.[49] In Virginia, Old Light clergy dominated the Valley pulpits while New Light evangelists itinerated through the Piedmont and Tidewater. After Robinson's visit came John Blair, followed by John Roan, who aroused tremendous anxiety and furious opposition in the mid-1740s because of his fiery attacks on the established clergy. As the Reverend Patrick Henry informed William Dawson, these "new Preachers" had "seduc'd some unwary people." They had even charged Henry with being a "stranger to true religion" and "an unconverted graceless man" incapable of preaching the gospel or helping those who sought out his ministry.[50]

Up to that point Gooch had treated the Hanover Presbyterians with cautious approbation. Early on, he had summoned Morris and his companions to Williamsburg and, at least according to some reports, was the first to identify them as Presbyterians. Born and educated in Scotland, Gooch knew that since the Glorious Revolution, Presbyterianism had become the established church in that portion of Great Britain. Therefore its adherents, though perhaps not on a par with members of the Church of England, deserved a respect not afforded to other dissenters. After counseling them to act discreetly, the governor sent them home. But John Roan's extravagant attacks on the established church forced a confrontation with local authorities that eventually pulled the governor into the fray. In April 1745, speaking to a grand jury in Williamsburg with Roan clearly in mind, Gooch charged this "new light" heterodox clergy with leading "innocent and ignorant people into all kinds of delusion" by "blaspheming our sacraments" and "reviling our excellent liturgy." The next day the grand jury returned indictments against Roan and some of his most vociferous backers for vilifying the established church and failing to obtain licenses to preach. They had blasphemed by charging that "at church you pray to the Devil" and "that all your ministers preach false doctrine, and that they, and all who follow them, are going to hell."[51]

Roan's career in Virginia ended abruptly, and after he left the colony the conservative Synod of Philadelphia wrote to assure Gooch that he had never belonged to them. Soon afterwards the New Light Synod of New York dispatched emissaries to patch up relationships with Virginia's colonial government.[52] But Gooch and his advisers decreed that from then on, the General Court, composed of the governor and his council sitting as one body, would have sole authority for approving all licenses for dissenting clergy and determining their places of worship. For the next few years the Presbyterians in Hanover and neighboring counties had only occasional services. George Whitefield arrived in Hanover for four or five days in the summer of 1745 to an enthusiastic welcome from both New Lights and "church people." Henry allowed the Anglican itinerant to preach in St. Paul's Church and was particularly pleased when Whitefield "advised the dissenters to return to the Church and some of the chief of 'em" announced that they would.[53] But dissent was evidently growing. In April 1747 the council issued a proclamation that local magistrates should use every legal means to forbid "Itinerant Preachers whether New Light men Moravians or Methodists" to preach, teach, or hold meetings anywhere in Virginia.[54] But interestingly it did not single out Presbyterians.

This policy had just gone into effect with the sheriff's notice posted on the meetinghouse doors when the Reverend Samuel Davies arrived in Virginia. The New Castle Presbytery had ordained him in February 1747 to visit Hanover and explore the feasibility of a pastorate there. In April the young clergyman appeared before the General Court in Williamsburg, swore the required oaths, and "after some Delay" was licensed to preach in four meetinghouses in Hanover and Henrico counties.[55] Not all the council members favored granting him permission to preach, but license in hand, he proceeded to Hanover to begin his ministry. Parson Henry reported to the commissary in June that Davies had been traveling about "preaching at certain appointed places" with "circular Letters and Advertisements" to broadcast his arrival and sermon dates. In Hanover he had celebrated "the Sacrament of the Lords Supper" with "a great many Communicants."[56]

The welcome had been warm, but after about a month of preaching, Davies left Virginia. His health, always precarious, had worsened, and then in September his young wife died in pregnancy after less than a year of marriage. Depressed and ill, he thought he was dying also, and it was not until spring of the next year that he could respond to the renewed call for his services from Hanover. This time he brought with him another clergyman and good friend, John Rodgers. The two arrived in Hanover, preached at one service, and continued on to Williamsburg to secure a license for Rodgers. While Governor Gooch received them pleasantly, the meeting with the council was a disaster. The timing was not auspicious because the cases of the men indicted by the grand jury three years earlier were finally being tried before the General Court. Samuel Morris, for example, would be fined twenty shillings for hosting John

Portrait of Samuel Davies (1723–1761). (Virginia
Historical Society, 2003.292.8.A–C)

Roan's sermons. And the religious name-calling had not abated. Another grand
jury had presented several individuals for blasphemy and impiety: they had
called the sign of the cross in the baptismal ritual "a whore's mark" and lambasted the established church's ministry.[57] The local clergy were furious, and
a Hanover clergyman, almost certainly Patrick Henry, had followed them to
Williamsburg "and complained that Mr. Rodgers had preached in the province
without a license, and demanded the rigorous enforcement of the law." Gooch,
who had favored the two Presbyterians, then turned on Henry and declared, "I
am surprised at you! —you profess to be a minister of Jesus Christ, —and you
come and complain of a man, —and wish me to punish him for preaching the
gospel! For shame, Sir! Go home, and mind your own duty. For such a piece of
conduct, you deserve to have your gown stripped over your shoulders."[58]

Perhaps because of his Scottish background, Gooch was known to Presbyterian historians as a man of "mild and amiable character" who was "strongly opposed to the persecution of dissenters." But although he, Commissary Dawson, and one or two other council members favored the young ministers' cause, the majority was unalterably opposed. When Rodgers told the governor afterwards that he was not requesting "a favour, but pleading a right," Gooch agreed and proposed that the ministers draw up a petition to that effect and present it the next day while he absented himself. But it had no sooner been read than Thomas Lee, the senior member of the council, announced, "We have Mr. Rodgers out, and we are determined to keep him out."[59]

Davies bid goodbye to Rodgers and assumed responsibility for the growing flock in Hanover and environs. The following autumn Presbyterians in Caroline, Louisa, and Goochland counties successfully petitioned the General Court for three more licensed meetinghouses for Davies. Thus by the middle of the eighteenth century, after just a few years of ministry, the young minister was caring for seven growing congregations in five Piedmont counties. In addition to "300 Communicants," many more people including numerous Anglicans were turning out for his services, and he also had baptized about forty slaves.[60] The powers in state and church became alarmed. When the New Kent County Court in April 1750 licensed still another meetinghouse for Davies, the General Court abrogated that license on the grounds put forward by Peyton Randolph, the colony's attorney general, first, that the county court had no right to issue it and, second, "that a dissenting minister has no legal Right to more Meeting-Houses than one."[61] Davies protested that ruling, but Gooch had recently retired to England, and the council's president, Thomas Lee, acted in his stead. Lee promised to ask the London government for its judgment on the matter. A transatlantic conversation now ensued that lasted for several years.

In July 1750 Commissary Dawson expressed his concerns in a letter to Thomas Sherlock, the bishop of London. Randolph had followed royal instructions in granting "liberty of Conscience to all persons except papists" with the proviso that they behaved quietly and peacefully without "giving offence or scandal to the Government." Dawson wanted Sherlock's advice. Did the Toleration Act or those instructions intend that one dissenting clergyman could multiply meetinghouses? Davies had become too successful, and Dawson was deeply concerned that "Schism" was "spreading itself through a colony which had been famous for uniformity of Religion." An awareness of class also crept into the commissary's letter. Davies particularly appealed to "poor people who generally are his only followers." Preaching to them on weekdays when they should be working violated the "religion of labour whereby they are obliged to maintain themselves and their families." If this "neglect" continued, it could impact the government.[62]

In October, Davies, suspecting that Lee would misrepresent his situation, sent a long letter to Philip Doddridge, a highly respected dissenting minister in England, asking his intercession. Doddridge in turn wrote Bishop Sherlock enclosing an extensive extract from Davies's letter. From Davies's perspective, he and his followers had been treated shabbily. Laboring under the "odium" of both the state and the established church, they were regarded "as incendiaries and promoters of Schism." The authorities had thrown all sorts of obstacles in their path, infringed on Davies's "Liberties," and prevented other Presbyterian clergy from ministering in Virginia. Some were still saying that the Act of Toleration did not apply in the colony, despite the Virginia legislation that exempted dissenters from attending church services. But the most immediate cause of Davies's anxiety was the council order confining his ministry to one meetinghouse. If the English government let this stand, it would create an "intolerable hardship" for his congregation given the distances people would have to travel. He had sworn all the oaths and met all the requirements of the Toleration Act. He only claimed the "liberties" that statute offered.[63]

The bishop of London was not persuaded. The Toleration Act, he explained to Doddridge in May 1751, was designed "to ease the consciences of them who could not conform," not to encourage dissenting clergy "to disturb the consciences of others, and the peace of a Church acknowledged to be a true Church of Christ." Davies was an "itinerant preacher" attempting to convert members of the established church in a place where few dissenters had existed before his arrival. Sherlock also voiced his own frustrations in attempting to supervise a church at the other "end of the world."[64] In his quick reply Doddridge commiserated with the problems the bishop had enumerated, but he also elaborated on the comfortable situation of dissenters in England as contrasted with Virginia. If three people in England petitioned for a licensed meetinghouse, the courts readily granted the request, and any licensed minister could preach there. The position of Davies and other dissenters in the colony was not comparable.[65]

In 1751 Virginia's government wrestled with two diametrically opposed positions. As Dawson explained to Sherlock in August, Parson Henry and four other Anglican ministers had drafted an extraordinary memorial to the House of Burgesses, which the commissary enclosed in his letter. In effect the Virginia clergy denied that the Toleration Act extended to Virginia. "Lay Enthusiasts" and "strolling pretended Ministers" such as Davies in Hanover claimed to be Presbyterians, though the Synod of Philadelphia refused to acknowledge them. Another clergyman named Clennick, a Whitefield associate, had moved into other Piedmont counties. But no Virginia statute authorized either him or Davies to preach. The Anglican clergy urged the assembly to enforce its own laws, particularly the 1642 statute that forbade any clergyman to operate in the colony unless he had been ordained by an English bishop and had sworn to conform "to the orders and constitutions of the Church of England." Undoubtedly some highly placed laity including Peyton Randolph agreed with Henry and his friends, but the Burgesses never entertained this petition because it contradicted the Toleration Act. That became glaringly evident later in the summer when the response of the Lords of Trade to Lee's query was finally communicated to the council by his successor. Lee had died, and Lewis Burwell had replaced him as president. Dawson quoted the text in his letter to Sherlock. Referring directly to the "affair of Mr. Davies the Presbyterian," the Lords had pointed out that "Toleration and a free exercise of Religion is so valuable a branch of true liberty, and so essential to the enriching and improving of a Trading Nation, it should ever be held sacred in His Majesty's Colonies." The Virginia government must do "nothing . . . which can in the least affect that great point." But the Lords wanted Davies admonished "to make a proper use of that indulgence which our Laws so wisely grant" and "not to afford any just cause of complaint to the Clergy of the Church of England or to the people in General."[66]

The prospects for Britain's economic gain trumped the desire for religious uniformity, but the London authorities had set down only general guidelines. Colonial authorities would have to implement them. Davies had argued that he was no more an itinerant preacher than the Anglican parson who provided services in different churches and chapels in a multicongregational parish. Further, to the complaint that a dissenting clergyman should only officiate in the county in which he had been licensed, he replied that since he had been licensed by the General Court, the "supreme court" in Virginia, he should be able to preach in any licensed meetinghouse in the colony.[67] The new lieutenant governor, Robert Dinwiddie, and the council disagreed, and it was only with "much difficulty" that Davies was able to gain permission to have John Todd assist him by taking over four of his seven meetinghouses. Dinwiddie challenged Davies's capacity to care for additional preaching stations, but he did not confine him to only one.[68] The Virginia authorities accepted that in principle the Toleration Act applied in the colony, but they disagreed on what it meant. Most important, they rejected the pleas of dissenters for more licensed meetinghouses and the capacity to call "any qualified dissenting minister whom they shall invite" to preach for them. Doddridge had died in 1751, so Davies wrote Benjamin Avery for information on the practice in England.[69] After consulting lawyers and Sir Dudley Ryder, the attorney general and chief legal adviser to the Crown, Avery advised that Virginia's dissenters were entitled to all the meetinghouses they desired and enclosed Ryder's judgment for the Virginia authorities to "consider."[70] They were not swayed.[71]

Davies used the occasion of Todd's installation in November 1752 to reach out to his antagonists. The previous year, in a published letter to Joseph Bellamy, a Connecticut clergyman and a leader in the New Divinity movement, Davies had lambasted Virginia's ministers for the "very low State" of religion in the colony. Sunday religious services were far too casual for his taste, but the Presbyterian's chief complaint was the Anglican clergy's rejection of "the Calvinistic" doctrines of their own Thirty-Nine Articles of Religion, including human depravity and predestination. Instead of an *experimental* piety that taught the need for and process of *"Regeneration,"* Virginians heard from their pulpits curious preaching that mixed Arminian doctrines on grace and free will with a small helping of genuine religion. Following these introductory remarks, Davies recounted the history of his evangelical efforts in Virginia and the obstacles and frustrations he had encountered at every turn.[72]

Now, however, he had John Todd by his side and the prospect of other Presbyterian clergymen joining them. The installation sermon, which Davies later published and "Humbly Dedicated to the Revd. Clergy of the Established Church in Virginia," appealed to a basic ecumenism by pointing out the common doctrinal ground that Anglicans and Presbyterians shared. Surely their similarities in faith and order were far more important than their differences, he argued. By recognizing their "essential Agreements," the clergy of both churches could promote "a Spirit of Candour and Moderation." The task of a minister was to preach the gospel in a peaceful manner, without stirring up contentions or insisting on a narrow orthodoxy. Moreover, Presbyterians had not withdrawn from the Anglican Church out of "a *schismatical Spirit*" or religious hostility, but only from a conviction that they would find "Means . . . better adapted to [their] Edification" elsewhere. They retained only "benevolent Wishes for the spiritual Prosperity of the church [they had] left."[73]

Despite this olive branch, Virginia's elite in state and church was not seduced. From Governor Dinwiddie and his council down to the gentry sitting on county courts and church vestries, the growth of religious dissent posed a major threat not only to the established church but to the whole national ideal of uniform doctrine and worship. The commissary thought that a radical religious revolution was taking place as Davies caused "a great defection" from Anglican services. In former times without places for worship, the dissenters had "quietly conformed to the Doctrine and discipline of our Church." William Dawson was angry, worried, and probably ill.[74] He died later that year, and his brother Thomas Dawson, the rector of Bruton Parish Church in Williamsburg, replaced him. The new commissary wrote Bishop Sherlock of his desire "to see that uniformity of religion restored, for which this Colony was once famous; and peace and quietness established among us."[75]

How extensive was dissent in Virginia by the middle of the eighteenth century? We have no reliable statistics, and historians disagree, but a reasonable case can be made that religious diversity was gradually becoming more widespread even before the Separate Baptists exploded on the scene in the 1760s.[76] In the first place, although most of the white inhabitants of the colony may have attended Anglicans services more or less regularly, at no time did the number of Anglican communicants represent more than a small fraction of parishioners.[77] When the itinerants came through and later when dissenting ministers received licenses, they could always draw a curious and often a friendly crowd. Competition sparked religious interest but endangered the monopoly of the established clergy.

Second, a tithe list exists for one important county that is suggestive for others. In 1742 Truro Parish included all of Fairfax County when it was separated from Prince William County. This area encompassed what today is Fairfax, Arlington, and Loudoun counties and the city of Alexandria, that is, the upper portion of Virginia's Northern Neck that borders the Potomac River as far as the Blue Ridge Mountains. In 1749 soon after Truro Parish was divided by the creation of Cameron Parish in the recently formed Loudoun County, the Reverend Charles Green drew up an elaborate tithe list of the two parishes. It demonstrates both the population increase and the presence and diversity of dissent. When Green became Truro's rector in 1738, the parish numbered 621 tithables, white and black. Eleven years later, the number had grown to 2,035 (1,122 white, 913 black), an increase of 1,914. Of the total number, Truro now included 1,207 tithables, and the new parish of Cameron held 828. Each parish possessed two churches. Green detailed by name the householders in each parish, their religious affiliation, and the number of tithables in each family. Quakers, for example, formed a significant community in Cameron Parish with sixty-seven men and two widows as heads of households. Quaker preachers numbered four men and four women. The growing antislavery movement within the Society of Friends obviously had borne fruit because only one Quaker, Elisha Hall, is listed with black tithables and by his name is the cryptic notation, "Sometimes comes to Church."[78]

Cameron Parish also had five "Anabaptist" and fourteen Presbyterian male heads of households. Fifteen more Presbyterian householders lived in Truro Parish, and some were important figures in their community. John Carlyle, for example, was a wealthy Alexandria merchant who married Sarah Fairfax of the Northern Neck's first family; and Colonel John Colville was the collector for the Alexandria port, a major landholder and slave owner, a member of the House of Burgesses, and formerly vestryman of Truro Parish.[79] Over the mountains in the Valley, Presbyterians frequently served as vestrymen, but Colville held this position in an area where Anglicans were numerous. That Presbyterians might serve on vestries in such places indicates how socioeconomic position might be more important than religious affiliation even at the heart of Anglican polity. It also indicates the somewhat ambiguous position the established Church of Scotland held in British dominions.

No ambiguity existed, however, when it came to papists. Though the Toleration Act specifically excluded them, in fact Catholics maintained a visible religious identity in Britain and its colonies.[80] Governor Gooch knew of their presence in Fairfax County. In April 1746, before word of the decisive defeat of the Jacobite rebellion at Culloden had reached Virginia, the governor issued a proclamation warning that "Roman Catholic Priests" had "lately come from Maryland to Fairfax county" and were attempting "by crafty Insinuations, to seduce" Virginians "from their Fidelity and Loyalty to his Majesty King George, and his Royal House." He called on the authorities and all "His Majesty's Liege People" in the Old Dominion to capture them "so that they may be prosecuted according to Law."[81]

Green's 1749 tithe list identifies as Catholics twenty-three householders in Cameron Parish and twenty-five more in Truro and also names adult Catholics living in other households and working, for example, as overseers. But the uproar over the Scots' rising for the Stuart pretender, Gooch's proclamation, and the fines levied for nonattendance at Anglican services had done its work. Next to about half of the Catholic names, Green made such notations as "formerly Papist, now Churchman," "of late comes to Church," "comes sometimes to Church," and "often comes to Church." There is a careful calibration of loyalty, and in some cases it carried rewards. Former Catholics John Turley and John West had gained places on the vestry.[82]

Green was able to identify the religious affiliations of almost all of the householders, though a few names bear the vague label "sectaries of some sort." His tithe list demonstrates the existence of significant dissent in the upper Northern Neck and also the potential for more. In identifying his churches, the hardworking clergyman wrote "about 120 Constant Communicants" in Truro, but the note for the Cameron church at Goose Creek states tellingly, "I never had one Communicant."[83] For a charismatic preacher moving through the Northern Neck, these were fields lying fallow for the gospel seed.

Green's labor identifies religious diversity in one area of Virginia, just as it suggests why Anglican authorities, both clerical and lay, sought to stem the explosive growth of Davies's Presbyterian communities. On the other side of the Blue Ridge in the Valley of Virginia, Presbyterians, Quakers, Mennonites, Lutherans, and German Reformed lived in tolerant harmony far removed from the center of power in the Tidewater, but the congregations of Davies and Todd in Hanover and neighboring counties operated under the General Court's noses. Though the government had allowed Davies the help of Todd, it repeatedly denied his requests for more meetinghouse licenses.[84]

Frustrated by the intransigence of Dinwiddie and his council, Davies sailed for England in 1753 as an agent of the Synod of New York to raise money for what would be the College of New Jersey but also to ease the situation of Virginia dissenters by a personal appeal for support from the English dissenting ranks. The fund-raising proved successful; however, Davies soon learned that the London committee which represented dissenter interests at court could provide little assistance. To the minister's surprise, after reviewing his writings on the position of dissenters in Virginia and the pertinent colonial statutes, the committee thought that the only provision in the Toleration Act applicable to the colony was the exemption of dissenters from attendance at Anglican services. They advised him to draft a petition to the king and royal council and have it signed by "educated Dissenters" out on the Virginia frontier. Their social standing and their valuable presence as "a good Barrier against the French and Indians" meant that their request would carry "more Weight" in London than one from Hanover Presbyterians. When Davies discovered that his "old Adversary," Peyton Randolph, was also in London on other business, he realized the difficulties he faced. But with the committee's help he drafted the petition and sent it to Virginia. The signed document was back in his hands before he sailed for home in November 1754. Davies passed it on to the committee, though he left England without great hopes that it would be successful.[85]

In fact, the committee decided not to present the petition but to pursue a different strategy. In February 1755 the committee's secretary instructed Davies to apply for meetinghouse licenses through the county courts first. If the courts refused, then he should request them from the General Court, and if turned down there, then he should appeal to the governor. If this approach proved fruitless, the committee proposed civil disobedience. The clergy should preach in unlicensed meetinghouses, and if the Virginia authorities prosecuted them, the London committee would represent them in an "appeal to the King in Council."[86]

But British troubles made confrontation unnecessary. While Davies was in Britain, the French and Indian war broke out along the Virginia frontier. He arrived home in Hanover to find the whole colony engulfed in feverish military preparations. The fighting on their colony's borders forced Virginia Anglicans to recognize the value of the dissenters. At the clergy convention in 1754,

Thomas Dawson inveighed against the "blind Zeal of Fanaticism" that challenged the established church's hegemony in Virginia, but that danger was now outweighed by the "furious malice of popery" that threatened to overrun the king's dominions.[87] Virginians had experienced the defeat of Colonel George Washington's forces at Fort Necessity in 1754 and then the disastrous outcome of General Edward Braddock's attempt to capture Fort Duquesne the following summer. The drive for religious uniformity yielded to the exigencies of military defense and the fight for survival. Dissenters made good soldiers, and Samuel Davies excelled as a passionate recruiting parson. Over the next few years, he delivered a series of fiery sermons linking religion to the patriotic struggle against the "French Papists" and "blood-thirsty savages." If not stopped, they would make Virginia "a conquered, enslaved province of France."[88] The government in Williamsburg found the Presbyterian preacher to be a valuable ally.

During Davies's absence in Britain, the Synod of New York had dispatched additional ministers to the southern colonies, and late in 1755 it authorized Davies to organize the Presbytery of Hanover with six clergymen. The advent of more clergy answered the government's formal objections against licensing further meetinghouses, for these preachers would be settled pastors rather than itinerants.[89] On behalf of the presbytery, Davies and Todd drew up in 1756 a flattering address to the new governor of Virginia, John Campbell, earl of Loudoun. Three points were central: First, their unabashed loyalty to George III and "his family." Second, decrying the "inhumane Barbarities and Depredations perpetrated upon our Frontiers" by "a mongrel Race of French and Indian Savages," the ministers promised to "exert our utmost Influence" to rally their congregations with a true patriotic "Spirit, and the love of their Country, and to animate them by our Instructions and Example, bravely to hazard their lives and Fortunes in its Defense."

Finally, while "cheerfully" accepting their status as dissenters with its requisite "Tests of Loyalty and orthodoxy," they asked the new governor to "continue in us those Liberties we have enjoyed, particularly the free Exercise of our Religion, according to our Consciences, and the Practice of the established Church of Scotland." In the past they had suffered "some Restraints" from which dissenters in England were freed. They asked for "all the Liberties and Immunities of a full Toleration ... according to ... the Act of Toleration."[90] Two years later, responding to a similar address from Hanover Presbytery, the new lieutenant governor, Francis Fauquier, as deputy for the earl of Loudoun, "assured" them of his "support" for the Toleration Act and the "peaceful Enjoyment of its Immunities."[91]

Meanwhile, Davies had found a new field for his labors in the Tidewater region of the Northern Neck, particularly Northumberland and Lancaster counties where some Presbyterians from Northern Ireland had settled. Following the strategy proposed by the dissenters' committee in London, he applied to the county courts for meetinghouse licenses, which he received in May 1757. The next month on a Sunday he preached in the Northumberland courthouse and then preached outdoors during the following week there and in Lancaster to "a considerable Concourse of People." In November he was back again, and by April 1758 a sizable meetinghouse had been constructed in Lancaster County and John Todd had shown up on circuit. The growth of the dissenter population alarmed the local Anglican clergy, John Leland and David Currie. They in turn complained to Commissary Thomas Dawson about these "Conventicles and Field preachings" that were "drawing off the People from the established Church." One of Currie's vestrymen, Colonel Edwin Conway, also wrote to Dawson and enclosed a brief statement for the council to forward to the House of Burgesses. The self-identified "Oldest Freeholder in the County" was a staunch Anglican and had been shocked by the appeal Davies had made to the slaves.[92]

But the council was focusing on a much more threatening concern for which Davies and Hanover Presbytery were providing an immediate remedy. Under Davies's leadership the ministers had quickly established the Society for Managing the Missions and Schools among the Indians, an initiative which received the hearty endorsement of the governor and his council. Despite the urgent calls for clerical services in growing congregations across Virginia, during the next two years the presbytery dispatched two of its newly ordained young ministers to work among the Cherokees. Virginia's government was delighted with this venture, which promised to produce "the greatest Good" for relations with the Native Americans. Just after Conway, Currie, and Leland had lodged their protests against the Presbyterian incursion into the Tidewater, a much greater crisis occurred when the Shenandoah Valley came under direct attack from former Cherokee allies who committed "Robberies and Murders." Tense months followed until early in 1759 when Indian leaders arrived in Williamsburg to restore peaceful relations. In response, the governor and council ordered trading goods given to the Indians with presents for the chiefs. The peril had lifted, but throughout this period the missionaries proved invaluable in maintaining contact with the Indians and providing information about their activities to the Virginia authorities.[93] The Presbyterian clergy had displayed their civic usefulness precisely at a time when the colony's very existence had been seriously threatened.

Thus Anglican protests against the Presbyterian presence came too late. By January 1759 Benjamin Waller, the clerk for the council and the General Court and a longtime member of the House of Burgesses, advised Edwin Conway "that the Dissenters have power to build a house and enjoy their religion by act of Toleration."[94] Although major issues remained, including the tithes that dissenters paid for the salaries of the established clergy, the struggle for basic religious toleration was largely complete. When in 1759 the College of New Jersey called Davies to assume its presidency upon the death of Jonathan Edwards, he reluctantly accepted. In a valedictory sermon to his Hanover congregation, he urged an ecumenical spirit. It would be beneficial, he thought, if Presbyterians from time to time attended services in the established church, maintained "catholic principles," and found their "spiritual good . . . wherever it may be obtained." Their objective should be to "live peaceably with all men . . . and never let differences in religion" create bad feelings "or interrupt the good offices in civil life." From Davies's perspective, the Presbyterian "cause" had always been "liberty and the gospel," not factionalism or schism.[95]

No doubt Davies preached that sermon because his congregation needed to hear it. The journal of a devout Presbyterian, Colonel James Gordon, provides a window into a mixed society of Anglicans and Presbyterians in Tidewater Virginia between 1759 and 1763. Gordon had emigrated from Northern Ireland to Lancaster County in the 1730s and become a prosperous planter and tobacco merchant. His first wife was Millicent Conway, a daughter of the old colonel. The two men clashed over religion, and Gordon described his father-in-law as "so great a bigot that people who are religiously inclined despise his advice."[96] But the younger man also displayed a narrow range of sensibilities. Periodically he would accompany his wife to the local Anglican church of St. Mary White Chapel, but invariably he found the sermons distasteful and a waste of time. The local rector, David Currie, was "much against Presbyterians," and he and other Anglican ministers such as John Leland and Adam Menzies, who each had a parish in neighboring Northumberland County, made no bones about "ridiculing the Dissenters" when they preached. When Gordon challenged Currie on his sermons at a vestry meeting, he not surprisingly found the minister defensive.[97] Currie was probably intimidated by the public rebuke the Presbyterian offered in a setting dominated by some of the most important laity in his parish. But he undoubtedly knew that Presbyterian preachers had found sympathetic listeners among his parishioners.

Between 1759 and 1763 Gordon recorded the names of eight visiting ministers who preached at services in his neighborhood. While they attracted sizable congregations of "common people and negroes," he noted that "very few gentlemen" attended. Members of the gentry who might want to come stayed away, he thought, because they were afraid "of being laughed at." After all, presence at Sunday worship was a social act that helped to define membership and rank in the local community, as well as an acceptance of the church establishment. To go elsewhere could be problematic for one's reputation. Indeed, Parson Menzies had decried attendance at dissenter services as "scandalous" to the parish.[98]

But though the clergy and members of the established church might contest such preachers and preaching, civil authorities no longer hampered the ministry of licensed dissenting clergymen at licensed meetinghouses. Those legal provisions were critical. When, for example, Presbyterians in Lancaster County and its environs determined to invite James Waddell to become their pastor in 1763, he took "the oaths agreeable to law" in Williamsburg and then "read the articles of religion" as specified by the Toleration Act before the two local Anglican ministers, Currie and Menzies.[99] One can only imagine the scene and the conversation afterwards on both sides when these two clerical protagonists of the church established by law witnessed the young Presbyterian minister pronouncing his acceptance of the Anglican articles with the exceptions privileged by the Toleration Act. Ecclesiastical competition had become legitimate in Virginia. The world as they had known it was passing away.

2

Toleration

"The Free Exercise of Religion"

The genial William Gooch, Virginia's most successful colonial governor, began his tenure in Williamsburg in early 1727 in the conciliatory tone that would mark his administration. Addressing the assembly, he expressed his own "peculiar felicity" to govern a colony "where the Doctrine, Discipline and Worship of the Church of England is not only established but almost universally received and complied with." Yet the new governor also pointed out that should any "dissenters" happen to exist in Virginia, "an indulgence" toward them was "so consistent with the genius of the Christian Religion that it can never be inconsistent with the interest of the Church of England."[1] The legislators were not persuaded. When it came to indulging dissenters, Gooch represented London's perspective, not Virginia's. In an address to George I two weeks later, the Burgesses informed the monarch that it was their "peculiar happiness" that the Old Dominion was more "united in the Religion of the Church of England" than any other British colony in America, and they were grateful that the king had made "the establishment in Church and State" his "first and always . . . chief care."[2]

These laymen formed the heart of that establishment. The clergy, while essential to the church, worked for them. Virginians expected their ministers to preach and to administer the sacraments of baptism and Holy Communion, to witness their marriages, and to bury their dead, but the laity as much as the clergy comprised the Church of England in the Old Dominion, and the gentry managed the church's affairs in the colonial assembly, the county courts, and especially the parish vestries. Robert Carter Nicholas, the treasurer of the colony and a major figure in Virginia at the outset of the Revolution, explained in a published letter in 1773 this mentality and his sense of obligation: "The Vestries in this Colony, I consider, as the civil Guardians of our Church. . . . In as much as the Clergy are not amenable to any ecclesiastical Jurisdiction in this Colony, surely the Vestries ought to be the more circumspect and attentive to their Duty. The only Instance . . . in which they can serve their Parishes, in any important Degree, is to be prudent in the Choice of their Minister. Upon this depends, in a great Measure, the Happiness of the People."[3]

The laity's sense of entitlement in church polity would outlast the Revolution. By a law enacted in 1748 and approved by the king, the vestries had full authority to hire clergy for a year after a vacancy occurred. Though governors, commissaries, and bishops of London might wring their hands over this infringement of the bishop's jurisdiction and the governor's instructions, there matters stood.[4] Dissenting calls for complete religious liberty and church disestablishment, therefore, not only attacked the ecclesial uniformity that Virginia's churchmen thought necessary for a healthy society; they threatened the foundations of their own power and position in the community. The presence of dissenters also challenged the hegemony of the established church's clergy, who benefited from the fact that the "national church," as one of Jefferson's clerical teachers styled it, was "incorporated and blended with the state." As such it formed "a necessary and essential part of the political system of the nation."[5] Both laity and clergy stood to lose by the growth of dissent.

The Parson's Cause

A shared concern for the church's welfare did not mean, however, that relations between the clergy and the laity within Virginia's Anglican establishment were always cordial. Nor did the church in England always move in sympathy with its coreligionists in the colony. In 1759 the new lieutenant governor, Francis Fauquier, reported to the Board of Trade in London that "the establishment of the clergy in this Colony" was an obstacle to the much desired settlement of foreign Protestants on the frontier. In the midst of the French and Indian War, Scotch-Irish Presbyterians and German Lutherans made good soldiers. But establishment meant clerical salaries, so these dissenters would have to maintain clergymen of their own persuasion while simultaneously paying taxes to support an Anglican minister.[6]

Only a few years earlier the General Assembly, in response to the petition of ministers in two frontier counties, had passed a law that fixed their salaries at £100 per year.[7] Since few Anglican clergy actually made their way to the west, Fauquier's worries may not have been shared by many settlers; but by the time he wrote to the Board of Trade, a serious dispute over clerical salaries roiled Virginia. As it developed over the decade from 1755 to 1765, the so-called Parson's Cause involved constitutional, imperial, legal, and economic issues. Some historians such as Rhys Isaac, following the lead of Bishop William Meade's sharp criticism of the colonial church, have placed the dispute within the context of a growing opposition by the laity to the established church and its clergy, particularly in public affairs. According to this interpretation, the clerical-lay contest over salaries fomented an anticlerical mentality. This in turn provided the backdrop for the religious turmoil of the Revolutionary era that ultimately ended with Jefferson's Statute for Religious Freedom and church disestablishment.[8] So the Parson's Cause deserves attention from a church-state perspective, and the issue of anticlericalism bears examination.

Throughout Virginia's colonial era taxes for various purposes generally were paid in tobacco and were levied on the basis of tithables, that is, the number of free males and slaves, men and women, over sixteen years of age, per household. Virginia law provided that each minister be paid 16,000 pounds of tobacco per year, and each year the parish vestry would apportion the levy for this and other parish expenses among the parishioners. When a severe drought threatened to drive up the value of the tobacco crop, the assembly passed a law in December 1755 that allowed people over the next ten months the option of paying their taxes in coin or paper money rather than tobacco at the rate of two pence per pound. The law did not single out the clergy but included them by allowing the payment "for public, county and parish Levies, or for any secretaries, clerks, sheriffs, surveyors, or other officers fees."[9]

Eighteen ministers led by John Camm, the rector at York-Hampton Parish and professor of divinity at the College of William and Mary, signed letters to the bishop of London protesting against the so-called Twopenny Act.[10] Unlike the law fixing their salaries, this act became operative upon Lieutenant Governor Robert Dinwiddie's approval without the king's approbation. The clerical protest dissipated, however, when the average value of the crop that year approximated the monetary equivalent fixed by the law. Then in 1758 another threat to the crop produced a second Twopenny Act effective immediately for twelve months.[11] As the value of tobacco shot up to six pence a pound, the clergy watched the colonial law slice their salaries to one-third of what their income would otherwise have been that year. A conference of clergymen convened at the college and deputed Camm to represent their views in England.[12] After Bishop Sherlock added his objections to the Virginia law and disparaged the clergy's situation in Virginia, the Privy Council disallowed both Twopenny Acts in August 1759.[13]

Camm immediately instructed his attorney in Virginia to bring suit against his vestry to recover his full salary. While he tarried in England for over a year, tensions rose in the colony. As a new session of the General Assembly opened in November, the Reverend Isaac William Giberne attempted to soothe the situation by preaching a timely, hopeful sermon on "The Duty of Living Peaceably with all Men." From the pulpit of Bruton Parish Church in Williamsburg, he urged his congregation to recognize that "the Duty of Peace, Love and Charity, is universal and always obligatory." Virginians should "strive" to be "exemplary" in "their Zeal for the true Welfare both of Church and State."[14]

Only recently ordained in England and new to Virginia, the young clergyman had managed to strike just the right note; the Burgesses were so pleased with his sermon that they ordered it published at House expense. They were not trying to pick a fight with the clergy. Giberne soon became acquainted with several burgesses including Landon Carter, and in 1762 when the minister relocated to Carter's parish in Richmond County, the parson and the planter became good friends. Within a few months of his sermon, both Carter and Richard Bland published pamphlets defending the Virginia church and refuting Bishop Sherlock's low estimate of its condition. Neither document carried an anticlerical tone. Neither writer attacked the clergy en bloc. Rather, the tone Carter adopted and Bland followed in this and subsequent pamphlets appeared designed to isolate Camm from the rest of Virginia's clergy, including those he had led astray. In a reference obviously directed against Camm, Carter attributed the entire controversy to "some turbulent Genius" who had hoodwinked a small number of ministers into collaborating in a scheme "destructive to the Welfare of the Community, and the Peace of the Church."[15] Bland's pamphlets adopted the same argument. Only "a *small* part" of Virginia's clergy was disaffected, and in their attack on the legislature for failing to maintain them, they had ignored or forgotten the numerous favors the assembly had done for them, particularly in recent years. Bland detailed these benefits, insisting that the assembly had acted correctly in passing the Twopenny Act. The welfare of the people had required it. "The Clergy," he pointed out, "is of great Consideration in the State; as Instructors of the People in that Religion upon which the Salvation of Souls depends, they ought to be held in high Estimation; but yet the Preservation of the Community is to be preferred even to them."[16]

When Camm returned to Virginia in the summer of 1760, he found himself as welcome as a skunk at a garden party. Despite his obvious qualifications, William and Mary's Board of Visitors refused to select him as the next president of the college. When he delayed in presenting himself and the British government's documents to the governor, Fauquier was so furious that he publicly ordered his slaves never to admit Camm to the palace again—by all accounts an extraordinary insult.[17] The General Court repeatedly postponed his suit against his vestry. Finally, when he attempted to publish his rebuttal to Carter's and Bland's attacks, Williamsburg's public printer rejected his pamphlet on the grounds that it cast aspersions on the legislature. Ultimately he had to find a printer in Annapolis.[18]

Much to Camm's disgust, the assembly also passed a resolution to support whatever vestries were challenged in court.[19] Several cases involving the back payment of these salaries had begun moving slowly through the county courts. One of these provided a young, self-educated lawyer with an opportunity to display his oratorical skill. When the Reverend James Maury of Fredericksville Parish sued the tithe collectors in Hanover Court for back payment of his salary, Patrick Henry Jr., named for his clergyman uncle, represented the defendants. The trial created a sensation in the colony. Because the court ruled that the British government had repealed the law, the only issue at stake was the damages Maury might collect. In his lengthy address to a packed courtroom, Henry attacked the parson and the established clergy generally as "enemies of the community" who deserved to be "severely punished," and he charged that King George had behaved tyrannically in disallowing a just law passed by the Virginia assembly and signed by the governor. At this some in the crowd murmured "treason," but the jury—the "vulgar herd" as Maury later styled them—included several "New Light" dissenters. Anticlericalism was here with a vengeance, but Henry placed it within a challenge to the British government's authority over the Virginia legislature. Maury later reported that Henry had apologized to him immediately afterwards and remarked that his attack was not personal but only designed to enhance his own popularity. He achieved that objective. The jury awarded the furious clergyman one penny in damages, but more important, the Parson's Cause propelled Henry into the colonial assembly, where he quickly seized center stage with inflammatory resolutions against the Stamp Act in 1765.[20]

Patrick Henry and Quaker Dissenters

In the legislature Henry also encountered the religious, legal, and financial disabilities that dissenters suffered and took their side. Why? What motivated this man? To understand Henry's views on religious liberty and the situation of the dissenters, we must appreciate the influences that marked his formative years, and especially the unusual combination of church establishment and dissenter that distinguished his own family. The values of both would resonate throughout his life. Consider the environment in which he grew up as a boy in the 1740s and lived as a young man coming to adulthood in the 1750s. Baptized in the Church of England as an infant, he was named for his uncle, the rector of St. Paul's Parish in Hanover County and therefore the religious leader of the local community. John Henry, Patrick's father, was a vestryman for the parish. By the 1740s Hanover County was becoming more religiously pluralistic under the influence of Samuel Davies, the most influential dissenting clergyman in the colony. His converts included John Henry's wife, Sarah, and her father, Isaac Winston. On Sunday mornings, Patrick Henry Jr. found himself driving his mother and sisters in the carriage to Davies's meetinghouse and sitting in the congregation spellbound by the preacher's sermons. Historians have stressed the impact the Presbyterian evangelist made on the impressionable boy and speculated on the effect of Davies's rhetoric on Henry's oratorical style.[21]

But what did young Patrick observe and learn at home? What did it mean for him to grow up in a household in which his parents, who by all accounts loved and cared for one another, attended religious services in opposing churches? How did these tolerant domestic arrangements of his formative years affect his later outlook on religion and religious liberty? Rhys Isaac has emphasized the threat the evangelical movement posed not only to the established church but to the whole hierarchical gentry-dominated society of Virginia.[22] Other historians have highlighted the patriarchal qualities of that society before the Revolution. Yet in the Henry family, where the husband's adherence to the Church of England was sealed even by ties of blood, the wife elected an alternative service and took her children with her. Patrick Henry never joined his mother's church but remained an Anglican throughout his life. After his death, his relatives and friends testified to Henry's personal religious convictions.[23] But his family background gave him a practical experience of religious tolerance and a respect for different faiths that few politicians of his generation understood, much less shared, at the outset of the Revolution. He was, as his son-in-law Spencer Roane noted, a "plain, practical man . . . emphatically one of the people."[24] In matters of both church and state, his policies and politics were based on a profound understanding of human nature rather than any philosophical premises or theoretical presuppositions. He knew what was necessary and what worked.

Henry was in the assembly in 1767 when Quaker pacifists sought relief from the militia laws. During the French and Indian War, they had been under enormous pressure to participate in colonial defense when Virginia came under attack on the frontier. Then the House of Burgesses had rejected their petition to be excused from military service on conscience grounds.[25] Now their petition to be exempted from militia musters without being fined received a sympathetic hearing. The law that Henry helped to draft provided for the peacetime exemption for Quakers who could prove their religious affiliation.[26] Henry's few surviving papers do not mention this event, but he was on exceptionally good terms with Quaker leaders, including members of the influential Pleasants family. Before the Revolution, Roger Atkinson, an Anglican who married Ann Pleasants, described Henry to his brother-in-law, Samuel Pleasants, as "a real half Quaker . . . moderate and mild and in religious matters a Saint but ye very Devil in Politicks—a son of Thunder."[27]

Lieutenant Governor Fauquier died in 1768, and Norborne Berkeley, baron de Botetourt, arrived to replace him. In an address published in the *Virginia Gazette*, the Quaker community welcomed the new governor and expressed their "gratitude" for the "free exercise of religion" they enjoyed and the "great indulgence lately granted to our society." In his published reply Botetourt assured them that their "free exercise of religion" would continue.[28] But what did that vague phrase mean to the Quakers and to the governor? At best a degree of religious toleration. It did not mean freedom from parish tithes or the other dimensions of life regulated by a church established by law. A year later, encouraged perhaps by the Quaker success, the Mennonites requested similar exemptions from military service and war-related taxes. But this time the assembly rejected the petition.[29] This shift in the legislature may have resulted from a growing concern over the expanding presence of dissenters in the colony signaled by the arrival of the Separate Baptists in the 1760s. They posed a distinctly new threat.

The Separate Baptists

As early as 1714 some General (Arminian or Six-Principle) Baptists could be found in the lower Tidewater region of the colony. Their numbers increased slowly on the south side of the James River, and eventually they spread into neighboring North Carolina, formed the Kehukee Association, and became Regular (Calvinist) Baptists. Other Regular Baptists migrated into Virginia from Maryland and established churches in the Northern Neck. They were called "Regular" to differentiate them from the "irregular" Separate Baptists who originated in New England during the Great Awakening and then expanded into the South, especially Virginia and North Carolina, after the middle of the eighteenth century. Itinerant Separatist preachers formed "New Light" communities, and by the late 1760s their lively preaching attracted numerous converts. On the eve of the Revolution, their association included some thirty-four churches spread around the Tidewater and Piedmont.[30]

Alarmed by the rapid Baptist growth, Anglican clergyman James Maury criticized these preachers as "wild orators" and attacked their "Pretensions to an extraordinary Mission from Heaven to preach the Gospel." His good friend and fellow minister Jonathan Boucher complained bitterly about the "swarms of separatists."[31] Some members of the laity shared their concerns. In August 1768 a group of Maury's parishioners appealed to the clergyman "to preach them a sermon or two by way of Antidote."[32]

Other Virginians wanted stronger measures than sermons to handle men they considered disturbers of the peace. Earlier that summer the first imprisonment occurred in Spotsylvania County where the authorities clapped three Separatist preachers in jail. None of them possessed licenses to preach. The English Toleration Act permitted Protestant dissenters to worship at their own services. Although some magistrates thought this law did not apply in the colonies, Virginia authorities generally interpreted it to approve a limited number of licensed meetinghouses for dissenting preachers who would apply to the General Court for preaching permits. Initially it appeared that the Separatists also would apply to this court, as the Quakers, Presbyterians, and Regular Baptists did. John Blair, the acting governor following Fauquier's death, expected them to do so after he met with two preachers and received their assurances. But the ministers soon changed their minds, perhaps because the General Court met only twice a year and its licensing system would stymie their freewheeling itinerancy. They rejected any limitations on a ministry conducted by God's mandate. The scriptures said nothing about waiting for the approval of human law. Perhaps they also knew what Blair suspected: that their persecution would draw sympathetic attention and win converts.[33]

But the Baptist preachers were not wedded to any single position. By 1770 they were petitioning the assembly for relief from laws that required them to train for military duty and limited their preaching to specific meetinghouses. When the legislature refused, the resisting clergymen endured accordingly.[34] The harassment occurred on the local level. When magistrates like Edmund Pendleton, a justice of the peace in Caroline County, enforced the licensing laws, Baptist ministers suffered fines, whippings, and incarceration. But something more was at stake here than the issuance of preaching licenses. Baptist preachers provoked a reaction that was often violent and abusive far beyond any apparent aggravation and much worse than that suffered by earlier dissenters. Why was that? Four related factors appear to have motivated their persecutors.

First, Baptist worship did not conform to the decorous religious patterns embodied in the rituals of the Anglican Book of Common Prayer. One layman explained his admiration for the established church's worship this way: "Our Happiness [is] that we have so excellent a Form of Prayer prepared for us; . . . adapted not only to the general Exigencies of the Church, but . . . suitable to almost every particular Case. We think it a signal Advantage to know what these Prayers consist of; we can meditate on them in our Closets; and when we come into Church, and join in them, as it were with one Voice and one Heart, we find that this is the greatest Excitement to our Devotions."[35]

Baptist services produced a very different style of "excitement." The raw, spontaneous rhetoric of the "New Light" preachers appealed directly to the heart and the emotions, and their hearers responded with demonstrable enthusiasm. They became people who appeared to be out of control. This aroused the scorn and perhaps the fear of unconverted onlookers.

Second, Baptist doctrines, especially their opposition to infant baptism and insistence on immersion, directly challenged Anglican belief and practice. Their outspoken verbal attacks on the established church's position on these issues encouraged its defenders to respond in kind. Moreover, their strict norms for personal behavior and the social discipline Baptist churches maintained over their members set them apart from their Anglican neighbors. Excommunications and suspensions of members were common occurrences for such varied offenses as adultery, intoxication, "disorderly walking," and even "Playing the Violin."[36]

Third, the success of Baptist preachers in converting numbers of slaves aroused hostility, and the radical equality implied in the early covenants of Baptist churches challenged a slave society. White Baptists treated black converts as spiritual "brothers" and "sisters" in close communities of faith. In some Baptist churches Afro-Virginian preachers, sometimes free, sometimes slave, ministered to mixed congregations. Though spiritual equality did not translate into racial equality, yet the practices of Baptist churches in the years before the Revolution defied the social conventions of a slaveholding society.[37]

Fourth, Baptists had an "in-your-face" approach to evangelization. Often their preachers were accused of being vagrants, heretics, and "disturbers of the peace" who deceived poor, ignorant people by their incessant, enthusiastic preaching. "They cannot meet a man on the road," one complaint went, but that they have to "ram a text of Scripture down his throat."[38] These preachers brought religion into the marketplace and out on the courthouse green—outside the fixed boundaries of church or meetinghouse.

So some county authorities went after them. In 1774 Andrew Glassell, a Fredericksburg merchant who had emigrated from Scotland at midcentury, described the arrest of an unnamed preacher to an English correspondent. The Scotsman was listening to a Baptist sermon when the local sheriff "went boldly up to the pulpit with his hat upon his head and asked the preacher . . . to Come along with him. The preacher desired him to let him finish his discource; he would not." Nor would he permit the Baptist to say any prayers. "How it did melt my heart," Glassell wrote, "to see how warmly he prayed for his very per[se] cuters." As the sheriff carted him off to jail, "the whole Congrigation Cry'd after him." The Scotsman added, "Such a shoking sight I was never witness to before, as people suffring for rightousness seak." As a staunch Presbyterian, Glassell disagreed with certain doctrines of the Baptists, but he was enormously impressed by their religious zeal. "I love them much," he wrote, "because I find a Great many of them To be very Good men."[39]

Other Virginians obviously agreed. By this time Glassell had been attending Baptist services for at least a year and had witnessed the phenomenon that "the more they persecute thim the more they Grow." Because everything depended upon how local magistrates interpreted the law, enforcement varied from county to county.[40] In the early 1770s Archibald Cary, a no-nonsense Anglican and the presiding judge of Chesterfield County, repeatedly fined and imprisoned Baptists on charges of preaching without licenses.[41] But slap the preacher into jail, and he could turn his cell into a pulpit for the congregation that gathered outside. After John Weatherford started preaching through a grated window, the Chesterfield County authorities built a wall higher than the window, but the Baptist found a way around this obstacle. Whenever a crowd gathered, someone would put a handkerchief on a stick and wave it above the wall, and Weatherford would sound forth.[42] Though lodged behind bars, James Ireland managed to so enrage his persecutors that, failing to stop his sermons by climbing up on a table and urinating in his face, they attempted to kill him by various means: a gunpowder explosion, suffocation with smoke, and finally poison. Ireland survived and, shortly after his discharge, Governor Botetourt received him in Williamsburg "with all the graces of a gentleman" and granted him a license to build a meetinghouse.[43]

In addition to fining and imprisoning unlicensed preachers, the magistrates could also harass their congregations. That appears to have been a favorite approach in Caroline County where grand juries regularly presented individuals "for not frequenting their parish church," for hosting illegal preachers in their homes, and for attending their services.[44] When the pressure from dissenters became simply too much, the jailer might release a troublesome exhorter to get rid of him and the congregation he collected at the jailhouse door. Historians have not exaggerated the significance of this period for Virginia Baptist history. Preaching through the barred windows of county jails won the Separate Baptists support and enhanced their stature, particularly with the "lower sort," while magistrates, desperate to maintain religious homogeneity and bolster the established church, effectively transformed these preachers into Christian martyrs.[45]

During the years immediately before the Revolution, controversy over religious toleration and the status and rights of dissenters repeatedly roiled the assembly, the College of William and Mary, meetings of Baptist and Presbyterian leaders, and the press. The sides were not always predictable. James Maury is a case in point. Well educated at William and Mary and thoroughly orthodox in theology, he took his clerical duties seriously. But like many other clergy he was also comfortable with the language of natural rights that marked the American enlightenment. He favored enlisting reason in the service of religion and the defense of the establishment. In response to the challenges of the Separatist preachers, Maury laid out his case for the reasonableness of Christianity as embodied in the established church in a pamphlet published posthumously in 1771. He attacked Baptist claims to a divine call on both rational and scriptural grounds. The Christian, he argued, "is not required to believe an article, or perform a precept," until he had "received rational satisfaction of the credibility of the one and obligatory force of the other. His religion then may justly be termed an address to his reason."[46]

The Anglican clergyman also proposed a legitimate basis for religious dissent and a valid rationale for separating from the established church. In 1755 he had described "Liberty of Conscience" as a "natural right of mankind."[47] Then the issue had been Presbyterians without preaching licenses; now it concerned Baptists who did not want them. But Maury's guiding principle remained the same: the rights of conscience. One could—in fact, one should—leave the Church of England if he or she was sincerely convinced "that conformity is sinful and contrary to the laws of God." The minister was certainly unhappy with the growth of the Presbyterians and Baptists at the expense of the Church of England in Virginia, but he supported toleration and rejected coercion. Reason was crucial. He called upon those who had separated from the church to revisit that decision and make it not "as the result of giddiness, humour or caprice," but rather by "deliberation, principle and judgment." Accept no one's assertion of "an immediate mission from God" unless he could prove it; instead, "consult your own reason" and the scriptures, Maury urged.[48] Maury was the first real teacher of Thomas Jefferson and the future bishop James Madison. If this is what he taught them, they learned their lessons well.

Given the fact that the church establishment solidified lay control over society, it is not surprising that the most vigorous defenders of the status quo in church and state were the laity, and particularly the vestrymen. Edmund Pendleton, for example, a leader in the House of Burgesses, a vestryman, and a justice of Caroline County, had no qualms about harassing Baptists. Pendleton probably wrote "An Address to the Anabaptists imprisoned in Caroline County, August 8, 1771," which was published in the *Virginia Gazette* six months later. The very title was designed to insult. By calling them "Anabaptists" the author linked the Separatist Baptists to the followers of Jan of Leiden and the excesses of sixteenth-century Münster. He argued that common law required "every member of the Community" to obey the laws that the assembly determined were needed "for the Good" of all. Because every state needed to "conciliate the Divine Favour," an established church which fixed "Modes of Piety and Devotion" was integral to a healthy society. It supported the government, and everyone must accept it. "Opposition" to such "religious Establishments . . . must be considered as heresy and Schism, and a Breach of the Laws." Having laid out his case for religious uniformity, the author then drew back a bit. He favored a broad "Toleration" for "scrupulous Consciences," but the assembly should determine its "Limits" with a due regard for "the publick Peace," and "Dissenters must conform." Neither "Law or Government" should take cognizance of "private Opinions" that were kept to oneself; however, people who "go about publickly preaching and inculcating their Errours, raising Factions tending to disturb the publick Peace, or utter Doctrines which in their Nature are subversive of all Religion or Morality" deserve "civil Punishment."[49] If Pendleton was the author, he was simply justifying his treatment of the Baptists who had come before his court.

Toleration and Episcopacy

When the *Virginia Gazette* published this address in February 1772, the assembly was in the midst of debating a proposed Act of Toleration. Although the governor and General Court had sometimes behaved as if the English Toleration Act extended to the colonies, in fact that issue remained in dispute. For example, annoyed that Presbyterian clergymen Davies and Todd were preaching in his parish, Maury had written Commissary Dawson in 1755 that the question should be "indisputably solved" and "the Privileges of both Churchmen & Dissenters so precisely ascertained, as to leave no Room for Controversy."[50] But nothing happened until the Baptists burst onto the scene and forced the issue. By 1769 the concerns surrounding religious dissent had become so important that the House of Burgesses created a new standing committee for religion, and that year the legislators considered a bill "for granting toleration to . . . Protestant Dissenters." That proposal went nowhere, but the issue surfaced again during the controversy over an American episcopate for the Church of England in the colonies.[51]

That concern originated among northern Episcopalians, particularly missionaries of the Society for the Propagation of the Gospel (SPG), who were pushing for the introduction of episcopacy into America. Their letters persuaded John Camm to become active in the cause, and he won over Commissary James Horrocks. In May 1771 Horrocks called for a clergy convention to consider "the expediency of an application . . . for an *American* episcopate."[52] Only a dozen ministers bothered to attend, so the idea probably lacked much clerical support, but the gathering voted to draw up and circulate among Virginia's ministers for their support "an Address to the King for an American

Episcopate." Four clergymen, however, opposed this motion, including two junior members of the college faculty, Samuel Henley and Thomas Gwatkin. Shortly after the convention adjourned, the two published a formal protest in the *Virginia Gazette*. Among the various reasons for their opposition, they argued that "for the Clergy to make such an Application without the Concurrence of the PRESIDENT, COUNCIL, and REPRESENTATIVES of this province" was "extremely indecent" and a "Usurpation directly repugnant to the Rights of Mankind." When the Burgesses assembled in July 1771, they formally thanked Henley, Gwatkin, and the two other clergymen for their "wise and well timed Opposition . . . to the pernicious Project of a few mistaken Clergymen, for introducing an American Bishop."[53]

Was it only a "few" who desired a resident bishop in Virginia? In poor health, Horrocks sailed for England that summer and would die there the following year. In his place he left Camm as acting president at the college and William Willie to act as commissary. In an advertisement sure to rouse the suspicions of the laity, Willie soon called a convention to meet in October to consider "Matters of very great Importance (to the Clergy only)." That meeting determined that a fuller assemblage of the colony's ministers was needed to determine whether or not "a bishop should be settled among us." So Willie put out a call for yet another convention on February 20, 1772, with the express hope that the "number . . . who shall appear . . . will be respectable, [or] at least not contemptible." He asked those who could not attend to submit their views by letter.[54]

On the appointed date for the meeting, however, instead of the clergy assembling at the college, the *Virginia Gazette* reported a new pamphlet hot off the press, *A Letter to the Clergy of New York and New Jersey* by Thomas Gwatkin. In it he responded to a letter written by Thomas Bradbury Chandler to the "Episcopalians in Virginia" which had attempted to win their support for an American bishop without secular powers. Gwatkin reprinted the "protest" he and Henley had made against the clergy convention of the previous summer and elaborately refuted the arguments in Chandler's proposal. The northern clergy, he claimed, sought "a Civil Establishment of Religion to the Destruction of the Rights and Liberties of other Christian Communities."[55] A Virginia episcopate would do the same.

The same issue of the *Gazette* also contained some verse criticizing the quarrel that enveloped the college. The author urged:

> Let Camm and Henley drop an angry Pen,
> Discord forbear, —— Oh! Turn out loving Men,
> Write gently, without too much Gall in Ink,

Blessed Calvin did calmly write and think.
A House divided 'gainst Self must decline,
Then all Strife abhor, and in Peace combine.
Let Christian brotherly Love abound,
Nor talk of Pistols in that College Ground;
In Tutors let good Example be found.

. . . .

Learned Institutions are in vain,
Where Churchmen the most sacred Rules profane.[56]

As the controversy over the episcopate raged in the press, both Gwatkin and Henley also weighed in on the contents of a toleration bill that the assembly considered the following spring.[57] When the Baptists came forward in 1772, petitioning the assembly that they might enjoy "the Benefits of the Toleration Act," the Committee for Religion headed by Nicholas drafted a bill that would have definitively extended the English law to Virginia.[58] It promised that all "Protestant" Virginians "dissenting from the Church of *England* . . . shall have and enjoy the full and free Exercise of their Religion, without Molestation or Danger of incurring any Penalty whatsoever."[59]

The meaning of "full and free Exercise" remained undefined, but the debate had scarcely begun in the legislature when Henley preached a sermon to the House of Burgesses that attacked the entire basis for an established church and treated religious dissent as a matter of indifference to the state. Robert Carter Nicholas was dumbfounded that a clergyman of the church would treat "her Rules and Orders . . . with Levity and Disrespect." It was not the kind of sermon he would have given. "Were I a Minister of the Church of England . . . I would think it my bounden Duty to endeavour to display the superior Advantages of our Establishment, and the various and striking Beauties of our Liturgy. By such Means, I should hope that those already of our Communion would be still stronger attached to it, and that Strangers might be induced to join with us." Instead, the "chief Tendency" of Henley's sermon had been "to beat down and destroy that necessary, that friendly and amiable Alliance between Church and State."[60] That position together with Henley's lackadaisical handling of church doctrine in conversations with influential parishioners ensured that Nicholas and other vestrymen would reject his application for the coveted pulpit of Bruton Parish Church in 1773.[61] Richard Bland, who had been drawn into the controversy, accused Henley of "Self-Adulation and Vanity" and thought his explanations of scripture smacked of Socinianism.[62]

A few days after Henley's sermon to the Burgesses, Thomas Gwatkin, writing in the *Virginia Gazette* as "Hoadleianus," proposed that rather than subscribing to any of the church's articles of religion as the English Toleration Act required, dissenters should only have to accept "a Supreme Being, his government of the universe, . . . the obligations of morality," and if thought necessary, "the truth of the christian religion."[63] Nicholas was aghast at a clergyman's minimalist approach to the church's doctrine and his casual treatment of Christianity. But the treasurer acknowledged that the discussions in the Committee for Religion favored a more liberal toleration than the English law provided. The Burgesses decided, for example, to drop all the subscription requirements to various articles of church teaching, leaving only a statement accepting the Hebrew Bible and the New Testament as true and divinely inspired along with the requisite oaths to the king and British government. Quakers would be permitted to substitute simple declarations for sworn oaths. The county courts rather than the General Court would license dissenting clergy and whatever meetinghouses their congregations used. The committee, however, also added certain strictures, some of which torpedoed the bill. No services were allowed at night or in any private home for more than ten people beyond the family living there. Nicholas reported that a concern that these restrictions on "*Times* and *Places*" would dissatisfy the dissenters led some burgesses to urge that the bill be postponed and published, so that it could receive more mature consideration in the colony.[64] No doubt Nicholas welcomed the postponement. So also did the author of "An Address to the Anabaptists imprisoned in Caroline County." He argued that the English Toleration Act extended to Virginia and worked fine. The General Court had proper jurisdiction until the assembly directed otherwise, which he obviously thought unnecessary.[65]

Patrick Henry disagreed. Like the Quakers before them, the Baptists found in this rising political star a major ally as he volunteered his services in their cause in the courtroom and the assembly. Edmund Randolph, his contemporary and Nicholas's son-in-law, thought that contact with the "sufferings" of religious dissenters "unlocked" for Henry "the human heart" and noted that his political rhetoric contained the same "bold licenses" that marked evangelical preaching. As Robert Semple, an early historian of Virginia Baptists, wrote, Henry "only needed to be informed of their oppression, when, without hesitation, he stepped forward to their relief. . . . Baptists found in [him] an unwavering friend."[66]

Judge Spencer Roane, who married one of Henry's daughters, later recalled his father-in-law's description of the contests in the Caroline County Court where he defended "several Baptist Preachers" after Pendleton had slapped them into the county jail. To secure their release Henry paid their fines out of his own pocket.[67] He also encouraged civil disobedience. One of the irritating disabilities imposed on dissenting ministers was the inability to witness marriages. To be valid in Virginia, a marriage had to be performed by an Anglican clergyman using the ritual in the Book of Common Prayer. According to Semple, Henry proposed that Baptist preachers perform marriages anyway and argued that this would be "the most certain method" to reform the law. The conscientious Baptist questioned "*whether this was not doing evil that good might come,*" but he wrote his history after that liberty had been won.[68]

Henry had been one of the burgesses who drafted the toleration bill proposed in 1769; and as a member of the Committee for Religion in 1772, he gave a lengthy speech in support of "a general toleration." In it he insisted that the law would provide Virginia with "a virtuous clergy" who would be free "to reprehend vice." That was, from the beginning, the major sociopolitical role he urged for religion. His chief argument, however, was shrewdly calculated to appeal to the colony's economic elite who sat with him in the legislature. For their benefit he stressed Virginia's future prosperity, which he tied to encouraging European immigration. Two years earlier Henry had made his first trip to Philadelphia and New York. Now, on the floor of the House of Burgesses, he enthusiastically endorsed the practical advantages of the religious freedom he had observed in Pennsylvania: "A Dutch, Irish, or Scotch emigrant finds there his religion, his priest, his language, his manners, and everything, but that poverty and oppression he left at home." Virginia should encourage a growing immigrant population, including artisans who would manufacture the products people needed and enhance the colony's prosperity. "A general toleration of Religion," he wrote, "appears to me the best means of peopling our country. . . . The free exercise of religion hath stocked the Northern part of the continent with inhabitants." That policy would do the same for Virginia, drawing in European Calvinists, Lutherans, and Quakers.[69] James Madison would incorporate those same arguments in his *Memorial and Remonstrance against Religious Assessments* a dozen or so years later. But despite Henry's eloquence, the Burgesses flinched. After passing the toleration bill through two readings, they postponed sending it to the governor's council and instead had it published in the *Virginia Gazette.*[70]

Ecclesiastical Jurisdiction

While the Burgesses mulled over the terms of the toleration bill, another church-state matter of intermittent though long-standing concern surfaced once again: the supervision of the clergy. By the law of 1748 the vestry had clear authority, when a vacancy occurred, to select the minister to fill it. But they had no power to discipline or remove him from office. Nor, as it turned out, did anyone else in Virginia. As Nicholas pointed out, "The Clergy are not amenable to any ecclesiastical Jurisdiction in this Colony."[71] The bulk of the

Anglican clergy were hardworking ministers of good character who were respected by their congregations. But there were exceptions, men unfit for the office, a scandal to the church and a burden to their parishioners.[72] English canon law reserved the deprivation of a clergyman to the diocesan bishop operating in a church court. In the case of the colonies, although the bishop of London had jurisdiction from the king, the distance between England and the colony rendered that procedure unsatisfactory. Bishop Edmund Gibson had granted ecclesiastical jurisdiction to Commissary James Blair and then to his successor, William Dawson. During his long tenure Blair did not attempt to set up a church court. Instead, he worked through the Council of State, which included the governor and his council. This body heard and decided complaints against parsons. From the perspective of the church's canon law, it was irregular for laymen to sit in judgment on the clergy, but Blair's system worked in a colony where the laity expected to govern the church, and it kept the clergy clearly under their thumb. Naturally he was much more popular with the former than the latter.[73]

His successor, William Dawson, held one ecclesiastical court, which in his view had not gone well because officials were unfamiliar with procedures.[74] After his death in 1752, he was succeeded by his brother, Thomas Dawson. But Bishop Thomas Sherlock failed to renew the commission that Bishop Gibson had granted his predecessor, so he lacked ecclesiastical jurisdiction.[75] Dawson was present when the case of John Brunskill Jr., the rector of Hamilton Parish in Prince William County, came before the council and governor in 1757. According to the public record, the vestry complained about Brunskill's "drunkenness, profane swearing, immoral Practices, frequent Neglect of Duty, and indecent Behaviour in Church." Dinwiddie expanded on the charges in a letter to Sherlock. The minister was "almost guilty of every sin except murder and this last, he had very near perpetrated on his own wife, by tying her up by the legs to the Bed Post, and cutting her in a cruel manner by knives, and guilty of so many indecencies, that modesty forbids my troubling you with a detail of." After hearing numerous witnesses, the council agreed that Brunskill was "a Scandal to his Profession." The Crown's instructions to Dinwiddie stated that "if any Parson . . . shall appear to you to give Scandal, either by his Doctrine or Manners, You are to use the best means for the Removal of him." The commissary wanted to call the clergy together to decide what to do. But the council had heard quite enough. Ignoring Dawson's objections against this infringement on the "rights and privileges" of the ministers, they advised the governor to "remove and deprive" Brunskill of officiating in any church in Virginia.[76]

Several more cases of a similar nature came before the council in the ensuing years before the Revolution, but none of the bishops of London after Gibson sought the kind of royal commission that would have allowed them to delegate jurisdiction to their commissaries. The latter were therefore unable to exercise authority in difficult circumstances involving an unworthy minister.[77] Casting about for an alternative solution in the face of London's frustrating inactivity, the council took up a suggestion from Lord Hillsborough, secretary of state for the colonies and head of the Board of Trade, that the ecclesiastical jurisdiction of the bishop of London did not require a royal "Commission" but rested upon "ancient usage and practice" from the beginning of the English colonies.[78] But the bishop still needed to authorize his commissary to act on his behalf. Advocates of an American episcopate were quick to point out that the appointment of a bishop in the colonies would in fact establish in America the church's ancient and correct government. According to Camm, their plan envisioned a bishop whose principal tasks would be to confirm, ordain, and preside over a "Court of Clergymen to be held for the single Business of punishing Clergymen according to the Nature of their Offense."[79]

During these contentious years Camm, as the chief apologist for the clergy's position, and after 1772 their commissary, emphasized the distinction between civil and religious responsibilities. The clergy in their civil capacities accepted responsibility to secular law and civil authority. But in terms of their clerical duties and responsibility, they rejected "Episcopal Authority in the Hands of Laymen."[80] The legislature made one attempt at a compromise. While the toleration bill was making its way through the House, the Burgesses also initiated an inquiry "into the State of the established religion." A month later Nicholas reported back from the Committee for Religion its proposal that "for superintending the conduct of the Clergy," the assembly institute "a Jurisdiction consisting of laymen and Clergymen." After discussion by the whole House, the Burgesses resolved to formulate a law "to establish a Jurisdiction for superintending the conduct of the Clergy, to be exercised by Clergymen with an appeal to a Court of Delegates." Nicholas, Bland, and Benjamin Harrison were to prepare the bill. The measure received a first reading but went no further.[81]

Two years later in April 1774 another case arose when Edmund Pendleton and the vestry of Drysdale Parish accused the rector, Andrew Morton, of "divers Immoralities" and asked the governor, John Murray, earl of Dunmore, and his council, which now included Commissary Camm, to hold a trial and deprive him. The governor and council issued a citation to Morton to appear before them in June.[82] The minister never appeared. Instead, some of the clergy including probably Camm retained Richard Bland as counsel. In his published legal opinion, Bland quoted extensively from King George II's commission to Bishop Gibson to demonstrate that the governor was not authorized by the Crown to exercise any kind of visitation rights or ecclesiastical jurisdiction, and therefore the citation to Morton "for giving scandal by his doctrine and manners" was "illegal and void." In the course of his statement, Bland pointed out that the absence of any regulatory power over the clergy of the established church was a "defect in the constitution to the disadvantage of religion." In his view the assembly should correct it by legislation or by appealing to the king to make the proper delegation of authority for the church.[83] In the end, the legislators did neither. The issue of ecclesiastical jurisdiction would outlast the Revolution.

Toleration or "Free Exercise"?

By the mid-1770s the relentless petitioning of dissenters and the political solidarity needed to face the looming confrontation with Britain made the question of church establishment imperative. Was religious uniformity—at least as near as Virginia could get it—essential to a successful society? Defending himself against the charge of heterodoxy leveled by Bland and Nicholas, Henley argued in 1774 against "uniformity of belief as the greatest of all desiderata." Instead, he declared that "a diversity of opinion, maintained with charity, [was] preferable to a unity of exoteric faith, kept together by the bond of superstition, arrogance, and hypocrisy." The college professor took heart that "the rational Christian, the true Friend of freedom . . . is convinced that civil and religious liberty are inseparably connected."[84] Henley certainly did not win over his conservative opponents by quoting D'Alembert on his title page and citing Pierre Bayle's *Pensées* at length. Yet by the time he retired to England in 1775, he had made a lasting impact on at least some of his students.

A few years earlier, in 1772, one of them, the future bishop James Madison, had delivered the annual lecture commemorating the college's foundation and dedicated it to Henley. His speech offered a tribute to liberty in both church and state. Speaking soon after the proposed Act of Toleration had been published for the public's consideration, Madison recognized that people were generally nervous about "a free Toleration, in Matters of Religion" and took for granted that "civil and religious Affairs" appeared "almost inseparably dependent on each other." But relying on "the judicious Locke," the young graduate assured them that society was originally organized solely for "civil Interests," and that the authority of civil authorities extended "only to civil Concerns." The "free Exercise of Opinions" benefited both political and "religious Societies," but "one is the proper Object of the Magistrate, the other will not admit of his Interference. . . . 'In this 'tis God directs; in that 'tis Man.'"[85] Jefferson would echo those views and Madison's equation of religion with opinion in his Statute for Religious Freedom. It would become the perspective of the next generation.

Two years younger than his cousin, the future president James Madison had recently graduated from the College of New Jersey when he returned to Virginia. Disgusted by what he observed, he wrote to a college chum in January 1774 from his home in Orange County:

> That diabolical Hell conceived principle of persecution rages among some and to their eternal Infamy the Clergy can furnish their Quota of Imps for such business. This vexes me the most of any thing whatever. There are . . . in the adjacent County not less than 5 or 6 well meaning men in close Gaol for publishing their religious Sentiments which in the main are very orthodox. I have neither patience to hear talk or think of any thing relative to this matter, for I have squabbled and scolded abused and ridiculed so long about it . . . that I am without common patience. So I . . . pray for Liberty of Conscience [to revive among us].[86]

That year the House of Burgesses had another opportunity to enlarge the boundaries of toleration when it received petitions from Baptist and Presbyterian dissenters. Nicholas had accurately forecast the Baptist objections to the proposed act of 1772. Their association meeting in Loudoun County wanted freedom "to preach in all proper places, and at all Seasons, without restraint."[87] From Peaks of Otter Presbyterian Church in Bedford came a request that the elders of the church be incorporated so that the property in land and slaves that had been given for the support of the minister would be securely held and managed for that purpose. Their sole intention, the petitioners assured the Burgesses, was to promote "Religion and Virtue amongst the Presbyterians" in Bedford County.[88] So the requests that year involved two distinct dimensions of religious liberty: freedom to preach and security to exist and prosper. Dunmore's early dissolution of the assembly, however, stalled the proposed legislation.

In June 1775 the Presbytery of Hanover, appealing on behalf of all Virginia Presbyterians and "all Protestant Dissenters" and lacing their petition with New Testament references to the practice of the early church, asked that the proposed toleration act be amended to allow ministers to itinerate freely and to hold services in private homes and at night—just as the Anglicans did. The conclusion expressed their confidence that "the liberal sentiments" of the Burgesses would never force them to disobey "the Laws of our Country" in order to obey "the laws of Christ."[89] Five days later the Mennonites requested the "same liberty" the Quakers enjoyed of making a simple affirmation rather than swearing an oath. The next day the Baptists repeated their petition of the previous year.[90] But other events overwhelmed these concerns in the colonial legislature. The battles of Lexington and Concord had already occurred in April; the Second Continental Congress had met in Philadelphia in May; and now in

June, Washington took command of the Continental Army two days before the battle of Bunker Hill. The House of Burgesses ended that month, and the government of Virginia moved into the hands of the Revolutionary Conventions.

The exigencies of wartime mobilization finally broke the dike of opposition to greater religious toleration. In August 1775 the Virginia Baptist Association petitioned the Convention to permit Baptist preachers to minister to Baptist soldiers. In response Henry drafted the resolution that the Convention approved to instruct the commanders of the Virginia regiments "to permit dissenting Clergymen to celebrate divine Worship and to preach . . . or exhort" the soldiers.[91] Some sort of guarantee of religious liberty was overdue when the Convention met in Williamsburg in May 1776 to recommend that the Continental Congress declare the colonies' independence from Great Britain and to draw up a state constitution and a Declaration of Rights. Edmund Pendleton chaired the session, and the committee that drafted the declaration included George Mason, Edmund Randolph, Nicholas, Madison, and Henry. Mason had the principal role in the composition, and the drafts of the articles are in his handwriting. But as Pendleton and Randolph attested, he did not act alone.[92] We know also that Henry was vitally concerned with the "portrait of Government" that the convention would approve because he wrote John Adams of his anxieties that it be done properly. When Randolph composed his *History of Virginia* in the 1780s, he credited Henry with proposing what became the fifteenth and sixteenth articles in the declaration.[93] That Henry first urged the inclusion of an article on religious liberty is not inconsistent with the premise that Mason composed the actual draft. In fact, given Henry's outspoken advocacy of religious liberty for dissenters from the outset of his political career and the leadership role he held in the assembly, it would have been completely out of character for him to be silent. After all, the sixteenth article with its ringing affirmation of the rights of conscience more than achieved the promise of the proposed toleration act of 1772 that he had so vigorously supported.

As originally published in the *Virginia Gazette*, the text stated: "That religion or the duty which we owe to our CREATOR, and the manner of discharging it, can be directed only by reason and conviction, not by force or violence, and therefore all men should enjoy the fullest toleration in the exercise of religion, according to the dictates of conscience." During the debate young James Madison attempted to take the convention much further. His first draft of an amendment replaced "toleration" with "the full and free exercise" of religion and added "and therefore that no man or class of men ought, on account of religion to be invested with peculiar emoluments or privileges; nor subjected to any penalties or disabilities." At one stroke that would have disestablished the church. Serving in public office for the first time in his life, Madison did not offer this proposal himself. Instead, he asked Patrick Henry to move the amendment, perhaps with the hope that Henry's rhetorical ability could carry the majority. But when the guardians of the establishment accused Henry of proposing to end the church's standing in law, he denied that intention. He probably thought that the amendment's language simply guaranteed equality to all religious groups. When that amendment failed, Madison drafted a second amendment which replaced "toleration" with "the free exercise of religion" and dropped any mention of emoluments or penalties. This time he asked Edmund Pendleton, among the established church's strongest defenders, to move the change, and this time it passed.[94]

"Free exercise of religion" sounded acceptable to a Virginia churchman's ear in 1776. The phrase had recurred regularly in the discussions involving toleration and church-state relations in the years leading up to the Revolution. For many if not most of the Convention's members, it may well have appeared as simply a more felicitous expression. But what did it mean? "Free exercise of religion" was susceptible to multiple interpretations. The Quaker claim in 1768 that they already possessed it and Governor Botetourt's agreement in his response to their message demonstrated the ambiguity. That had become evident again in the Convention when Henry proposed Madison's addition about emoluments and privileges. At that point in the debate someone asked whether the amendment was "a prelude to an attack on the Established Church." Henry denied that objective. But the challenge to Henry was understandable at this time in his career. Randolph wrote of his "partiality for the dissenters from the established church." Henry "often listened to them," sympathized with "their sufferings," and brought their issues into the political arena. So supportive had Henry been that some of his political confreres in the Revolutionary Convention actually thought he was a dissenter himself, perhaps a Presbyterian.[95] Madison, on the other hand, envisioned something else. Had his amendment passed, it would have justified ending immediately the tax system that supported the established church and its clergy and seizing all church property. But neither Henry nor the majority in the Convention desired so radical a course of action.[96]

The next fall the new state legislature began the slow process that would eventually end in disestablishment many years later, but Henry was not there. In June, after approving Virginia's first constitution, the Convention had elected the firebrand from Hanover as the state's first governor. The dissenters must have been delighted at the advancement of their good friend and ally, but they would have been even happier that Thomas Jefferson was returning from Philadelphia and taking his seat in the House of Delegates if they had known what he had in mind.

3

Statute

"Establishing Religious Freedom"

A caustic letter in the *Virginia Gazette* from "A Preacher of the Gospel" greeted the new General Assembly as it settled into its first session in October 1776. In a slashing attack on the clergy of the established church, the author characterized the ministers as "dumb dogs" and "drones, who have long lived on the sweets of the land, unprofitable to, and an heavy charge on the public." The same day the House of Delegates, as the lower house of the assembly was now styled, received a petition praising the sixteenth article of the Declaration of Rights as "the rising sun of Religious liberty, to relieve them from a long night of Ecclesiastical Bondage." The petitioners asked for an end to religious taxation and the laws supporting the Church of England.[1] As the session continued, multiple petitions arrived from various groups of dissenters, including one reportedly signed by ten thousand people and another from the Presbytery of Hanover. All of them demanded religious equality for all denominations and the abolition of the church establishment.[2] They were portents of things to come.

During the next quarter century, literally hundreds of other petitions reinforced these demands for fundamental change in Virginia's church-state relationship. Eventually the combined weight of the unleashed frustrations, resentments, and anger these petitions embodied pushed against the assembly until it shattered a once proud establishment, and Virginia produced the most sweeping social revolution in the new nation. The entire process occurred in two distinct movements. The first resulted in the passage of the Statute for Establishing Religious Freedom. The second ended with the seizure and sale of the glebes, the farmlands that had previously belonged to the established church. Both outcomes, and particularly the second, were produced primarily by those who had been dissenters from that church. This chapter and the next examines this process.

The Travail of the Clergy

No one in the legislature in 1776—not even Thomas Jefferson—could have envisioned what was in store for church and state in Virginia. The Albemarle lawyer belonged to the Committee for Religion, whose membership that autumn also included Robert Carter Nicholas and Richard Bland. In that body and on the floor of the House of Delegates, Jefferson made a strenuous attempt to dismantle the entire legal apparatus that surrounded religion, and his effort produced "the severest contests" he ever faced. At his side stood young James Madison in his first session in the assembly and a minority of delegates sympathetic to the dissenters' grievances. Ranged against him were the state's most powerful legislators, including Speaker Edmund Pendleton, Carter Braxton, and Nicholas.[3] From their perspective the sixteenth article's promise of "free exercise of religion" guaranteed toleration to dissenters and nothing more. The clergy of the established church also fought back. In a lengthy memorial they defended their legal rights to the "Tenure" and "Emoluments" that came with their clerical profession and parishes, and they also argued for the beneficial effects of religious establishments in general and Virginia's in particular. Throughout the colony's long history, the church had helped to provide "order and internal Tranquility, true Piety and Virtue," while showing a "mild and tolerating Spirit" toward dissenters. Dissolving the establishment, they warned, would produce a "Contest" among the religious groups for "Superiority" and likely would result in "civil Commotions," an ominous prospect for the assembly to consider in wartime. Confident that a "Majority" of Virginians was satisfied with the established church, the ministers suggested that in such an important matter the legislature pause and canvass the "sentiments" of the people at large before proceeding to disestablish the church. Their position gained support when the *Virginia Gazette* published a petition signed by 260 people in nearby Charles City County expressing alarm at the "rapid progress" of those outside the church in "seducing the ignorant and unwary to embrace their erroneous tenets" and their efforts to overthrow the religious establishment. Let there be a "well regulated toleration," they conceded, but with "the church . . . maintained in all its legal rights."[4]

The assembly was too preoccupied by the war to do anything more than end religious taxation for dissenters and suspend it for Anglicans (who were now calling themselves Episcopalians). In what some would later term a "compact," the law freeing dissenters from church taxes also provided that "in all time coming" the glebes and all other church property were to be "reserved to the Use of the Church by law established."[5] There was no hint of disestablishment. Instead, the church remained tied to the state by a network of laws that effectively kept the clergy under the thumb of the assembly and the vestries, while at the same time restricting the dissenters. Only Episcopal clergy, for example, could legally perform marriages.

The war years marked a period of "great confusion and disorder" in the church-state relationship.[6] Numerous requests poured into the legislature for the division of parishes, the sale of glebes, the readjustment of parish boundaries, the dissolution of vestries, and the election of new ones. Because the Revolution necessarily separated the church from the mother country's ecclesiastical system, the situation of the established clergy changed dramatically. For some ministers their ordination oath of allegiance to the monarch created a crisis of conscience. Some returned to England while others resigned from the ministry and changed occupations. A combination of resignations and deaths severely depleted clerical ranks during the war years, and there were no replacements. Those men who remained in their pulpits found their incomes cut and their social status diminished. One unhappy but persevering minister complained bitterly to his brother in Scotland of the result: "The Establishment abolished, every sect upon the same level, and every man at liberty to contribute or not to the support of the Minister of his own persuasion as he judges best." From his perspective, the Revolution had proved "fatal to the Clergy of Virginia."[7] Those ministers who continued in their parishes lived off their glebes, school tuitions, and whatever people contributed. The voluntary system of church support did not catch on quickly. Newspaper advertisements for clergy invariably pledged "liberal," "handsome," "genteel," or at least "moderate" salaries, but the reality never quite matched the promises.[8]

The financial insecurity of Charles Clay at St. Anne's in Albemarle County was by no means unique. In 1777 Jefferson gave generously to the subscription for his patriotic rector who had strenuously commended the American cause to the "God of battles." But a running battle with his vestry who refused to pay the arrears of his salary discomforted the clergyman, and then a division of his parish with the creation of Fluvanna County in 1777 left his glebe outside St. Anne's. While Clay continued to minister to his former parishioners in Fluvanna Parish as well as care for two other churches in St. Anne's, the assembly acted upon a request from some dissenters and arranged for the sale of his glebe. His situation steadily worsened as the legislature rejected his petition for redress. Then he became so furious at the meager collection in 1782 that he insisted the vestry try again, and they refused. Clay switched parishes, perhaps in hopes of better remuneration, but ultimately resigned from the ministry in 1786 in order to make a living.[9]

The dissenting clergy faced not only economic challenges during wartime but also a continuing discrimination both legal and extralegal. Despite the guarantees of the Declaration of Rights, Virginia justice was relentlessly local. Baptist evangelist Elijah Baker spent almost two months in the Accomack County jail in the summer of 1778. The churchwardens had hauled him before the county court on the charge of "Vagrancy"—a typical accusation used against itinerant ministers—and the justices forbade him "to preach" in the county until he showed them the "proper Credentials." Ultimately they dismissed the charges, but a vigilante group forcibly put Baker aboard a boat in an effort to deport him. The vessel's captain, however, was so impressed by the preacher that he brought him back to land, and Baker proceeded to form the first Baptist church on the Eastern Shore.[10]

Jefferson's Statute for Religious Freedom

Jefferson's persistence matched Baker's. Despite his legislative defeat in 1776, he would not let the religious liberty issue rest. Two years later, as a member of a small committee assigned to revise all the former colony's laws to accord with the new state's independence, Jefferson drew up his statute "for Establishing Religious Freedom," a law that would guarantee freedom of conscience as laws had once guaranteed a state church. The establishment he envisioned was one of complete religious liberty. As John Noonan remarks, "Conscience, not church, became by law established."[11] The preface offers the clearest statement of his thoughts on rights of conscience:

1. Religion was an opinion one formed by the use of human reason.

2. Because "Almighty God hath created the mind free," belief must be based upon the evidence submitted to the intellect. Belief, therefore, was not an act of the will but rather must "follow involuntarily the evidence proposed" to people's minds. God had chosen "to extend [religion] by its influence on reason alone."

3. Consequently, civil government had no authority in the realm of religious thought and its expression, either to coerce or to support (which was often a form of coercion). Religious freedom was part of one's natural rights that were antecedent to any rights of government.

4. Church and state must remain separate, though Jefferson did not use that term; what he wrote was that "to suffer the civil magistrate to intrude his powers into the field of opinion and to restrain the profession or propagation of principles on supposition of their ill tendency is a dangerous fallacy, which at once destroys all religious liberty."[12]

5. The preface concludes with a sweeping affirmation of the power of unfettered reason over ignorance and error: "Truth is great and will prevail."

This bold statement of principles is followed by a brief enabling clause that provides for complete freedom of belief and worship. In conclusion the proposed bill warns that while future legislatures could repeal or amend this statute, any effort to limit the freedoms enunciated in it would violate "natural rights."

During that same session of fall 1779, the legislature also debated an opposing measure: a bill concerning religion. Closely modeled on a measure already approved in South Carolina, this proposal would establish the Christian religion in Virginia and tax everyone to support the religious group of their choice. This idea of a religious assessment had first been broached in 1776 when the legislature ended state support for clerical salaries. Now it returned as a fully developed proposal for the assembly to consider as an alternative to Jefferson's draft of a religious liberty statute for the revised code.[13]

Alternative Positions on Church and State

As the lawmakers debated these measures in Williamsburg for the last time before the capital moved to Richmond, virtually all of them might be found on Sunday morning in Bruton Parish Church worshipping at services conducted by an Episcopal minister according to the Book of Common Prayer. Yet though the legislators might pray together, their views on religion and the church-state relationship were worlds apart. By this stage in the Revolution, four distinct positions on the place of religion in society and the appropriate church-state relationship had developed or were in the process of emerging.

First, traditionalists such as Robert Carter Nicholas, Archibald Cary, and Edmund Pendleton championed a proestablishment position. They represented an older generation who were devoted to independence but also wanted to maintain the established church in its accustomed role as an essential component of their society. Religion was not someone's opinion but the "duty we owe to our Creator," as the sixteenth article expressed it. Their responsibility as civil magistrates was to see that duty carried out by the state. Devoted to the religious traditions in which they had been raised, they shared a genuine love for the church and its liturgy. While accepting a right to the "free exercise of religion," they understood that phrase in the Declaration of Rights as a grant of religious toleration to people they still regarded as dissenters. Disestablishment was anathema.

Their position, however, admitted of gradations. Most appreciated the need to amplify the conditions under which toleration might be exercised in order to cope with the religious pluralism rapidly developing in Virginia, and they recognized the need to conciliate the Presbyterians and Baptists to ensure their support for the Revolution.[14] Some were willing to free dissenters from religious taxation; others would go further and admit dissenting preachers on an equal basis with the established clergy in the performance of marriages and exempt them from jury and military duties. But none of these men were willing to give up the power they had enjoyed over the religious affairs of Virginia from the outset of their public lives. In the Old Dominion those who ruled the state ruled the church. Disestablishment meant divesting themselves of a significant measure of social control over Virginia society. Most men of this mindset were unwilling even to consider this eventuality for almost a decade after 1776.

Jefferson, Madison, and their allies represented a second position, directly counter to the traditionalists. By and large a younger group of legislators with a strongly rationalistic religious perspective, they supported immediate disestablishment and complete religious equality. Churches could fend for themselves with voluntary support. The key to Jefferson's thought is his definition of religion as a matter of private opinion formed by the use of one's reason. Unlike some of his close friends such as John Page, a wealthy planter and devoted churchman, Jefferson regarded the church as an institution of little value, nor did he see the clergy as fulfilling a significant role in society. As governor in 1780 he worked closely with the Reverend James Madison, president of the College of William and Mary and cousin of the other James Madison, to revise the college's curriculum. In the process they eliminated the chair of theology that had prepared so many of the established clergy. The following summer Madison proposed to Ezra Stiles, a Congregational clergyman who had recently become president at Yale College, that such an academic position which had been put in place when the church was established was "incompatible" with a republic.[15] That decision would prove a devastating blow to the Episcopal Church, which now had no place in the South at which to train its clergy. But that did not concern Jefferson. Though he attended religious services regularly and contributed to his local clergyman's salary, such behavior represented an assertion of his place within Virginia's gentry rather than the fulfillment of a religious obligation. While he remained a public Episcopalian, his personal religious views developed, changed, and occasionally reversed throughout his lifetime.[16]

Evangelical groups of dissenters, particularly in their multiple petitions to the assembly, spelled out a third position on church-state relations. In some respects these Presbyterians and Baptists echoed Jefferson in their republican calls for "equal liberty." But they based their case much more on religious arguments that were part scripture and part history. "When our Blessed Saviour declares his kingdom is not of this world," the Presbytery of Hanover informed the legislature in 1776, "he renounces all dependence upon State Power." More-over, the successful advance of Christianity before Constantine linked it with his empire demonstrated the benefits that would accrue to religion by disestab-lishment.[17] Over the next decade petitions from church groups and ordinary Virginians would draw upon these arguments repeatedly.

The assembly had responded first by ending taxation for the established church and by adjusting the marriage laws to permit dissenting clergymen to witness marriages under certain circumstances. By 1780 the evangelicals be-came even more insistent. They attacked as fundamentally unjust the law that restricted membership on the vestries to those who swore to conform "to the Doctrine and Discipline of the Church of England." Because the vestries lev-ied taxes for civil as well as religious purposes, this restriction embodied, as one Baptist memorial stated, "taxation without a fair and equal Representa-tion." They wanted all vestries throughout Virginia to be dissolved immediately and new ones elected by all patriotic freeholders regardless of religious affilia-tion. Thus, as a measure of the church-state relationship, even dissenters still thought of the church's vestries as integral to the government. To the vestrymen and their confreres who sat in the assembly, the social and political implica-tions of recasting the vestries in this fashion must have been breathtaking. But evangelicals demanded that all the state's laws "accord with that Republican Spirit which breathes in our Constitution and Bill of Rights."[18] They creatively extended the fourth article of the Declaration of Rights to include the estab-lished church and its clergy. The article stated: "That no man, or set of men, are entitled to exclusive or separate emoluments or privileges from the com-munity, but in consideration of public services; which, not being descendible, neither ought the offices of magistrate, legislator, or judge be hereditary." The 1776 Convention had deliberately rejected Madison's efforts to use this argu-ment to disestablish the church. But now evangelical petitions interpreted the declaration precisely in those terms.[19] Evangelical groups would continue to develop their position in the postwar world and to insist upon a social revolu-tion far beyond what even Jefferson and his allies had envisioned.[20]

To Form a Virtuous People

Those revolutionaries who agreed with Patrick Henry represented yet a fourth position on the church-state relationship. They favored the equality of all religious groups and were not necessarily opposed to disestablishment, but the hallmark of their thought was their insistence that the Christian religion provided an essential support for republican government. Therefore, the state should support religion, principally by guaranteeing its financial security. Dur-

ing the Parson's Cause, Henry had insisted that the established clergy's principal function was to promote civic responsibility. Later, in the colonial assembly,
he argued that the duty of the ministry was to "censure vice."[21] Moreover, he
shared the mentality of the proestablishment forces that adhered to the definition of religion in the Declaration of Rights as "the duty we owe to our Creator."
The intellectual gap between Jefferson and Henry can be measured by the distance between the two words they used: *opinion* and *duty*. As Daniel Boorstin
has pointed out, Jefferson's first concern was human rights, not duties. Rights
were the gift of the Creator in nature. This focus gave his thought a highly
individualistic cast. Governments existed essentially for the sake of liberty, to
protect each person in the exercise of natural rights, rather than to care for the
public interest or the general welfare of the community. The state had no social
purpose or responsibilities, and a person's duties remained undefined.[22] In contrast, people who thought like Henry, while accepting the necessity for religious
freedom, wanted the government to support the Christian ministry as it had
always done but on a broader basis.

The new situation of republicanism made such support even more necessary. A central tenet of this generation maintained that the success or failure
of the republican experiment depended ultimately on the virtue of the people
and the leaders they selected. That subject occurs repeatedly in the founders'
correspondence. As early as May 1776, when Virginia's Revolutionary Convention met to draft a plan of government, Henry became outspoken on the issue. Carter Braxton, one of the state's delegates to the Continental Congress
meeting in Philadelphia, had published an "address" to the Williamsburg meeting "on the Subject of Government in general, and recommending a particular
Form to their Consideration." Braxton favored the British system. In making
his case against a democratic form of government, he distinguished between
private and public virtue. Democracy, which he equated with a republic, was
unworkable because it depended upon the "public virtue" of the citizens, that
is, a concern for "the public good independent of private interest." According to
Braxton, if citizens wished to be truly virtuous in public life, they must abandon the pursuit of wealth, ambition, popularity, and every other self-interested
motive. But most people would find this impossible. Therefore, Braxton concluded, a democratic government was not feasible. In private life, on the other
hand, the cultivation of private virtue produced human "happiness and dignity."
So self-interest, which rejected public virtue, placed private virtue within the
realm of human possibility.[23]

Henry rejected Braxton's premise outright. Writing to his friend John Adams, he criticized the pamphlet as a "silly Thing" and "an Affront and Disgrace"
to Virginia. Virtue was indivisible, and he found Braxton's "Distinction" be-

Portrait of Patrick Henry (1736–1799) by Thomas Sully,
19th century. (Virginia Historical Society, 1851.1)

tween private and public virtue to be "weak shallow [and] evasive."[24] That same month, according to Edmund Randolph, Henry proposed in committee what became the fifteenth article of the Declaration of Rights. Unlike the other articles, which outlined the principles, purposes, and structures of government and enumerated the rights that citizens retained, the fifteenth article imposed an obligation on Virginians and linked virtue to the success of the republican experiment. It states: "That no free Government or the Blessing of Liberty can be preserved to any People but by a firm adherence to Justice, Moderation, Temperance, Frugality, and Virtue and by frequent recurrence to fundamental Principles."[25] The Convention had designated their new republic as the Commonwealth of Virginia, a political society established to maintain the common weal—the common good—of the people who comprised it. To promote the virtue vitally needed in this new form of government, Henry insisted on the value of religion. For eighteenth-century republicans, virtue meant allowing the common good to set the standard for individual behavior.[26] Success or failure would depend, in the ultimate analysis, on the virtue of both the people and those they elected to govern them.

Henry's conviction about the connection between virtue and religion grew even stronger toward the end of his life. In January 1799 he wrote an old friend, Archibald Blair, that only "virtue, morality, and religion" would protect America.[27] Before his death later that year, he devoted time and effort to preparing his will. After disposing of his property, Henry concluded: "This is all the inheritance I can give to my dear family. The religion of Christ can give them one which will make them rich indeed." Together with this document, Henry's executors found a small envelope containing a copy of the Stamp Act resolutions, one of very few papers that he had saved. On the back of the resolves, Henry inscribed his last testament to the American people. Speaking of the successful Revolution that his resolutions had initiated, he wrote: "Whether [Independence] will prove a blessing or a curse will depend upon the use our people make of the blessings which a gracious God hath bestowed on us. . . . Righteousness alone can exalt them as a nation." "Reader!" he concluded, "whoever thou art, remember this; and in thy sphere practice virtue thyself, and encourage it in others."[28]

Jefferson agreed with Henry upon the need for virtue in a republic, but they disagreed on how it should be fostered. For the sage of Monticello, education rather than religion was the key. In his view of human nature, all people possessed an innate "moral sense, or conscience" that enabled them to know right from wrong and disposed them to be attracted toward virtue.[29] Advising his daughter, he urged her always "to obey . . . this faithful internal Monitor" implanted by "Our creator."[30] The exercise of virtue transformed it into a habit of one's life, while education refined one's virtuous sensibilities. Moreover, "nature hath endowed" some people "with genius and virtue." If they could be identified, educated, and placed in positions of authority in government, such individuals would be the best protectors of the "rights and liberties of their fellow citizens" and would assure "the happiness of all." For this reason, along with the reform of the College of William and Mary, Jefferson proposed a "Bill for the More General Diffusion of Knowledge" that would initiate a comprehensive system of public primary and secondary education for the commonwealth. This measure he regarded as "the most important bill" in the entire revised legal code, the one that would assure the people's continued "freedom, and happiness."[31] It never became law, but late in life Jefferson found great satisfaction in founding the public University of Virginia.

The Postwar Religious Situation

After considering both Jefferson's statute and the bill for religion that would have established Christianity in general and provided for a general assessment, the 1779 legislature ultimately tabled both proposals. Following a lengthy debate, the assembly repealed the colonial law that provided for the support of the established church's clergy. But, on the third reading of the repealing act, the legislators struck out the preamble that referred to "the former established Church," warned its members against "the Expectation of any Re-establishment thereof," and urged them to adopt "proper Measures, among themselves, for the Support and Maintenance of their own Religion and Ministers."[32] While formally ending financial support, the legislators refused to set the church free. The results would prove disastrous for the once proud establishment.

Henry had completed the limit of three successive one-year terms as governor; and now the assembly elevated Jefferson into that honorific but largely powerless position, which he found humiliating when Banastre Tarleton and his British raiders invaded the state in 1781 and chased him out of Monticello.[33] But the defeat of his Statute for Establishing Religious Freedom had hurt more. A few years later, while serving in Paris as American minister to France, Jefferson published his *Notes on Virginia* and poured out his frustrations at the failure of the legislature to approve his statute. Discussing the state of religion in the Old Dominion, he distinguished between activities appropriate to civil government and to the individual: "The legitimate powers of government extend to such acts only as are injurious to others." Then came the zinger: "But it does me no injury for my neighbor to say there are twenty gods, or no god. It neither picks my pocket nor breaks my leg." That separation of belief from action would cause him major political problems during the presidential election of 1800. Yet Jefferson was supremely confident that left to itself reason would discover the truth. Only "error," he wrote, "needs the support of government. Truth can stand by itself."[34]

During the Revolution, Virginia's leaders necessarily focused their attention on fighting and winning the war. After Yorktown and the Treaty of Paris, the assembly could again consider domestic policy. This concern was also uppermost in the mind of George Mason when the war finally ended in 1783. Henry had resumed his place in the legislature as its preeminent leader, and Mason appealed to him as the one man above all others who could guide Virginia into a new era. "Justice and Virtue," he wrote, "are the vital Principles of republican Government." Henry agreed, and like most Virginians he linked virtue with religion and morality. In that triumvirate, if one declined, the other two suffered. Mason worried about "a Depravity of Manners and Morals," and in

America many thoughtful people related such corruption in the body politic to the blows organized religion had suffered during the war.[35]

Some attributed the widespread inattention to religious practice to the growing influence of deism, a theological perspective that denied divine revelation and traditional Christian doctrines such as the Trinity and the divinity of Christ. Henry was among those concerned. Apart from his treasured Bible, his favorite theological works were two important refutations of the deist position: *The Analogy of Religion: Natural and Revealed* by Anglican bishop Joseph Butler of Durham and *The Rise and Progress of Religion in the Soul* by Philip Doddridge, a prominent dissenting clergyman in England. Henry also had read with enthusiastic approval a small book by English Baptist Soame Jenyns, a member of the British House of Commons and no friend to Henry's politics or the American cause. In 1776 Jenyns published a *View of the Internal Evidence of the Christian Religion*, a vigorous antirationalist defense of Christianity. The sphere of reason was narrowly restricted, Jenyns argued. Only the superior doctrines and ethics of the New Testament, which "must derive its origin from God", could produce morality and a virtuous life. Henry was so impressed by Jenyns's work that he paid to have the volume reprinted, and he personally distributed several hundred copies wherever he thought they would do the most good.[36] One wonders if he gave a copy to Jefferson.[37]

Few women or men of Henry's generation would disagree with his perspective. Though they argued about the best method of forming a virtuous society, many Virginians shared Henry's concerns. Apart from challenges from deism, organized religion faced practical problems in the Old Dominion after the Revolution. A European visitor found Virginians "freely and openly" admitting that "zeal for religion, and religion generally" were in a sorry state. What was now called the Protestant Episcopal Church no longer enjoyed financial support from the state. Almost half of its clergy had died, resigned, or retired. Many church buildings were in disrepair or ruins.[38] Adding insult to injury, the church was still legally tied to the government and so was unable to manage its own affairs without legislative approval.

The Incorporation Issue

The church's legal standing preoccupied the Reverend David Griffith. The dynamic forty-one-year-old rector of Fairfax Parish in the Northern Neck was a native New Yorker who had been educated as a surgeon and practiced medicine before turning to the ministry. Ordained in 1770 for the SPG, he served in various parishes in New Jersey for about two years before becoming rector of Shelburne Parish in Loudoun County. When the war broke out, he enlisted as a surgeon and chaplain to a Virginia regiment and then in 1780 accepted the vestry's invitation to become rector of Christ Church, Alexandria.[39]

As soon as the war ended, Griffith seized the initiative. Writing to John Buchanan, the rector of Henrico Parish, which included Richmond, he pointed out the imperative need to institute church government. Griffith urged that all the Episcopal ministers meet in Richmond in April 1784. Only "the united zeal and efforts of her clergy," he wrote, could save the church from entire destruction. Buchanan's cautious reply reflected the pervasive mentality of utter dependence that distinguished Virginia clergymen who, unlike Griffith, had grown up under the establishment. He had conferred with several clerical and lay friends, and they all agreed that the responsibility to support religion belonged to Virginia's government, though none of them believed that the state would act. Therefore, if Griffith should find himself in Richmond in April, Buchanan would gather the local clergy, and perhaps something might come of it. As Bishop William Meade argued years later, this exchange illustrates the central problem Episcopalians faced in Virginia. The voluntary principle had not dented their collective consciousness. They could not envision acting on their own without the direction and approval of civil authorities.[40] And the laymen at the helm of the Old Dominion shared that perspective. Griffith laid out the situation to his friend William White, a Pennsylvania minister and future bishop: "The [Virginia] Clergy could not, with propriety, and indeed without great danger to the Church, empower any Person to agree to the least alteration whatever."[41]

Because of Griffith's leadership, however, a group of ministers submitted a petition to the legislature in June.[42] The assembly responded by drafting a bill "for incorporating the clergy of the Protestant Episcopal Church." A lengthy measure, it provided the clergy with corporate status and control over the church's "public Worship" and "spiritual concerns." The ministers were "to make Canons, bye laws & rules for the regulation and good Government of that Church" so long as these did not violate Virginia's "Laws & constitution." The proposed bill also empowered vestries, which were to be elected only by the church members in each parish, to select the ministers and manage all church property. The care of the poor was transferred from the vestries to the county courts. Reaffirming the "compact" of 1776, the bill repeated earlier guarantees to the church of all its buildings, glebes, and other property. The bill passed two readings in the House of Delegates before it was postponed.[43]

Had this "notable project" passed, James Madison informed Jefferson in July 1784, the clergy would have been rendered independent of the church's lay members. Like most Virginians, the young politician could not imagine a church which the laity did not dominate. Madison thought the bill "Extraordinary" and noted that only Patrick Henry's "talents" had saved it from defeat.[44]

Samuel Shield, the rector of Drysdale Parish in Caroline County who had presided at the clergy meeting, called Henry "the great Pillar of our Cause" when the House debated the bill in the fall session. It was probably due to Henry's rhetorical skills that an incorporation act finally passed that year, but only after extensive revisions, which provided for the incorporation of the minister and vestry in each parish to hold the church's property. A convention composed of a minister and a lay delegate from each parish would manage all the church's affairs.[45] No mention was made of a bishop, but the convention was free to do whatever it wished in that regard. Much to Madison's dismay an amendment in the House of Delegates that the convention seat two lay delegates per parish rather than one failed to make it into the final act. Even "more singular" in his view was that the vestry in each parish lacked the "uncontrouled" authority to select its minister unless the convention passed canons fixing this procedure.[46] He did not quibble, however, with the renewed guarantee of the church's property.

Madison's concerns demonstrate the attitude of even the most liberal politicians in Virginia. Despite a rationalist commitment to personal religious freedom for individuals, he apparently never questioned whether civil government should determine a church's polity. Incorporating a group—any group—for the sake of holding and managing its property was one thing, but determining how a religious body should govern itself was quite another. The fact that the assembly passed this law without seriously raising this issue demonstrates the extent to which Virginians accepted the Episcopal Church's complete subjugation to the state. The church's situation would worsen in the coming years.

As a palliative to the former dissenters, especially the Presbyterians who were infuriated by the assembly's apparent concern for the former established church, the legislature also offered to incorporate any other religious groups that asked.[47] None did. The Presbyterians explicitly rejected the idea of incorporating a group of ministers apart from the church they served. Moreover, their "Authority" over the "care of souls" derived from a "higher source than any Legislature on earth."[48] Madison was not particularly happy with the final Incorporation Act, although he had voted for it, he told Jefferson, in order to prevent what he considered a much more dangerous proposal, a general assessment or tax on everyone to support "Teachers of the Christian Religion."

The Assessment Proposal

The cessation of public funding had proved devastating for the established church during the Revolution. In 1783 news of the Peace of Paris formally ending the Revolution had scarcely arrived in Virginia when interested parties began organizing in support of what one petition to the legislature called a "just, equitable, and Adequate" assessment "for the support of the Christian Churches."[49] Maryland and South Carolina provided for such measures in their new state constitutions, and a section drafted by John Adams in the Massachusetts constitution of 1780 provided state support for "public Protestant teachers of piety, morality, and religion."[50] In Virginia some individuals and groups who wanted the Episcopal Church disestablished openly advocated a tax system that would support all Christian clergy and churches. In July 1784 "Pacificus" in the *Virginia Gazette* argued for a religious settlement that would provide "general satisfaction to all."[51]

An important part of that "all" would be the Presbyterians. Their laity and clergy had wholeheartedly embraced the Revolution not only for the independence it offered the state but also for the freedom it promised the church. But while welcoming the end of taxation for the religious establishment, their leaders disagreed on the question of how far church and state should be divorced. Because of their education and socioeconomic status, Presbyterians found themselves in a good position to rival or even supplant the Episcopalians. Their schools, for example, were thriving. On the eve of the Revolution, Hanover Presbytery had encouraged the foundation of Hampden-Sydney in Southside Virginia; and across the mountains in Lexington, Augusta Academy became Liberty Hall (later Washington) College. While concerned to provide the proper training for budding clergymen, the ministers also were convinced of the value of education in preparing virtuous leaders for the new republic. Moreover, the development of two educational centers under Presbyterian auspices provided solid alternatives to Anglican-sponsored William and Mary. As the war ended in 1782, the assembly invited Presbyterian minister John Todd to preach for them on a day appointed for public thanksgiving. That gesture eloquently signaled their new status in Virginia. They had arrived.[52]

After an October 1784 meeting, the Presbytery of Hanover dispatched Todd and three other ministers to represent their views to the legislature. Though the clergy and elders rejected church incorporation or any meddling in the "spiritual" aspects of the church, they thought it "wise policy" for the legislature to form an "alliance" with religion and gain its assistance "because of it's happy influence upon the morality of the citizens." Provided it be done on "the most liberal basis," an assessment would be acceptable to the Presbyterian leaders. Several county petitions that fall reinforced the idea that religion would benefit from the "Smiles, and Support of Government."[53] Leading politicians including Patrick Henry and Richard Henry Lee agreed.

In the fall assembly Henry headed the campaign to enact an assessment bill. According to its terms, each person would designate the religious group to re-

ceive the tax, and it could be used to support both clergy and church buildings. In its final form the bill was to establish "a Provision for Teachers of the
Christian Religion." The clergy were educators, teaching the religiously based
moral values and virtues essential to a healthy republic. "A general diffusion of
Christian knowledge," the proposal argued, would help "to correct the morals
of men, restrain their vices, and preserve the peace of society." Such an assessment could be effected, moreover, while maintaining the fundamental equality
of all the churches and religious groups in Virginia.[54] That law might well have
passed, but its most influential supporters were not on hand. First, Madison
maneuvered Henry out of the assembly and back into the governor's seat, thus
depriving him of his leadership role in the legislature. Lee had also strongly
endorsed the assessment and would have replaced Henry as its chief advocate
in the House, but he was busy presiding over the Continental Congress in New
Jersey. Under Madison's careful guidance, the assembly passed the Incorporation Act for the Episcopal Church, and then on Christmas Eve the canny politician persuaded the House to postpone the assessment bill until the people of
Virginia had been consulted.[55]

The Debate over Assessment

During the spring and summer of 1785, the assessment controversy produced
a political campaign that exceeded anything Virginia ever experienced before
the Civil War. On county court days and on Sundays in churches and meetinghouses, thousands of Virginians signed petitions to the legislature. Advocates
for the assessment produced over a dozen distinct memorials. These individual
compositions developed the standard arguments for the importance of religion
in society and the need for government to support it. In a normal year such
an outpouring of support for a bill would have impressed the legislature. But
for every person who signed his name or put his mark at the bottom of a pro-
assessment petition, more than ten others subscribed to a protest against any
assessment. The best known of these today was composed by James Madison.
His *Memorial and Remonstrance* elaborated fifteen carefully reasoned arguments against the proposed assessment and the dangers it posed not only to
religious freedom but to religion itself. Madison's composition was printed and
circulated in about a dozen counties in the Piedmont and Northern Neck for
signatures.

But the explicitly religious petitions drawn up and disseminated by church
groups proved much more popular. Furious with the assembly because of its
care for the old church establishment, Presbyterians and Baptists waded into
the fray. They viewed the Incorporation Act and the assessment proposal as a

combined effort to restore the Episcopal Church's preeminence. The old alliance of church and state endured. The great bulk of adult Virginians who would be liable for the assessment had been baptized by a minister of the established church. When asked what minister or church should receive their assessment, as the proposed law required, most probably would default to the Episcopal Church. That church, therefore, would reap the tax largesse, hire more clergy, and regain its former dominance. Its formal reestablishment would follow. Incorporation had been the first move in that direction. Assessment practically guaranteed its success.

Confronted by angry challenges from its congregations, Hanover Presbytery reversed its position and called for a church convention in August 1785. The long petition approved by those who attended this heated meeting condemned the assessment and attacked those portions of the Incorporation Act that determined church polity and awarded the church property of the former establishment to the Episcopalians. The sympathetic attention that the Episcopal Church received and the power it commanded in the legislature infuriated the Presbyterians. Ten years after independence the assembly still displayed a preeminent concern for one religious group, they complained, exalting it "to a superior pitch of Grandeur" and making it effectively "the Church of the State."[56] The Presbyterian convention's petition circulated among their congregations, particularly in the Valley, and was well subscribed.

Virginia's Baptists were even more electrified by the incorporation and assessment issues. The pre-Revolutionary persecution they had experienced now conditioned their reaction. The suffering of their preachers, the oppressive religious taxation, and the restrictions on their worship had left them with a profound hatred for the established church and all that it represented as the favorite of the gentry-controlled government. This attitude deepened their emotional commitment to absolute freedom of conscience and placed them in the mid-1780s among the strongest supporters of Jefferson's statute. In the postwar era the slightest indication of legislative assistance for the Episcopalians always would rouse Baptist fury. That would not ease until the state had seized the last vestiges of the establishment, the church's farmlands, or glebes. But the long memory of pre-Revolutionary oppression, repeatedly revived in books, sermons, and tracts, would keep most Baptists extremely wary of church-state ties throughout the nineteenth and well into the twentieth century.[57] When other denominations in later years attempted to enlist state support for the Christian empire, Virginia Baptists showed themselves much more cautious. They knew their past better than most, and they had a proud historic legacy to uphold.

At the time of the Revolution, Virginia Baptists overwhelmingly favored the break with Britain and recognized the singular opportunity it provided to redress their grievances and secure religious freedom. During the war they participated vigorously in the church-state controversies, repeatedly petitioning the assembly to end religious taxation, discriminatory marriage laws, and the secular power of the vestries. To respond to these concerns in what they recognized as a highly volatile political climate, the Separate Baptists organized a General Committee composed of representatives from their four district associations in the state. Despite their belief that the local church was the only proper instrument of ecclesial government and their consequent distrust of any hierarchical or centralized church polity, they appreciated the need for concerted action. The task of the General Committee was to oversee "political grievances" as well as other matters involving Baptists that might be referred by the associations. Composed of the most influential preachers, this organization functioned as the political-action wing of Virginia Baptists until the end of the eighteenth century. During the massive petition campaign of 1785, it did yeoman service in galvanizing resistance to the assessment and organizing support for the passage of Jefferson's statute.[58]

The formulaic petitions Baptists drew up emphasized that the assessment was "Contrary to the Spirit of the Gospel; and the Bill of Rights." Christianity had flourished before Constantine and would do so again if the clergy demonstrated by pure scriptural preaching and blameless lives that the Holy Spirit had called them to the ministry. As for the government's role, "let the laws punish" the contemporary "Vices and Immorality" and the magistrates faithfully "scourge the Growing Vices of the Age."[59] In both longer and shorter forms these petitions circulated throughout Virginia east of the Blue Ridge and were the most extensively signed that year.

The Methodists Become a Church

While the assembly tinkered with the incorporation bill and debated the general assessment, Griffith traveled to New York for the first convention of what would become the Protestant Episcopal Church in the United States. Eight states had sent clerical and lay delegates, and they agreed to seat Griffith though he lacked regular delegate standing. As a Richmond newspaper pointed out, Virginia ministers were "restricted by law" and "not at liberty to send delegates or conse[n]t to any alteration in the order, government, doctrine, or worship of the Church."[60] Virginia held the Episcopal Church bound in a way that the other denominations failed to appreciate. Griffith and his allies could not begin the process of ecclesiastical reconstruction until the assembly passed an incorporation act; but as that was happening, their church was losing the brightest promise of its renewal.

The final weeks of 1784 marked a critical moment for American Episcopalians when the Methodists met in Baltimore and withdrew from the church. What had been a vibrant reform element within the Church of England now became a new denomination, the Methodist Episcopal Church. The break had been coming for almost a decade. Though George Whitefield had promoted Methodist ideas, this evangelical movement only became widespread in the British colonies after 1769 when John Wesley began sending out from England a series of lay itinerant preachers. They evangelized the colonies by applying Methodist techniques of practical piety, discipline, and Christian fellowship.[61] Success was immediate, especially in those areas of the South where the established church held sway. The preaching of Joseph Pilmore was so popular that reports from Norfolk described the church on Sunday as "deserted" while thousands flocked to hear him preach "in the Fields." Though "the Ladies" came in droves, his appeal seems to have been universal. Rather than the moralizing sermons and liturgical formalism of Anglican worship, Pilmore and the other preachers encouraged a religion of the heart. Their exhortations sought to awaken their hearers to conversion. Describing his own father's spiritual transformation, Jesse Lee, a major figure of post-Revolutionary Methodism, summarized the religious experience: "One day, when his conviction was very deep, and his distress very great, he went into the woods, and continued travelling about, and mourning for his sins, till at length he claimed the promises of God, and by faith beheld the Lamb of God that taketh away the sin of the world, and was justified by the blood of Jesus Christ. The joy he felt in his soul he could not describe with words. He had an inward evidence, that his sins were forgiven, and that he was born again."[62]

Personal accounts of such conversion experiences are strikingly similar in their morphology. They began with an awareness of one's own sinfulness and the need for God's grace. Often a period of intensely private self-scrutiny preceded this awakening. Ultimately the person experienced an intense feeling that God offered his personal forgiveness and love, and that he or she had been "saved" by Jesus Christ. The sensible relief and joy were overwhelming, and this deep consolation would be renewed repeatedly, not only in the solitude of private devotions and scripture readings but more especially in the communal warmth of love feasts, class meetings, watch nights, and quarterly conferences. Methodism offered a path to individual salvation with the support and assurance of a faith community expressed most fully in the conference. Community was vital, both for validating the religious experience and assisting personal growth in holiness. Conversion only initiated the process. Arminian in his theology, Wesley urged his followers to pursue and achieve Christian perfection, a freedom from all sin and union with God in love.

This doctrine of human perfectibility through cooperation with God's grace pitted the Methodists squarely against Calvinist groups, and particularly the Presbyterians and Separate Baptists. They also faced opposition from within the ranks of the established church's clergy, principally because of the preachers' style of exhortation. Anglican ministers identified the Methodists as "New Lights," uneducated products of the Great Awakening that still rumbled across Virginia on the eve of the Revolution. Although Methodists regarded themselves as members of the established church and depended upon its ministers for the sacraments of baptism and Holy Communion, relations between the Anglican clergy and Methodist preachers were often uneasy. Some Methodists refused to receive the sacraments or even to attend the services conducted by a minister of whose life they disapproved or whose sermons lacked evangelical fervor.

Some Anglican clergymen reciprocated. Archibald McRobert, for example, considered Methodists "a designing people, void of the generous and catholic spirit of the gospel," controlled by "Pope John" Wesley, and "illiterate creatures" who lacked "prudence and discretion." The most notable exception was Devereux Jarratt, the minister of Bath Parish in Dinwiddie County. An evangelical himself, Jarratt welcomed the Methodist missionaries and rejoiced in the religious revivals that accompanied their preaching and swelled their numbers in Southside Virginia. Francis Asbury, one of Wesley's chief lieutenants and the principal leader of American Methodism, wrote of Jarratt in 1781 that "there have been more souls convinced by his ministry, than by that of any other man in Virginia."[63]

The distinctive feature of Methodism, however, lay not in its theology or evangelical preaching but in its organizational structure. Methodism was truly methodical. Wesley drew up extensive rules of discipline for his followers and instituted a system of classes, each composed of about fifteen people with a trained lay leader. These small groups provided an opportunity for each member to share the salvation experience. The process of communal discernment tested the individual's spiritual insights while mutual correction checked external conduct. Those capable of observing the strict personal discipline Wesley laid down were eligible for membership in these classes. Methodist societies were formed from them and grouped together geographically into circuits served by itinerant preachers. Beginning in 1773, these preachers met annually in conferences to certify new preachers, assign circuits, resolve difficulties, and provide a time of prayer and mutual support in their labors. As the number of societies increased, circuits were enlarged or new ones created. Thus even before the separation from the established church, Methodism possessed a pragmatic and flexible polity, well suited to the religious needs of a rapidly expanding and widely dispersed population. On the eve of the Revolution, nine circuits served more than two thousand members, and by 1776 the membership doubled, mainly in Virginia and principally due to the tireless assistance rendered by Jarratt in the Southside.[64]

In helping the Methodist preachers, the minister trusted their protestations of loyalty to Anglicanism. Soon after the American colonies declared their independence from Great Britain, Virginia Methodists reiterated their position as a "Religious Society in Communion with the Church of England."[65] The first significant indication of ecclesial separatism appeared three years later. Despite the wartime dislocations, the departure of most of the English Methodist preachers, and the embarrassment created by Wesley's public opposition to American independence, Methodism spread steadily during the war years. But the shortage of Episcopal clergymen due to retirements, resignations, and deaths presented a serious problem. For a group of young Methodist preachers in Virginia and North Carolina, this presaged the demise of the established church. But because their converts needed the sacraments, or ordinances, as they called baptism and the Eucharist, they decided to take matters into their own hands. A conference of southern preachers met in Virginia and ordained four of their number to administer baptism and the Lord's Supper. This threatened Methodist unity, and Asbury eventually persuaded them to postpone dispensing the sacraments, but the problem only grew worse. "If we had an itinerant clergyman," he informed Wesley, "all our wants of ordinances would be supplied, but such a clergyman is a miracle."[66]

The large number of non-Episcopalians joining Methodist societies created yet another difficulty. Were they to attend Anglican services and take communion? Moreover, how could Methodists insist on the importance of baptism and the Eucharist if clergy were lacking to supply them? Anglican ministers cared for territorial parishes, but Methodists often enough lived outside of them. As a frustrated Asbury wrote his spiritual leader in England, the issue boiled down to the ordinances. They had been "the tools of division and separation" ever since the Reformation.[67] Thomas Paine had asserted that an island should not rule a continent. It seemed equally wrong that an outmoded and unnecessary dependence upon a moribund church should hamper the growth and operation of a dynamic Christian community. By 1784 more than eighty preachers cared for fourteen thousand members in Methodist societies in America, mainly in the southern states. In spirituality, ministerial style, theological emphases, and popular appeal, a wide divergence already existed between Methodists and the great bulk of their nonevangelical Episcopalian brethren. No matter what administrative decision might be made, "a separation of heart and practice," as Asbury noted, had already occurred. New wine demanded new skins.[68]

Recognizing reality, Wesley dispatched Thomas Coke and two elders whom he had personally ordained with instructions for organizing a new church in America. They met with a group of preachers assembled in Baltimore for a special conference at Christmas 1784. The Americans selected Asbury to serve as a superintendent with Coke over the new Methodist Episcopal Church. After Asbury's ordination to the orders of deacon, elder, and superintendent, other preachers were selected and ordained as elders and deacons. The superintendents would function essentially as bishops, while the elders would administer the sacraments and the deacons would assist them. All of them—bishops, elders, and deacons—would travel on circuit with the lay preachers. The conference also approved a liturgy which Wesley had proposed and *The Discipline*, a book containing norms for Methodist life and behavior which evolved in a few years into *The Doctrines and Discipline of the Methodist Episcopal Church in America*.[69] Under Wesley's guidance the Methodist leaders had formulated a hybrid ecclesiastical polity. It contained a flexible, itinerant ministry within a tightly organized hierarchical structure ultimately governed by the democratic procedures and processes of a conference. While traditionally Christian in its theology, Methodism had adopted a distinctively American style.[70] For the Episcopal Church, however, the results of the Christmas Conference spelled catastrophe because it lost the brightest promise for its own revitalization.

The exodus of the Methodists had a direct bearing on the church-state challenges Virginia Episcopalians faced over the proposed assessment and their own recent incorporation. The new Bishop Asbury had once predicted that America would be "the glory of the world for religion." Liberated by its independence and throbbing with evangelical fervor, Methodism prepared to make the most of the opportunities the new nation offered. A connection with the state was not one of them. Following Virginia's incorporation of the Episcopal Church, some friends of the Methodists in various states suggested the new church apply for incorporation also, but Bishop Coke, fresh from England, thought differently. "We have a better staff to lean upon," he wrote, "than any this world can afford."[71] Asbury agreed. A few years later when some ministers proposed an incorporation act in Maryland, he thought it a "Jesuitical plan" that would alienate the people. "We have no church property but our churches; who will contend with us for these," he asked, "or put us out of the possession of them?" Opposition to government assistance of any kind quickly became Methodist policy.[72] That marked a dramatic reversal from 1776 when Methodists had strongly supported the establishment. Now in the midst of the assessment debate, Bishop Coke publicly rejoiced that American independence had "broken ye antichristian union . . . between Church & State."[73] In 1785 the Methodists would neither endorse the general assessment proposal nor defend the Episcopal Church's incorporation.

The Protestant Episcopal Church

The Episcopalians themselves were divided, particularly over assessment. While that controversy raged across the state, they held their first convention in Richmond. The decisions their leadership would make over the next few years in the formation of their own church would prove critical for the future of church-state relations in Virginia. Once again Griffith took the lead in organizing this meeting, as he had energized efforts for an incorporation act. More than a hundred delegates, two-thirds of them laymen, assembled in a makeshift building serving temporarily as the state's capitol in May 1785 and elected as their presiding officer James Madison of the College of William and Mary. The convention assumed three major tasks: the election and instruction of delegates to the General Convention of the Episcopal Church scheduled for the coming fall in Philadelphia, the composition of an address to the church's membership in Virginia, and the approval of canons for church government and discipline.[74]

The controversy over the upcoming Philadelphia meeting exposed the fault line between conservatives and liberals in the Virginia church. The New York meeting Griffith had attended the previous year recommended that each state send representatives to a General Convention, and set out some general principles designed to preserve church unity. The majority at the Richmond convention objected to two of these principles: first, that the church retain the doctrine and worship of the Church of England except for those modifications required by political independence; and second, that the clerical and lay delegates meet together but vote as separate bodies with the concurrence of both bodies needed to pass any proposal.[75] The reason for these objections became apparent when zealous lay reformers dominated the meeting.

In the discussion of the church's liturgy, Edmund Randolph, the state's attorney general, and Jefferson's friend John Page led the forces advocating change. Known for his interest in theology, Page had eagerly looked forward to this meeting and relished his role as "an Elder of the Church." Encouraging St. George Tucker, a prominent Williamsburg attorney, to lend a hand in this "great work" of reformation, Page spelled out in glowing terms his expectations for the meeting: "Religion may be restored to its primitive Purity, everything not essential to the support of genuine Christianity" eliminated, "and all Sects of Christians may be heartily reconciled to one another." America's "Golden

Age" had dawned with the opportunity to deliver "Mankind from the Shackles of Tyranny and Superstition."[76]

But one person's superstition is another's dogma. Writing to Griffith months before the convention, Samuel Sheild, the rector of John Page Jr.'s parish in Caroline County, warned against an "innovating spirit" loose in the church. The younger Page had informed his conservative pastor of his father's hopes and dreams for reforming the liturgy. Sheild feared that misguided individuals in a vain exhibition of their "Ingenuity" or "critical Talents" might wreck "a Form of Prayer which has been established for Ages."[77] Much to the dismay of some clerical delegates, the senior Page's agenda dominated the deliberations. The eager lay theologian recommended sweeping liturgical alterations in the Book of Common Prayer, including the elimination of the Nicene and Athanasian creeds and the words "descended into Hell" from the Apostles' Creed. Page also wanted to erase the rubric that permitted the minister to use his discretion in refusing the Eucharist to certain categories of people.[78] Heated debates ensued. Led by Griffith and John Burgess, the respected rector of Southwark Parish in Surry County, most of the clergy objected; but the laity had the votes. Page and Randolph took turns moving and seconding each proposed change, and they always carried the majority. In the presiding officer's chair, they had an important ally. Madison's theological liberalism was well known, and his convention sermon demonstrated that his sympathies favored reform. Perhaps for balance, the convention elected Griffith and Page to represent Virginia at the General Convention.[79]

Reforming forces also influenced the forty-three canons that the convention approved for governing the Virginia church. Following the policy laid down in the Incorporation Act, this church law concentrated authority in an annual convention in which lay and clerical delegates would vote together. The canons effectively emasculated the office of bishop. He was to be "amenable to the Convention" and restricted to the tasks of ordaining, confirming, and presiding at church functions. Although nominally responsible for "superintending the conduct of the clergy" and required to make triennial visitations of every parish in the diocese, his role was purely advisory. He had no authority to regulate, discipline, or enforce. The vestries kept control of hiring the clergy. Moreover, the canons insisted that the bishop also be a regularly inducted minister of a parish responsible for all his parochial duties in addition to those expected of a bishop.[80]

At the end of the weeklong meeting, the guiding hand of President Madison showed itself. Before adjournment, the convention resolved that in the intervals between its meetings, the real power in the diocese would reside in a standing committee of two clergy and two laymen. They would "correspond" with other

Episcopalians, run the day-to-day affairs of the church, and call conventions as appropriate. They also would investigate how a bishop might be obtained for Virginia and report their findings to the next convention. All four men— Robert Andrews, John Bracken, John Blair, and John Page—hailed from Williamsburg or nearby and belonged to the circle around the college president. Though Griffith might attend the convention in Philadelphia, Madison effectively eclipsed him in Virginia. This would become even more apparent in the succeeding years.

Reactions to the meeting varied. Page left quite satisfied, while Randolph sniffed that he would never go to one again.[81] From the northern states Episcopalians had watched the proceedings of their Virginia brethren with interest and, at times, alarm. One New Jersey minister, after reviewing the published *Journal* of the 1785 convention, thought it contained "such a motley mixture of Episcopacy, Presbytery and Ecclesiastical Republicanism as before was never brought together and incorporated, and must surprise the whole Christian world."[82] The church's General Conventions over the next few years would demonstrate that Virginia Episcopalians were liturgically and theologically out of step.

The Passage of Jefferson's Statute

Even more serious for the immediate future of their church, they were not in tune with most Virginians. In a public address to church members, the Episcopal convention stated its desire to work with other religious groups "to bring the Christian Church to unity." A Richmond observer applauded the progressive tone but thought a reunion of Christian denominations unlikely. The closer they came to one another, he noticed, the more hostile they became. The years 1785 and 1786 witnessed the bitterest interreligious feuding of the decade. Ignoring the ecumenical enthusiasm voiced by liberal Episcopalians, the growing ranks of evangelicals, and particularly Baptists and Presbyterians, had read the Incorporation Act as a sign of renewed legislative preference for what had once been the state church.[83] The Episcopalian convention reinforced this opinion by symbolically demonstrating the special relationship that church enjoyed with the government. The lay delegates were drawn largely from Virginia's political and economic elite. They met with the clergy in the tobacco warehouse turned temporary capitol in Richmond and invited the governor, the council, and the Supreme Court judges to join them "within the bar."[84] No wonder evangelicals feared that the assessment was designed in reality to revive the former established church's preeminent position. That summer they threw their full weight behind the petition campaign that effectively doomed that proposal. When the legislature met that fall, the assessment bill never came to a vote. Instead, Madison brought forward Jefferson's proposed statute for establishing religious freedom, and the assembly passed it by a wide margin in January 1786. In retrospect, that proved one of the great defining moments in the history of religious liberty.[85]

Some Virginians could not quite fathom what had happened. Trying to understand the assembly's opposition to the assessment "for the support of Religion," John Page mused in verse:

> Have Christians all remembrance lost,
> How much their ancestors it cost,
> To support their church and preachers,
> And to encourage holy teachers?—
> Or recollecting what was done,
> Wish they all such expence to shun;
> Thinking it would be far better,
> Their teachers knew not single letter—
> By inspiration pray and preach,
> And congregations gratis teach.
> This plan some sect'ries taste would hit,
> And just as well free thinkers fit;
> They the prevailing sect would be,
> These triumph by their sophistry—
> Learning with learned sects decline,
> And impious wit triumphant shine,
> 'Till bigoted enthusiast zeal,
> Break forth and crush the common weal.[86]

Over forty years later John Marshall explained to a northern Presbyterian clergyman how different the church-state relationship was in Virginia from that in New England: "Previous to the revolution we had an established church and all were taxed for its support. From one extreme we passed to the other," and it became "purely voluntary." He then described the proposed assessment bill and pointed out "its supporters incurred so much popular odium that no person has since been found hardy enough to renew the proposition." As a young member of the House of Delegates in 1784, the chief justice had voted in favor of the Incorporation Act and against Madison's proposal to defer consideration of the assessment bill.[87]

The coalition that controlled the assembly the following year and passed Jefferson's statute was largely composed of Episcopalians of a rationalist cast of mind and Presbyterians. Episcopalian churchmen like Page found themselves outnumbered. Baptists and Methodists were practically absent.[88] The same division between traditional believers and rationalists existed within clerical ranks, and they also disagreed on church-state polity. In his sermon to the convention in May 1786, the future bishop Madison praised the passage of Jefferson's statute as providing a "glorious instance, wherein religion and policy are no longer connected."[89] Griffith saw nothing to celebrate in that development. John Swanwick, a prominent Philadelphia Episcopalian, published a pamphlet warmly attacking Jefferson's work as "a general declamation against all religion." He charged that "under the specious appearance of establishing religious freedom," the statute actually "tends to remove the necessity of any religion whatsoever among the people." Soon after Swanwick dispatched multiple copies of his work to Griffith, the minister wrote him an encouraging, appreciative letter.[90]

The split within Episcopalian ranks, the passage of an ill-conceived Incorporation Act for their church only, and the massive petition campaign launched especially by the Baptists against the assessment proposal enabled Jefferson's bill to become law. In a single decade the religious situation had changed more dramatically in Virginia than in any other state in the confederation. Where once the established church had reigned supreme, religious pluralism had become an accepted fact. From a position of preeminence with full government support in 1775, the Episcopal Church had been reduced to the status of a denomination locked in competition for adherents with those who had once been classified as dissenters. The latter, and particularly the Baptists and Presbyterians, had become major players on the religious landscape; and the Methodists had emerged as a vibrant independent religious body. Perhaps less obviously, the state also had been significantly changed because of the self-denying quality about the statute "for establishing religious freedom." It remained to be seen, however, exactly what the statute meant. That would be determined in the political order by what the evangelicals and particularly the Baptists wanted.

4

Property

"To Reconcile All the Good People"

News of the passage of his Statute for Establishing Religious Freedom left Thomas Jefferson in a state of sensible consolation. Though James Madison noted that Senate amendments had "slightly mutilated" the preface, the bulk of the bill had survived intact. Writing from Paris, the proud author announced that across Europe it was being translated and published to widespread acclaim. At last, he wrote, "the standard of reason" had been "erected," and how sweet it was that his own Virginia had done it.[1] The boundaries of that law, however, remained undefined. For the next decade and a half, more contests would be waged at courthouses and churchyards, in the press, and in the legislative chambers, until yet another resolution had been attempted "to reconcile" Virginians to a new definition of the church-state relationship. The leadership in that movement would come not from Jefferson or Madison or their erstwhile rationalist allies from Virginia's political elite but from the evangelical forces that had defeated the assessment.

The Repeal of Incorporation

A major theme of the anti-assessment petitions of 1785 had been the evils of the Episcopal Church's Incorporation Act. The Baptists resumed the attack the following year with a fresh wave of petitions. Two issues consumed them, and both underscored the elevated position they supposed the former established church still maintained in Virginia, thanks to the General Assembly. First, by fixing the church's governing polity, the incorporation law had violated a "divine prerogative," created the Episcopal Church as "the Church of the state," and privileged it with "Peculiar distinctions and the Honour of an important name." Equally galling was the issue of church property. By awarding one religious body all the churches, church plate, and glebes that by right belonged to the public at large, the law had placed the "Episcopal Society" in "the Lap of the Legislature." The Baptists were furious. Coordinating the political efforts for the four Separate Baptist associations in Virginia, the General Committee sent Reuben Ford and John Leland, two of the most influential preachers, to represent their views to the legislature. The petition they submitted elaborated their objections and attacked incorporation as "pregnant with evil, and dangerous to religious liberty."[2] In the next weeks almost thirty similar petitions arrived in Richmond, mainly from Tidewater and Piedmont counties where Baptists were numerous. Following the strategy used to pass Jefferson's statute, the General Committee had circulated these memorials at church events and on court days. They called for the repeal of the Incorporation Act, the sale of the "public property" occupied by the Episcopalians, and the application of the resulting funds to "public use."

These petitions laid bare the anger and stored-up resentment of previous decades. While varying in style and language, they advanced a common interpretation and historical perspective on the Declaration of Rights. Colonial governments had originally wrested this property from their ancestors by force. Instead of returning it to the people at the time of the Revolution, the legislature had transferred it to one religious group that not only bore no intrinsic connection to the now defunct colonial church but differed from it in name, laws, and forms of worship. Baptists saw this as oppression pure and simple. "Tyranny is not the better," one petition complained, "for being on this side of the Atlantic."[3] The fourth article of the Declaration of Rights stated "that no man, or set of men, are entitled to exclusive or separate emoluments or privileges from the community, but in consideration of public services." By awarding the Episcopalians the exclusive use of all property once held by the Church of England in Virginia, the legislature trampled on that article.[4] "Good God," exclaimed another memorial, "can this be equal for a man that has five or six children to will fi[f]ty or a hundred thousand pounds to one; and not one English Shilling to the rest of his Children; when all the Children Labour'd alike to Raise that hundred thousand pounds?" This Albemarle petition bluntly warned the assembly of the Baptists' political clout: "Our whish is this, that our own delegates . . . should be as free giving their own Sentiments as the Water that Runeth down the Brook: but if this Our Petition should meet with any Opposition and it comes to be debated in the house, pray Gentlemen be so kind as to let us see the ayes and noes."[5] The Presbyterians stayed quiet that year, perhaps because of their own internal reorganization, as the western portion of Hanover Presbytery beyond the Blue Ridge broke off to become the Lexington Presbytery. But the Baptists demanded results.[6] With an irritation that his letters seldom displayed, David Griffith wrote to William White from his Fairfax Parish glebe, "It wou'd seem that nothing will satisfy these people but the entire destruction of the Episcopal Church."[7]

This year, however, the Episcopalians were ready for them. Earlier a realistic Edmund Randolph had been prepared to concede the failure of the assessment proposal. But from his perspective the Incorporation Act had forged a sacred trust. "I cannot but consider" that law, he wrote, "in the light of a compact; which legislative authority may dissolve by the arm of power, but not by the rules of justice and honour."[8] The key concern was the church's property. The May 1786 Episcopal convention drafted a petition to the legislature and asked the parishes to do the same. In the greatest demonstration of postwar solidarity, more than thirty-five parishes responded. As with the Baptist memorials, emotional currents of hurt, anger, and resentment ran deep beneath the reasoned Episcopalian arguments. They advanced an interpretation of events at sharp variance with that proposed by the Baptists. According to the Episcopalian perspective, Virginians had built most of the churches and purchased the bulk of the glebes when virtually everyone belonged to the established church and "scarce any such thing as a Baptist" or other dissenter existed in the colony. With the Revolution, Episcopalians had "cheerfully" accepted the abolition of the establishment, even though their numbers "far exceeded that of the Dissenters." But "as a compact" for the church's acceptance of the end of state financial support, the 1776 legislature had guaranteed the security of its property, not as a fresh grant but as a confirmation of what the church already owned.[9] Randolph and the convention were not inventing this compact theory. In 1781 Leland had applied to Madison's father to use a church in St. Thomas Parish in Orange County. Denying the request, James Madison Sr. pointed to the 1776 act and noted that the dissenters had then accepted the reservation of "the glebes, churches, books, plate, ornaments, donations" to the established church in exchange for the "privilege" of no longer having to contribute to its support.[10]

Episcopalians also rejected the Baptist interpretation of the Declaration of Rights. The fourth article, they insisted, referred not to churches or glebes but to hereditary offices inconsistent with republican principles. Apart from history or legislation, they based their case on the rights of private property. If the assembly could seize the glebes and churches, then no one's property remained secure. Indeed, "with equal propriety, and with the same justice, all grants for Lands under the Kings of England, now held under those grants; and all donations, from any former Assembly, may by this, or any succeeding Assembly be declared null and void."[11] That autumn the House initially appeared to side with the Baptists when it considered a bill that would open all the Anglican churches to "common use" and authorize the sale of the glebes in those parishes where no Episcopal clergy resided or where the majority of inhabitants, under certain restrictions, desired it.[12] In December a concerned Episcopal standing committee dispatched a letter to the assembly to supplement their convention petition. In a notably more serious and even threatening tone, the church's leadership insisted on the Episcopalians' property rights. The church could not be "deprived" of its buildings and glebes except "by Violence"; and such an assault, they warned, would extinguish "public Faith," violate "the Principles of all Government," and shake "the Foundation of the State." Anyone tempted to so disturb "the Peace of the Episcopal Church" should reflect first on how its members, "who compose so considerable a Part of the State" were likely to feel and react. The signatories included John Page, a member of the assembly that year, and John Blair, one of Virginia's most respected jurists. Madison later told Jefferson that the church property issue "involved the Legislature in some embarrassment."[13] The angry exchange betrayed the profound hostility that had been building between Baptists and Episcopalians for at least a generation.

In the face of the Episcopalians' threats, the politicians retreated and compromised. A brief act authorized all religious societies to appoint trustees to hold and manage their property and repealed the Incorporation Act as well as any other acts that inhibited the church from regulating its own affairs. Griffith thought repeal had placed the Episcopalians "in a very embarrassing situation," probably because it revoked their church polity. But the next Episcopal convention simply passed legislation providing for the church's internal government and reenacted the church canons of 1785.[14] More important, while removing itself from regulating "spirituals," the government left the Episcopalian property intact. In effect the lawmakers reconfirmed the "compact" of 1776 and gave the evangelicals the smaller half of the loaf. The next year's legislature reinforced that decision. Despite the Baptists' petitions and a resolution from Lexington Presbytery, the assembly defeated a limited proposal to sell only those glebes that lacked a resident minister in parishes that approved the sale. In a roll-call vote, 62 to 45, George Mason, James Monroe, George Nicholas, and other key figures that had supported the passage of Jefferson's statute now deserted their evangelical allies. Valley Presbyterians had always been more liberal than their Piedmont brethren in their approach to religious liberty, perhaps because relatively few Baptists lived there. The Baptist General Committee may have eased their decision because only by a one-vote margin did the members at their annual meeting accept the proposition that the glebes and churches were "public property," and it submitted no petition that year. Some Baptists even admitted the bargain struck in 1776.[15] Though the Episcopal Church no longer enjoyed a special standing in law, its title to the glebe lands and churches appeared secure.

Revivalism and the Changing
Religious Landscape

Between 1784 and 1790 the four principal denominations in the Old Dominion reorganized themselves to cope with the radically new situation of civil and
religious freedom. Each approached the task somewhat differently depending
upon its history and the polity it judged to be theologically correct. Common
to all these churches, however, were the concessions made to the American environment in three important respects. First, in Virginia, as in the other states,
the laity developed a significant role in church councils that their counterparts
in Britain and Europe could scarcely imagine. To a degree this represented continuity with the colonial experience, but now it became solidified in such formal
arrangements as the Episcopalians' canon law and its equivalents in the other
denominations. Second, democratic procedures for decision making determined outcomes in and for these churches to a degree unimaginable in the Old
World across the sea. Lastly, the Revolutionary generation of churchmen had
discovered the usefulness of petitioning and interest-group politics. Though
some had been more actively engaged than others, all the denominations had
participated, and some had honed political skills they would not hesitate to
wield in future contests. In that respect the passage of Jefferson's statute was
simply a prelude to the religious politics of the 1790s.

Apart from the challenges to their incorporated status and property, the
Episcopalians had other troubles related primarily to their own internal divisions. When their second convention met in May 1786 to complete their polity and select a bishop, the protagonists were evident. On one side clergyman
James Madison of the College of William and Mary urged the delegates to
abandon "every system, as the fallible production of human contrivance, which
shall dictate articles of faith, and adopt the gospel alone." He lost that battle
when the convention accepted the changes to the Book of Common Prayer
as the Episcopal General Convention had proposed them and selected David Griffith, a thoroughly orthodox clergyman, to be Virginia's first bishop.
But Madison emerged as the ultimate victor when the convention enlarged
the powers of the diocesan standing committee consisting of Madison and a
group of his Williamsburg friends. They rather than the bishop would govern
the Virginia church. Moreover, the committee never raised the funds to send
Griffith to England for consecration. After Griffith resigned and died in 1789,
another convention elected Madison as bishop, and within two months he was
sailing to London. He returned to serve in that office until his death in 1812, a
tenure that marked the nadir of the Episcopal Church in Virginia.[16]

While the Episcopalians deliberated and divided, the Methodists, Baptists, and Presbyterians were experiencing waves of revivalism and raking in the converts. By 1788 the Methodists were riding the crest of the biggest religious awakening Virginia had ever seen. Even the older preachers who fondly remembered the pre-Revolutionary glory days were overcome by its magnitude. At a Southside conference in 1787, Thomas Coke preached to "the largest congregation I ever saw in America," estimating the crowd in the thousands. Jesse Lee, the future apostle of New England Methodism, described the effects of one sermon he gave in Petersburg: "One woman dropped down from her seat like a person struck dead; but in a little while she was enabled to rise and praise a sin pardoning God aloud, and many shouted for joy." Praying aloud had become common, and American preachers were accustomed to such emotional piety, but it took Bishop Coke aback at first. In his journal he noted that people would simultaneously be "praising God, praying for the conviction and conversion of sinners, or exhorting those around them with the utmost vehemence." He found such religious enthusiasm most prevalent in Maryland and Virginia. "What shall we say?" Coke mused. "Souls are awakened and converted by multitudes; and the work is surely a genuine work, if there be a genuine work of God upon earth." Down on the Williamsburg circuit, a dedicated young preacher rejoiced over the success of his sermons and the evidences of personal conversions in his classes and confided to his diary, "Glory be to God for his great and wonderful Love to his poor Creatures in this howling Wilderness."[17]

At the Christmas Conference in 1784, separation from the Episcopal Church had seemed a precipitous step to some Methodists. "Oh how tottering I see Methodism now," one anxious preacher had scrawled in his journal. But the numbers belied such fears as the revivals of 1787 and 1788 swelled Methodist ranks. By the end of that decade, the conference counted more than 57,000 members, one-fifth of them African Americans. More than 15,000 Methodists lived in twenty-three circuits located entirely or mostly in Virginia. However recent its origins, the Methodist Episcopal Church was emerging as one of the dominant religious bodies in the state. Writing from Virginia to an English friend in 1788, Asbury expressed the sentiment of his fellow Methodists: "We enjoy real liberty here, no denomination hath any preeminence over another, and I hope never will have. I wish we may all stand on equal ground." So Methodists avoided the activity directed against the Episcopalians. Perhaps the old ties of affection still lingered for some. Early in the 1790s Coke and Madison even proposed a reunion of their two churches, but nothing came of it.[18]

The Presbyterians also largely eschewed politics after 1787 and focused on growth. What developed into "a glorious revival" began at Hampden-Sydney

College with student prayer meetings encouraged by the school's able president, the Reverend John Blair Smith. The religious enthusiasm spread to nearby churches served by Hanover Presbytery and then spilled across the mountains into the Valley where Liberty Hall Academy caught fire.[19] The theological content of Presbyterian preaching did not vary significantly from the sermons of other ministers, whether they belonged to the Reformed tradition or were Arminians. All preached the need of conviction of sin and the importance of salvation, the love of God manifested in the redemptive suffering of his Son, and the dangers of eternal damnation. But revival styles differed. Smith and the other Presbyterian clergy did not permit the kinds of emotional outbursts, vocal prayers, and bodily exercises that so distinguished the more spontaneous, less controlled Methodist and Baptist revivals. Undoubtedly, this restraint appealed to some individuals who might be generally contemptuous of evangelistic religion.[20] The most important effect of these genteel revivals was the increased number of applicants for the ministry. Because of their insistence that ministers possess a classical education and extensive theological preparation, the Presbyterians would never rival in numbers the Baptists and Methodists, but they would have enough clergy to replenish their ranks and maintain the church's growth. Thus they emerged from the postwar awakening with the promise of renewal for decades ahead.[21]

Baptist Unity and Politics

The Baptists offered the Methodists their greatest numerical competition. In order to strengthen the political campaign for religious freedom and equality, the General Committee of Separate Baptists promoted denominational unity. Efforts at cooperation with Regular Baptists had been made during the war, and in 1786 representatives from the Ketocton Association attended the General Committee meeting, which in turn recommended that all Virginia Baptist associations send delegates to a unity conclave the following summer. Six associations responded, and after extensive discussions of theological positions and the value of doctrinal formulations, the representatives reached "a happy and effectual reconciliation." The Separates had been reluctant to accept the Philadelphia Confession with its Calvinist emphasis on predestination and the doctrine of election. The Regulars objected to the overt Arminianism of some Separate preachers. If conformity to a normative theology defined unity, the divisions would continue. The Separates responded by pointing out that the ministers about whom the Regulars complained were frequently men "of exemplary piety and great usefulness in the Redeemer's kingdom."[22]

"Swearing Jack" Waller offered a case in point. One of the most notorious of early Virginia Baptists, Waller spent his formative years studying law and learning how to gamble. His neighbors tagged this hell-raiser from Spotsylvania County as "the Devil's adjutant" for his reckless and often violent antics. But after his conversion Waller directed all his energies and enthusiasm into his new vocation. Ordained in 1770, he preached tirelessly, baptized numerous converts, and warmed several county jails for refusing to seek a preaching license. Influenced by a Methodist preacher, Waller turned to Arminianism in 1775 and attempted without success to persuade his brethren in the Dover Association to that position. The hotheaded evangelist then broke with the association for a few years and declared himself an "independent Baptist." Throughout the war years he carried on a whirlwind ministry, baptizing, ordaining, and instituting "camp-meetings" for his followers. Tiring eventually of his dissenting status, Waller sought reconciliation with the Separates. For their part, his former colleagues recognized his value to the churches. To cut this zealous preacher off from their association, they explained to the Regulars, would be tantamount to "tearing the limbs from the body."[23] Thee Separates agreed to take in Waller.

The General Committee sought to be as comprehensive as possible. To achieve this inclusivity, the ministers decided to accept the Philadelphia Confession as containing "the essential truths of the gospel," but not to require anyone to observe it in its entirety. The critical agreement was that all would maintain "the doctrine of salvation by Christ and free unmerited grace alone." Arminians could affirm this teaching, and thus the meeting resolved "that the names Regular and Separate, be buried in oblivion; and that, from henceforth, we shall be known by the name of the United Baptist Churches of Christ, in Virginia." Baptist polity was now complete. They would cooperate in matters of common concern, exchange associational letters, and send representatives to the General Committee. Thus the Baptist leadership allowed latitude in theological matters, at least theoretically.[24]

As representatives of churches that jealously guarded their prerogatives, they had reached the best possible compromise. Throughout the discussions the vast bulk of Virginia Baptists clung to the traditional church polity of an independent local covenanted community, free to judge its own members and to ordain its own ministers. Even the association was simply "a combination of churches," a forum for ideas and advice to preserve the member churches from error, "reconcile differences," and "remove difficulties." And if the time-honored association was only an "advisory council," forbidden "to lord it over God's heritage," so much more so was this new creation, the General Committee.[25]

Soon after this compromise was announced, a letter from Morattico Baptist

Church to its association expressed clearly what its members would accept. While these Baptists rejoiced over the "happy union" achieved by the General Committee, they insisted that it held no "legislative power, for the government of the baptist Churches." Nor would they accept it as "a high Court of Appeals." So far as they were concerned, their own association remained "the Great Council in this District, to advise in matters tending to Spiritual Knowledge." The purpose of the General Committee should be to promote "communication, where we shall be informed of the success of the Gospel, the increase of Society and the advancement of the Redeemer's Kingdom." Finally, these independent-minded Baptists recalled that "where either episcopal or synodical government had been adopted, . . . tyranny, persecution and oppression" surely followed.[26] That covered the Episcopalians, Methodists, and Presbyterians, as examples they did not choose to follow. Such restrictions, however, did not dampen the enthusiasm of the members of the General Committee. For the next dozen years church-state politics would keep them fully occupied.

The merger of Regulars and Separates occurred simultaneously with the outbreak of revivalism. Writing to Baptist associations in New England the following spring, the General Committee saw a direct correlation between the two events. The effect of Baptist unity in Virginia had been a "downpouring of his Spirit in many of our Churches." The preachers had baptized more than a thousand awakened souls, and at last Virginia was becoming "a Goshen for Israel to dwell in." What worked for the Methodists also worked for the Baptists. Despite different theologies and polities, both denominations had similar preaching styles, worship services, and effects on the congregations. One Baptist minister commented favorably on a "New Light Sermon" he had heard at a Methodist meeting and approved of the resulting "disorder" that had as many as seven people talking at once, put two persons flat on the floor "in distress," and lasted three or four hours. He felt perfectly at ease, because it was not unusual at Baptist revivals to see people collapse on the floor or ground, incapable of moving their arms or legs, and praising God aloud or crying out for mercy. While not all preachers favored such exercises, one clergyman observed that those who announced their conversion during such sessions were much more likely afterward to provide "clear, rational accounts of a divine change of heart" than those who converted more sedately.[27] Both Baptist and Methodist services also featured singing. Wesley insisted on the importance of hymns, composed a number of them himself, and mandated singing at all Methodist meetings. Baptists revivals rang with the "sweet singing" of the people that at times was "more blessed . . . than the preaching."[28]

Similarities heightened competition between the two denominations. Intrigued by reports of the Virginia awakening, Isaac Backus, New England's most important Baptist leader, toured Virginia for five months in 1789, preaching more than a hundred sermons and attending two association meetings. Writing to his wife in Connecticut to explain his delay in returning home, Backus emphasized the "zeal" of the Methodists, their assault on the "most essential doctrine of the gospel," and his responsibility to expose "their errors." His diary records impressions of a dynamic, rapidly expanding family of Baptist churches, exultant in the accession of new members and emboldened by its freedom from state control. The role reversal of Baptists and Episcopalians particularly delighted this pietist advocate of church-state separation. "The church of England," he wrote, "is now fallen into contempt," but "the baptists are in the best credit with their rulers of any denomination in Virginia." Praising the Old Dominion for its revivals and its enactment of Jefferson's statute, he wrote that the state had experienced "the greatest revolution about baptism and religious liberty, that ever I heard of in any government upon earth."[29] John Asplund's *Register* for 1790 trumpeted the extent of Baptist growth: 204 churches in Virginia with 262 ordained ministers and licensed preachers and 20,443 members. Considering the state as a whole, John Leland, another itinerant clergyman, thought that "more people . . . attend the Baptist worship than any" other.[30] They represented a substantial part of the new evangelical majority.

The political arena already had begun to experience the newfound clout of the Baptists. The congressional elections felt their impact first. Alarmed by the failure of the new federal Constitution to provide "sufficient provision for the secure enjoyment of religious liberty," Baptist ministers and congregations invested heavily in the 1788 campaigns. Recognizing their importance to his efforts to gain a seat in the House of Representatives, James Madison composed a careful letter to George Eve, pastor of Blue Run Church in Orange County, stating his support for amendments and "particularly the rights of Conscience in the fullest latitude." Madison already had gone out of his way to meet with Leland, who itinerated within his district. Remembering Madison's role in the passage of Jefferson's statute, both preachers supported his election. Evidently Baptist votes made a difference there and elsewhere. As one supporter assured Madison in December, "The Baptist Interest seems every where to prevail." And the ministers expected to play a continuing role. Congratulating the congressman-elect, Leland bluntly stated, "One thing I shall expect; that if religious Liberty is anywise threatened, that I shall receive the earliest intelligence."[31] Organized and united, the Baptist ministry was ready for new battles as the last decade of the eighteenth century began.

The Church Property Issue Revisited

On a fine spring day in 1787, Baptist preacher Jack Waller boldly approached the Episcopal vestrymen of Berkeley Parish in Spotsylvania County and invited them to sign his petition to the legislature for the sale of the parish glebe. Like many Episcopal parishes, Berkeley lacked a resident minister. Waller confidently informed the vestry that he expected the assembly would approve the disposal of "all the Vacant Glebes" and would authorize the sale of the others one by one as their incumbent ministers died or retired. When he was accused of attempting to eliminate the Episcopal clergy, Waller retorted that "true Ministers of the Gospel . . . would preach as well without Glebes." The confrontation ended when one of the vestry's leaders declared bluntly "that I would Neither Sign for nor against it; that I believed the assembly was very full of it and needed no further information, and, whatever they did I Should Submit to."[32]

Waller served regularly on the Baptist General Committee, and when the assembly met that fall, his petition was among several urging the sale of the glebes. Another from Lyttleton Parish in Cumberland also asked that the church building there be opened to all denominations and attacked the pretensions of incumbent minister Christopher McRae, "who, exercising a power given by the law which was in force before the Revolution, conceives, that he alone may lock the door and that he alone has a right to keep the key." To a legislature bone weary of religious bickering, the Baptists pointed out that these "feudes and jealousies" resulted from a preferential system that "tends only to sow seeds of Discord and crumble us into parties."[33] Alerted to the threat, Episcopalians countered with petitions decrying any "Act of Violence" against their property, and from Waller's county the Berkeley vestrymen announced that they planned to hire "an orthodox Minister" and desired no further "oppression or Molestation" from anyone.[34]

The property issue was not insignificant. East of the Blue Ridge, the Episcopal church buildings and chapels, communion plate and liturgical books, and glebe lands set aside for the ministers' use together with their homes, barns, and slaves were often extensive and sometimes quite valuable. When, for example, Elizabeth City Parish sought a clergyman in 1788, the newspaper advertisement promised a "house of brick with four rooms and a passage above, and as many below stairs, all convenient and necessary out houses, the land very good, and contains 200 acres, with plenty of rail timber," and twenty-four slaves. The Henrico Parish vestry in 1791 estimated the worth of its 196 acres at £1,000. They rented out the glebe for £40 a year.[35] In short, the Episcopalians occupied a gold mine, and the erstwhile dissenters, particularly the Baptists, deeply resented it. Though largely ignored by historians, the struggle that ensued held enormous importance for the future of church-state relations and religious politics.[36]

The Battle Joined

Aware of their communion's growing numbers and electoral influence, the 1789 Baptist General Committee prepared a long petition dealing with church property and added two arguments that carried increased weight in the next decade. The ministers first pointed out that glebes were "not such inchanted Places" that previous legislatures had refused to sell them. They had been sold before, "and if they can be sold for one good Purpose we hope they will be for a better." Second, they argued that the basis for land claims was "Social Right," not "Nature" or "Grace." In a free government the majority decided what should be done. Therefore, "if a Majority of Voices, governed by the Principle of Right, say, that the Episcopal Church ought to have all the Property, . . . than said church is entitled to it; otherwise the Law by which they hold it, may be as easily repealed as any other Law whatever." The Baptist leaders claimed to represent a majority of Virginians who wanted the church property laws revoked.[37]

Some politicians, however, were concerned about the potential dangers of majority tyranny in their new situation of republicanism. Private property was sacrosanct to the Virginia gentry. Writing to Jefferson in 1788, Madison warned of "the danger of oppression" from majority rule. While the country debated whether the new Constitution needed a bill of rights, he had little confidence in "parchment barriers" erected to safeguard liberty. Virginia's Declaration of Rights, he pointed out, had been "violated in every instance where it has been opposed to a popular current." The supreme danger to "private rights" came "from acts in which the Government is the mere instrument of the major number of the constituents." And he advised his friend "that if a majority of the people were now of one sect, a religious establishment would still take place and on narrower ground" than had been proposed by the assessment bill and in spite of the passage of the Statute for Religious Freedom.[38] The will of the majority did not necessarily yield liberty or justice.

Legislative supporters of the Baptist position proposed that the assembly refer the matter to the people by printing the General Committee's memorial and soliciting popular opinion. This strategy had defeated the assessment, but defenders of the Episcopal Church fought back from the high ground of private property. The legislature voted to postpone the whole business.[39] Determined to impress the assembly with the Baptists' numerical strength, the General

Committee made an even stronger effort in 1790 to arouse public support, but despite an outpouring of petitions, the lawmakers rejected a resolution for the sale by a crushing 52 to 89. Undoubtedly the legislators knew of the division within Baptist ranks. Earlier in June the Roanoke Association, an important Southside group of more than thirty churches and 2,100 members, had objected to the General Committee's circular letter. While accepting its "spirit and intent," these ministers believed that "Compassion" required them to leave incumbent Episcopal clergymen and their families alone. They wanted all the churches opened to general use but only vacant glebes sold, and they would endorse no petition that said otherwise. No memorials were submitted from counties in the Roanoke Association that fall.[40]

But the Baptist leadership would not abandon the issue. Instead, they shifted strategies during the next five years, searching for weaknesses in their adversaries' positions while trying to keep their own forces united. In 1792 they had an initial success when by a single vote the House approved a resolution to permit the sale of glebes in parishes where a majority of freeholders wished it, provided that incumbent ministers retained their rights to the land. But a draft bill failed on its first reading.[41] In a major change the General Committee in 1794 did not request the immediate sale of any church property. Instead, the Baptists asked simply for the repeal of all legislation assigning it to the Episcopal Church. But the House defeated a resolution to repeal the glebe laws by a vote of 52 to 80. Two days later Thomas Evans, a delegate from Accomack County on the Eastern Shore, explained the "principle" that guided the majority's vote: did the church's title to the property involve "private rights vested in bodies corporate capable of holding such rights"? If the individual parishes with their trustees were corporations, then the assembly could not legally "divest them." Moreover, only the courts, Evans argued, could properly settle that question. The state could not touch the church's holdings until and unless it received a favorable judicial ruling. The conservative politician decried the efforts of some petitioners to make judges out of legislators and give them "an absolute power over the rights of property."[42]

The Baptists, however, did win a precedent-setting assembly battle in 1794. Buckingham County petitions, no doubt sponsored by Baptist churches, had requested the sale of Tillotson Parish glebe. In calm, dispassionate tones they depicted an Episcopal Church in collapse. Although the people had been taxed to buy a glebe and construct a residence, the last minister had died and had not been replaced. Before the buildings completely decayed, the petitioners wanted the property sold and the money applied to reduce parish taxes. Though the Episcopal convention had known trouble was brewing in Buckingham and authorized the parish to elect a vestry, no one there had acted, and Tillotson's

Episcopalians, if any existed, presented no counterpetition.[43] A few days after refusing to repeal the glebe laws, the assembly completed work on a bill appointing commissioners to sell Tillotson glebe. Legislative support for the Episcopal Church's absolute title to its property was eroding.[44]

The act approving this sale only expanded government intervention in church affairs, for state regulation had never really ended. Even after the assembly passed the 1787 law that authorized Episcopalians as well as other religious bodies to manage their own business, the legislators continued to approve requests from parish trustees to sell glebes and purchase new ones. Aware of potential problems, Episcopal leaders endeavored to assert their authority. Their 1790 convention claimed that the church was the "exclusive owner" of the property, that the legislature had no right to sell or dispose of it "to any other purpose," and forbade vestries or trustees to do so "without the consent of a Convention." But that same winter, in response to county petitions, the lawmakers in Richmond took it upon themselves to divide a parish and create a new one, to order the Episcopalians to elect trustees for both parishes, and to give instructions for the disposition of glebe lands in the old parish and the purchase of new ones.[45] This was exactly the kind of actions the legislature routinely took before the Revolution. Old habits die hard. Despite Jefferson's statute and the other acts passed by subsequent legislatures to relinquish authority over religious bodies, the General Assembly clearly considered itself in charge of the temporal affairs of the Protestant Episcopal Church in Virginia.

This situation became even more apparent two years later in the case of St. Patrick's Parish in Prince Edward County. A county petition from this Presbyterian center pointed out that the parish had neither an Episcopal vestry nor "any people who call themselves Episcopalians." Some years earlier a fund had been raised by the sale of the glebe, church furniture, and plate. The petitioners asked that the money be spent "for some public use." After two months of intermittent discussions, votes, and amendments, the legislature passed an enabling law.[46] If this could be done with parish funds, a case could be made for selling other church property and using the money, particularly in places where few if any Episcopalians lived or that lacked incumbent ministers. In authorizing the sale of Tillotson glebe, the 1794 assembly accepted this argument. By both state and church law the Episcopal vestries owned and managed all church property, but at least in parishes without vestries, the assembly filled the vacuum and assumed control of the church's property.

The parish-by-parish approach seemed to work best. So, the next fall Baptists in four parishes, two of them with incumbent Episcopal ministers, requested the sale of church property. One petition also proffered a new argument designed to meet the objections against repealing the glebe laws that had been raised in the 1794 legislature. This petition maintained that the vestries of the old established church had indeed been corporations. But when the Revolution dissolved them, all their property had reverted to "the original Donors," the people of the state. Thus the assembly's allocation of this property to the Episcopal Church in 1776 was a "usurpation."[47] The Episcopalians fought back with memorials defending their property rights.[48] Caught between the opposing religious forces and immersed in the politics of the Jay Treaty, the legislature temporized. A resolution of support for the Baptist petition failed by the slender margin of seven votes.[49]

Alarmed by the erosion of support in the legislature, a well-attended Episcopal convention in May 1796 devoted much discussion to the glebe issue and then arranged to submit a memorial to the next assembly. When the legislature convened that fall, it referred this petition together with the regular missive from the Baptists' General Committee to the Committee for the Courts of Justice, the body responsible for questions of property and constitutionality. The committee report to the floor of the House was a forceful defense of the church's historic title to the glebes and churches. The property was "vested in the respective parishes as members of the Church of England and not as professors of any other religious persuasion." The legislature of 1776 had promised that the property would continue to be held by the Church of England, and the Protestant Episcopal Church "is the same in its rights" with that church. It mattered not how the property had been acquired. If the state had granted it in 1776, it was now private property like any other grant. To settle the dispute permanently, the committee recommended an assembly declaration guaranteeing nonintervention in the church's property. Robert Andrews from Williamsburg, a former Episcopal clergyman, reported the committee's recommendation to the House.[50]

The Tide Turns

The supporters of the Baptist position immediately proposed to replace Andrews's report with an amendment that directly addressed the property issue. The central point was whether the glebes in fact had been "invested in the parishes as members of the church of England." An analysis of Virginia's colonial laws dealing with vestries, ministers, and glebes showed that the parishes had never been incorporated. Strictly speaking, parishes designated geographical boundaries rather than people. Though vestries in every parish were "incorporated," they never had been "invested with any species of property, personal or fiduciary in the glebes." A vestry could buy a glebe and present a minister to the colonial governor for induction, but once that had taken place, the minister held the land "independent of all persons." Yet he was not free to dispose of the glebe on his own or even acting with the vestry and parish. Therefore the real trustees remained "the original grantees." And when the object of the trust, the established church, ended at the Revolution, all church property reverted to them. Because the people were sovereign in Virginia, they, together with the heirs of private donors, were entitled to the property. This ingenious argument was calculated to turn the Episcopalians' claim to "private property" on its head. If the property had reverted to the state (i.e., the people), that enormously strengthened the Baptist case that the assembly had acted improperly in giving it to one church.

After reviewing the disestablishment legislation since 1776 and pointing out the limitations inherent in the laws incorporating the Episcopal Church and endowing its vestries with control over the church's property, the amendment shrewdly noted that during the past ten years the legislature had approved bills disposing of glebes. Clearly, the assembly had exercised "legislative right," thus showing "the insufficiency of any private title." Therefore, in awarding all the church property to Episcopalians, the lawmakers in 1776 "either violated private property . . . or devoted public property to the exclusive use of a particular sect." The advocates of the Baptist position proposed three resolutions: that the legislature should repeal the church property laws, that incumbent ministers should retain their glebes for their lifetimes, and that vacant glebes should be sold and the money applied to the education of "poor children." This sweeping rejoinder to the Episcopalian position left the House at an impasse, and the matter was later postponed until the next session. But the Baptists and their allies had finally offered the legislature a plausible argument to justify the repeal of the glebe laws. The House ordered two thousand copies of the committee report with proposed amendments to be printed and circulated for a full discussion by Virginians.[51]

Baptist leaders smelled victory. "The Business was put in such a Train," David Barrow wrote Isaac Backus early in 1797, that he thought it "more than probable, it will be effected the next session."[52] The assembly had referred the glebe issue to the people, and although overshadowed by reaction to the Jay Treaty, it was warmly canvassed in at least some of the spring elections. Anticipating the arguments of the Episcopalians, an eventually victorious candidate in Fairfax County declared that the glebe laws probably violated the Declaration of Rights but that decision belonged in the legislature, not the courts. Only "the Assembly itself," he wrote in a published statement, could repeal or block a legislative act.[53] Legislative supremacy was crucial to the Baptist position, because supporters of the Episcopal Church dominated the bench.

Preachers and politicians alike prepared for the assembly session of 1797–98, but a petition war did not break out across the state. The Baptist ministers drafted their regular memorial, a brief document that lacked the passion of earlier petitions.[54] Perhaps they realized they had already won. Nor did the Episcopalians deluge the legislature with memorials, though Edmund Pendleton suggested a petition campaign and personally drafted an elaborate defense of the church's property. As president of the convention that had approved both the state constitution and the Declaration of Rights, and as Speaker of the House of Delegates in the fall of 1776, he wrote with unique authority of the intention of Virginia's founders. Moreover, he was an able and learned judge and a shrewd politician who commanded immense respect in the state. Reviewing the work of the first state assembly, he stated that an understanding had existed that "by common consent, and with a view to avoid all future contest," the same act that ended religious taxes had reserved the property to the Episcopal Church. Further, the assembly had been "declaring a subsisting right and not creating a new one." Such property rights were "sacred."[55]

The sagacious old judge proposed that for the sake of "uniformity," the church circulate a memorial in the parishes for signatures, but Episcopal leaders had determined on a different strategy.[56] Instead of their usual May convention, they would meet in Richmond at the same time as the opening of the assembly session and lobby directly for their cause. When the legislature convened in December, thirty-one clerical and forty lay delegates met next door in the General Court room in the Capitol. The distinguished assemblage included Governor James Wood, three state senators, and thirteen members of the House of Delegates. At the outset Bishop James Madison produced a letter from three of Virginia's most esteemed lawyers: Bushrod Washington, nephew of the first president; Edmund Randolph; and John Wickham. The church was "the exclusive owner" of its property, they asserted confidently. Its title stood "upon the same grounds with the rights of private property," and only "the judiciary, and the judiciary alone," could decide a property issue. This legal opinion, together with Pendleton's defense, formed the basis for the convention's resolutions and memorial to the assembly. The Episcopalians appointed a committee to present their petition and to propose that the assembly submit the issue to "a proper tribunal of justice."[57]

The Legislature Redefines the Church-State Relationship

When the House discussed the matter in January, it rejected the Episcopalian position by an overwhelming vote of 97 to 52 and by the same margin passed a resolution to repeal the glebe laws. This represented a dramatic shift from earlier voting patterns in the House.[58] Several days later a bill was presented "To repeal certain acts[,] declaring the construction of the Bill of Rights and Constitution concerning Religion, and directing the disposition of Glebes and Churches." The preamble criticized previous legislatures in blunt terms. Since 1776 they had approved a series of laws that, among other things, "bestowed property upon" a church and "incorporated religious sects." Such acts were "inconsistent with the principles of the Constitution, and of Religious Freedom," and were leading "to the reestablishment of a National Church." To halt this development, the first section of the bill repealed all such laws and declared that Jefferson's statute contained the "true exposition of the principles of the Bill of Rights and Constitution."

The second section treated the disposition of church property. In parishes that lacked incumbent ministers, a majority of the parishioners could decide to elect commissioners to sell the property for "the general benefit" or "the education of poor children." But they could not eject an incumbent minister from his glebe, parsonage, or church. After lengthy discussions the House dropped this entire section and rewrote the bill's title to omit any references to glebes and churches. Reporting to his constituents, Gideon Spencer reflected the exhaustion many delegates must have felt: "I hope it will meet with no opposition in the Senate and that we shall at length get rid of a subject that has cost the state such an immensity of money both from its being so often agitated and from the lengthy debates which it has occasioned."[59]

In its truncated form the repeal bill passed to the Senate. Senators tended to be older, wealthier, and more conservative; and their Speaker, Ludwell Lee, had participated in the Episcopal convention. So it was probably no surprise to the delegates when the senators sent the bill back with two substantive amendments, which the House rejected. The first amendment coupled repeal of the laws with a commission to the state's attorney general to take the question of ownership to the courts. Until the issue was settled there, the parishes, vestries, and incumbent ministers would retain all church property. The House vote rejecting the first amendment was 36 to 79. Second, the Senate wanted a declaration that the act did not imply "a legislative opinion" about who held title to church property. The impasse killed the bill for that session. For the Episcopalians, however, legislative defeat had only been postponed, and the Baptists knew it. The following year the House bill was reintroduced and glided smoothly through to passage. A single amendment calling for the judiciary to decide the question of church property ownership was defeated 57 to 86.[60] The opposition had been routed. The legislature had established Jefferson's statute as a sole standard for interpreting the church-state relationship in Virginia and had voided every other law that pertained to religion or the churches.

Although the act in January 1799 only repealed the church property laws and did not order the seizure of any buildings or glebes, a movement in that direction was inevitable. The Episcopalians knew it. Their May convention instructed John Ambler, the lay delegate from Williamsburg, to confer with lawyers on the best defense for the property and authorized the bishop and standing committee to take all necessary steps to bring about a judicial proceeding. The repeal act did not inhibit the church leaders from acting on other property concerns. Among other actions the convention authorized the "vestry and trustees" of Bristol Parish in Dinwiddie County to sell the glebe and purchase a better one and approved a revised canon on polity which reiterated the vestry and minister's ownership and control over all the parish property as "trustees" of the church's interest.[61]

From the evangelical perspective, however, glebes stood ripe for the picking. Petitions from several counties called for seizing the lands and giving the proceeds to the overseers of the poor. The assembly had previously acted on such bills individually. Some legislators favored a more systematic approach, but the House tabled a sweeping resolution to transfer the glebes in all parishes without incumbent pastors to the overseers of the poor. The 1799–1800 assembly eventually authorized the overseers of the poor to take over the glebes in three parishes. Two of them apparently had ministers residing in them, but no formal protests against the seizures were forthcoming.[62] But what if an incumbent minister did object? A Halifax County petition asked the legislature to appoint trustees to sell the Antrim Parish glebe, slaves, and all the other Episcopal Church property there for the sake of educating "poor Children" in the county. Obviously annoyed, the Reverend Alexander Hay and his vestry counterpetitioned.[63]

An immigrant from Scotland, Hay had tutored the children of several prominent Virginia families before his ordination by Bishop White in 1790. Soon afterwards the Antrim vestry inducted him as its rector, filling a vacancy that had existed since the outbreak of the Revolution. Hay set to work vigorously. In 1792, the first year he kept records, the minister baptized eighty-nine whites and thirty-five blacks, married eleven couples, and conducted one funeral. His parish contained four churches, but they were in a dilapidated condition, so in 1793 parishioners subscribed £125 to build a new church and a few years later raised about half that amount to restore another. Hay had gone to great personal expense to fix up his glebe, and his congregation had helped repair its buildings. Their lengthy memorial began by pointing out that though the 1799 law had placed the church's holdings in a "peculiarly singular" situation, Hay occupied a "freehold for life." For the state to authorize a confiscation of the church's property held "revolutionary" implications for private property rights. It also would deprive the Episcopalians of a place to worship. They named their enemies. The Baptists, who formed the largest religious group in the county, were behind this effort. Their language of "civil rights" masked a "rancorous spirit." Though most people in Halifax were unchurched and "indifferent" about the issue, some had been importuned to sign the petition to sell the glebe. The Episcopalians were counting on the assembly's justice and good judgment to safeguard their religious worship and property rights. They pointed out that "the question respecting the sale of Antrim Glebe involves the question respecting the sale of every Glebe in Virginia."[64]

Eventually the legislators would have to face this question. Perhaps because of the protest, a bill to sell the Antrim Parish glebe failed on the first reading, though the next year the assembly authorized the sale of a vacant glebe in Martin's Brandon Parish in Prince George County. The problems with this seriatim approach became obvious in December 1801 when six counties submitted petitions for the sale of church property. The onslaught had been foreseen. One of the new delegates, William Brockenbrough, had noticed the previous June that a cabal was being formed to "lay Warrants upon them as upon vacant Lands." That was too extreme for the ambitious young lawyer-politician, and he thought the legislature should act quickly. On the third day of the session, he found himself appointed to a select committee to draft a general law. Within two weeks the House of Delegates approved by a margin of 126 to 39 a bill "concerning the Glebe lands and churches of this commonwealth."[65]

This House bill essentially turned control over the issue to the "Freeholders and Housekeepers" in each parish. If a majority in a parish lacking an incumbent minister petitioned the county court, the magistrates had to appoint commissioners to sell the glebe and all other church assets except those churches occupied by the Episcopalians or property acquired by private donations. The proceeds were to benefit the inhabitants of the parish by reducing taxes, caring for the poor, or supporting local education, as local voters decided. Several petitions had asked that the churches be opened for general use. The House bill provided that wherever a majority of the parish desired it, those buildings should be considered the common property "of all religious sects."

The Senate made significant amendments on both the theoretical and practical levels, and for the next month senators and delegates argued over the bill's provisions. The House had operated on the premise that with the 1799 repeal act the church property belonged to the individual parishes. But the Senate insisted that it reverted to the state. Other Senate amendments were designed to reduce local religious animosities. The overseers of the poor were to sell vacant glebes without consulting the parish, but all churches, churchyards, liturgical books, and communion plate were specifically excluded from sale. By implication these remained the property of the Episcopalians. However, the preamble embodied the Baptist position. At the time of the Revolution, it declared, "all property formerly belonging to the Episcopal church, of every description, devolved on the good people of this commonwealth ... And although the general assembly possesses the right of authorizing a sale of all such property indiscriminately, yet being desirous to reconcile all the good people of this commonwealth, it is deemed inexpedient at the time to disturb the possession of the present incumbents." Only a diehard remnant remained in the legislature to defend the property claims of the Episcopal Church. Now they would have to rely on the courts.[66]

Why the Baptists Won

The Baptists had won a decisive victory. In repealing legislation that had guaranteed the glebes and churches to the Episcopal Church, the General Assembly repudiated the judgment of virtually every assembly since the Revolution and of some of Virginia's finest legal minds. No other state acted in this fashion. In Maryland and the Carolinas, where the Church of England had also been established in colonial times and the glebes and church buildings transferred to the Episcopalians at the Revolution, the governments never seized the church's property. That it happened in Virginia was due principally to the Baptist General Committee: to its shrewd political intelligence, strong organizational ability, a willingness to search out allies wherever they might be found, and untiring persistence despite repeated rebuffs.

Baptist political skill produced the outcome. Almost every year the legislature could expect a memorial from the General Committee complaining of the church property laws. These appeals were not simple repetitions. The preachers varied their arguments and demands, probed for weakness in their opponents' case, and ingeniously responded to every defense offered by supporters of the Episcopal position. The fact that evangelicals—the Baptists, Methodists, and Presbyterians—had gained adherents while Episcopalians lost them did not by itself turn the tide on the glebe issue. The major shift toward the Baptist side in the assembly occurred only after they presented a plausible rebuttal to the Episcopalian argument for the rights of private property. Once conservative legislators accepted the logic that the Episcopal Church's property originated in a grant from the people to a church that had ceased to exist at time of the Revolution, they could vote for seizure without fear of setting a dangerous precedent. In fact, by wrapping themselves in the mantle of the Revolution, Baptists gained the patriotic high ground in this debate as they had during the decade between independence and the passage of Jefferson's statute.

Their adroit verbal maneuvering in Richmond was matched by a carefully orchestrated public appeal throughout the state. Operating particularly through the General Committee, Baptist ministers mastered techniques of effective lobbying and developed mass support. In 1790, for example, their circular letter promised that the preachers would campaign vigorously "for the sale of the glebes, and free occupation of the churches by all religious societies," and asked local churches to send in petitions with "as many subscribers" as possible. On the local level they creatively developed county petitions and passed them around for signatures at church meetings. Published handbills, reprinted in the press, reiterated the arguments against the glebe laws, expressed frustration at the assembly's repeated refusals to repeal them, and urged popular opposition at each legislative session.[67] When members of the Roanoke Association objected to a direct attack on all the Episcopal glebes, the General Committee restored rank-and-file unity by delicately changed the pitch to request only the repeal of oppressive laws. As a group, the ministers became highly effective politicians.

Nor did it hurt their cause that both preachers and congregations embraced the majority party of Republicans in Virginia. Like most Virginians, Baptists naturally gravitated to a party whose emphasis on decentralized government and social equality harmonized with their own style of polity and worship. Republicanism embraced the egalitarianism that formed the central theme of so many of their legislative petitions. A major objective of their struggle, wrote John Leland, was to place "all sects . . . upon a level." For them, as for other religious groups who had once been called dissenters, the hope for "equal religious liberty" had been a crucial factor in their support for Jefferson's statute. Repeal of the glebe laws was necessary to fulfill the implicit promise of that act. The laws regarding glebe lands and church buildings represented the last vestiges of the old establishment: a continuous reminder of a colonial past when "through the adulterous connection between Church and State, the imposition of king craft and priest craft, . . . cherish'd and supported each other." Allowing the Episcopal Church to retain its colonial properties implied that within Virginia there still existed "a favorite Church in a Republican Government," an intolerable denial of the freedom and equality secured by the Revolution.[68]

Baptists openly identified with Republican viewpoints on domestic and foreign policy. In the 1790s certain policies of the Federalist administration, particularly Washington's neutrality proclamation in the war between Britain and France and the use of force against the Whiskey Rebels, provoked strong negative reactions in Virginia. Then the appointment of John Jay as American negotiator with Britain and the resultant treaty of 1795 sharply heightened partisan tensions. Throughout these conflicts the Republican friends of Jefferson dominated state politics while Federalists remained a distinct minority. Baptist churches and clergy did not hide their political affiliation. A Caroline County congregation deplored the Jay Treaty's tendency "to draw us smoothly, swiftly and dreadfully into the whirlpool of oppression—oppression Civil and Religious," and the Goshen Association appointed a day of fasting and prayer "for a deliverance from the dangers we apprehend" from the treaty with Britain. "I am strongly convinced," wrote one Baptist minister, "that the people of Virginia are unanimously in favour of the French Republic." From his perspective a war against France would destroy "our liberties and union."[69]

The General Committee's petition in 1795 reflected the charged political atmosphere. The ministers' chief argument became the clash between the inequalities of the glebe laws and the "grand leading Principles of Republicanism," and they attacked the glebe laws as "inconsistent with the dignified Character which true Republicans ought to sustain." Once the church property issue was thrust into politics, the ministers astutely emphasized their political affiliation and concentrated their pressure on Republican delegates from counties where evangelicals were numerically powerful. Some legislators undoubtedly came over to the Baptist cause in order to strengthen their own political position, and some Federalists, too, probably changed their views in response to pressure from evangelical constituents. One contemporary church historian claimed that Baptists in some counties were able to decide the election and place "a worthy and useful member" in the legislature.[70] The political efforts of the Baptists were well rewarded.

But despite the identification of Baptists with Republicans, party lines did not determine the glebe fight. When the House passed the 1797 proposal to repeal the glebe laws, thirty-two Federalists and sixty-four Republicans supported it, while twenty-five Federalists and twenty-seven Republicans voted in opposition. The next year, when the House turned down the Episcopalians' plan to refer the glebe issue to the courts, thirty Federalists and twenty-seven Republicans favored the motion, but eighteen Federalists and sixty-eight Republicans rejected it. The Federalists' conservative instincts, as well as their concentration in older counties where Anglicanism had been strong, may have encouraged a higher proportion of them to support the Episcopal Church. Yet an astute politician like Madison noted in a letter to Jefferson in 1798 that the glebe issue was not a party issue.[71] The split was not political but geographical and cultural. Some of the staunchest advocates of the church's property rights were Republicans like Bishop Madison and the future governor John Page who were devoted to the political fortunes of Jefferson. Both Jefferson and the other James Madison sensibly avoided taking sides in this battle.

The General Committee also mobilized popular support among other evangelicals across Virginia and even attempted a formal alliance with Methodists and Presbyterians. The last offered the richest prospects, because both of Virginia's presbyteries at one time or another had discussed the issue and drafted petitions. In the Shenandoah Valley the ministers and lay elders of Lexington Presbytery in 1787 composed an elaborate memorial against the "exclusive appropriation of the glebes and churches" by an "infant church." Three years later the General Committee sent agents to enlist Hanover Presbytery in the glebe fight, but the eastern Presbyterians turned them down "on account of some Circumstances." They had declared the Baptist proposal "reasonable and just," yet they backed away from a coalition. The next year Hanover Presbytery passed a motion to join the Baptists "in a remonstrance and petition to the General Assembly . . . to sell the Glebes and open the Church Doors." A committee was appointed to draft a memorial and present it to the legislature, but nothing happened. When Hanover Presbytery considered the issue again in 1792, the committee presented a petition that was initially approved, yet two days later, "after deliberating fully," the presbytery rejected it. It did not discuss it formally again, nor did Lexington Presbytery or the Synod of Virginia.[72]

The Hanover Presbytery minutes do not explain the "Circumstances" of 1790 or its refusals to support the sale of the glebes, but these probably related to other petitions the church leaders had submitted to the assembly. Throughout this period two Presbyterian colleges, Hampden-Sydney and Liberty Hall, sought help from Richmond. So also did various Presbyterian congregations. In 1789 the state gave land for a church building to the Presbyterians in Lexington, and the next year the legislature authorized lotteries to build Presbyterian churches in Alexandria and Shepherdstown.[73] The presbyteries could hardly petition for the seizure of the Episcopalian property while asking the assembly for financial assistance and other favors for themselves.

The Baptists also reached out to their biggest rivals in the business of salvation, the Methodists. Numerically, Methodists were right behind Baptists with more than 15,000 members in twenty-three circuits located entirely or mainly within Virginia. Two Baptist emissaries presented their case to the Methodist conference at Petersburg in June 1790 but failed to gain any declared support. Facing a schism led by James O'Kelly, the Methodists may have been too deeply preoccupied with their own problems and internal divisions.[74] But even if the preachers considered the Baptist proposal, it is unlikely that they would have cooperated. First, the Methodists had only separated from the Episcopalians a few years before, and since then both Bishop Coke and Bishop Madison had expressed a desire for denominational reunion.[75] But more important, Arminian Methodists would have found an alliance with Calvinist Baptists unnatural. The two churches were competing against each other for adherents.

Yet though their churches' policy-making bodies refused to take a public stand, many individual Presbyterians and Methodists rallied to support the seizure of the church property. Areas in the Southside and Shenandoah Valley where Presbyterians were numerous consistently favored the sale of the glebes. A petition from Prince Edward County, for example, carried the signatures of Archibald McRoberts and Drury Lacy, two ministers from Hanover Presbytery. Where it counted most, in the assembly, Presbyterians voted 19 to 1 to repeal the glebe laws in 1797. Rank-and-file Methodists also circulated petitions and sided with the Baptist position in the assembly. Thus the Baptist General Committee successful enlisted other evangelicals in their cause.[76]

Throughout the struggle Baptist tenacity was as important to the outcome as political acumen. Their "unreasonable and unparalleled Obstinacy," as Episcopalians saw it, is particularly striking. For the first eight years of the campaign, the assembly easily and overwhelmingly rejected their petitions,[77] but the preachers refused to drop the issue. Such persistence requires explanation. In terms of Baptist polity, the church property issue was important to their organization and unity as a religious denomination in the 1790s. Unity had finally been achieved in 1787 when conflicting groups of Regular and Separate Baptists came together in the General Committee and the General Association. When this association was dissolved the following year, the General Committee remained as the single common agent for all Virginia Baptists precisely at a time when revivals were enlarging their ranks. Composed of the most influential ministers, the committee functioned well as a central organization responding to issues and questions arising from the associations.

Not all congregations or preachers were comfortable with this arrangement, because Baptists were wary of anything that threatened the "liberties of the Churches."[78] Major resistance surfaced after the committee condemned slavery in 1790, and the storm of opposition that action provoked seriously threatened the committee's existence. In a circular letter the following year, the Baptist leaders quickly backpedaled: "We desire you to view us, only as your political mouth, to speak your cause to the State Legislature, to promote the interests of the Baptists at large, and endeavour the removal of every vestige of opposition." Though the ministers renounced any intention of interfering with slavery, which was not yet a political issue, some Baptists still questioned the legitimacy of a General Committee. Two years later the ministers protested that their sole concern was the "external interest" of Baptists and denied any "power over the liberty and independence of the Churches." Some committee members disliked this limitation on their discussions, but the glebe issue was the only matter that they negotiated successfully after 1792. Thus, for those ministers to whom the survival of the General Committee was important for Baptist unity and organization, the church property question proved extremely useful. It justified the committee's continued existence. In the spring following the repeal of the glebe acts, the members gathered one last time to congratulate themselves on the victory. They then dissolved the committee with the recommendation that the nine associations consider holding "a general annual meeting . . . for promoting the cause of Religion, and for preserving union and harmony amongst the churches."[79] The next year Virginia Baptists instituted the General Meeting of Correspondence.

A more emotionally compelling reason for pursuing the glebe issue was the historic antagonism that scarred the relationship between Baptists and the former established church. Charged by Episcopalians with an "exclusive self-love," Baptist leaders felt obliged to explain to the public that they were not moved by "impure motives" but by concern for "principle." Their petitions, however, betrayed profound antagonism and resentment. They blamed Episcopalians for the oppression they had experienced before the Revolution. One minister who had once been imprisoned later wrote that every "persecution" invariably had "a priest at the end of it, and received the hearty concurrence of their parishioners." An Episcopalian responded in kind: "Actuated by the malicious and revengeful spirit of Haman who erected a gallows in his own house to hang Mordecai thereon, [Baptists] have also erected in [their] imaginations one on which we too are to swing."[80]

Social disparities, real or imagined, widened the gap between the two denominations. The Baptists were justly proud of their own growth and development. Certainly by the 1790s their ministers were no longer, if they ever were, a poor or crude segment of the population. Though to the unconverted they might appear as stump ranters, Baptist preachers held land and slaves like any other comfortably fixed, middling sort of citizens in the commonwealth.[81] Yet despite their secure economic position, status anxiety pervaded their petitions. They knew that Episcopalians tended to belittle them as members of an uneducated, lower class and ridiculed their enthusiastic style of worship. They could have had Edmund Pendleton in mind. In a private letter to Madison in 1788, he commented to the politician on how "Methodist and Baptist preachers swarm thro' the State, exhibiting daily and nightly, and struling hard for the Episcopal Flock." The old judge acknowledged their success "since their hearers fall down and go into the Waters by 50's at a time," and he described their preachers' "influence" over them as "more than Papistical." Given the upcoming elections, some thought them motivated by politics or an effort to grab "the Glebes and Churches." The Episcopalians felt the pressure. As Bishop Madison wrote in 1790, "Ignorance and Enthusiasm are Hydras which require a powerful Arm to oppose them." According to Bishop Meade, Madison himself repeated a story about an old Federalist gentleman who remarked to a church elder that "there are many roads to heaven, and he was in favour of letting every man take his own way; but . . . no gentleman would choose any but the Episcopal."[82]

Baptists reciprocated with an intense dislike that bordered on hatred. To Baptist William Price, the Episcopalians were "too aristocratic and overbearing," possessed of "English airs" and "arrogance of demeanor among neighbors." "Such a Church," he wrote, "is not suited to a liberty loving people."[83] Thus the slightest indication of legislative concern or preference for the old establishment inevitably provoked a strong reaction. Baptists deeply resented an assembly that spent time "brooding over this Egg of Priest-craft" while discriminating against them and disregarding their repeated memorials.[84] They had never willingly tolerated "oppressions," and they would not do so now when they represented, in the words of one legislative draft, "a numerous and respectable part of this Community." It galled them that a "Deaf" assembly treated the Episcopalians as "a favorite Church."[85] Thus the Baptists stayed with the church property fight until they prevailed; and this persistence together with their political acumen, effective organization, and popular support from other evangelicals eventually persuaded the legislature to resolve the issue in their favor.

Why the Episcopalians Lost

If strong, coherent, and persistent leadership was noteworthy among the Baptists, its conspicuous absence on the Episcopalian side was also crucial to the result. The former established church had inevitably declined in numbers and influence since the Revolution, and problems accelerated in the 1790s. A growing shortage of clergy exacerbated the difficulties in maintaining Episcopal control over church property. Deaths and resignations thinned clerical ranks, even though Bishop Madison ordained at least twenty-four men to the ministry in the 1790s, and other clergy migrated in from states to the north. Sixty-six ministers occupied parishes in 1796, but the number shrank to fifty-three incumbents four years later. What kind of men were they? The scarcity of records has driven historians to rely heavily on Bishop William Meade's two-volume compilation of notes, memories, and reminiscences pulled together in the 1840s. A staunch evangelical, Virginia's third bishop regarded the clergy of his youth with a jaundiced eye. Through his tinted lenses, he saw them, all in all, as a sorry lot whose "defective preaching" and "evil living" seriously hampered the church. Their lay contemporaries, however, might have disagreed with the bishop's later vision. Consider, for example, Abner Waugh, rector of St. Mary's Parish in Caroline County until his death in 1806. Meade excoriated him for gambling at cards. Yet Edmund Pendleton, his parishioner for thirty years, liked Waugh's preaching, admired his personal character, and recommended him in 1801 as chaplain to the U.S. House of Representatives.[86]

More than from any deficiency on the part of the average clergyman, the church's decline stemmed from the contemporary culture. Even a zealous minister such as Jarratt wrote discouragingly in 1794, "In my own parish also, I have the mortification to behold those, who were once my near and dear friends, yea my children in the gospel, fall off from me, and join with my most notorious enemies." By the end of the decade, the devout old minister lamented to another clergyman about the wretched prospects for "religion and morals" and the "degenerate times." The crowds to whom he once preached were gone. But the evangelical clergy had not necessarily siphoned them off. When another Episcopalian condemned the "gross, destructive and heathenish infidelity" abounding in Virginia, he echoed the evangelical lament of the era. The revivals had ended by 1791, and clergy of all churches anguished over the spiritual torpor of congregations and the coldness of their preachers' sermons. "Religion is at the lowest ebb that ever it has been among us," one Baptist leader reported to Backus, and his witness was confirmed by other ministers. The enemies were deism and infidelity. Thomas Paine's *Age of Reason* had become the "Bible" of the "ungodly"; across Virginia "error and vice" displayed a "Brazen face." "With what boldness they blaspheme," another Baptist complained. "Even the very children appear to ketch it from their Parents."[87]

When a traveling businessman attended church services in Richmond one Sunday, he was disgusted by the "levity" and "indecorum" of young men and women in the congregation, particularly when the minister spoke of the "depravity of human nature." Friends told him that this was typical behavior, deliberately intended to display "contempt for religion." Working as a tutor in Richmond in 1798, the future Unitarian leader William Ellery Channing noted the neglect of scripture and the growth of "Infidelity." Frustrated by his failure to find anyone with whom to discuss religious topics, he complained that "religion is in a deplorable state. Many of the people have wondered how I could embrace such an unprofitable profession as the ministry."[88] The times were not propitious for churchmen.

Weakened by its losses to evangelicals as well as to the growing forces of irreligion, the Episcopal Church split over the glebe issue in the 1790s. The solidarity so noticeable a decade earlier eventually collapsed before the Baptist assault. In the crucial legislative sessions of 1797–98 and 1798–99, only half of those delegates positively identified as Episcopalians defended their church's title to the glebes and other church property, while at least a third voted against it. Some of the latter may have accepted the argument that by the dissolution of the Church of England at the Revolution, the church's property had reverted to the commonwealth. Others may have feared the antagonism toward the church that the continuing controversy evoked. Repealing the glebe laws, after all, did not sell a glebe or seize a church. Any attempt to do that could be settled in a law court.[89]

Bishop Madison's Rule

Certainly the Episcopalians disagreed among themselves, and in that respect Bishop Madison's leadership left much to be desired. Shortly after his consecration in 1790, his promise to Bishop White that he would "not be deficient" in serving the church contained a warning that his own "Exertions" could be but "feeble."[90] They grew weaker as the years passed. His strategy to lobby the legislature at the session of 1797–98 failed utterly. The next year he made no efforts to organize resistance to the repeal of the glebe laws. No Episcopal convention assembled in 1798 to combat the threat. Nor did the bishop support or individual parishes follow the tactic that Pendleton suggested and submit legislative petitions. A well-organized campaign might conceivably have prevented church support from hemorrhaging. Episcopalians had rallied before. But this would have required vigorous leadership and persuasive politicking, and the bishop had no heart for such activities. The House votes reflected the internal division. The church was of two minds, as was its bishop.

Madison's reluctance to rally public support may have stemmed, at least partially, from the novelty of his position. Many post-Revolutionary Virginians thought bishops out of place in the new nation. Their introduction would ultimately yield "an alliance between Church and State." As "the creatures of Kings" and inherently unfriendly to republican forms of government, one writer argued, they belonged with an established church in a royal realm. Bring them into America, and the ultimate result would be a return to British domination.[91] In 1795 a satirical newspaper article, commenting on a monument to be erected at Halifax County Courthouse, described the principal figure as "a Republican Bishop. . . . He has the head of an ass, the feet of a Bull, and the tail of a Monkey." And the attack on episcopacy continued in verse: "Lo! a Bishop without a King! / Poor lifeless, senseless, Popish thing." Madison himself was never completely accepted by the people he was ordained to serve. Episcopalian John Tyler, a future governor and friend of Madison, expressed sentiments shared by many in the gentry class: "When I speak of the Bishop I feel the highest veneration for his character as a Man, but I like him not the better for his canonicals, they will not let men be enough of Republicans—besides he went to Great Britain for the exaulted station. Now who wou'd ever be sent to Heaven by such a people."[92]

Madison evidently wondered that himself. He often betrayed an ambivalence toward his episcopal calling, particularly when the church was under pressure. Although his public exhortations in conventions and his private correspondence with Bishop White in the 1790s displayed a pious concern for the church's welfare, ecclesiastical affairs did not intrude into his letters to public figures who might have offered political advice or support in the legislative battles.[93] While lambasting "immorality" and "impiety" at church meetings, he presided over a college that became notorious for those qualities.[94] And despite the limitations placed upon the bishop by the Virginia canons, Madison neglected even basic responsibilities. He did not make the prescribed parish visitations regularly, nor did he attend the triennial General Convention of the Episcopal Church after 1795.[95] Actually his own public religion probably rendered Virginia's bishop distinctly uncomfortable in the company of his episcopal brethren.

Madison's published address to the clergy and laity of his diocese after the convention of 1799 revealed his chief pastoral concerns as well as his theological orientation. After decrying "the dreadful prostitution of religion and moral principle, which we everywhere experience," he outlined a reform program. First on his list was an exact observance of the church's canons. That had become, in his words, "a dead letter," and he urged his flock to shake off that "fatal lethargy" destroying the church. For example, some parishes had failed to elect vestries, yet vestrymen as "the guardians" of the churches and glebes represented a crucial element in Episcopal polity. Many church buildings had fallen into disrepair, in part because congregations feared that the state would seize them. Based on the evaluations of some of Virginia's finest lawyers, Madison encouraged his brethren to restore the churches confidently and to support the clergy with decent, reliable subscriptions. In terms of explicit religious exhortation, the bishop praised fidelity to Sunday and family worship and a commitment to morality and virtue. Reason yielded belief in the existence of "one Supreme Mind" whose laws were manifested in the physical and moral universes. There men could examine God's "beneficent design" and discern their religious "duties." Religion guaranteed "virtue and genuine republicanism."[96]

Madison was far more comfortable in the realm of moral philosophy than theology or scripture. Though he quoted at length from an unnamed "modern moral philosopher," his address contained hardly any biblical references. It reflected the rationalist cast of mind that made the company of Jefferson and his cousin Madison so pleasant. Writing to his relative, the bishop suggested he pick up a copy of the address at the Richmond printer's and take it to his father. His fellow Episcopal bishops, however, would find it less congenial. They worried about Madison and the church under his care. The triennial convention of

1808, which was deliberately placed in Baltimore in a vain hope that Virginia would send a delegation, expressed the fear that the Virginia church was "depressed" almost to the point of "total ruin." After the meeting the bishops published a pastoral letter, possibly with the president of the College of William and Mary in mind. In it they insisted on the importance of the fundamental "evangelic truths" contained in the church's Articles of Religion and the Bible. Urging morality apart from the basic principles of Christianity they thought ineffective. Moreover, "we suppose a fallacy in every modern scheme of religion, which professes to make men virtuous without the motives to virtue supplied to them in the Gospel; and we think, that in every endeavor of this sort, in which infidelity is not avowed, we discover it in disguise."[97] Long before this, Bishop Madison had evidently ceased writing to Bishop White.

He also dallied repeatedly with the idea of resigning. He wrote his cousin in 1794 that he had been considering "retiring to some comfortable little Farm in a healthy Part of the County." In the spring of 1798 at the height of the crisis over the church's property, a correspondent in Kentucky informed one of Madison's neighbors that the bishop "proposes to visit Kentucky in the fall with a view of procuring a farm for his future residence." Finally, in 1800 and 1801 Madison seriously considered property for sale in the central Piedmont near Jefferson as well as his cousin. Ultimately the price was too high, but he still might have found a farm and moved there if Gabriel's revolt had not terrified his wife. She feared living in a rural area surrounded by a multitude of slaves. The bishop also weighed the advantages of becoming a candidate for the presidency of Columbia College in New York. Even after someone else filled that spot, rumors continued to circulate in the Tidewater that he was resigning his position at William and Mary. In none of his letters discussing a change of residence did Madison mention his episcopal responsibilities.[98]

Although clerical chores apparently awakened little interest in the bishop, he threw himself enthusiastically into Republican politics. As the Baptists were launching their final assaults against the glebes in 1797, the bishop called a meeting of freeholders to protest the policies of the Adams administration, and the following spring he drafted a special prayer to be used throughout his diocese against the possible war with France. He admired Jefferson's "pure and enlightened Views," rejoiced in his election as president, and paid him an extended visit at Monticello in 1802.[99] But the bishop's passion for Jeffersonian Republicanism was not matched by an equivalent vigor in the cause of his church. Although his intervention might not have affected the outcome of the church property struggle, his apparent indifference outside of the conventions did not rally support, particularly when the church was already divided and apathetic. At least two state conventions in 1799 and 1805 urged the bishop to "pursue to the end" the defense of the church's right to the glebes. Madison expressed confidence in 1799 that the courts would prove a "shield against every attack."[100] His hopes were misplaced.

What the Glebe Contest Revealed

Though historians have generally ignored or minimized this fight over church property, it revealed the future in four important respects. First, on the most basic level, the outcome demonstrated the social transformation that the Revolutionary era had worked on the balance of religious forces and especially the newfound strength and confidence of the Baptists. Convinced of the justice of their cause, their clerical leaders were determined to trumpet their grievances until the assembly acted. The earlier struggle to defeat the assessment proposal and to enact Jefferson's statute honed their political skills. They learned how to develop broad coalitions of popular supporters and to represent their views to the assembly both in person and by petition. That experience now paid off. But this time the ultimate success of their argument and their persistence was their victory alone. Thus when it was over and won, there was a strong note of self-congratulation among the Baptists, a sense of "we did it" that was not present after Jefferson's statute had passed. Then Madison had taken the applause. Now at the beginning of the new century, the evangelicals had their day in the sun, and they found it a heady experience. After struggling more than a quarter century, they had achieved "liberty and equality with all religious societies" and emerged with a newfound political clout.[101] They would not hesitate to transfer their political skills to other causes. In fact, they had only just begun.

Second, unlike earlier contests over church-state issues, the glebe fight was not a coalition effort with experienced politicians like Madison in charge. Instead, in the House a collection of young men largely new to politics controlled the business,[102] while Baptist clergy outside the Capitol set the agenda and the timetable. Their experience had taught them to compete on their own. Their ultimate success in this contest helped to lay the foundation for an organized evangelical bloc ready to impose, by legislation if necessary, their values and culture on the American body politic. The triumph of Baptist-led forces in the glebe struggle foreshadowed this critical development of evangelical politics in Virginia and elsewhere in the United States.

Third, the glebe fight also differed from earlier church-state battles in another important respect. The seizure of these lands that the assembly repeatedly had guaranteed by law to the Episcopal Church was the most radical step taken by any one of the new republics against the property rights of any individual or group in the aftermath of the Revolution. In some states Loyalists had their property taken from them, but the Anglican Virginians had overwhelmingly supported the Revolution. That their church's property should be seized was unprecedented. That it should have happened in a conservative slave state where the right to hold property in human beings was sacrosanct is nothing short of amazing. Nothing like it would be seen again in the United States until the Emancipation Proclamation.

Finally, the assembly thought that by repealing all laws pertaining to religion and defining the Statute of Religious Freedom as the authoritative statement on church-state relations, it would solve the church property fight and bring reconciliation to Virginia's warring religious groups. But the legislators' solution created new problems. The laws of 1799 and 1802 did not separate church and state or prevent the government's involvement with religious issues or the churches. At practically every session petitions dealing with church matters or religious concerns arrived at the capital from individuals, churches, and groups; and the lawmakers wanted to respond to their constituents. For example, in 1804 the assembly obliged Abner Waugh, the popular incumbent of St. Mary's Parish in Caroline County, who asked that his glebe be sold and the money invested for his support as long as he remained at his post.[103] Because the law providing for the sale of vacant glebes did not specify the purposes for which the overseers of the poor should allocate the funds, various memorials asked that they indeed be used for the poor or directed toward the building of schools or workhouses. The assembly generally granted those requests.[104] But repeatedly it repulsed efforts to take churches, furniture, and plate that remained in the possession of the Episcopalians or to require the churches be made available to all denominations.[105]

After a drawn-out series of fierce battles that embittered church members and particularly the Baptists and Episcopalians against each other, the law of 1802 was a legislative effort at reconciliation. As the years passed and the legal cases involving the glebe lands were adjudicated, both the courts and the Episcopal Church became increasingly reluctant to tamper with the arrangements made when the nineteenth century began. Yet the potential for religious division remained just below the political surface. It quickly erupted at the end of 1802 when a new assembly narrowly elected as its chaplain John Courtney, a local Baptist preacher, known for his pastoral care of Richmond's African American population, over the urbane and popular Presbyterian John Blair. The result probably turned more on Blair's outspoken Federalism than either man's denomination, but it roused much comment in the press and demonstrated once again the power of religion to divide.[106] Thus it made Virginia politicians all the more determined to keep church and state as far apart as possible. For forty years after 1808, the legislature would decide repeatedly against selecting any chaplain.[107] Civic peace required the expulsion of religion and its spokesmen from the public square. Yet peace would not come. Instead, Virginia's approach to the separation of church and state created enormous conflicts and problems in the years ahead. The Virginia glebe fight demonstrated the possibilities for the entanglement of church and state, religion and politics that would follow throughout the nation's history.

5

Litigation

"Nursing Fathers to the Church"

As the spring of 1803 ripened along Virginia's Eastern Shore, Elizabeth Bowdoin McCroskey scribbled a mournful letter to her old friend St. George Tucker. Her husband, Samuel Smith McCroskey, had died in April, leaving her in desperate straits. McCroskey had been the rector of Hungars Parish in Northampton County for more than a quarter century. One of Virginia's more distinguished clergymen, he sported a DD after his name and numbered among his closest friends Tucker, Joseph Prentis, and Robert Andrews. All three were Williamsburg jurists and staunch Episcopalians. Tucker and Prentis sat on Virginia's General Court, and Tucker was also professor of law and police at the College of William and Mary and the most highly regarded legal scholar in the state. A former minister, Andrews had shed his clerical garb almost twenty years earlier and become a lawyer in order to feed his family. Now McCroskey's widow turned to her late husband's old friends for help, and especially to Tucker. The deceased minister had confided in no one on his side of Chesapeake Bay, his financial affairs were terribly snarled, and Elizabeth McCroskey was living alone on the plantation and distrusted the overseer. Writing from her home at Charlton Glebe, she begged Tucker to come and qualify before the county court as executor of the estate.[1]

Years before, the minister and his wife had treated Tucker's son, Henry, with enormous kindness. Elizabeth had tutored the boy in Greek while he lived with them at the glebe. But Tucker could not respond to her pleas immediately. Together with his judicial duties he was busy putting the final touches on his edition of William Blackstone's *Commentaries*. The first volume was just going to press in May, and the publication of all five volumes would be completed by October. Meanwhile, the widow grew increasingly frantic over the situation on the glebe and her fears that the slaves, worried over being sold, would all run away. Eventually she sent Tucker an itemized list of the estate's debts and debtors. Regarding himself as "the guardian of the church property," McCroskey had employed lawyers to defend the glebe, confident that his vestrymen would support his decision. Now the lawyers pressed their claims, and the widow wanted the vestry to pay the bills. After the court session ended, Tucker crossed the bay to comfort Elizabeth and take charge of Samuel's affairs. He also composed a fulsome gravestone inscription for his old friend. It was a sad business, and by the time he sailed home, the judge was weary to the point of sickness.[2]

Tucker would have been even more exhausted had he known of the legal contest that awaited him. The legislators had hoped that by defining Jefferson's statute as the sole law concerning religion in Virginia, repealing all other religious or church-related laws, and providing for the gradual seizure and sale of the glebes, they had definitively settled the relationship between church and state. They wanted reconciliation in the commonwealth. Instead, they had created a legal situation that would vex the churches, courts, and legislatures throughout the nineteenth century and well into the twentieth. Within a short time Tucker would find himself at the center of a major court battle, the results of which would reverberate for decades. This chapter first considers those legal disputes and then examines the fight over the incorporation of religious groups that preceded the Civil War. Both were direct results of the church-state legislation of 1799 and 1802.

The Glebe of Hungars Parish

The death of the incumbent rector had left Hungars Parish vacant, and the overseers of the poor in Northampton County had been asserting a claim to the glebe property. A lawsuit was in progress, as St. George Tucker warned Thomas Davis, another clergyman friend, after his visit to Elizabeth. Davis had considered applying for the parish a few years earlier when he heard that McCroskey was thinking of retirement. At that time Davis was rector of Fairfax Parish, but like David Griffith years before, he found the glebe poor and the congregation parsimonious. Hungars possessed an excellent location on Chesapeake Bay and almost 1,600 acres of land, a large brick manor house, outbuildings, orchard, and garden. Two years later, however, Davis informed Tucker that his income had improved. He was living in Alexandria, which held the principal church of Fairfax Parish, and was receiving, in addition to the glebe revenues, $2,000 a year.[3] In the past clergymen could play musical chairs to gain a better parish; however, the new glebe law had stopped the tune. Incumbents were safe. But when a parish became vacant due to the death or resignation of a minister, the law now required the overseers of the poor to take over the land, slaves, and buildings. A newly inducted clergyman would have to live on whatever subscription the vestry might raise and perhaps teach school on the side.

Hungars glebe, however, presented an unusual situation. In 1654 Stephen Charlton had died, leaving his home, mill, and lands to a daughter with the proviso that if she died childless, this property should then be used to maintain "an orthodoxe devyne" in the parish. When she died years later without leaving children, the parish's incumbent minister fell heir as residual legatee. Because of the terms of the Charlton will, the state could not seize the glebe lands when McCroskey died in 1803. The dozen glebe slaves, however, had to be sold because when the Charlton farm came to the parish, the vestry had sold the original glebe and purchased slaves to work the new property. Consequently, their descendants came under the terms of the glebe law and now reverted to state ownership.[4]

At one point the overseers, seeking to understand their duties and the proper extent of their claims under the new law, wrote for advice to Philip Norborne Nicholas, the state's attorney general. When Elizabeth McCroskey got wind of this move, she was outraged. Thinking she was entitled to remain on the glebe, she once more begged Tucker's intervention. He sailed across the bay again in the fall of 1803, in his capacity as one of her husband's executors, hoping to help Elizabeth come to grips with the realities of her situation. Ultimately the Charlton property appeared safe for the Episcopal Church so long as a clergyman remained in the parish. According to the will's terms, if a vacancy occurred for more than six months, the house, lands, and mill reverted to a Charlton nephew's heirs. Aware of this provision, the vestry moved quickly in 1803 and hired a new rector, Walter Gardiner.[5] Evidently he preferred not to live on the glebe, because when Elizabeth finally had to move out at the end of the year, a Methodist couple with nine children rented the house. She had not left happily. Another gloomy letter to Tucker described the rainy night when the new occupants had turned her out of "dear Charlton." Her brother had found her somewhere to live, a place called the ferry house which she described as miserable.[6]

Turpin v. Lockett (1804)

Toward the end of 1803, Robert Andrews had become Elizabeth McCroskey's chief adviser,[7] and Tucker was engrossed in the politics of a judicial election. The ambitious judge had long hoped to sit on Virginia's Supreme Court of Appeals, the state's highest tribunal. The death of the venerable presiding judge, Edmund Pendleton, in September 1803 had created a vacancy, and the legislature would select his replacement. Tucker's greatest desire now appeared within his grasp. Potentially strong opposition existed, however, from western delegates who wanted a judge from their part of the state and even more from others vitally concerned about the decision in an extremely important case pending before the court. When Manchester Parish became vacant shortly after the passage of the glebe law of 1802, Edmund Lockett and the other overseers of the poor in Chesterfield County started proceedings to sell the glebe. The vestry brought suit in the Superior Court of Chancery for an injunction to prevent the sale. Their bill made several key assertions: First. that the church had been vested with the property before the Revolution, and though the Revolution had "destroyed" the religious establishment, the Protestant Episcopal Church was essentially the same as the colonial Church of England. Second, Virginia statutes during and after the Revolution recognized this church and confirmed its property rights, and their repeal could not divest the church of its property. Therefore, the law of 1802 was unconstitutional. After examining the arguments on both sides of the case, Chancellor George Wythe dismissed the suit. The vestry then took its case to the Supreme Court of Appeals.[8]

Turpin v. Lockett, as the Manchester glebe case was formally titled, was first argued before the judges in the spring of 1803. This hugely controversial case was widely regarded as the most important issue the Supreme Court of Appeals had yet faced. Of the five members of the court, Judge William Fleming disqualified himself because of his residence in Chesterfield. Three of the other four, including Pendleton, were expected to sustain the church's claim to the glebe. Only the court's youngest member, Spencer Roane, was known to support the 1802 law. During the summer, while the judges were preparing their decisions, Roane consulted William Brockenbrough, who had been a member of the assembly that approved the glebe law. Brockenbrough explained to the judge that the legislators believed that the 1799 act repealing all laws pertaining to religion except Jefferson's statute had effectively dissolved any corporation of the Episcopal Church that might have existed. He also defended the decision to award the money arising from glebe sales to the parishes. Roane's opinion would not have mattered, however, except that on the night before the court was to render its verdict, Pendleton suddenly died. The case would now have to be reargued after the assembly elected his successor.[9]

Before casting their ballots, however, some legislators wanted to know Tucker's views on the constitutionality of the glebe law. The judge could not, of course, reveal how he might vote on the case, but he gently suggested to James Semple, a Williamsburg neighbor in the assembly, that he consult Tucker's new edition of Blackstone's *Commentaries* for its appendix entitled a "Summary View of the Laws Relative to Glebes and Churches." After a fulsome account of the glebe law and Chancellor Wythe's dismissal of the vestry's bill, Tucker had inserted a proposal for a general assessment "for teachers of religion and morality, and for the erection and keeping in repair places of worship and public schools." Tucker saw in his proposal, which closely resembled the practice in

Massachusetts and Connecticut, nothing "incompatible with the most perfect liberty of conscience in matters of religion." A tax scheme on a nondenominational basis violated neither Virginia's constitution nor the Statute for Establishing Religious Freedom. His friend Bishop Madison concurred. At a church convention shortly after the passage of the 1799 act that had made Jefferson's statute normative for the church-state relationship, the bishop in good republican fashion had linked morality and virtue with the support of religion and urged consideration of a "general assessment." Reading Tucker's account of the legal history and his assessment plan, a thoughtful person might well infer that the judge agreed with the constitutionality of the 1802 law and was suggesting a way to apply the funds raised by the sale of the glebes.[10] Tucker obviously had reassured the lawmakers because early in January they elected him over Archibald Stuart, the western candidate, by a vote of 115 to 82.[11]

In May 1804 two impressive legal teams reargued the case before the Supreme Court of Appeals. Edmund Randolph, John Wickham, and Daniel Call, who was also a legal editor and brother-in-law of John Marshall, spoke on behalf of the plaintiffs. Much to the delight of the Baptists, George Hay had volunteered his services and joined Philip Norborne Nicholas, the state's attorney general, in defending the constitutionality of the glebe law. Thomas Ritchie, editor of the *Richmond Enquirer*, reported the contents of the debate in an extensive series of articles. With the positions of the other judges already known, the outcome depended on Tucker's decision.

He began his opinion on an unusual personal note.[12] After expressing his "regret" that this case had ever arisen, the judge opened with an encomium for the established clergy at the outbreak of the Revolution. Without "selfish" regard for their own welfare, they had zealously promoted the cause of independence "by precept & exhortation" and even "by example." Was he thinking of his late friend Samuel McCroskey, or David Griffith, or his own rector, Bishop Madison? "If ever men in their station deserved the esteem of their County," he wrote, it "was due to the Clergy of the established Church in Virginia," and he openly wondered why the Revolutionary Convention had failed to guarantee "the security of their Rights by a constitutional declaration." Tucker also criticized the legislature for not settling "this Question" by a law while the Revolutionary generation was still alive. But "most of all" he lamented the unfortunate death of the "distinguish'd" Pendleton, whose "Decision . . . would probably have reconciled the doubts of all who doubted, and would have produced acquiescence, at least, in those who were not convinced." Without a doubt Pendleton's opinion would have been very different from that which the newest member of the court was about to render.[13]

Tucker then laid out the basic history and principles of English common law regarding "Parishes, Glebes, Parsons, Churchwardens, Parishioners, & Vestries." Essentially the glebes originated under the feudal system of medieval England with the parson holding his glebe as a tenant like other vassals. In the ceremony of induction, he was invested with the title to his glebe. By common law he became a corporation, but an ecclesiastical rather than a civil one. In colonial Virginia ecclesiastical corporations existed "for the purpose of perpetuating the Rights of the established Church"; but the Revolution had dissolved them when the new constitution failed to provide for a religious establishment, thus effectively abolishing the established church, as the plaintiffs had admitted in their bill.[14]

By colonial laws the vestries were "a body politic, capable of purchasing, & holding lands for the use of the Ministers of their respective parishes; and capable of a perpetual succession." At the Revolution the vestries held "the legal titles to all the glebes." The issue was whether the vestries still held those titles. Tucker concluded they did not. Reviewing the laws passed since 1776, he pointed out that the dissolution of all vestries by the Incorporation Act of 1784 and their acceptance of that law effectively dissolved those "former bodies politic." Despite the plaintiffs' vehement assertions, the church incorporated by that law was substantially different from the former established church, at least in the eyes of the law. The latter had been "part of the general body politic, or State." But the Protestant Episcopal Church was simply a "private Incorporation" of the minister and vestry in each parish "with power to hold lands, to a certain amount, for a special purpose."[15] After the assembly repealed that act in 1786, the property was then held by a new corporation called "Trustees"; and in 1788 another act referred to these ministers and vestries in each parish as "Successors." The assembly had repealed all these laws in 1799, and the corporations were thereby dissolved. Tucker found legal precedent for such sweeping legislative authority in Parliament's dissolution of the monasteries during the reign of Henry VIII. Virginia's government had acted in similar fashion on other occasions.

Throughout the Revolution and its aftermath, the struggle of the Virginia legislature to define the church-state relationship had proved to be a complex and sometimes contradictory business. Now Tucker called his responsibility of reconciling "the conflicting, and even opposite, acts of the legislative body" an "unpleasant" and "arduous task." As he saw the issues, the most important were "the *Dictates of Moral Justice*, and the principles of the *Constitution of the Commonwealth*." Moral justice demanded that any funds resulting from the glebe sales should belong to the parishioners as the 1802 law provided. Specific articles of the Declaration of Rights were also at stake. Tucker determined, for example, that the legislative acts that bestowed on the Episcopal Church "the *exclusive Emoluments* of the Glebes, purchased at the common Expence of *all* the parishioners," violated "the fourth Article of the Constitution." The Presbyterians and Baptists had voiced this complaint for several decades. On this same point Tucker noted that "the *Dissenters*" were "infinitely more numerous" than the Episcopalians and revisited his assessment proposal: "If the legislature had thought proper to appropriate the Glebes & Churches, purchased, & built, at the Expence of *all the parishioners,* in each parish, for the use of such Minister, or Teacher of Religion, as a *Majority* of the *Parish* should chuse, without any regard to sects or denominations of Religion, whether Christian, Jew, Mahometan, or other whatsoever, *This Article,* I apprehend would not have stood in the way of such a *general appropriation.*"[16]

Finally, Tucker undercut the plaintiffs' claim that the 1802 law violated the rights of private property. The glebes had never been private property but were purchased at general parish expense. If the incumbents had a right to the glebes, the law safeguarded their title so long as they occupied the farms. But as the repeal of the laws in 1799 had been valid, so also the law providing for the sale of the glebes was constitutional. The Manchester Parish vestry had no legal title to the glebe in Chesterfield County; and because no incumbent minister occupied the parish, the overseers could proceed to sell the property. With the four judges hearing the case evenly split, Chancellor Wythe's dismissal of the plaintiffs' bill was upheld. A devoted Episcopalian judge on Virginia's highest court had vindicated the Baptist cause; and the youngest son of Robert Carter Nicholas, the great defender of the established church, had argued their case. Baptist associations joined in expressing their gratitude to the two Episcopalians, Hay and Nicholas, "for their signal and zealous services" as attorneys for Baptist defendant Edmund Lockett.[17] The religious revolution was complete.

Terrett v. Taylor (1815)

But the legal contests continued. A split decision did not definitively resolve the issue. Jolted perhaps by the *Turpin v. Lockett* decision, enough Episcopalian delegates assembled in 1805 for a "Special Convention" to discuss ways of strengthening church polity. They delegated Bishop Madison and the standing committee "to pursue to the end the rights and the property of the churches." But nothing came of it. The increasingly infirm Madison asked the convention for an assistant bishop, but his request was ignored.[18] No further conventions were held during his lifetime. Nor did Virginia send any representatives to the church's General Convention during the first decade of the nineteenth century. By 1811 the convention meeting in New Haven reported that the Virginia church was "so depressed, that there is danger of her total ruin."[19] Madison died in April 1812 and was eventually succeeded by an outsider, Richard Channing Moore, the fifty-two-year-old rector of a thriving parish in New York City with a reputation for diplomatic skill and evangelical preaching.[20] He would need all his talents in his new position.

As Moore was installed in the diocese of Virginia, a glebe case involving one of his parishes was making its way through the federal court system. In 1770 the churchwardens of Fairfax Parish had purchased a tract of 516 acres as a glebe. Originally located in Fairfax County, Virginia, the property fell within federal jurisdiction following the creation of the District of Columbia in 1791.[21] When the parish vestry later attempted to sell the land, the overseers of the poor of Fairfax County claimed the property under the 1802 glebe law. Edmund Jennings Lee, a member of the diocesan standing committee from one of Virginia's first families, had encouraged Moore to come to Virginia. The two would become steadfast friends and allies in the coming years. As a churchwarden of Christ Church in Alexandria and highly respected lawyer, Lee challenged the Fairfax County overseers and successfully argued the case before the U.S. Supreme Court.[22]

In his verdict Associate Justice Joseph Story reviewed the history of Virginia's church-state relationship and blistered the legislature on several counts. By common law and the assembly's statutes, he argued, property of various kinds had been legally vested in the colonial church; and despite the demise of the establishment with the Revolution, the assembly's law of 1776 had confirmed the church's title. Further laws passed in the 1780s had incorporated the minister and vestry of each parish, reiterated their ownership of the property, and later provided for trustees and then their successors. Story found this completely appropriate, and he strongly criticized the 1799 law repealing the state's repeated guarantees of the church property as an unconstitutional violation of contractual obligations: "The doctrine that a legislative grant is revocable . . . would uproot the very foundations of almost all the land titles in Virginia, and is utterly inconsistent with a great and fundamental principle of a republican government, the right of the citizens to the free enjoyment of their property." In sweeping terms Story attacked the state's action as an infringement of "natural justice, . . . the fundamental laws of every free government, . . . the spirit and the letter of the constitution of the United States, and . . . the decisions of most respectable judicial tribunals."[23]

What weight would Story's opinion carry in the Virginia courts? By the time that case had been decided, most Virginia vestries had accepted the inevitable seizure of their glebes. On two occasions state courts repelled efforts by eager overseers to sell glebes out from under incumbent ministers; however, when the clergymen died or retired, the church normally lost the property. But after the U.S. Supreme Court had determined that the Virginia church laws of 1799 and 1802 were unconstitutional and awarded the Fairfax glebe to the church, some vestrymen of neighboring Shelburne Parish in Loudoun County determined to test that decision's applicability in Virginia.[24]

Selden v. Overseers of the Poor (1840)

The Shelburne vestry originally had purchased a glebe of 465 acres for David Griffith before the Revolution. After a succession of ministers, John Dunn served the parish from 1801 and proved by all accounts a competent and edifying rector until his death in 1827. The parish church of St. James in Leesburg had been constructed during his tenure. The overseers had first attempted to seize the glebe when his predecessor had died in 1801, but they lost in court. Now their successors could cite the 1802 law, and a majority of the vestry was prepared to cede the property. After the overseers sold it to a Maryland resident, four vestrymen decided to pursue the issue legally with the support of the newly inducted parish minister, Thomas Jackson. With Story's decision in mind, they thought that even though they might lose the case in Virginia, it could be successfully appealed to the U.S. Supreme Court.[25]

The lawsuit, however, placed the Episcopal Church in a potentially awkward situation. As Bishop Moore explained in a letter to Jackson in 1829, he appreciated the financial problems the minister faced and the hardships the loss of the glebes had created for his clergy throughout Virginia. The homes and farmlands their predecessors had enjoyed had been sold. Their incomes now depended precariously upon the hopeful promises of vestries and subscriptions circulated among their parishioners. Moore had agonized over these concerns since the beginning of his tenure in the state. Yet the church had survived and was now prospering. While the Shelburne glebe matter was of recent vintage and a court victory might create "little noise" in Loudoun County, if success in this case encouraged other parishes to claim property that had been sold decades earlier, the bishop feared the "opposition and tumult" involved in such suits would bring Episcopalians into disrepute just when their reputation was rising. "I would rather trust to the goodness of God," Moore wrote, "than risk the happiness and prosperity of the Church."[26]

Selden and Others v. The Overseers of the Poor of Loudoun County began in the Winchester Court of Chancery. The plaintiffs argued that the overseers had sold the property "without legal authority" because according to the *Terrett* decision, the 1802 glebe law violated the U.S. Constitution.[27] The chancellor who delivered the ruling in 1830 was Henry St. George Tucker, once tutored in Greek by Elizabeth McCroskey and the oldest son of the judge who has cast the deciding vote in *Turpin v. Lockett* in 1804. He began by examining the position of bishops and parsons in common law and argued that from a legal perspective colonial Virginia had neither. Rather than being founded on the common law, the whole religious establishment from the beginning of the colony had been "a statutory system." The colonial church was "a public civil institution, ordained by the government for public purposes, instead of being a private ecclesiastical establishment, or, like the Church of England, a co-ordinate and co-equal estate of the realm."[28]

Although father and son agreed on the conclusion, the son's opinion assumed a very different judicial tone. Absent was any indication of sympathy for the Revolutionary clergy or regret for the failure of government to safeguard their interests. Instead, the younger Tucker boiled with righteous indignation at the infringement of "the rights of religious liberty, and freedom of opinion in matters of conscience" at the hands of an "oppressive" church establishment throughout the colonial period. Rewriting Virginia's colonial history, the chancellor was "certain" that the colony possessed "large congregations of dissenters, with pious and learned pastors"; and he singled out "the Presbyterians" as "a flourishing sect . . . under the powerful ministry of Samuel Davis." Echoing the sentiments and vocabulary of Jefferson's statute, he charged that the laws requiring them to support the established church were "sinful and tyrannical." The very first state legislature should have repealed them immediately, and the glebes should have been seized and sold at once, instead of waiting until 1802.

Indeed, the legislative guarantee of the property to church in the laws of 1776 and 1786 had been "VOID" because the Episcopal Church was not a corporate body. Although those laws provided for a grantor (the assembly) and a grant (the property), no grantee (legal body) existed to receive the grant. Tucker went further to deny that any grant could ever be made to a religious society even through trustees because the beneficiary remained "uncertain." He accurately summarized the result: "There is not a religious society in Virginia, which has not felt the difficulty, nay the impossibility, of any valid and binding arrangement of their property for the uses of their sects."[29]

When Tucker wrote this opinion, it was the common practice in Virginia for trustees to hold property on behalf of the churches. Baptist and Presbyterian churches had followed this practice in the colonial period.[30] The county deed books testify to the explosion of evangelical congregations in the early national period, particularly the Baptists and Methodists along with the continuing Presbyterian presence and the renewed growth of the Episcopalians. Most interesting, perhaps, is the land deeded in trust for churches that were to be open for the use of multiple denominations. Such property grants chart the religious revival that swept across the state in the nineteenth century.[31] The law validated most of these grants in 1842.

The key for Tucker was the act of 1786 that repealed the church's incorporation and thus "completely annihilated" its "rights." In fulsome terms he praised this law "passed in the plentitude of the power of our venerated commonwealth, when her sovereignty was untrammeled, and her will alone determined the validity of her laws." Therefore, the chancellor asserted, "the question in this case *is not touched by the constitution of the United States*, which was not adopted until two years afterwards; . . . this *is a subject over which the supreme court of the United States have no manner of jurisdiction.*" Contradicting Story's judgment on the 1799 and 1802 laws, Tucker found them "not only constitutional and just, but politic and wise." In the concluding pages of his opinion, Tucker extended his historiographical reach beyond colonial Virginia to the dangers displayed by European religious establishments with their penchant for acquiring wealth and property. The papacy and Catholic religious orders presented "a history of the cupidity of monks and devotees, veiled under the sacred garb of our holy religion." The notorious riches of the church in France had fostered a revolution that "shook the civilized world to its very centre." Nor were Protestant countries immune from the dangers. Britain's "church establishment" displayed an "overgrown wealth" and a hierarchy living in "luxury and indolence." Even the United States provided an instructive example in the extraordinary wealth possessed by the "Episcopal Church of New York." Virginia had chosen wisely, Tucker argued, and a decree by the court of appeals nullifying the 1799 and 1802 laws would unleash a multitude of practical as well as theoretical problems.[32]

The chancellor's unusually personal decision was published in the newspapers and in pamphlet form. It did not go unanswered. Writing under the pseudonym of "A Layman," Edmund Jennings Lee published a "review" of Tucker's "opinion." Forty-three pages in length, it was almost twice as long as the judgment it challenged. The chancellor had claimed that his court lacked jurisdiction and that the vestry's suit belonged in a court of law rather than one of equity. But instead of simply dismissing it to a county court, he had proceeded to argue that legally the case had no merit, thus prejudging it for any future tribunal. Even more outrageous, though Tucker sat on an inferior state bench, he had presumed to review and reject a U.S. Supreme Court decision. "It is difficult," Lee averred, "to account for this departure from *judicial dignity.*"[33]

Tucker's rendition of church history and particularly his assault on the Episcopal Church infuriated Lee, a devout vestryman. Invoking a litany of Episcopalian patriots from Griffith to Washington, Lee objected vigorously to Tucker's inferences that the adherents of Virginia's mother church had been lukewarm in their commitment to the Revolution, or that they lacked concern for religious liberty and desired "a union of Church and State." Virginia stood in no danger of that, though he suggested a worse alternative: "an alliance between *infidelity* and the State." Every state guaranteed religious freedom, but only Virginia had seized the church's property and refused to incorporate religious groups.[34]

The principal portion of Lee's pamphlet offered a detailed exposition of the assembly's laws pertaining to the Episcopal Church and its vestries and clergy from 1776 to 1802. Lee noted in particular that they referred repeatedly to the church and its ministers by title, thus contradicting the chancellor's claim that both church and clergy were legal "non-entities." Quoting Tucker page by page, he rebutted his arguments against the legal existence of the church and challenged that aspect of the glebe law of 1802 whereby the overseers could seize and sell church property "without an inquest of office," as they had done most recently in Loudoun County. Ominously, Lee warned that if Tucker was correct and the Declaration of Rights "prohibited the Legislature to pass any law securing to any religious community the means of protecting their rights as a society—that they all exist by *courtesy* alone," then all denominations were at risk; and "the same principles which are now attempted to be applied to the rights and property of the Episcopal Church, if countenanced by the public, may, at some future time be applied to them, their rights and their property." Was this what Virginia's founders had meant by "religious freedom," he asked? Lee concluded by quoting Patrick Henry's last will and testament on the value of Christianity and urging "every department of our government" to embrace Henry's values and "use their talents and influence in upholding instead of pulling down the institutions of Religion."[35]

Virginia's Supreme Court of Appeals did not hear the case until 1840. Tucker had been elected as that court's presiding judge, but because he had ruled on the issue in chancery court, he recused himself from the unanimous decision of the four judges who upheld *Turpin v. Lockett*. The relatively brief report of the case did not recount the arguments of Chapman Johnson for the Shelburne vestry or John Robertson in defense of the Loudoun overseers because the judges prescinded from them.

Instead, speaking for the court, Justice Robert Stanard made three points. First, in the thirty-five years since the Manchester glebe case, almost all the property had changed hands with the general acquiescence of the Episcopal Church. Second, the issue of incorporation for churches and religious groups had been settled repeatedly in the assembly and also in the constitutional convention of 1829. The Episcopal Church had no corporations, and "incorporations of religious sects, providing for church government of the members, and the election or appointment and institution of ministers, are without the scope of legislative power, and incompatible with the principles of [Jefferson's statute] now incorporated in the constitution." Considering the general acceptance of the operation of the glebe law over many years, the sale of virtually all the glebes and the development of new and varied interests in that property, and the decisions made in the legislature and the constitutional convention, the court judged that "the injunction of *stare decisis* is of the most commanding authority." Despite the fact that *Turpin v. Lockett* had decided nothing, the court would let it alone.[36] Nothing was said, however, about *Terrett v. Taylor.* The Virginia justices had resolved the ownership of the glebes by ignoring the nation's Supreme Court.

The Politics of Incorporation

The incorporation issue would not be solved so easily. In his decision in *Terrett*, Justice Story also attacked a crucial assertion of the Virginia assembly in its 1799 law of repeal. After specifying Jefferson's statute as the sole criterion for interpreting Virginia's church-state relationship, the legislature had proclaimed that the incorporation of churches was "inconsistent with the principles of the constitution, and of religious freedom, and manifestly tends to the establishment of a national church." After that, the legislature routinely rejected incorporation petitions from churches and religious bodies.[37] Story found this position incomprehensible. In his view corporate powers were obviously necessary to facilitate the ordinary ministries of a church or religious organization, and no "public or constitutional principles required the abolition of all religious corporations."[38]

The justice's opinion resonated with various denominations in Virginia who remained perplexed about their situation. The repeal of all laws save the statute had placed them in a legal limbo without secure property titles or a recognized status in civil society. Virginia Presbyterians provoked the first major test of this policy when their synod in 1815 appointed trustees for a theological seminary and instructed them to obtain an act of incorporation.[39] John Holt Rice, pastor of Richmond's Presbyterian Church, was the driving force behind this effort. Speaking before a legislative committee and later in the press, Rice insisted that the state should encourage religion on a nonpreferential basis. "In our country Christianity is the religion of the nation," he asserted. The government should "give us authority to do, that which we have a natural right to do, namely erect schools, and educate our youth for . . . the ministry of the gospel." Other states, he pointed out, had incorporated churches and seminaries and even mandated religious tests and tax support for churches and ministers. The opposition, however, successfully argued that seminary incorporation would create "an establishment of religion" and would violate Virginia's Declaration of Rights, state constitution, and Statute for Religious Freedom.[40] Ultimately the Presbyterian leaders solved the problem by placing the seminary and its endowment under their church's General Assembly, which had been chartered by Pennsylvania. The General Assembly's trustees would control the fund, while the Virginia and North Carolina synods would jointly manage the seminary.[41]

Although some Presbyterians attributed the assembly's refusal to incorporate their seminary to "ignorance and . . . prejudice," Virginia's intense post-Revolutionary debate on church and state had sensitized its political leadership to a degree unmatched elsewhere in the new republic. The bulk of the legislators shared the views of one assemblyman who bluntly informed his constituents, "I protest against all incorporations for religious purposes." In the constitutional convention of 1829–30, which wrote Jefferson's statute into the revision of the state's fundamental law, only twelve votes supported a proviso to permit the incorporation of seminaries and religious benevolent associations.[42] As the court of appeals reaffirmed in the Selden case, regardless of what the U.S. Supreme Court thought or other states did, churches had no legal standing in Virginia.

This intransigence created serious problems for religious groups. When, for example, Joseph Gallego, the wealthy owner of Gallego Mills in Richmond, died in 1818, he left a large number of bequests including $1,000 to support the city's Catholic chapel and a city lot and $3,000 to build a church. But because the Catholic Church and its trustees were not incorporated, the court of appeals ruled in 1832 that there was no legal entity that could receive the bequest. By far the longest of the three written opinions came from the pen of the court's recently elected president, Henry St. George Tucker. In their rulings he and Justice Dabney Carr followed the precedent set by Chief Justice John Marshall in a similar case before the U.S. Supreme Court in 1819. But Tucker roamed outside the matter at issue to praise "the decided hostility of the legislative power to religious incorporations." Knowing that "wealth is power," the assembly wisely feared "that the grant of any privilege, however trivial, might serve but as an entering wedge to greater demands." He then quoted verbatim but without attribution from his version of European religious history in Selden v. Overseers that pointed out "the dangers of ecclesiastical establishments."[43]

Virginia's legislators obviously found Tucker's perspective persuasive. When Samuel Butcher died in 1778, he left Ebenezer Baptist Church in Loudoun County two acres for a burial yard, meetinghouse, and school. A church was already on the site, and for more than fifty years a Baptist congregation continued to worship there. Butcher's will, however, had not provided for trustees, so no individual or group held legal title to the land. Church members petitioned the assembly in 1833 to appoint trustees in order to guarantee church ownership, but the legislature refused.[44] Church property titles remained precarious for an-other decade until finally, in 1842, the assembly passed a general bill that granted title to church buildings, burial grounds, and parsonages to trustees and their successors; but the law did not mention bequests or grant corporate status.[45]

During the 1830s the assembly regularly incorporated railroad, canal, steam-boat, and turnpike companies; savings and insurance institutions; gold, copper, and coal mining enterprises; iron and steel manufacturers; academies and col-leges; library, literary, and scientific societies; and even mineral springs. But no religious groups could apply. In a dispute over a parish glebe, a petition hostile to the Episcopal Church's claim to the land accurately summarized the church's disabilities: "Under our laws, a society of persons cannot take or hold lands without both an act of incorporation and a grant. . . . No one would seriously attempt to prove that in Virginia an Episcopal minister is a corporation, or that the church itself is a corporation. . . . The church possesses but few, if any, of the requisites of a corporation, and the ministers have still fewer. It has no name, in law, no capacity to sue and be sued, grant or receive by a corporate name, and has no common seal; all of which are incidents to corporations."[46]

Episcopalian frustration spilled over in a petition that Bishop Moore and a group of ministers submitted to the assembly in January 1840. From the mid-eighteenth century, the clergy had regularly contributed a portion of their sala-ries to a fund to support the families of deceased ministers. Without corporate status for this association, however, they had no assurance that the fund's ob-jectives actually would be accomplished. Other states had readily incorporated such societies, and the ministers were clearly aggravated: "Whilst the Legisla-ture are continually granting Charters to Companies and Associations of every kind, and description, your Petitioners cannot believe that they will refuse one to a Society which has for its object the *relief of the Widow and the Orphan*! It is *Fathers* and *Husbands*, who are appealing, not in behalf of themselves, but of their Wives and *Children* to *Fathers* and *Husbands*!" But the assembly denied the Episcopalian appeal, and the next year it overwhelmingly rejected a similar Methodist proposal to incorporate a society for "Superannuated and Disabled Ministers."[47]

The Great Debate over Church Incorporation

The Episcopalians did not give up. The 1842 law, which had granted trust-ees legal title to church property, seemed to suggest a shift in the assembly. Urged on by Bishop William Meade, Moore's dynamic successor, the clergy campaigned vigorously for church incorporation and, in particular, for the legal standing to receive bequests. Meade thought the legislature could hardly refuse this "reasonable" request, particularly if all Virginia churches cooperated in the appeal. After the assembly brushed aside both private appeals from prominent Episcopalians as well as a formal petition to permit "literary, charitable and religious associations to hold property to a limited extent," the bishop pledged himself to an ecumenical effort. Throughout 1844 a committee of Baptists, Episcopalians, Methodists, and New School Presbyterians solicited support across Virginia.[48] Their common petition protested that the denial of "the corporate privilege of acquiring and holding property, and of entering into contracts" seriously hindered educational and charitable work. Even organizations for "mere amusement" enjoyed legal rights denied religious groups. They asked for equal, unprejudiced treatment for all denominations. Underlining the benefits their churches provided the community at large, they warned that rejection of their request would severely jeopardize Virginia's "prosperity and morals."[49]

In order to drum up support and silence objections, four Richmond clergymen drafted an elaborate explanatory tract. They pointed out that although wealthy benefactors frequently included church and benevolent groups in their wills, an "*unincorporated* Institution or Society" could not legally inherit such bequests, and they enumerated cases in which grants to education, missionary, and Bible associations had been canceled. To deny the benefits of legal protection to church groups that other organizations possessed was unjust; to refuse assistance to institutions vital to the state's development was shortsighted. Appealing to the practice elsewhere, the ministers detailed the incorporation permitted to religious bodies in neighboring Maryland, Ohio, Kentucky, and North Carolina. "Why, it may be asked, should Christians in Virginia be denied privileges granted them in almost every other State? . . . We ask, respectfully, but we ask it as a *right*, that we should not be disfranchised because we profess allegiance to the God of the Universe!" Citing resolutions passed at Baptist and Episcopalian meetings, the four ministers emphasized the interdenominational aspect of their appeal and asserted that they spoke for all churches "as far as we know or have any reason to believe."[50]

Had the churches been united, the outcome might conceivably have been different. Instead, major opposition surfaced within clerical ranks in the person of William Swan Plumer. Even his critics admired the minister's oratorical skills and imposing figure in the pulpit. A head taller than most men and endowed with a magnificent speaking voice, the pastor of Richmond's First Presbyterian Church was considered Virginia's foremost preacher in the 1840s. In addition to his pastorate, he edited the *Watchman of the South* and dominated the Old School faction that comprised the bulk of Virginia Presbyterians.[51] The Old School–New School division of 1837–38 had split the state's Presbyterians, leaving the Old School clergy in the majority.

William Swan Plumer (1802–1880). (Virginia
Historical Society, IMG07478)

When the Old School synod debated the incorporation appeal in October
1844, it did not help the case that one of the pamphlet's authors was Joseph
Stiles, the New School pastor of a Richmond congregation that had separated
from Plumer's church.[52] Under Plumer's leadership a majority of the Virginia
Synod repudiated the pamphlet and voted to oppose "any *general* law for the
indiscriminate incorporation of institutions claiming to be Literary, Benevolent
or Religious." While acknowledging that "gentlemen" of "piety, talents, and high
character" favored the proposal, the synod thought the idea was filled with potential dangers for both state and church. There was no need, the majority argued, for the assembly to alter its policies toward religious groups. A minority
disagreed. In recalling John Holt Rice's failure to obtain incorporation for their
theological seminary thirty years before, the pamphlet had struck a nerve. They
warned that the synod's resolutions would create the misleading impression
that Presbyterians approved of the rejection of their seminary's incorporation

and the failure to protect bequests to religious groups. Their objections were overruled, although the majority accepted the principle that the legislature might incorporate individual churches or religious groups, considering each case on its merits. The synod appointed Plumer to represent its views.[53]

The Episcopalians had led the campaign for incorporation, but the group most visibly outraged by the Presbyterian position was the Baptists. Though Baptist polity emphasized local church autonomy, most adherents favored associational meetings of churches for advice and mutual support. In Virginia a third and more controversial administrative layer also existed, the General Association, which spearheaded cooperation among Virginia Baptists in the establishment of Sunday schools; Bible, education, temperance, and tract societies; the preparation of candidates for an "enlightened ministry"; and other "great plans of christian benevolence." Great plans cost money, however, and finances were extremely strained. As the Education Society pointed out in 1844, "To educate the rising Ministry of the State, we must have more money, for it cannot be done without it." The managers of the Foreign Missionary Society, Bible Society, and Sunday School and Publication Society voiced similar complaints of meager collections and inadequate revenues.[54]

In response to these problems, the Baptist General Association had been pushing for a law to secure bequests. Now the Presbyterian opposition triggered a vigorous protest from the association's executive board. The Baptist leaders especially resented the insinuation that the legal changes they had requested violated church-state separation. The identity they had carefully constructed for themselves was at stake. No group had suffered "greater persecution" under the colonial establishment, they remonstrated, or shown greater antipathy to any union of church and state. They had not sought incorporation or vast endowments. Whatever funds they received were immediately spent. They wanted only the right to receive bequests to support their works of benevolence. The Baptist board pointed out that the source of these unjust charges was "the Jealous Whispers of those who having obtained by another and more comprehensive Means all they need or desire, are unwilling that any others shall enjoy like privileges." Pennsylvania's incorporation of the Presbyterian General Assembly amply secured that church's property throughout the country. "How strange," the Baptists observed, that "those who cry out most loudly against our moderate request are the very persons who enjoy this wholesale and sweeping power." If the assembly could not equalize the situation among the churches, they suggested it render the Presbyterians "impotent."[55]

James B. Taylor, Virginia's foremost Baptist minister, presided at this meeting, and in January 1845 he sent a respectful letter to the legislature contrasting the legal situations of Baptists and Presbyterians. The Baptists had not requested the "general . . . incorporation" that the Presbyterians opposed but only the same capacity to receive bequests that the latter already enjoyed. Taylor had to state his case carefully, because he knew that some Baptists disagreed. Noting that "a few Baptists Churches . . . styling themselves 'Old School,' will probably oppose this measure," he claimed to speak for "70,000 communicants" who comprised the vast majority of Baptists in the state.[56] In fact, eight Old School or Antimission churches had already protested against any change in the laws. Though a minority, they prized their independence and rejected the collaborative efforts of the General Association as unscriptural.

In petitions strongly reminiscent of the Baptist memorials that sixty years earlier had supported the passage of Jefferson's statute, they informed the assembly, "The teaching of Religion of any kind whatever, is a matter, which our legislature has no constitutional right to meddle with: the wise framers of our constitution have left it where it belongs 'Between each Citizen and his God.' The religion of Heaven will sustain itself without the strong arm of civil law, and that which requires legislative patronage to sustain it, can not fail to involve our country in anarchy[,] hierarchy, despotism and blood." They attacked the General Association as a "religious party" bent on obtaining "corporate priviledges" so it could teach that "Religion" was "a science, and inseperably connected with the spread of the Bible, sabbath schools, and evangelizing our own as well as other lands." The assembly should repudiate "any legislation that may strengthen a religious aristocracy, or have a tendency to unite Church and State, or to encourage even an idea that false benevolence, or religion, is to receive the fostering care of any legislation whatever; further than is now abundantly extended."[57]

Throughout winter and spring of 1845, friends and foes of church corporations vigorously sparred in the pages of the *Richmond Whig and Public Advertiser*.[58] Meanwhile, the legislature tabled the petitions. A disappointed Bishop Meade blamed the "luke-warmness" of his forces, though a more realistic opponent of incorporation thought they had made "great efforts." Undaunted, both Baptists and Episcopalians renewed the struggle in the next legislative session.

That May the Baptists had confronted a typical problem. In her will Elizabeth Thornton Dabney had left the General Association $500, but she specified that her brother Robert Dabney was to have use of the funds for two years. His health was poor, however, and if he happened to die within that period, his legal heirs could claim the money. Therefore, Baptist officials arranged that Dabney would turn over the funds to them immediately, after first deducting two years' worth of interest. Shortly before adjourning, the association decided to ask for an act of incorporation, although its brief petition later requested only the passage of whatever law would lift its disability to receive bequests.

The longer Episcopalian memorial presented at the same assembly session pointed out that religious groups were "unknown to the laws," without legal redress, "disabled and disfranchised." The church leaders were concerned for the welfare of their theological seminary and the need to support the clergy, the church buildings, and the widows and orphans fund. Christianity would survive without state assistance, they argued, but Christians were still entitled to legal protection.[59]

The unusual public hearings conducted the next January by the Committee on Courts of Justice reflected the opposing opinions of Virginia's evangelicals. The advocates for the proposed law, James Lyons and William Hamilton Macfarland, were respected lawyers as well as active Episcopalians, and Lyons was also a state senator. Jeremiah Tinsley, a Richmond minister, represented Baptist interests. But while a capable team, they were no rhetorical match for Plumer. More than a year earlier, he had publicly challenged Lyons and Macfarland to a debate. Now almost nightly for several weeks the two sides presented sharply contrasting perspectives on the proper interpretation and application of Jefferson's statute.[60]

The proponents of incorporation argued that churches should receive, not special privileges from the commonwealth, but only the same rights and equal treatment that virtually every other state in the United States already granted religious groups. The proposed law, Macfarland argued, did not violate the Jefferson's statute. Rather, Virginia's denial of incorporation to church groups infringed upon religious freedom and the "rights of conscience" by refusing the legal protection necessary for church groups to function effectively, receive bequests, and manage their own finances.[61]

Plumer argued in opposition that a general incorporation law for churches and religious groups would create a formal relationship between church and state. The act of 1842, "public sentiment," and "public manners" provided sufficient security for the churches' property. The contest was not "between religion and irreligion, but . . . the best mode of promoting religion." The civil government could not "tolerate religion or irreligion, nor . . . aid either" without creating itself into an agency "to determine what is and what is not true religion and safe opinion." Neither side would benefit from a closer relationship, he claimed; while "independent" and "in most respects unallied," each had prospered. Indiscriminate church incorporation would damage the state and bloat Virginia with rich church corporations possessing extensive tracts of nontaxable property. Neither would such a law benefit the churches, the minister warned, because "a powerful State never grants privileges to the church without requiring sooner or later, heavy payment. A State nursing a church, has always been like a she-bear hugging a lamb." Reciting the sordid tale of ecclesiastical power, wealth, and abuse since the reign of Constantine, the minister emphasized the evils in Virginia's colonial establishment, attacked the blasphemy laws of other states, and dismissed their experience with religious incorporation laws as unreliable and untested.[62]

Lyons and Macfarland responded as best they could, though the latter decried the public setting and averred that normal committee sessions would have been fairer. Rebutting charges that the incorporation of religious groups would lead to a church-state "alliance," Macfarland accused Plumer of exaggerating potential abuses. Fears of "swollen wealth, theocratic pretensions, and ambitious priests" were unjustified. "What kind of toleration," the lawyer asked, "refuses to recognize the social rights of pious men, associated in a common undertaking for conscience sake?" And he decried the "negative, suicidal policy" that denied citizens the right to control their own property and, through bequests, to benefit "present and future generations."[63]

At the outset Plumer had promised not to limit his remarks. Committee member Robert E. Scott later reported that he "spoke until the candles were burnt down and called loudly for more light." Asked how much longer he planned to talk, the minister responded that "he made no provision as to time, and then that he was in the middle [of] his speech he could make no provision." The legislators had heard enough that night, but the debates continued until almost the end of January. Presbyterian minister Moses Drury Hoge attended several of the sessions, found his friend Plumer's arguments both "able and amusing," and thought he emerged the winner. Although the contest became nasty at times, with Lyons questioning Plumer's "consistency, & honesty," Hoge noted that the two opponents "rode home in Lyons carriage."[64]

In addition to his allies among Old School Presbyterians, Plumer also drew support from other ministers and churches. Expressing its satisfaction with the 1842 church property law, the Virginia Methodist Conference wanted no endowments that would render its ministers "independent . . . of the people they serve." Realizing the visceral reaction the term *incorporation* aroused, Macfarland ultimately proposed a simple law authorizing religious groups "to accept donations and bequests within . . . prescribed limits." Even this compromise failed, however, when the legislature sustained a unanimous committee recommendation: "*That the policy of the laws of the commonwealth by which the power to take and hold property is withheld from religious congregations, is founded on the highest wisdom, as well for the safety of the state as for the purity of the church.*"[65] The language is noteworthy. Absent is any explicit mention of church-state separation or Jefferson's statute; rather, the legislature conceded that its function was not only to ensure civil society's welfare but to preserve "*the purity of the church.*" Perhaps without realizing the irony of their words, the legislators had constructed a self-identity as, in some attenuated fashion, "Nursing-Fathers to the Church."[66]

That resolution effectively ended the debate. During the ensuing years the assembly remained intractable. The Baptist association renewed its petition in 1846, complaining that even "Free Masons and Odd Fellows" held rights denied to Christian groups and recalling that Virginia had incorporated the Bible Society in 1813 without evil consequences. But the legislature sided with the opinion of the Antimission Baptists that religion should be "left alone."[67] In 1848 the assembly refused to incorporate St. Joseph's Female Orphan Asylum in Richmond; and the next year, when Ahavath Israel, a Jewish benevolent society organized to care for the poor, sought a charter, the legislators considered such a law would be tantamount to "substantially incorporating a religious sect."[68]

In January 1850 a fresh petition from the Episcopalian clergy dramatized the dangers faced by unincorporated bodies. William Williams, the treasurer of their society for the support of widows and orphans, had been responsible for managing its $10,000 in assets. Unfortunately, he had recently died before the cash and stocks could be transferred to someone else. According to the petition, these assets became liable for his debts and other claims against his estate. Even if not lost in that fashion, the society had no legal means to claim the money. "As citizens and not as clergymen," the ministers pleaded for a law to protect their wives and children and insisted that their organization had "no intrinsic or essential connection with or dependence on, the Church as a Church." The assembly, however, rejected a bill to incorporate "the Virginia widows and orphans insurance company" 50 to 34.[69]

Virginia's third state constitution, approved the following year in 1851, explicitly stated: "The general assembly shall not grant a charter of incorporation to any church or religious denomination, but may secure the title to church property to an extent to be limited by law." Significantly, it said nothing about religious agencies, schools, and seminaries. Interested legislators recognized the possibilities. In 1854 they incorporated the "Protestant Episcopal Theological seminary," in Alexandria, and the following year the assembly gave the Presbyterians' Union Theological Seminary in Richmond the charter it had refused John Holt Rice forty years earlier.[70] The courts, however, stood fast. On the eve of the Civil War, Presiding Justice Richard Cassius Lee Moncure, an "ardent Episcopalian," upheld the *Gallego* pronouncement in voiding a bequest to build two Baptist churches and support their clergy. In his decision Moncure reiterated a concern of previous Virginia courts, namely, "the danger of an excessive and inordinate alienation of property to religious uses, so jealously guarded against by the policy of our law and the provision of our constitution."[71] The legislation of 1799 once more operated against the current interests of those who had been its strongest supporters and now formed by far the largest denomination in the state.

The Case against Incorporation

For more than fifty years, the Virginia legislature had considered and rejected, usually by lopsided margins, a series of proposals: individual and general incorporation acts for churches, theological schools, and religious benevolent societies; compromise measures to permit supervised and restricted incorporations associated with churches and religious groups; and finally, a law to guarantee bequests made for religious purposes. Why did the Old Dominion refuse to follow the practice of other states and accede to what many people considered eminently reasonable proposals?

Certainly the disagreements within and among the various Christian bodies played an important role in stalling change on incorporation, as both Plumer and Meade acknowledged. Despite church and pulpit swapping at church conventions, conferences, associations, and synods, the "Race of Religion," as one observer characterized the denominational competition, strained ecumenical relations. Baptists, Episcopalians, Methodists, and Presbyterians further publicized their disagreements about church incorporation in extensive press battles and lobbying efforts.[72] But sectarian rivalries were not the only or even the most important factor in stalling Christian unity on this issue.

Some clergymen disagreed with the proposed law on strictly religious grounds. Religious "confessionalists" such as the Old School Presbyterians and Antimission Baptists valued theological distinctions and mistrusted evangelical ecumenism. States' rights Democrats in their politics, they favored a church-state polity that removed government as much as possible from interfering with religion. Moreover, as Mark Y. Hanley has argued, antebellum ministers in general feared conflating Christianity with the world and resisted attempts to accommodate the gospel to the development of liberal democratic culture after 1830. Religion meant salvation from sin, preparation for the next life, something to be prized and kept separate from secular civilization.[73]

These concerns provided a subtle undercurrent in Plumer's objections to church incorporation. In his mind church wealth spelled corruption and threatened the voluntary principle in religion. Even more important was his conviction that "Christ's kingdom is not of this world." Disparaging popular assumptions about the advance of civilization, the Old School preacher inveighed against the "depravity of human nature" and the embrace of secular culture implied by the term "Christian Commonwealth." Even more forceful in denouncing rapprochement with the world were the Old School Baptist associations, which rejected the idea of accommodating Christianity to civil society by, as one put it, "encorporating light and darkness together." Reminding the legislature of their identity as "the same patriot Baptists" who allied with Jefferson and Madison in the battle for religious liberty, they urged the assembly to uphold "republican doctrine" and safeguard minority rights. The heart of their petitions vigorously rejected any benefits of material or intellectual progress to the salvation of souls. Wealth posed a special danger, because "the love of money is the root of all evil" and a rich church yielded a "licentious ministry." One unusual petition even concluded by boldly threatening civil disobedience: "Where Conscience begins empire ends."[74]

Equally of concern to some was the specter of an incorporated Catholicism. Religious nativism was enjoying luxuriant growth just as the politics of incorporation reached a climax. Shortly before his death in 1831, the aging John Holt Rice had warned Virginians that a "class of religionists whose fundamental principles are utterly incompatible with freedom of thought and inquiry, and the right of private judgment," was on the march in the Old Dominion and threatened religious liberty.[75] When the House of Delegates debated an incorporation act for a society of retired Methodist ministers in 1842, Whig conservative Robert E. Scott warned that such a benefit to one religious group would establish a dangerous "precedent . . . under cover of which another society would gradually advance itself, untill if not the whole foot print, at least the great toe of the Pope would be plainly visible."[76]

Plumer himself was noted for his anti-Catholic addresses and writings. In 1843 he packed the galleries of his large Richmond church for a highly successful lecture series attacking Catholicism. "Popery is an unsheathed sword," he concluded, "its hilt in the hand of the Pope at Rome, and its point in the United States."[77] Plumer was no more enthusiastic for church hierarchies than he was for church incorporations; concerns for the spread of one fed into his speeches against the other. Indiscriminate incorporations, he maintained, would enhance an already existing ecclesial "aristocracy," which considered itself "the Church!!!" and identified its leaders by "the city or commonwealth where they happen to reside. Thus we have the 'Bishop of New Jersey,' and 'the Bishop of Richmond,' and the 'Bishop of Virginia.' It speaks of other churches, which outshine it in talents, piety and numbers, as being at best 'religious societies.' It refuses its houses of worship to other communions, even to preach a sermon over their dead." All this was "hideously anti-American and anti-Christian," he avowed, under whatever guise it be found. "Well did Luther say: 'Every man is born with a pope in him.' Let us not then by legislation, foster and fatten this pope."[78]

Apart from ecclesiastical competition and denominational anxieties, however, Virginians rejected church incorporation for reasons based on the relationship between religion and politics in the state. After the revised state constitution of 1830 included the Statute for Religious Freedom, the first line of public argument became constitutional. Church incorporation advocates asserted that Jefferson's text permitted the state to support religious groups provided the government treated them equally. Opponents insisted that any state incorporation of a church or religious society created an establishment of religion and therefore was unconstitutional.[79]

They based their position not only on the legislative opinion expressed in the law of 1799 but also on President Madison's rejection of a bill incorporating Christ Church Parish in the District of Columbia. When Congress passed that act in 1811 against the strong objections of many Virginia congressmen, Madison promptly vetoed it as a violation of the First Amendment's establishment clause. First, he argued that it gave "legal force and sanction" to church polity by specifying voting qualifications for church members, regulations for church officers, and procedures for selecting and removing ministers. Second, the act stated that the church's vestry or governing body could provide for the care of the poor and the education of children. The president thought such matters of "pious charity" might be considered "a precedent for giving to religious societies, as such, a legal agency in carrying into effect a public and civil duty."[80] The strength of his reasoning was demonstrated when the House attempt to override failed by the lopsided margin of 29 to 74. Only two of the twenty members in the Virginia delegation voted against the president. A few years later, while seeking incorporation for the Presbyterian seminary, John Holt Rice asked his friend William Wirt in Washington, D.C., to explore the reasons behind the veto, because he knew that Madison's views heavily influenced the Virginia legislature.[81]

In his "Detached Memoranda" former president Madison repeated his warning against the incorporation of religious groups, but this time coupled it to another, more powerful consideration: the potential wealth that corporate status might bring to churches. His concern derived not only from the established church's position in colonial Virginia but, like Henry St. George Tucker, from a particular interpretation of European church history. He cautioned that "the indefinite accumulation of property from the capacity of holding it in perpetuity by ecclesiastical corporations" posed a potent threat to republican society. Although any kind of unrestricted growth of corporate wealth was dangerous, the "excessive wealth of ecclesiastical Corporations" had demonstrated historically its capacity for evil. "How enormous were the treasures of religious societies, and how gross the corruptions engendered by them," Madison wrote.

Warning against the "multiplied incorporations of Religious Congregations with the faculty of acquiring & holding property real as well as personal," the elder statesman argued that endowed wealth would grow "beyond its object and the foresight of those who laid the foundation of it."[82]

Virginia's legislators agreed. Their 1842 church property act stipulated that no church could own more than two acres in a town or thirty acres in the countryside. State court rulings echoed Tucker's and Madison's concerns.[83] Incorporation advocates were aware of the suspicion of church wealth and tried to dispel it. The Episcopalian clergy proclaimed that they had neither "the desire nor the means of becoming a great moneyed Institution" and asked only for "the power of holding funds to a limited amount." The interdenominational petition in 1844 proposed that the apprehension of ecclesiastical wealth could be solved by legislative limits. Baptists protested that they sought no "increase of Mortmain property."[84]

The Continuing Entanglement of Church and State

But fears of an establishment of religion and the growth of wealthy churches were not the only issues; and even if the clergy had united in seeking incorporation for their churches, the assembly might well have rejected the appeal. At the heart of resistance to incorporation was the relationship between religion and politics in antebellum Virginia. Unlike the situation in the North, the planter class rather than the evangelicals dominated Southern political culture.[85] In religious affairs as in politics, the laity was accustomed to control. In essence incorporation was a self-denying ordinance. If the assembly recognized the churches as legal entities, churchmen could organize church polities, govern church properties, and manage church business without the oversight of civil authorities. Although some laity held responsible church positions and participated at meetings and conventions of the major Protestant denominations, they were relatively few in number. Acts of incorporation would give the clergy and their closest lay associates such as Episcopal vestrymen and Presbyterian elders a dominant role in church affairs that had previously been exercised by the legislators and the men who elected them.

By threatening the existing planter hegemony over the churches, incorporation portended a radical departure from the politico-religious culture that had prevailed since the beginning of the colonial period. Antimission Baptists shrewdly charged that clergymen, "not [church] members nor the people generally," were the ones who wanted incorporation. Plumer asserted that no one offered him "more aid and comfort" in his opposition than Episcopalian church members. Watching from the sidelines, two Jewish merchants in Richmond summarized the prevailing sentiments: "Virginia would not permit power of any Sort to be gradually acquired by the Clergy or lay Managers of the various churches and sects in which its citizens are divided." As the Episcopalian ministers acknowledged, at one time "the very name of 'Clergyman,' if sounded in the Halls of Legislatian, served as a bugbear, to fill some minds with a host of undefined and indeterminate alarms."[86]

Despite its supportive stance toward Christian belief and expression, the Old Dominion would not cut the churches free. Old traditions die hard. Lay control of the church had been an established principle of church-state polity since the beginning of the colonial period. Thus the government took a different tack toward believers when they attempted to organize and function as societies, churches, synagogues, and temples. Of course, they were technically free to do so, but religious bodies had only carefully limited and controlled legal standing. Virginians might toast church-state separation, but churches and civil society did not operate as separate, independent agencies. As John Holt Rice trenchantly observed, the state's treatment of the church "as a nonentity" put religious groups at a severe disadvantage.[87]

The text of the 1842 church property law illustrates the extent of continuing state control. It severely limited the amount of land churches could possess and made no provision for them to buy or sell property. By refusing incorporation to the churches, the state also ensured that they would not receive bequests, sue, or be sued.[88] Religious benevolent organizations were even more sharply curtailed, because they had no legal property titles or endowments.[89] Nor did Jefferson's statute or any law passed before the Civil War prevent civil government from managing church property or disposing of church acreage, structures, and plate, including that acquired by private donations rather than public grants or taxes.[90] Churches wishing to acquire or dispose of property first had to seek legislative approval. Sometimes this was easily granted.[91] It was just as easily denied.[92]

Rather than building a wall of separation, antebellum Virginians kept the churches and their organizations firmly under the state's thumb. The situation strongly resembled the colonial period, when the House of Burgesses oversaw the acquisition and alienation of Anglican church holdings, save for one glaring exception: the fact that these legislators might not be members of the churches they regulated. Before the Revolution, the overwhelming majority of the gentry who sat in the colonial assemblies were adherents of the Church of England. By the nineteenth century, however, the governing class included men of almost every Christian persuasion or none. They repeatedly became embroiled in complicated disputes over the respective rights of conflicting congregations or factions within a congregation; for example, between Lutherans and German Reformed in Wythe County, "old Regular" and "Reformed" Baptists in Morgantown, and Presbyterians and German Reformed in Martinsburg. Still another celebrated quarrel involved the ownership of Christ Church in Richmond and led to an act permitting members of a congregation to sue church trustees in court.[93] Not until the 1850s did the assembly provide an alternative to its own immediate involvement in church property issues. In 1851 the trustees of Mount Carmel Baptist Church in Page County asked to sell their old meetinghouse in order to finish a new building. As "a body unknown in law," the church requested "the interference" of the legislature. For two sessions the lawmakers proposed, passed, tabled, amended, and reamended a bill to let the church trustees sell a bit of property. Ultimately, House and Senate could not agree on how to draft the legislation, so they authorized circuit courts to oversee such sales.[94] Churches had finally gained another venue for property management, but the state had not renounced involvement in religious affairs.

By continuously meddling in church business, Virginia's politicians regulated the collective ecclesial expression of belief and bound religion and politics, church and state ever more closely together. Though formulated by conservative legislators who claimed adherence to the principles of Jefferson and Madison, the resulting policy of civil control and state intervention in collective religious life and practice was hardly what those two men or the text of the statute had envisioned in 1786. Instead, during the decades after the law's passage and apotheosis, Virginia constructed a hybrid church-state polity that selectively combined liberating elements from the statute with the colonial tradition of lay control, while embracing the evangelical culture that enfolded the state by the third decade of the nineteenth century.

Rather than a judicious application of the Statute for Religious Freedom, this settlement demonstrated the enduring power that a conservative planter class maintained over both state and church in antebellum Virginia. It would take the Civil War to break that hammerlock. To understand their mentality, we need to look more closely at the evangelical culture that dominated nineteenth-century Virginia.

6

Culture

Making Virginia "a Christian Country"

On the day after Christmas in 1811, Richmond's only theater caught fire during an evening performance. A candle in a chandelier brushed against the hanging scenery in the rafters of the wooden structure and touched off the blaze. Thick black smoke rapidly filled the building, and panic ensued as the terrified audience trampled one another trying to exit through the single door or jumped from open windows on the balcony and box levels. Within a few minutes the roof collapsed in flames. About six hundred people had jammed the house that night. A city that normally held about ten thousand people, Richmond was crowded because of the annual meeting of the General Assembly. John Campbell, a member of the House of Delegates, was reading in his hotel room when the alarm sounded. He wrote to his brother the next day that as he rushed to the scene, his "ears were stun'd with cries and shrieks and screams! I saw numbers that were carried away half burnt up—The husband supporting his wife and the child his dying parent. Don't suppose the picture is too highly colour'd. O! my God I wish it was!" More than seventy people died, including the newly elected governor George William Smith, former U.S. senator Abraham Venable, and some of the "brightest ornaments" of Virginia society. "The whole City is bath'd in tears," Campbell wrote, "almost every person having lost a Father a mother a child a wife or a sister." The assembly had suspended its session. "Shew this letter to all my friends," he urged. "May heaven preserve you all from the woes and calamities which are now seen here in every part of this place."[1]

The young politician had not exaggerated the fire's effect.[2] As one clergyman wrote two decades later, "It was truly a calamity unparalleled in the history of our state." Drawn together by the personal dimensions of the disaster, Richmond became, as businessman Joseph Marx described it, "one Family." Normal life ceased. "Our time generally is engrossed, by visiting and nursing the maimed and Fractured," he wrote, "attending Funerals and processing and a unanimous endeavour to supply the wants of the afflicted."³ Initially a communal funeral service was to be held at the Baptist Meetinghouse, but it was moved to the site of the fire where John Buchanan, the Episcopal rector of St. John's on Church Hill, intoned the "service for the dead." As the New Year began, Richmond paused for "a day of humiliation and prayer." Businesses shut down, and the churches "filled to overflowing."

Evangelical clergymen grasped the opportunity to read into the disaster the judgment of God. John Durburrow Blair, the Presbyterian pastor of Pole Green Church in neighboring Hanover County, selected his text from Amos 4:12, "Prepare to meet thy God, O Israel." "We are a sinful people," he warned, "a people laden with iniquity."⁴ His confrere, President Moses Hoge of Hampden-Sydney College, described the fire as a "Salutary Chastisement" that had not occurred accidentally. He urged his congregation to forgo "vain amusements" and to find their "pleasure" in "God and his Son Jesus Christ, and the exercises and hopes of genuine religion." In Alexandria, Presbyterian James Muir entitled his sermon, "Repentance, or Richmond in Tears."⁵

Burning of the Theatre in Richmond (December 26, 1811), published by B. Tanner, early 19th century. (Virginia Historical Society, 1993.214)

The city, the state, and in fact the entire nation was profoundly shaken by the disaster. Richmond banned all "public amusements" for four months of mourning.[6] The Alexandria City Council, "impressed with a deep sense of the late awful visitation of Divine Providence," called for a day of public prayers, while Norfolk processed a funeral urn with "solemn dirge" through the city streets to the Presbyterian and then the Episcopal churches. The "Roman church" held a separate service a few days later.[7] Similar memorials were staged in cities and towns throughout the nation. News of the fire caused shock waves in Washington, D.C. Flailing about for some suitable response, William Branch Giles, Virginia's senior U.S. senator, urged President James Madison to consult with Congress.[8] In Philadelphia a contingent of more than a hundred medical students from Virginia attending the University of Pennsylvania asked Archibald Alexander to hold a memorial service.

"The System of Infidelity"

Alexander had been recruited from the presidency of Hampden-Sydney in Virginia's Prince Edward County to become the pastor of Philadelphia's Third Presbyterian Church. In his sermon the minister commented on the tragic event, the worthiness of the victims, and the shock of their passage. Such a catastrophe, he argued, demonstrated the value of Christianity in contrast to "the system of infidelity." Those who explained the "Christian religion" as "a fable" had nothing to offer people "overwhelmed with calamity and suffering." Infidelity, he told the future doctors, could not console "the distressed and dying." And he went on to analyze the religious skepticism that had become rife among the educated classes in Virginia by the end of the eighteenth century:

> Infidelity was the product of pride and licentiousness combined. Its object was to break down the restraints of conscience, to separate remorse from crime, and to banish fear from the guilty. It never ought to be considered as an evidence of superior understanding or information; for it has been repeatedly proved that the balance of genius, learning and worth, were greatly on the side of revelation. And every young man should repel every solicitation to embrace this deadly system, with horror and indignation. For skepticism, once admitted into the soul, may not be so easily cast out, even when we desire it, and stand in need of better consolations.[9]

As a Virginian, Alexander knew his subject and his audience. He had begun his ministry in the 1790s when virtually everyone acknowledged that religion was at low ebb in the Old Dominion. Young Joseph Carrington Cabell, a student at the College of William and Mary at the end of that decade, bragged that he and his friends had rejected "old-fashioned precepts and doctrines" and now bordered "on the gloomy verge of Atheism." This younger generation embodied what Pastor Blair condemned as "the vice of infidelity." They "set up their own philosophy as the rule of life," refused to admit their need for Christ, and ridiculed "the precepts and the practice of religion."[10] A businessman attending Sunday services in Richmond was amazed by the brazen behavior of a group of young men and women who chuckled throughout the sermon and roared with laughter when the minister spoke of "the depravity of human nature." Afterwards friends told him that such conduct was commonly done "for the express purpose of showing their contempt for religion."[11]

Even when the behavior was not deliberately offensive, Virginia church services appeared to be more social events than religious worship to an English visitor. Baptist sermons, associational letters, and private correspondence for the decade before 1800 are filled with concern over the "languishing state of Zion." Even while the dispute over the glebes raged, their prime enemy was not the Episcopalians but the infidels; and the latter appeared to be winning. Baptist preacher David Barrow thought that in all his twenty-five years of ministry, he had never seen religion so dead. The revivals of the late 1780s were only blissful memories. One of his fellow preachers compared Southside Virginia to Sodom, and still another summarized the results of their preaching by quoting Peter's statement in the Gospels, "We have toiled all night and caught nothing."[12] Though a brief revival might appear here or there, "the winter of religion" prevailed throughout the state. Bishop Madison, who preached a rational religion, considered Virginia in 1803 to be awash in "the bitter waters of infidelity." Religious figures, both clerical and lay, agreed. That same year in a newspaper column that became a best seller, Presbyterian layman William Wirt warned against "the noxious weed of infidelity." Hanover Presbytery issued the same complaint four years later and noted its prevalence among "the rising Generation." Instead of joining the church, young people were wallowing in an ever-widening stream of "profanity, impiety, and dissipation; of pride, luxury and Infidelity" spreading across the state. "The churches of God are greatly deserted. The Institutions of the Gospel are treated with contempt." Even professed Christians displayed "an unaccountable apathy and listlessness."[13] As the War of 1812 came home to the Chesapeake Bay region, the Virginia Synod instructed its churches to observe a formal day of prayer and fasting. While eschewing "political discussion" and disclaiming "all interference with the affairs of state," the Presbyterian leaders read "the anger of God" in the British invasion and enumerated the multiple sins that had merited the "divine displeasure." These included the sale and consumption of liquor, "fornication, & even adultery," blasphemy, the hunger for making money, and the neglect of religious duties and religious instruction.[14]

Episcopalian William Meade would have nodded in agreement with the Presbyterian concerns. Ordained to the deaconate by Madison earlier in the year of the theater fire, he had attended the College of New Jersey. He found William and Mary a "hotbed of French politics and religion," he later explained. "In every educated young man of Virginia whom I met, I expected to find a skeptic, if not an avowed unbeliever."[15] Alexander wanted to turn his congregation of future doctors into fervently committed evangelical Christians. Meade's ministry had the same objective.

Creating a Christian Empire: The Second Great Awakening

Jefferson's statute had set the clergy free to pursue such goals. In retrospect it is clear that Virginia's evangelical leadership had far different reasons for supporting that measure when Madison brought it before the assembly in 1785 than did its author or his rationalist allies in the Richmond legislature. For the evangelicals the statute spelled freedom not only from state control and the threat of a revived establishment but also the freedom to transform the Old Dominion into, in the words of one Methodist minister, "the Christian Empire." Many a preacher longed to remake Virginia, and the whole United States for that matter, into "a Goshen for Israel to Dwell in."[16] These evangelicals were not ambiguous people; they suffered no identity crisis. Their purposes were as transparent in the 1790s as those of the New England Puritans in the 1630s. They did not conceive of religion in Jeffersonian terms as a private affair. Nor did they want the church separated from society and culture. Rather, they envisioned a Christian America, a nation remodeled through their efforts and the grace of Christ into God's Kingdom. In one of the great ironies of American history, Jefferson's work would help them pursue that goal.[17]

Though Alexander and Meade may not have appreciated it, the waves of irreligion had already begun to recede under the impact of revivalism. What historians later called the Second Great Awakening began by most accounts at Cane Ridge in Kentucky in August 1801 and then filtered back across the mountains to the east.[18] The following April a Richmond newspaper published a long account of the Kentucky revival. Virginia's evangelicals must have thrilled at that article's conclusion: "It has confounded infidelity, awed vice into silence, and brought numbers beyond calculation under serious impressions."[19] That is precisely what they desired for the Old Dominion, and the Methodists soon initiated camp meetings there. Led by a team of ministers from various denominations, these revivals were held outdoors in an easily accessible rural location and lasted for several days or even a week. In the early decades of the

nineteenth century, such religious awakenings broke out more or less spontane-
ously across the state until most of the commonwealth caught fire. Eventually
this led to the institutionalization of the revival as a technique deliberately designed to whip up religious sentiment. At such gatherings the clergy put a high
premium on producing an emotional reaction. If a satisfactory response was
not forthcoming, the minister might even leave the stage and move among the
crowd, urging them *to let the power come.*[20]

Clerical reaction varied. Methodists and Baptists were the most enthusiastic.
"There are glorious Times among us," reported a Baptist preacher from Norfolk County in 1801. "The Lord is here." Richmond's Baptist Church testified
that year to the "Marks of Gods favour" as "Affected" people crowded services
and membership increased rapidly.[21] Presbyterians were more cautious. Their
Virginia Synod initially had welcomed the news of the revivals as an indication of "the outpourings of the spirit of God." As the awakening spread across
the mountains and worked its way into their own congregations, the ministers
noted the "great mercies" God displayed among them.[22] But then Lexington
Presbytery expressed its disapproval of "extraordinary bodily exercises which
appear voluntary and ostentatious" and the singing of "improper songs or
tunes" at "divine worship." People afflicted with the "Jirks" disrupted the services and disconcerted Samuel Wilson, newly licensed by the presbytery. He
also worried that other preachers were trying to siphon off his flock to their
congregations.[23]

The excitement of these outdoor revivals provided something for everyone.
While the devout found consolation, the bored were entertained, and the en-
terprising made profits. Vendors set up shop under the trees with wagonloads
of food and beverages, some quite ardent.[24] The social dimensions of the camp
also provided courtship opportunities for young men and women. Virginians
discovered that religion could be fun! In a critical article written for publication
in 1806, Blair captured the mixed flavor of the assemblage when he criticized
camp meetings as a "rendezvous for all the licentious and lewd."[25] By the end
of that first decade, however, the organizers had imposed more social control
over the event. A circular letter from the Dover Baptist Association insisted on
order and decorum, particularly at baptisms: "To permit the weak and ignorant
to toss themselves indecently in the water after they have been baptized, is very
improper, if it can be prevented."[26] Methodist Stith Mead reported in 1812 that
the Williamsburg Circuit had hosted a successful camp for five days with nine
preachers. He estimated that 4,800 people had been present on Sunday, and
forty-one had joined the church on the last day.[27]

By that time the religious renewal had spread from the countryside into the
city through the multiple sermons that occurred at the gatherings of Baptist

associations, Methodist conferences, and Presbyterian synods. Each denomination met at least annually for as long as a week in cities and towns across the state. In addition to conducting church business, the ministers spread out to the various churches and meetinghouses for extensive preaching to the local population. When the Dover Baptist Association met in Richmond in 1810, the *Enquirer* published an account of the meeting under the heading of "the Cause of RELIGIOUS TOLERATION" together with the complete text of James Madison's *Memorial and Remonstrance*. On Sunday a crowd filled up the chamber of the House of Delegates in the State Capitol to hear a sermon, while other preachers took turns at the Methodist and Baptist churches.[28]

A typical eight-day Methodist conference at Lynchburg in 1815 drew well over a hundred clergymen. Mary Pocahontas Bolling regretted that she had heard "only five" sermons; however, the "venerable" Francis Asbury, who was helped into the pulpit by another clergyman, had preached one of them. Because the toothless prelate could not articulate and his thoughts rambled, she found his overly long discourse disappointing, but she was enormously impressed by his appearance. Widely reported in the secular press, these denominational gatherings of the churches' lay and clerical leaders spoke eloquently to the surging power of evangelical religion in Virginia. An 1815 circular letter from the Baptist General Committee summarized the results as "a general increase of regard for religion and religious institutions. The fear of God seems to have fallen upon the minds of the people."[29]

The Monumental Church

Richmond's reaction to the theater fire exemplified this shift in religious consciousness. Within two days of the disaster, the Richmond City Council had determined that it would be impossible to recover and properly bury the bodies of those who had perished. So the site itself would be purchased, "consecrated as the sacred deposit of their bones and ashes," and a suitable monument erected to their memory. A fund drive was already under way to build an Episcopal church on Shockoe Hill where the Capitol stood. John Marshall among others had subscribed $200. St. John's on Church Hill was inconvenient for the expanding city, and John Buchanan only conducted services there on communion days three times a year. Otherwise, he and Blair alternated holding Sunday services in the Capitol. Now the city council and the commissioners for the projected church agreed to pool their resources and to build an Episcopal church on the site of the theater as a monument to the victims of the fire.[30]

The Presbyterians in Richmond were already in the process of forming a separate congregation. Because Blair was responsible for a church in Hanover, they had invited John Holt Rice from Charlotte County to become their pastor. He was considering that request when the theater fire occurred. A few years earlier he had bemoaned his "little Congregation" and the lack of education among the "Common people." Presbyterianism required "knowledge," Rice argued, and he thought the future in the rural county belonged to the Baptists whose "genius" was better suited to the "state of Society." Nathaniel Beverley Tucker considered Rice a "sober Presbyterian" but noted that the only other choices in Charlotte were a "factious Baptist or ranting Methodist." He was the only Episcopalian living in the neighborhood.[31] Rice's younger brother and fellow minister, Benjamin Rice, tried itinerating, but it was disappointing work. From Halifax he wrote in 1811: "At this place there are a few red hot Methodists and a great many red hot sinners. . . . The fact is that the Methodists, Baptists and the Devil have taken this whole country so that there is no room for a Presbyterian." The opportunity in Virginia's largest city beckoned John Holt Rice from his country pastorate, and Benjamin would soon follow suit and begin a church in Petersburg.[32] For the most part, Presbyterians would reap their harvests in an urban ministry.[33] Impressed by the capital's crowded churches, John Holt Rice wrote Alexander of the warm reception he received. In the pulpit of Richmond's First Presbyterian Church and later as a professor at Hampden-Sydney, he would become one of Virginia's most influential religious leaders.[34]

The Episcopal Revival

Another was Episcopal bishop Richard Channing Moore. Following Bishop Madison's death in the spring of 1812, an Episcopal convention met for the first time since 1805 and elected John Bracken as his successor. The pastor of Bruton Parish Church was well liked in his parish; but already sixty-three years old, he evidently accepted the position and then reconsidered his decision. He resigned at the May 1813 convention that elected a new standing committee. The center of authority in the Virginia church now shifted from Williamsburg to Alexandria. The new leadership team included that city's two youthful rectors, Oliver Norris of Christ Church and William Wilmer of St. Paul's, along with Justice Bushrod Washington, nephew of the late president, and Edmund Jennings Lee, an influential lawyer and scion of that distinguished Northern Neck family.[35] Together with William Meade of Winchester, this group took responsibility for finding a suitable bishop.

Even before Bracken's resignation became public, first Wilmer and then Meade wrote Moore, the dynamic rector of New York's St. Stephen's Church, urging him to visit Virginia and to consider the positions of bishop and pastor of the Monumental Church being built in Richmond. They thought that the diocese needed an outsider. While the clergymen did not minimize the "most deplorable" condition of the church in the Old Dominion or the challenges the new bishop would face, they emphasized the potential: Richmond was the largest center for Episcopalians in the South, and "a Bishop of real piety, zeal, and talents" would have a transforming effect on church members across the state.[36] Moore appreciated the situation, but he wanted assurances that the diocese's clergy and lay leadership were prepared to embrace the church's liturgy, doctrines, and discipline. He had evidently heard of aberrations. For example, Buchanan and Blair presided at the Capitol on alternating Sundays; and in order to accommodate the varied religious sensibilities of the congregation, the Episcopal minister modified his liturgy from the one prescribed in the Book of Common Prayer. Bishop Madison had accepted this situation; Moore would not. As he set out to visit Virginia in early 1814, the New York clergyman insisted to Wilmer on the restoration of "our incomparable liturgy," and he suggested that "mild and persuasive means" would induce the laity "to relax their opposition."[37]

The new Monumental Church opened for services on the first day of the Episcopal convention in May 1814. The sermon Wilmer preached on that occasion indicated the evangelical direction Virginia Episcopalians were heading. Speaking of the essential qualities for ordination to the ministry, he emphasized that "all knowledge, all human learning, is as nothing in comparison to the saving knowledge of Jesus Christ and him crucified." "What will it avail us in the sight of God," Wilmer pointed out, "to have been acquainted with the structures of all animals, the nature of meteors, the virtues of minerals, with all languages and roots of words, the subtleties of metaphysicians, the heights and depths of all science, if at last we are found ignorant in the science of salvation." This not so subtle critique of the preeminent interests of the late bishop Madison could not have been lost on his hearers. The shift away from preaching a rational morality to "the glorious doctrines of grace" would be a notable feature of the younger generation of clergy and the new bishop of Virginia. The convention chose Wilmer as its presiding officer; and after the vestry of the Monumental Church announced the appointment of Moore as their rector, the assemblage elected the New Yorker as their bishop. Two weeks later he was consecrated at the General Convention in Philadelphia and soon afterwards arrived in Richmond to a warm reception.[38]

The bishop's first episcopal act was the consecration of the new church shortly after the General Assembly convened in November. State Senator Burr Powell thought the event "grand and solemn" but maybe "a little too much bordering on the Popish order." He told his wife to keep his opinion a secret, however, lest "the Presbyterians" use it "to the prejudice of the good old establishment."

Obviously delighted by his church's revival, Powell had dinner with Moore and was impressed by the bishop's manners and behavior. He liked his preaching also, though he thought it better suited to a "city audience" than "a plain countryman." Not everyone was happy, however. After a confirmation service the following year, an old Episcopalian told Meade that Moore was "nothing but a Methodist," because his pulpit "style and manner" so broke with the staid tradition of Episcopal churches.[39]

But there was nothing of the Methodist camp meeting—of which he disapproved—in the bishop's liturgy. Moore distrusted the revivalist "new measures" designed to achieve conversions, and he insisted on an exact fidelity to the language and rubrics set forth in the Book of Common Prayer. He recognized, however, a legitimate place for the emotions. "I love feeling in religion," he wrote William Meade, "but then I love to see that feeling produced by a faithful disclosure of Evangelical truth. By preaching Christ as the power & wisdom of God."[40]

Theologically, the bishop desired a "moderate" Calvinism taught in the pulpits and the seminary in his diocese, with an emphasis on justification by faith and salvation through the sole merits of Christ. The contemporary author of an essay in *The Old Bachelor* may have had someone like Moore in mind when he suggested, "People go to church, not to doze but to worship; and it is not wonderful that they should prefer the man who makes them feel, to one who makes them sleep."[41]

Louisa Holmes was a committed Presbyterian who taught Sunday school at her church in Norfolk. Yet she regularly attended Episcopalian and Methodist services. At Christ Church she was much impressed by the solid sermons of the minister Samuel Lowe, which enabled the congregation to examine their "hearts, and enable us to see more of our inward depravity." After attending one of his prayer meetings, she wrote, "Surely this can be nothing but the power of God." One Sunday, Holmes also took communion at the Episcopal church and wrote afterwards of her experience: Lowe's "manner was very solemn and impressive, and the audience very attentive. The number of communicants was very great, many members from other churches uniting with them. I have reason to bless and praise God for the comfortable season I enjoyed." In the afternoon she attended another of Lowe's sermons; and that evening at the Methodist Meetinghouse, she found the sermon of "indifferent" quality. The devout Presbyterian was drawn by the vibrant religious life she experienced in the Episcopal congregations in Richmond and Norfolk. An admirer of Bishop Moore, she described him as an "eloquent instructor," "a most delightful companion," and "a great blessing . . . from the Lord," who "must do good wherever he goes." Politician John Campbell evidently agreed. He wrote his mother one Sunday

Portrait of Richard Channing Moore (1762–1841) by unknown
artist. Oil on fabric, 133.35 x 106.05 cm. (Virginia
Historical Society, 1995.152.3)

in 1816, "Every body is going this morning to the Monumental Church where I wish to go also." Over twenty years later his niece attended services there and described "a venerable old bishop with 'the hoary head' ripe for 'the crown of glory'" reading the Episcopal prayers "in a most impressive and touching tone." Though raised a Presbyterian, Virginia Campbell had joined a Methodist church; but when visiting Richmond she preferred to worship at the Episcopal church, perhaps because of its social status.[42]

Under Moore's leadership the Episcopalians joined Methodists, Baptists, and Presbyterians in expanding their state convention from an annual business meeting into an urban revival and a demonstration of denominational strength. Beginning in 1817, they adopted the pattern of the other churches and rotated among ten or more cities and towns. When they met in Fredericksburg in 1817, the press reported that "numerous congregations" came to the prayer services and sermons offered each morning and evening.[43] The Episcopal Church was well established there, but elsewhere the annual diocesan convention helped a congregation introduce itself to the local community. For example, a small group of Episcopalians organized a church in Lynchburg in 1822.[44] Four years later they hosted a convention that opened with Bishop Moore consecrating their new St. Paul's Church. During the meeting the Episcopal clergy were welcomed to preach in the Baptist, Methodist, and Presbyterian churches. Afterwards the local newspaper praised the bishop's "fervent yet liberal piety" and noted that the convention had dispelled historically rooted "prejudices" against the church's clergy and clarified its doctrines. Lynchburg was sorry to see the assembly disperse. A few months later the same newspaper published the section of his sermon in which Moore defended the church's liturgy.[45] Most important, during the convention the bishop had ordained five men for the ministry, products of the Virginia Theological Seminary, which had opened in Alexandria in 1823 under Moore's watchful oversight to prepare new generations of Episcopal ministers.[46] The revival of Virginia's mother church was complete.

Cooperative Evangelization

In promoting God's kingdom, the clergy and church members of all these evangelical denominations produced a full array of strategic organizations from Sunday schools to reform associations to missionary societies. They all fit nicely into the Christian ethos. As such organizations multiplied, the religious press supported them with tracts, sermons, religious books, and hymnals. By 1804 Richmond's John Holt Rice was editing the South's first religious periodical, the *Virginia Religious Magazine*, designed expressly to spread "the influence of Christianity."[47] That folded three years later, but he followed it in the next decade with the *Christian Monitor* and then the *Virginia Evangelical and Literary Magazine*. The Presbyterian minister wanted his publications to reach the largest possible audience, so he reported on the conventions and meetings of all the denominations in Virginia as well as the progress of missionary, tract, and Bible societies.[48]

All these efforts were designed to transform the state into a "Christian Kingdom." Voluntary societies are a well-known part of American religious life. The first two decades of the nineteenth century saw their multiplication in Virginia. Sunday schools were organized to spread "the doctrines of religion, and the precepts of morality."[49] The Jamestown (Prince Edward) Baptist Foreign and Domestic Mission Society began its address "to the people of Virginia" by quoting lines from the poem "Charity" by William Cowper: "God working ever on a social plan, / By various ties attaches man to man." John Gordon rejoiced that "sound morals and genuine religion" were replacing "vice and immorality." He solicited on behalf of "the young Men's Missionary Society of Richmond," the first Virginia organization "composed entirely of young men," and summarized its purpose by stating, "The immortal interest of our fellow men lays near our hearts."[50] Based on the friendship and cooperative work of Buchanan and Blair, Richmond's religious culture already possessed an ecumenical flavor. That developed further when in 1813 six Richmond-area clergymen proposed the formation of the Bible Society of Virginia. The group included Buchanan, Blair, Rice, Presbyterian James Turner, and Baptist clergymen Jacob Gregg and John Boyle. A successful British and Foreign Bible Society had been established in 1804, and the movement had spread from England to the United States. In June 1813 the ministers invited "the Liberal and Pious" among their fellow Virginians to join them "for the holy and benevolent purpose" of bringing "the blessed Gospel of our Lord and Savior Jesus Christ" to the "poor" and the "heathen in our own and distant countries."[51] A week later the press published the constitution that had been drawn up at the initial meeting. Buchanan had been elected president, the position Moore would later hold for many years. The society's managers included both clergy and laymen of various denominations. Their duties were to purchase Bibles with the dues of the members, to oversee their distribution, and to report to the members at an annual meeting. To avoid theological controversy, the constitution specified that "the scriptures distributed shall be without note or comment." That phrase, "without note or comment," would become a mantra in the massive nondenominational campaign. In a published address that September, the managers appealed for public support to make Virginia "an instrument in promoting the great designs of heavenly mercy to a lost world" and to provide "every family on earth" with a Bible.[52]

Over the ensuing years the annual meetings included religious services consisting of exhortations, prayers, and sermons, with a lengthy report published afterwards. The assemblage met in the large hall of the Capitol used by the House of Delegates. Within the first year the society was obviously a smashing success. The clergy of various denominations were involving their congregations as auxiliary societies formed in Norfolk and Fredericksburg as well as a Ladies' Bible Society of Manchester across the James River from Richmond.

Hundreds of Bibles had been distributed, and the managers were projecting enormous needs that would keep everyone engaged for years to come.[53] In 1813 the society's officers applied to the General Assembly and received a charter as an incorporated body, an extraordinary development given the refusal of the state to incorporate any religious group. But how could the legislators resist when Jefferson, Madison, and Monroe paid fifty dollars apiece to join as life members and even Catholics were included? The *Report* of 1824 pointed out the benefits of the Bible to human society by promoting "virtue" and restraining criminal activity. It guaranteed oaths and provided the "moral influence which human governments do not, and cannot exert." The scriptures were "the main pillar of the laws" and helped "make men wiser and better."[54] In this first great ecumenical venture, the Christian churches could work together to make them better known in their state and around the world. The Presbyterian Synod of Virginia in 1817 praised "the readiness of our brethren of other denominations to unite with us in services involving no difference of sentiment" and applauded the Bible societies.[55]

These formed only the vanguard of voluntaryism. Other societies were created to distribute religious tracts and prayer books and to support foreign and domestic missionaries. Evangelicals provided both leaders and members for a host of Christian benevolent organizations. Through them like-minded women and men from different churches could participate in a common effort without compromising doctrinal positions. As the Baptist General Meeting pointed out in 1817, the rapid expansion of Christian societies indicated "the dawn of that glorious day . . . when the knowledge of God shall cover the earth as the waters cover the great deep." When a local church asked the Dover Association whether Baptists could join in "religious exercises" with "other denominations," the association responded that "there are many excellent institutions set afloat by one denomination of christians in which all others can join with propriety, pleasure and great usefulness." Reflecting on the enormous variety of works in which the churches were engaged, another Baptist association in its circular letter for 1822 began, "The present is an age of wonders."[56]

The key to the long-term success of Protestant evangelization in the nineteenth century was not the frenzies of revivalist preaching, nor the outpouring of emotional religion, but organization. The Second Great Awakening became, as Donald Mathews has pointed out, an organizing process, a time of both renewed order and creativity. Evangelicals enlisted both clergy and laity and involved them directly in the work of evangelization. They reached out to the unchurched and indifferent, recruited them by the tens of thousands, and established local churches that remained after the revivals had ended.[57] As Jefferson watched with growing distaste from retirement at Monticello, all the major Protestant denominations were actively and apparently with good success engaged in the quest to win the Old Dominion for Christ. With slight variations, all espoused a reformed theology and advocated a common morality.

Yet evangelical cooperation and similar theological positions did not preclude competition and rivalry. Dr. Philip Barraud, an old-school Anglican who disliked the more emotional preaching of the young Episcopal clergy, was shocked by the "Contest" he observed in 1816 "among some of the dissenting Sectaries." When his "mother church" appeared to be joining the lists, the physician was dismayed and absolutely refused to become "a Methodist." A decade later, however, he had changed his tune. Bishop Moore had done his work. Delighted by the "correct and polished Deportment" of their minister and the quality of the new organ in their "beautiful Church," Barraud thought the Episcopalians were "getting on famously in the Roll of Religion." The laity generally displayed more tolerance of different theological views than did the clergy. Presbyterian Andrew Heron warned his congregations against religious indifferentism, the notion that all Christian sects were basically the same. Instead, they should carefully understand and observe their "Scriptural Profession" and catechize their families on the *"peculiarities of our public profession."*[58]

An outspoken evangelist, Methodist bishop John Early enjoyed giving "a broadside" to Baptist and Presbyterian doctrines when he preached, and he relished attacking the latter church's insistence on an educated clergy. When someone asked Early why he had skipped a sermon by a student from the Presbyterian seminary, the bishop replied that he "was not in the habit of going to hear a man exhort or speak who had to study divinity for five years before he could be licensed to preach, wore gold breast pins and who did not pray by the side of his bed." When an Episcopalian clergyman told some Presbyterians that they did not belong to any "church of Christ, but only one of the sectaries," and attempted to win over their "young clergymen," William Hill, the Presbyterian pastor in Winchester, responded with a vigorous sermon at the meeting of the Virginia Synod in 1819, arguing that all clergy were basically equal and no valid distinction could be made between presbyter and bishop. The press also aired religious controversy between denominations, though sometimes a critic would intervene. For example, an exchange in the Lynchburg *Virginian* between Baptist and Episcopalian controversialists was interrupted in midstream by excerpts from a clergyman's sermon on "Christian Peace and Unity."[59]

"Fashionable Amusements"

Unity was needed against the common foe: the values and lifestyles of the society that surrounded them. Practically from the outset of the Reformation, a major evangelical battle cry had been that real Christians should not conform themselves to "the world" but stand against it. Before the Revolution one of the most distinctive aspects of the dissenters was their rejection of many of the social customs and amusements acceptable in Anglican society. Methodist evangelist Stith Mead exemplified this mentality when he admonished his Episcopalian father in the 1790: "The Indulgeance of Fidling and Dancing, has ever been your beseting sin, and I fear will be your final and Eternal Ruin." In sending his young siblings to "dancing Schools" and "balls," he was "training them up for the Devil." Mincing no words, he warned his parent, "You need Evangelical repentance and faith."[60]

Presbyterians insisted that God wanted his church to be "holy and without blemish." That meant for Hanover Presbytery in 1791 that a "chosen peculiar People" should "separate" from "fashionable Follies and Amusements." The list of forbidden fruit included gambling and card playing, dances and balls, and the elaborate carriages, fashionable clothing, and social visiting identified with the gentry class. Ministers, church elders, and members who violated these prohibitions, failed to observe the Sabbath properly, or neglected "the Duties of Family Religion" would be excluded from communion.[61] With additional cautions against musical instruments and feasts, Baptists embraced similar norms and argued their way around such biblical objections as David's dance before the ark. Though some amusements might not be intrinsically evil, Baptists pointed out that they became "sinful . . . in their consequences."[62] Bishop Francis Asbury went even further in condemning races, theaters, fairs, balls, swearing, lying, foolish talking, liquor, superfluity in dress, and anything that fell under the heading of "play." For recreation he advocated that students at the Methodist Cokesbury College in Maryland work in the garden. No wonder the school closed after a few years. Other preachers added other items to the catalog—Bishop Early noted in his diary that he had attacked the "base practices" of the Masons and "rubbed the women about naked breasts and elbows"—but in general the list of prohibited pleasures was pretty much the same. In terms of condemning the world with its works and pomps, Virginia evangelicals were engaged in a united effort; and the theater fire renewed their energies. The author of a typical composition afterwards trembled "to think of the condition of their souls, for I think, had I been of their number, my portion this day had been in hell among the damned."[63]

John Holt Rice shared those concerns. In 1815 Richmond's hardworking Presbyterian pastor announced that he would edit a weekly newspaper, the *Christian Monitor*, "consecrated to the interests of religion" including "the enforcement of Christian duties."[64] He was quite willing to help Episcopalians fulfill their obligations also. As he peered over his denominational fence, Rice recognized the weeds luxuriating in the Anglican garden. Moore saw them also.

Realizing the challenge the formality of Anglican worship posed to people long accustomed to extemporaneous prayer, the new bishop had been gratified by his diocese's receptivity to liturgical renewal. His efforts to ensure conformity to the Book of Common Prayer were generally successful, and within a very few years the revival of Virginia's mother church was in full swing. The stickiest wicket Moore faced involved standards of conduct, particularly with regard to what many Episcopalians regarded as innocent recreation. Rice divided Christians into two groups: rationalists and evangelicals. He lodged Bishop Madison in the first class. But Moore clearly belonged to the second. In August 1817, in an essay entitled "The Theatre Again," Rice published a friendly letter he had received from Moore together with a portion of a pastoral letter the Episcopal bishops had addressed to their clergy and laity at the May General Convention. One of the items they singled out for special condemnation was "the Theatre." Two weeks earlier the *Christian Monitor* had denounced what were called "Innocent Amusements." Now, obviously delighted by the bishops' statement, Rice proclaimed that "the united voice of the Church of Christ in America, (including all Protestant denominations,) is decidedly against Theatrical representations."[65]

The Episcopal Church Divides

But the Episcopalians were actually split. No issue in the early republic created more acrimony in the Virginia church than the fight over "amusements." Ultimately the dispute pitted some of its most influential laymen against one another and against the bishop and his clergy, thus reinforcing a residual anticlericalism left from the colonial era when the laity had insisted on dominating the established church. The resurgence of that division in turn significantly impacted the church's influence in the legislature and the courts. It helps to explain Henry St. George Tucker's tone in the *Selden* decision and the opposition or indifference of many Episcopalians in the government to the evangelical churches' efforts to obtain incorporation for religious groups. Separation of church and state became a way of walling the clergy off from what some laity regarded as their excessive power in society. It further reinforced the division of the genders into separate spheres as men remained in the pews while their wives and daughters went forward to receive communion.

Let us trace the process. In the revised set of canons the Episcopal convention approved in 1815, the sixth laid out "crimes and misdemeanors" for which a lay communicant could be "reproved, publicly censured, or repelled" from the communion table. The list included "drunkenness, incontinence, profane swearing, general neglect of public worship, Sabbath-breaking, irreverent behavior during divine service, gaming, extortion, and any other open viciousness of life." The seventh canon explained the roles of the ministry, vestry, and bishop in taking such disciplinary action. These canons would not go into effect, however, until another convention had taken place a year later. At that 1816 meeting, after the vestry of St. George's Church in Fredericksburg lodged a protest against those canons, the convention returned to the previous norm by which members could be disciplined for behaving "in a manner unworthy of a Christian." The press noted that during the discussion, the issue of "theatrical amusements" was raised, but nothing came of it.[66]

Another year passed, and at the 1817 convention Edmund Jennings Lee brought up the communion rubric in the Book of Common Prayer. Lee pointed out that despite the repeal of the canon concerning lay discipline, the minister should apply the rubric to reprove, censure, or repel from communion "any member who may be guilty of the offenses" noted in the canon. The entire assemblage of lay and clerical delegates agreed that the minister should conscientiously execute the canon concerning communion, and that this should be done by the minister alone. The vestry had no role in this. That same month the Episcopal bishops issued their pastoral letter, which Presbyterian Rice approvingly published in August. Now Lee and those who thought as he did had the full weight of the American church behind them, and the zealous layman urged Moore to enforce church discipline. In principle the bishop agreed with Lee. In New York, giving up "Balls, the Theater, and card-table" had been the "sine qua non" for admission to communion. But he wrote Lee that after consulting "some truly excellent men" in his parish, he realized that he could not enforce such norms in Virginia. Indeed, as he gazed down from his pulpit in Monumental Church on a Sunday morning, the bishop could see in his congregation at least fifteen men including John Marshall and William Wirt who were planning to purchase stock in the new theater being built down the street. With good reason, Moore feared that no one in Richmond would support him, and he asked Lee to canvass the other members of the standing committee to see what might be feasible.[67]

When the convention met in Winchester in 1818, Lee offered a resolution that the convention state its opinion that communicants should abstain from gambling, theatrical performances, "public balls," and horse racing because they stained "the purity of the Christian character," offended "pious brethren," and endangered people's "salvation." While recognizing that different viewpoints existed about such entertainment, the resolution hoped that such a statement would produce "conformity of conduct and unanimity of opinion" in the church. That hope was wildly misplaced. Alfred Powell of Henrico Parish proposed that the convention effectively table Lee's resolution. That motion failed by a vote of 12 to 28. Powell then moved that the convention substitute the milder statement from the House of Bishops, one of the two governing bodies of the Episcopal Church's General Convention. That also was defeated. Then Charles Fenton Mercer, a U.S. congressman from Shelburne Parish in Loudoun County, offered another, much more elaborate resolution that sought to explain and differentiate among the various items of amusement and to conciliate the contrasting viewpoints. After rejecting that alternative, the convention approved Lee's resolution. When Powell, joined by three other delegates, called for a vote "by orders," the clergy were unanimous in supporting Lee's position, but the laity divided 17 in favor to 9 against.[68] The training of the young Episcopal clergy is significant. After the College of William and Mary eliminated the chair of theology in 1780, men desirous of entering the ministry prepared under the direction of a minister they respected. Meade, for example, had studied with Walter Addison, the Episcopal pastor at Georgetown in the District of Columbia who strongly opposed "fashionable amusements."[69] The clergy also knew where Moore stood.

Shortly after the convention ended, the battle for the future of the Episcopal Church broke open in the press. Styling himself as "Marcus," an Episcopalian who professed his love for the church in which he had been raised attacked the Winchester resolution for violating the church's traditional "liberality of spirit" and attempting to dictate what was essentially a matter of individual conscience. Was the convention simply aping "some other churches"? Would the clergy feel bound to enforce it? In measured tones he dissected the resolution. The convention had expressed an "opinion" but failed to support it by arguments that might have produced "conviction" with the resulting "conformity" and "unanimity" they desired. They expected church members to follow an opinion that others had formed for them, without using "the understanding" God provided "to light our steps." Moreover, the church leaders' approach appeared vague and undefined. For example, would the convention next set norms for clothing, food, and "furniture"? Did the ban on theaters extend to puppet shows, circuses, and "the East Indian juggler"? Marcus hoped that the 1819 convention would repeal the resolution.[70]

A few days later "Lucius" jumped into the fray, observing that the laxness Marcus praised had driven the "seriously pious" to join "the Baptists, Methodists, or Presbyterians." Those churches embraced "a rigid discipline" that drew "a line of separation between the followers of the Lord Jesus Christ" and everybody else. Now the Episcopalians were developing "a spirit of piety" that expressed itself in the convention's resolution. But this did not have the standing of "a canon," nor could it be used against someone who "generally" lived a "moral and religious" life. Lucius preferred Mercer's substitute, which he quoted liberally, because it offered a rationale and better language than the adopted resolution. Using his favorite pseudonym of "A Layman," Lee countered Marcus directly, arguing that the amusements named in the Winchester resolution had never been accepted by the Bible or "any Christian Church, since the days of the reformation."[71] And so it went, back and forth, in the pages of the *Richmond Enquirer* through June and July. Editor Thomas Ritchie had offered the opportunity for a single rebuttal following Marcus's original column, but he let the discussion run, perhaps because he knew his readers were interested.

Repelling from Communion

The conflict over "amusements" laid bare the turmoil in Episcopalian parishes and families. By private letters and from the pulpit, young rectors were challenging their parishioners: "Have you been to a ball or the theatre"? One disgruntled writer complained that promises to swear off such entertainment were being "extorted" from "young inexperienced, unprotected females."[72] This crusade by "fanatics and bigots," charged "Philo-Marcus," contradicted "the principles and practice of the Episcopal Church from its foundation to the present time." These "gloomy people" confused "vice with pleasure" and would "change Episcopalians into Methodists" by forbidding legitimate amusements that church members had always enjoyed. The convention had listened to "the wild rhapsodies of evangelical enthusiasts, who have nothing in common with real Episcopalians."[73] The theater could provide "a school of morality," an older writer argued, while the "ball room" offered "a school of good manners." He had witnessed George Washington in both settings. The rapid advance of the Episcopal Church could only be checked by "the mistaken but honest zeal of its friends and pastors." Another writer in the same issue developed that concern in an open letter "To the Reverend Dr. Moore, Bishop of Virginia." He expressed his "respect" for the bishop and his office and his joy at the "revival" of the Episcopal Church. For this to continue, ministers needed to gain the respect and love of their congregations. But over the past few years, he had observed some clergy with an "intemperate zeal" invoke the threat of withholding communion as a weapon to suppress "proscribed amusements." He wanted Moore to use his "influence and example" to correct "this growing evil."[74]

At times the discussion assumed the character of a generational quarrel. Older Episcopalians were delighted by Moore's renewal of the church but dismayed by the "new modes of things." Since Bishop Madison's death, it had become fashionable even in the conventions to attack the reputations of the colonial clergy and to blame them for the post-Revolutionary depression of the church. But writing in the *Richmond Enquirer,* "Cyprian" thought that those earlier clergy "would bear a fair comparison, in point of excellence, with any of our very zealous reformers." He also pointed out that realistically the revival of Episcopalian fortunes could also be attributed to the growing religious "sentiment" in America that was not connected to "any peculiar church or denomination of Christians."[75] Religion had become fashionable in the young nation. The older generation could still make a plausible case for "rational piety," but a new generation was calling for fidelity to the demands they perceived in the Gospels and stricter norms for church participation.

As the press debate ended that summer, Bishop Moore turned to the standing committee for advice. Did either of the resolutions from the House of Bishops and the Winchester convention or the communion rubric in the Book of Common Prayer justify the minister in withholding communion from those "who occasionally frequent theatres and public balls?" Lee and his confreres replied that the convention's resolution was advisory in nature; however, the communion rubric "required" the minister "to repel from the communion 'any whom he knows to be a notorious evil liver, or to have done wrong to his neighbours.'" While refusing to answer the bishop's question directly, they agreed that given the "circumstances" surrounding "public balls and theatres," such entertainment should be avoided by "all communicants." They called for a policy of "justice" that did not "forget mercy," that was "firm and independent, yet . . . cautious and moderate." In short, they left it up to the minister and his vestry to use their best judgment in each case.[76] Toward the end of July, Marcus advertised in the *Richmond Enquirer* that he had read everything written on the subject and changed his mind not a whit.

As the Episcopal convention prepared to assemble in Petersburg in May 1819, Marcus published another column urging the participants to cancel the Winchester resolution. They must remember where they lived. "Virginians are not Italians," he wrote. "They are not like the submissive slaves of a conclave of cardinals, who take their bulls as the Word of God. We think for ourselves; and the liberal part of this community are ready to repeat, that you have dared to exercise control over the rights of conscience which they will not submit to." They should move the church back to the way it had been before. "It is a triumphant Church only," he pointed out, "that can afford to abuse its authority." "Make friends, gentlemen," he warned them, "you cannot afford to lose any." The press would be there to watch them.[77] The Petersburg convention was sparsely attended, and nothing was said about the Winchester resolution.[78] Two years later young Episcopalian women frequented both the theater and the church without any apparent internal conflict, while Blair continued his invective against the theater as "a most pernicious nursery of vice."[79]

Yet, as "Philo-Marcus" predicted, that "formal and authoritative declaration" which resembled "a Papal Bull" had done its work. Episcopalians who enjoyed entertainment frowned upon by the clergy would simply not approach the communion table.[80] The list of communicants demonstrates the results. In 1829 the Monumental Church admitted 179 communicants, of whom 22 were men. Many of the women were the wives of prominent men, including "Mrs. Judge John Marshall" and Mrs. Thomas Ritchie; but their husbands did not come forward. When Bishop Moore gave his last report to a convention in 1841, he enumerated 201 communicants in his parish. Only 25 were men. During the next four years, 70 more women and 34 more men came to the communion table.[81] That represented something of an improvement, but women vastly outnumbered men in terms of full church membership in the Episcopal Church. That was true of all the evangelical denominations. Wives and daughters joined first; sometimes the men followed, but later in their lives.

Chapman Johnson is a case in point. A prominent lawyer educated at William and Mary at the turn of the century, he married and settled in Richmond where he had a distinguished legal career. In the *Selden* case before the Supreme Court of Appeals, he argued on behalf of the Shelburne Parish vestry. His daughter later testified to his attachment to Bishop Moore and the Episcopal Church. But while his wife was a communicant at least by the 1820s, he did not become confirmed and join her at the communion table until 1844 when he was in his mid-sixties and infirm.[82] By that decade Episcopal churches in Virginia were using a printed form letter with a dozen detailed questions to be answered in writing by those who wished to take communion. Pastors could thus verify that full church members possessed an evangelical faith and a lifestyle consistent with that confession. "What is your opinion," they were asked, of "the amusements of the world, such as theatres, balls, games of chance &c. and could you consistently engage in them?" In the public sphere the laity maintained their control, but inside the church the clergy had gained the upper hand.[83]

Jeffersonian Virginia?

A few years before his death, Jefferson confided his belief to Benjamin Waterhouse "there is not a young man now living in the United States who will not die a Unitarian." Never was the sage of Monticello further from the mark. The Unitarianism of New England was not the wave of the future for his Virginia or the South, or even the nation, for that matter.[84] Rather, the faith and order of evangelical Protestantism—identified first with Baptists, Methodists, and Presbyterians and later with the Episcopalians and the Disciples of Christ of Alexander Campbell—came to dominate Virginia; and from there, as well as other centers, it spread across the country and shaped the social, political, and economic development of the American people.[85]

From his observation post at Monticello, the author of the Statute for Religious Freedom was not pleased with the religious transformation taking place in his state. "In our Richmond," he wrote in 1822, "there is much fanaticism, but chiefly among the women." He decried their "night meetings and praying parties, where, attended by a hen-pecked husband, they pour forth the effusions of their love to Jesus, in terms as amatory and carnal, as their modesty would permit them to use to a mere earthly lover." Six months later he expressed his aversion to the missionary and Bible societies. Yet even as he watched, his own Albemarle County offered him a firsthand example of the impact of evangelical religion. In 1815 a Charlottesville petition asked the legislature to extend the jurisdiction of the town's trustees to include the "houses of ill fame" just outside its boundaries. Three years later the trustees complained that they lacked authority over "houses and tipling-shops" just across the city line; and a well-respected Presbyterian minister, Conrad Speece, found the town so ungodly and unreceptive that he observed, "When Satan promised all the kingdoms of the world to Christ he laid his thumb on Charlottesville and whispered, 'Except this place, which I reserve for my own especial use.'"[86] Yet in 1822 Jefferson remarked that Baptists, Episcopalians, Methodists, and Presbyterians were gathering for services in the Albemarle Courthouse, and during the ensuing decades the county witnessed a veritable explosion of church building.[87]

The culture, the ideas, values, and attitudes of Virginians had changed, even among the leaders of secular society. No matter how some clergymen might inveigh against the continuing threat of "infidelity," rationalism was everywhere in retreat before the forces of evangelical revivalism.[88] Not everyone was pleased by this transformation. Novelist John Pendleton Kennedy criticized the "stiff, awkward, and churchly morality" imposed on the Old Dominion by "pennysaving presbyterians." But perhaps the greatest howls of protest came from social critic Anne Royall, who had no use for missionaries like "Hallelujah Holdforth" and "Preacher Thunder."[89] From her perspective Virginia was engulfed in a "cloud of ignorance and Priest-craft." Visiting the capital during the constitutional convention of 1830, she lampooned the major denominations:

> Richmond above all places is peculiarly cursed with this bane of our land; the whole of it is parceled out amongst those ravenous wolves. Here is the *Episcopalians*, the *Presbyterians*, the *Baptists* and *Methodists*. It is certainly a painful sight to the Philanthropist to hear those stupid men and women—"Oh, I knows him, he 'longs to de Methodist church" "I is member o' de Baptist church," "I knows who you means, now he is member o' de Presbyterian church," "well I 'clare I diden know dat"—Member of the fools' church! Was there ever such a bigoted people! They are ten times more ignorant than when I was here last.

She reserved her greatest scorn for the Presbyterians. Visiting Charlottesville, she remarked: "The world must stand astonished to hear that this costly University has been completely overturned, by the treachery of the faculty, through the Presbyterians, and at this moment is worse than nothing! A Presbyterian Priest has sat himself quietly down, in the midst of it, and rules the whole." In fact, "the Presbyterians," she insisted, "have the whole of Virginia under their thumb." By the time she reached Lynchburg, she was calling them "terrorists."[90]

Even more telling, Nathaniel Beverley Tucker, the evangelical Presbyterian son of St. George Tucker, was called upon to preach a funeral sermon on the death of Adams and Jefferson. Casting his words in the context of a Reformed theology that would have sent both men revolving in their graves, Tucker portrayed Jefferson as the unwitting instrument of God's providence. By his Statute for Religious Freedom, Jefferson imagined that "he was inflicting a death-blow on . . . the errors[,] false doctrines & superstitions of Christianity." But his statute exuded a confidence that truth would prevail, and indeed it had. In Tucker's view the subsequent expansion of evangelical faith showed that Jefferson had done more to spread "the Christian Religion" than even "it's warmest advocates."[91] Tucker himself exemplifies a striking development in the early decades of the nineteenth century: the way in which one educated rationalist individual after another went over to evangelical religion in later life. John Hartwell Cocke, Edmund Randolph, John Randolph, William Wirt—these men and others of their class who had been at least skeptical about religion or flirted with deism all became evangelical Christians.[92]

Why did that happen in their lives? What was taking place? Consider the larger context: the gospel these evangelical churches preached had a significant message to convey, a view of life and the world that helped the post-Revolutionary generation of Virginians make sense of their situation. In a raw young society suffering acute social strain and economic dislocation, churches and religious societies furnished the crucial structures that provided a sense of belonging and identity, shared values, and an opportunity to participate in a larger social purpose beyond narrowly individualistic acquisition and aggrandizement. They taught mutual responsibility. Indeed, in a state without a public education system before the Civil War, the networks of churches and preachers provided, particularly through their Sunday schools, the only available statewide teaching institutions. Thus the churches were critically important in building a democratic civic community—arguably more real and more important than Jefferson's mythic independent yeoman farmers to the formation and maintenance of republicanism.[93]

Religious freedom gave evangelicals the opportunity not only to preach their faith but also to interpret the destiny of America as a Christian nation. They presented their perspective more consistently, more thoroughly, and more successfully than their rationalist opponents. By the time of Jefferson's passing, their religious values informed the culture of the Old Dominion and found expression in its laws and institutions. Denouncing infidelity in Virginia then was not unlike waving the bloody shirt in the North fifty years later or fanning Cold War fears of domestic communism in the 1950s. Infidelity made a useful enemy, when enemies were hard to find. Even in Charlottesville, however, the village infidel had become a scarce commodity by the end of the so-called Age of Jefferson.[94]

7

Politics

"Neither Hand nor Finger in the Pie"

Two years after Thomas Jefferson's death, the General Assembly finally yielded to the insistent demands from the western sections of Virginia and called a referendum on the question of writing a new state constitution. The voters approved the convention, but the document it produced during the winter of 1829-30 dashed reformers' hopes for extending the suffrage and reapportioning the legislature on the basis of the white population. Containing former presidents James Madison and James Monroe, Chief Justice John Marshall, Senator John Tyler, and Congressmen John Randolph of Roanoke, the distinguished gathering represented a last hurrah for the Revolutionary generation. As they had throughout Virginia's past, the slaveholding, tobacco-growing interests prevailed.[1] The Tidewater delegates at the convention were mainly Episcopalians, but religion did not figure in their votes opposing democratization.[2] Apart from the universal sentiment that favored the inclusion of Jefferson's statute in the new constitution, religion played little role in the convention except on two neuralgic issues: excluding clergymen from the legislature and the incorporation of seminaries and religious groups.

Incorporation proved the easier of the two issues for the politicians, and it would continue to be so until the legislative battles of the 1840s. In the initial discussion in the convention's committee, William Henry Brodnax proposed that the new constitution explicitly recognize the right of the legislature to incorporate theological seminaries, religious societies, and any "body of men created for charitable purposes or the advancement of piety and learning." But the Southside conservative added this hook: "The Legislature of this State, during all future time, shall possess the power to alter, re-model, or entirely repeal such charter, or act of incorporation, whenever they shall deem it expedient." When William Branch Giles objected that corporations were dangerous agencies and were "gradually absorbing to themselves all the powers of the Legislature," Brodnax pointed out that under present law corporate charters were perpetual

Virginia Convention of 1829–30 by George Catlin, 19th century.
(Virginia Historical Society, 1957.39)

instruments "unless legally forfeited." His amendment would rein them in by providing for legislative oversight and correction. He also argued that seminarians were now leaving Virginia for ministerial training at two seminaries built with Virginia money but incorporated elsewhere because the state refused to charter them. He rejected as a "chimera" the fear that such incorporations created an impermissible relationship with the civil government. Less than 10 percent of Americans were even church members, he claimed, and none of the denominations wanted a "Union with the State." Alexander Campbell was not satisfied. A reforming Baptist minister who would soon become the principal founder of the Disciples of Christ, Campbell had been elected to the convention from Brooke County on the Ohio River. He abhorred "religious incorporations" and thought they would force people to contribute to them. Brodnax rejoined that such compulsion was expressly forbidden. In his remarks Campbell had questioned the need for seminary education; but with a sarcastic swipe at "The Reverend, or the *Right* Reverend gentleman from Brooke," Brodnax proposed that seminaries could at least teach prospective ministers "good morals and good manners." But the committee supplied only a dozen votes for his amendment.[3]

Campbell had not won much of a victory, however. On the floor of the convention a month later, the minister proposed a sweeping amendment: "That no
incorporation for any ecclesiastical or religious purpose, shall ever be granted,
or have validity in this Commonweal." A number of members including John
Marshall spoke against this proposal as entirely too restrictive. The general sentiment was to leave the issue up to the discretion of the General Assembly.[4]
Most of the members of the convention were satisfied with the way the legislature had handled the incorporation issue in the past. They found no reason to
rock the boat. The clergy would do that without their encouragement.

"Gentlemen of the Cloth"

On issues such as the glebe lands and the incorporation of churches and
religious organizations, clerical entanglement in state politics had been evident
from the outset of the Republic. William Graham, an influential Presbyterian pastor in the Valley and founder of Liberty Hall Academy that became
Washington College, urged a "vigorous opposition" against the proposed federal Constitution in 1787. Shortly after its ratification Baptist preachers began
throwing their considerable weight behind candidates they favored for public
office. Other ministers joined the political fray with gusto. Even a strict separationist like James Madison sought their endorsement.[5] His cousin the Episcopal bishop Madison was an openly enthusiastically Jeffersonian Republican,
while Richmond's Presbyterian pastor, James Blair, was an equally ardent Federalist and backed President John Adams to the hilt.[6] A Baptist minister might
complain that "much Breath" was expended on "politicks," but his clerical brethren were not reluctant to interact with politicians or voice political opinions.
When Jefferson was about to leave the presidency, the Virginia Baptist General
Meeting of Correspondence offered their heartfelt "applause" for his conduct
of the office and added that "almost to a man" they favored his Republican successor.[7] Such political involvement became an integral part of the identity the
clergy of every denomination constructed for themselves as leaders in society.

Yet despite such cooperation a wall of sorts also existed between the clerical
and lay leaders of Virginia society. Like those of many other states, Virginia's
first constitution in 1776 excluded the clergy from political office, a ban that
would be continued through the Civil War.[8] The next year, when Monongalia
County elected a Baptist minister, John Corbley, to the House of Delegates, it
refused to seat him.[9] Madison wrote Jefferson shortly after the Revolution that
he thought such exclusion violated principles of liberty and justice, but the latter feared undue clerical influence. In 1785 in the midst of the campaign against
the assessment, Jefferson wrote a French correspondent that the clergy were ex-

cluded to keep them from taking over the legislature. He reasoned that because they were dispersed throughout the state, heavily influenced the people, and possessed multiple occasions to electioneer, they would gain a majority of seats. The assembly sided with Jefferson's original position even after he supposedly changed his mind.[10] Bedford delegate Thomas Mead considered himself a political reformer. In 1822 he argued for extending the suffrage and reapportioning the state to ensure equal representation in the legislature, but he wanted "the clergy to be eternally seperated from the civil or judicial powers" with "neither hand nor finger in the pie."[11]

The election of a licensed Methodist preacher, Humphrey Billups, to the House of Delegates in 1826 provoked a full airing of the argument for the restriction. The objective of the exclusion law, according to the Committee on Privileges and Elections, was "to keep separate Church and State." Drawing liberally on Jefferson's statute, the committee's report painted a grim picture of "sectarian" discord and theological wrangling if ever "ecclesiastical legislators and rulers" foisted "religious enthusiasm" on the state. Clerical "demagogues" would prey upon "the fears, prejudices and passions of their congregations," and the winners ultimately would overturn the Statute for Religious Freedom. The House denied Billups a seat by a vote of 179 to 2. Reelected three years later, he was refused again by a similar margin.[12]

By the time that second vote was taken, the legislature and the constitutional convention were both meeting in Richmond. Because the House of Delegates occupied its own hall in the Capitol, the convention had relocated to the new Presbyterian church nearby.[13] When the members turned their attention to religion, they unanimously agreed to incorporate the enabling paragraph of Jefferson's statute into the new constitution.[14] As law professor Henry St. George Tucker had pointed out to his students a few years earlier, even though the statute was simply a law "enacted by the ordinary legislative body, and therefore not binding on future legislatures," yet Virginians regarded it "with religious veneration."[15] They also endorsed the assembly's recent decision on Billups by continuing the provision that excluded clergymen from sitting in the legislature.

During the lengthy debate on this proposal, reform-minded delegates including Philip Doddridge and John Rogers Cooke objected principally on the grounds of consistency. Jefferson's preamble argued that civil rights and religious opinions were unrelated, yet now the convention was excluding an entire group of educated, "virtuous" citizens simply on the basis of their clerical occupation. But conservative voices outnumbered the liberal westerners. Their arguments varied and at times even contradicted one another. For example, Brodnax, while professing great "respect" for the clergy, thought ministers had no business in civil government; but he did not worry about the possibility of a church-state fusion. In his view the churches were too divided among themselves to be a threat to the state. A political career, however, contradicted a clergyman's "sacerdotal habits and sentiments." For good measure, Judge John Coalter tossed in the scriptural distinction between what belongs to Caesar and what to God. But Randolph of Roanoke wrapped up the discussion by charging that allowing "gentlemen of the cloth" into the assembly would "*ipso facto*" create a "union of Church and State." They should be excluded not because of their religious "opinions" but because their "occupation" was "incompatible" with a political career. Randolph considered the presence of ministers in politics, like that of women, to be indecent. Political involvement would cost both groups the "deference" they deserved. Those who favored keeping the clergy out of the assembly also voiced another concern: their influence over their congregations enhanced the likelihood of their election, and once in office "sectarian attachments" would determine their votes "on all questions where the interests of a sect were directly or indirectly involved."[16]

When the vote was taken, only twelve members including former president Madison wanted the exclusion struck from the constitution.[17] Another roll-call vote on this issue a month later ratified this decision, 81 to 14.[18] Madison was joined in the minority by the Reverend Alexander Campbell. The popular preacher could draw a crowd to the Baptist Meetinghouse in Richmond on a Sunday morning.[19] But his presence in the political gathering roused the ire of some observers as well as members. One member described his manner as exhibiting a "bold and unperturbable impudence." Hugh Blair Grigsby thought his speech on the issue of representation "failed dreadfully." When the clergyman cracked a joke, one critic thought that the audience had laughed at him, not with him. In the minds of many Virginians, "theologian Campbell" did not belong at the convention.[20]

Anticlericalism

The hostility Campbell encountered was almost palpable, probably because a hearty vein of anticlericalism throbbed just below the surface of the fervent evangelicalism of nineteenth-century Virginia. The reasons were multiple, and the Campbell brothers, who were not related to the minister, exemplify some of them. Raised in the Presbyterian faith but a regular attendant at Episcopal services in Richmond, John Campbell became disgusted by religious bigotry and what he regarded as the pretensions to infallibility of the various denominations. His brother David concurred. Like Jefferson, he thought that people would logically follow "the most rational" religion. But they did not. "We exercise our common sense upon all other subjects"; but when it came to religion, people generally proved to be "heretics to all faith or fanatics to some absurdity." They were too credulous "to investigate" religious claims, and denominations clung to "doctrines which they do not understand and which in fact are beyond comprehension."[21] Not David Campbell. When a favorite niece wrote in 1825 that she was becoming a Methodist, the future governor replied that while he respected her decision, it was not one he would have made himself. In his letter he distinguished between "being religious" and joining a "particular church." "Being religious" meant "To fear God—Walk humbly before him and perform our duties as he has required. *But there I would stop.*" And thinking perhaps of the Methodist camp meetings reported in the press, he added a caution: "Enthusiasm is not religion—There is no religion in external forms—None, in the cut of the frock or the kind of ribbon you put on it—nor in the length of ones face—nor in the frantic shrieks which are often utter'd to the great disturbance of religious worship." He also warned her against proselytism: "There is no religion, in an over zeal to bring others to our faith—When one does this, they shew that they have no knowledge of the human mind and that they have not read their bible to advantage. Christ did not over persuade—Because he knew that it was better calculated to make hypocrites than sincere christians." Campbell represented a Jeffersonian rationalism that was fast receding in the Old Dominion. "The great object of religion," he explained, "is to make us look into ourselves—correct our own errors and improve our own intellectual powers. When we have done this, we are fit subjects for good society and for the enjoyment of happiness."[22]

When he moved to Richmond as governor in 1837, Campbell was pleasantly surprised by the sermons he heard at the Methodist Church and impressed by the throng of people who filled the pews and galleries.[23] But when a Methodist preacher importuned another of his nieces to marry him, and a church elder and members of the congregation tried to persuade her to accept, the governor was outraged. While he regarded the ministry as a "sacred calling," he warned his niece: "The greatest knaves in the world are professional preachers, who are not at heart really religious men. Their calling enables them to impose." The Virginia politician thought that clergymen could easily be hypocrites. "His profession is to wear the garb of sanctity—He puts it on, and whether it is his own or borrowed no one can tell—Other men of any standing in society generally act with more sincerity because their motives for deception are not half so strong." Campbell feared the sway that preachers exercised over their flocks and maintained that apart from religious matters, they generally gave poor advice. "They are not acquainted with the world and have a very imperfect knowledge of men," he explained. "They do not mix with the world in the way to know it—

and men often put on a *false face* before them. They are also too presumptuous in their opinions and too self confident—The consequence is, they learn nothing from society and their sentiments, except so far as they can polish them from reading the Bible, are coarse." Campbell thought that preachers should stick to religion and deserved "the severest reprehension" when they wandered outside their chosen field.[24] Writing in the *Southern Literary Messenger*, one author argued that barring the clergy from the legislature was designed to preserve "the purity and simplicity of religion itself. Whenever the high priest descends from the altar to bedraggle his robes in the vile mire of an electioneering process . . . religion falls into contempt . . . and its ministers become the most profligate and the most contemptible of mankind."[25]

Despite their exclusion from the assembly and the hostility of at least some politicians, clergymen remained politically active. Preachers could be shrewd debaters, as William Swan Plumer demonstrated during the public contest over incorporation in the mid-1840s. "Under those black gowns there was a great deal of politics," avowed one legislator.[26] Methodist bishop John Early visited Washington, D.C., to observe the legislature and took an active interest in national Democratic politics.[27] Moreover, the press did not hesitate to twit prominent clergymen for their political affiliations. The *Richmond Whig*, for example, found it intriguing that Plumer, after he accused "organized Catholicism" of jeopardizing American "Liberty and Religion," had supported James Knox Polk in the election of 1844. How could this *"Democratic Divine"* vote with Catholic Democrats in the North while exposing the "abominations of Popery"?[28]

To be fair to the clergy, however, voting in Virginia was viva voce, and their flocks sometimes demanded to know their opinions and even rejected their preaching because of their political views. "The Lord knows how careful I have been not to act the politician," one Methodist preacher noted in his diary. Plumer argued correctly that incorporation was not a partisan political issue; Democrats and Whigs were found on both sides of the question. But the minister felt constrained to deny that he was a "political theologian" or a "theological politician." While acknowledging that he voted, he claimed never to have discussed party politics in the pulpit or the press.[29] Bishop Meade echoed those sentiments. When the *Protestant Churchman* suggested that he had introduced "political discussions" into his preaching, the leader of Virginia's Episcopalians denied it vigorously. Writing to the editors, he protested that he had only voted once in his life, when he was young, and he thought clergymen had no business participating to politics.[30]

Evangelical Issues in Politics

Yet practically from the beginning of the Republic, a symbiotic relationship existed between religion and politics. Alexis de Tocqueville's classic comments are well known, but he was not the only European observer impressed by the voluntary character of religion in America. The Bavarian émigré Francis Grund commented on the same phenomenon in the 1830s. He singled out the abundance of ministers, their energy in preaching Christianity in a variety of denominations, and most remarkable, the laity's willingness "to *pay* for it."[31] From his perspective "religion has been the basis of the most important American settlements; religion kept their little community together, religion assisted them in their revolutionary struggle; it was religion to which they appealed in defending their rights, and it was religion, in fine, which taught them to prize their liberties." "The Americans look upon religion as a promoter of civil and political liberty," he wrote, and they "have, therefore, transferred to it à large portion of the affection which they cherish for the institutions of their country."

Grund drew the inevitable contrast with Europe, where "liberal" forces strove to weaken religion's influence. In the United States, however, the government depended upon religion: "Its promotion is essential to the constitution. . . . Whatever is calculated to diminish its influence and practice has a tendency to weaken the government, and is consequently opposed to the peace and welfare of the United States." Morality rested upon religion; and by morality, Grund meant a person's "moral conduct," which he equated with "private virtue." On the whole he thought that Europeans were much more forgiving of the private peccadilloes of their artists, politicians, soldiers, and even clergy because of the overall good they bestowed upon society. The same was not true in America, where "private virtue overtops the highest qualification of the mind, and is indispensable to the progress even of the most acknowledged talents."[32] By religion he meant Christianity, a religion of *"the heart"* that focused on "Love and charity" and emphasized Christ's redemptive sacrifice "in dying for the sins of this world"; in short, evangelical religion and its concern for the kind of Christian lifestyle and behavior that would merit admission to the communion table.[33]

By the first decades of the nineteenth century, Virginians were well aware of these evangelical concerns and the pressure that churches and religious groups could bring to bear on legislation. Evangelicals had recognized that civil authorities could serve as a major support for their version of Christian morality, and they did not hesitate to seek assistance from state and local governments. Indeed, these expectations represented continuity with the church-state relationship under the colonial establishment. Thus in 1784 Hanover Presbytery requested legislative support for "preserving . . . the public Worship of the Deity," and the next year the Baptists petitioned the assembly to support Christianity by passing "those laws of Morality, which are necessary for Private and Public happiness."[34] Virginia's evangelicals saw no contradiction between these requests and Jefferson's statute. Nor did the lawmakers.

Other petitions urged the enforcement of laws against "Vice and Immorality."[35] Prodded by the evangelicals, the legislature responded. In 1798, for example, a bill was proposed "to suppress theatrical presentations." Evangelicals regarded the theater as a "most pernicious nursery of vice" where players used "smutty and obscene" language to titillate the audience, prostitutes circulated freely to attract customers, and men and women interchanged parts to play the opposite sex. The bill did not pass, but the publication of the roll-call vote indicated the commitment of its proponents. After the Richmond theater fire, pulpits across the country sermonized upon the event as God's judgment on theatrical performances.[36]

"The Greatest Gamblers in the World"

Another favorite evangelical target was the gambling that was epidemic in Virginia. Religious leaders regarded "Gaming" as "destructive to morals and religion." As one legislator noted with dismay, even "people of fashion and real merit" gathered around the loo table. French visitor Ferdinand Bayard was surprised to see the gambler treated with respect by other gentlemen despite Jefferson's strictures on the practice. To his amazement the Virginians he encountered considered the gambler to be much like a shipowner. Both took risks, one "on a gaming table" and the other "on the ocean."[37]

Richmond served as Virginia's gambling capital, particularly when the assembly was in session. Members of the House of Delegates, senators, county justices, and other government officials jostled with other citizens crowding into the city to try their luck at faro, dice, and pool. Those who enjoyed blood sport could always find a cockfight somewhere in the city, and horse races were well attended on weekends. Such vices were "fashionable" but sometimes turned violent when, well-watered by liquor, the gamblers settled their differences in a brawl. Observers noted with horror the fighting and gouging out of eyes, the efforts to rip out "each other's testicles," and the general mayhem that ensued.[38] The stakes were frequently high, and great sums changed hands with ease. In 1804 a match race between Miles Selden's colt and John Randolph's filly brought a wager for $1,000. In the warm summer months, the action moved to Virginia's springs with professional "Gamesters" in attendance.[39]

Evidently the 1792 law restricting gambling was deemed insufficient because legislators made repeated efforts to toughen it in subsequent decades.[40] Local law enforcement apparently winked at the antigambling statutes. A proposed law in 1815 would have required all justices of the peace, sheriffs, constables, and court prosecutors to swear an oath "so help me God" that they would do everything possible to "suppress, discourage and expose to punishment" violations of the law. Failure to do so would subject them to a hundred-dollar fine.[41] Church authorities as well as the press urged the passage and enforcement of such laws against gambling as well as those against adultery, fornication, blasphemy, dueling, drunkenness, and firing off guns on Sunday.[42]

Jefferson generally did not object to such measures to elevate the moral tone in society until toward the end of his life, when he was beset by bills that he could not pay. A series of financial misfortunes, a Southern generosity in underwriting the failed ventures of others, and an extravagant lifestyle that he refused to check ultimately put him in serious financial straits. At this juncture, reflecting upon the long service he had given to Virginia and the nation, the elder statesman decided that a state lottery with his property as the prize would serve best to free himself from debt and his family from an encumbrance that would cripple them financially after he was gone. The assembly had provided for dozens of these since the Revolution, but strictures against gambling had gradually extended to lotteries, and many evangelicals were opposed. After an extremely close initial vote in the lower house, Jefferson's lottery bill was eventually passed by what one legislator called a "puritanical and impolitic" assembly; but no tickets were ever sold, and nothing came of it before his death.[43]

The morality of lotteries occasionally provoked serious debates in the assembly and the press. Arguing in 1818 on behalf of a proposed lottery for the Agricultural Society of Virginia, John Taylor of Caroline insisted that each lottery should be evaluated solely on the basis of its merits. If the motives and purposes of the lottery were good, then who could possibly object that it was "vicious"? But the majority of the legislature did not accept Taylor's premise. In 1824 they even rejected a lottery to pay for the repair of a church.[44] An angry David Campbell informed his wife that a lottery requested by the trustees of Abingdon Academy near their home probably would fail to muster sufficient support in the legislature. Hundreds of thousands of dollars were flowing out of state each year to purchase lottery tickets in other states, he complained, but Virginia would reap no benefits from this cash outflow. "We are determined to suppress all gambling—and yet to be ourselves . . . the greatest gamblers in the world."[45] The Appomattox Baptist Association expressed in 1827 the accepted evangelical position when it condemned lotteries as an example of "covetousness" in violation of the tenth commandment and "pregnant with the most extensive evils to the community and to individuals." If a church member or preacher bought or sold lottery tickets, the Baptist leaders decided that *"he should be treated as if he had engaged in horse-racing, card-playing, or any other detestable species of gaming."*[46]

Even more than gambling, the great legislative cause that defined evangelical America in the nineteenth and early twentieth century was Prohibition. Virginia's evangelicals placed themselves in the forefront of that "noble crusade." The young Irish traveler Isaac Weld explained the issue to his readers in his section on the Virginia Piedmont. "Intoxication is very prevalent," he wrote, "and it is scarcely possible to meet with a man who does not begin the day without taking one, two, or more drams as soon as he rises." Weld noted the Virginians' partiality toward brandy and thought that most homes with at least two rooms also housed "a still." A generation later another visitor commented that some Virginians kept "their spirits up, by pouring spirits down," starting with the breakfast "mint-julap."[47] The clergy had noticed this also, and by the 1820s their objective had begun to shift from temperance to abstinence.[48] John Hartwell Cocke, a wealthy evangelical planter and friend and neighbor to Jefferson, led the crusade in Virginia. As he later explained to Bishop Meade, he had supported the antiliquor campaign from its inception, believing that it was "a great moral movement, prompted and adopted by divine Providence, as an auxiliary to the gospel, to prepare the hearts of men for the reception of his grace." Total abstinence would herald the "final triumph of God's kingdom upon earth," and he urged the bishop to abandon wine for grape juice at the communion service.[49]

Laws prohibiting alcohol were not feasible in the early decades of the nineteenth century, though a combination of taxes on liquor and fines for drunkenness was proposed.[50] The issue became controversial when prolonged evangelical camp meetings attracted sutlers selling a variety of food and beverages. A 1792 law provided penalties for those who disturbed worship services, but the explosive mixture of booze and religion raised the stakes substantially. In 1812 Stith Mead, a master impresario of camp revivals, forestalled any problems with a blunt press announcement that the Methodists managed all the property near the site of their planned meeting and warned that "no spirituous Liquors, Cyder, Beer or Cakes" should be "brought" or "sold at, or near the encampment."[51] Mead's event turned out well, but not all organizers maintained such control; and some evangelicals and particularly the Dover Baptist Association wanted state intervention. A bill "for more effectually preventing disturbance at religious worship" that would require sutlers to stay a mile away from any religious encampment passed the House in the 1819 session by a comfortable margin, 131 to 45, only to falter in the Senate.[52]

At the next assembly session, multiple petitions arrived with hundreds of signatures in support of such a measure. Baptist associations led the charge, protesting that "disorderly persons" were interrupting their worship services and insisting that the legislators as "Guardians of our morals" should stop "retailers of spirituous and other intoxicating liquors" from setting up shop adjacent to their revivals.[53] But that effort proved no more successful than the previous year's attempt. The intermittent petitions that followed over the next twenty years demonstrate the continued irritation some evangelical Virginians experienced over this issue.[54] A Methodist petition dropped the issue squarely in the lap of the legislature: "The political blessing of the right of conscience is indeed virtually defeated if professors of religion" could not worship in peace. But the legislature was not persuaded.[55] In 1838 a bill passed the House of Delegates only to fail in the Senate. A decade later a similar measure was tabled before it could receive a third reading, and in 1851 the House Committee on the Courts of Justice decided that a law providing "further protection to religious worship" was "inexpedient."[56]

Nor did the Virginia assembly protect the exercise of religion by the African American population, whether slave or free. Liberty of conscience for white Virginians had been an argument for removing the restrictions on manumission after independence. Proponents of change argued that to forbid masters to liberate their slaves violated the consciences of those who desired to do so on religious grounds.[57] Slaveholders converted by Baptists and Methodist preachers in the Revolutionary era and immediately after it often realized the inconsistency between "soul liberty" and bodily enslavement. For example, religion was the driving force in the decision of Robert Carter of Nomony Hall to liberate his almost five hundred slaves starting in 1791.[58] In the first decade of the nineteenth century, Virginia countered the threat posed by the growing free black population by requiring all newly emancipated slaves to leave the state within one year. Yet a sizable community of free American-Americans remained, particularly in urban areas. Their challenge was to find space to worship and a clergy to minister to them. Two documents in the archives of the Library of Virginia illustrate the religious discrimination they faced. In 1823 a petition from Baptist "Free Persons of Color" as well as slaves endorsed by Dr. John Adams, Richmond's mayor, asked for a law permitting their community to build a "Baptist African Church" in Richmond. They had drawn up a membership list that included some seven hundred names and turned it over to the city's head of police, who had "no objection . . . to their moral character." They were willing to accept "any restraints which are necessary," though they asked for "a voice in the choice of their teachers" with Adams having a veto over their selection. Nor did "they reasonably expect to hold night meetings or assemblages for Baptizing" without his approval. Along with Adams, who noted that this would benefit both whites and blacks in Richmond, the petition carried the endorsement of Governor James Pleasants Jr. and John Marshall as chief of police.[59] Despite such support, the legislature rejected the bill that would "incorporate" and "authorize them to build a Baptist Church." A York County delegate explained to his constituents his opposition: "I protest all incorporations for religious purposes, and especially against this unwise measure." He did not "in reality think that [the issue] is worthy of notice."[60]

Fifteen years later a large number of Petersburg citizens, including the mayor, petitioned the assembly to allow "free Colored Ministers to bury the dead, to marry and baptize persons of *their* own Color." The law stated that only white clergy could perform these services, but the "free colored population are generally . . . extremely poor" and unable to pay for "these ceremonies . . . important to all Christian Communities."[61] Clearly the Statute for Religious Freedom did not apply to the African American community. Nor did the white churches protest against the limitations on religious liberty their black brethren experienced. Despite their strictures on Sabbath breaking, gambling, horse racing, dancing, and the like, the evangelicals offered no fundamental challenge to the dominant socioeconomic structure. Even before the eighteenth century ended, they had given up the assault on slavery, and in the antebellum South evangelical preachers would be numbered among its most vocal supporters.[62]

The churches fell in line to support the dominant concerns of the state. But how far should the state go in cooperating with the churches and with which ones? This was easier to determine when all the Christian groups agreed. Yet camp meeting revivals were much more appealing to Baptists and Methodists, the largest religious bodies in Virginia, than to Presbyterians and Episcopalians. The convention, whose membership was heavily weighted in favor of the latter two denominations, undoubtedly realized which evangelical clergymen would enter the legislature if the constitution failed to bar their presence.[63] So regardless of what Jefferson wrote about the irrelevance of religious status to civil and political rights, the members overwhelming maintained the exclusion of clergymen from the assembly.

"The Chains" of Matrimony

But a reluctance to engage in politics did not inhibit the effort of both clerical and lay evangelicals to form America into a Christian nation. Jefferson's statute guaranteed that Virginians enjoyed freedom of belief and religious practice and the equality of all religious groups in the state, but it had not rendered the state neutral toward religion. Virginians expected their civil authorities to support a legal code reflective of Christian values. The General Assembly obliged.

For example, legislators repeatedly invoked scripture to justify the marriage laws and to refuse civil divorce. Their chief support came from the keepers of conscience and tradition, the clergy and the lawyers, who urged a necessary congruence between the laws of God and man. Indeed, as the years passed, they tended to conflate the two. When a great debate erupted in the 1826 legislature over the law that forbade a man to marry his deceased wife's sister, much was made about the prohibition in Leviticus. Delegate John Campbell remained unpersuaded. Indeed, he pointed to the slippery slope to which that argument led. "The Statute [forbidding such marriages] was not made to enforce the precepts of the Levitical laws," he wrote his brother. "There would be just as much reason that every other precept of the old & new testament should be enforced by human laws as this one in relation to marriage." But Campbell did not support the law's repeal. He believed it to be "essential to the good order and well being of society." What he wanted clarified was its place as good law, independent of scriptural warrant.[64]

Campbell's distinction was lost on many nineteenth-century Southerners. "The Bible contains in itself every lesson of morality and every rule of action," wrote a contributor to the prestigious *Southern Literary Messenger* in 1838; "it is engrafted upon the civil code of every civilized nation."[65] Drawing upon their Anglican tradition, Virginia's lawmakers argued that marriage should be indissoluble. In the New England and Middle colonies, Reformed Protestantism as expressed in the Puritan, Congregational, and Presbyterian churches dominated the religious culture. Adherents of the Reformed tradition regarded marriage simply as a civil contract. In their meetinghouses or wherever couples came together to be married, civil magistrates witnessed a legal ceremony; divorce was regrettable but accepted.

The Anglican clergy in the Southern colonies witnessed a far different ceremony. The established Church of England made no room for divorce. In England divorces could only be granted by Parliament. In Virginia the state legislature assumed that responsibility, and for decades legislative divorce was the only option for those who wished to shed a spouse legally. As in England divorces were extremely rare until well into the nineteenth century. Though Virginia comprised a society of diverse Protestant traditions, the Anglican canon law of marriage carried over into the state's civil code. Repeatedly the legislature rejected the passage of any general divorce laws until the mid-nineteenth century. Virginia evangelicals assumed the marital outlook of the old Anglican culture. Perhaps the most rigid in this regard was George Bourne, a Presbyterian clergyman and author of *Marriage Indissoluble and Divorce Unscriptural*. In his book only a preexisting marriage on the part of one party allowed a couple to divorce.[66] Yet the efforts to conform the statutes on marriage and divorce to the scriptures ultimately fell short. Gradually the assembly expanded the grounds for absolute divorce a vinculo, much to the distress of the distinguished legal scholar John Barbee Minor. From his lofty position at the University of Virginia, this devout evangelical Episcopalian decried the divorce law's violation of both the *"spirit"* and *"letter"* of the New Testament.[67] In his mind Jefferson's statute did not apply.

Make Holy the Lord's Day

Sabbath legislation is also pertinent here. A hallmark of evangelical preaching was an insistence on the need to observe the Lord's Day. A virtuous citizenry was, after all, crucial to the republican experiment. The same assembly that passed the statute in 1786 also approved a law which compelled Sunday as a day of rest and fined anyone found working or making his or her servants or slaves work on that day. And the law was enforced with the churches' strong encouragement. The Virginia Synod, for example, regularly told its presbyteries to enjoin church members who served as county justices to enforce the Sabbath laws.[68] One Presbyterian minister pointed out that not only work but any *"unnecessary* traveling" or even "carnal or worldly conversation" violated the Sabbath.[69] Yet did not that Sunday closing law violate Virginia's constitution after it included Jefferson's statute?

In February 1846 prominent merchants Jacob Ezekiel and Jacob Levy, members of Richmond's Jewish community, petitioned the assembly to remit a fine they had paid nine years earlier for working "quietly" in their offices one Sunday in violation of Virginia's Sabbath law.[70] They had evidently taken the argument over church incorporation seriously. At one point in the debate during the winter of 1845–46, Plumer had asked rhetorically, "Is this a Christian Commonwealth?" and answered his question in such a way that Levy and Ezekiel might well have anticipated a change in the law. "If by these terms be meant," Plumer said, "that the great majority of our people, who profess any religion, profess the christian religion, and that a great majority of the nation are prejudiced in favor of the christian religion, then I do not object to the language. But if it be intended to create a belief that christians ought to be by our laws entitled to any civil, political, or religious privileges except in common with Jews, Deists and Atheists, if there be any amongst us, then I utterly reject it."[71]

Ezekiel and Levy decided to test Virginia's acceptance of Plumer's views. The issue involved *"equal rights"* and religious freedom, they asserted, for the 1792 law forced them "to rest on a day which their conscience does not require of them." Hence they were "less protected" than Christians who kept Sunday in accordance with their consciences. The state had no business singling out any religion for special prerogatives. Sabbath observance was *"a religious enactment."* While the men acknowledged the justice in providing a day of rest for servants and workmen, they considered it an "intolerable oppression" when forced upon themselves. If the assembly had reflected on the "known jealousy" of Virginians "against religeous encroachment," it would never have passed the Sabbath law, since such matters of religious observance were inappropriate for "legislative enactment or judicial decision." The two merchants asked for the remission of their fine and a law that would keep them from being harassed for following their conscience. The issue was equality *"as Jews, with those who are Christians,"* but they also thought all faiths would be better off without "legislative interference."[72]

Their petition died in committee. The Sabbath crusade was in full swing in Virginia, and the assembly was in no mood to challenge it.[73] Ezekiel and Levy repeated their request two years later, but nothing came of it until the revised code of 1849 specifically exempted those who observed Saturday from the enforcement of the Sunday law.[74] The exception proved the rule. By midcentury Protestant Christianity increasingly assumed the characteristics of a functional establishment with ever-increasing state support for, and endorsement of, religion in general. Ministers were already exempted from state taxes. Then in 1847 the assembly authorized a chapel "for religious and moral and literary purposes" on government property next to the armory.[75]

Public prayer also returned to the General Assembly. Shortly after the Revolution, the House of Delegates had elected a chaplain and approved a resolution by Patrick Henry to begin each day's session with a prayer approved by the Committee for Religion.[76] The practice became most controversial in the 1802 dispute when, after a closely contested vote to continue the position, the House elected a local Baptist preacher, John Courtney, over the incumbent, Presbyterian John Blair, known for his Federalist sympathies. According to James Callender's newspaper, the *Recorder,* when the Jeffersonian faction could not eliminate the chaplaincy, they determined to elect Courtney, an "apostle of negroes," to ridicule the position.[77] The choice of Courtney might also be interpreted as evidence for the rising political and social status of the Baptists. They had triumphed in the glebe fight during the previous year's session.[78]

Within that decade the House stopped appointing a chaplain and thereafter regularly rejected the idea whenever it was suggested. During its 1848 session, however, the legislators decided to ask the local clergymen to begin their daily meetings with an invocation. During the next months twenty Protestant ministers from assorted Richmond churches took turns leading the lawmakers in prayer. The House renewed this system in 1849, but only after a lively debate over the merits of the practice. One feisty opponent, Nathaniel Charles Claiborne of Franklin County, pointed out that during the previous year various delegates were observed reading books and perusing newspapers during the prayers, thus making the service a "mere burlesque" insulting to religion. Instead of listening "uselessly" to a long-winded clergyman drone on for as much as three-quarters of an hour, he argued that the assembly should spend its time on legislation and end the session sooner. When his confreres voted to keep the prayers, Claiborne proposed that the legislators pay the minister four dollars a day for his services out of their per diems. That motion was roundly defeated 113 to 3.[79] Thus, without formally selecting a chaplain—or paying a salary— the legislators returned formal worship to their hall, for anyone who cared to participate.[80]

They saw no contradiction between these actions and what they increasingly called separation of church and state. The phrase had come into general use at least by the 1830s, but with a particular Virginia cast to it. For example, in an 1832 oration commemorating John Holt Rice a year after his death, Presbyterian minister William Maxwell stressed three dimensions of Rice's devotion to *"religious liberty"*: first, a commitment to "separation of church and state"; second, "a full toleration of all sorts of religious opinions"; and last, complete freedom "from all *ecclesiastical* domination." According to Maxwell, Rice wanted to keep "our clergy, as well as our rulers, in their proper places" and to maintain "the rights of the people in the church, as well as out of it—the sacred rights of reason and conscience—untrammeled alike by *secular*, and by *sanctimonious imposition*."[81] In this rendition, religious liberty could be threatened by both clerical and civil magistrates.

Six years later in a lecture for the Richmond Lyceum, James Heath, the first editor of the *Southern Literary Messenger*, argued that the United States was distinctive because of its "perfect religious liberty, and the entire separation of church and state." Yet the Virginia style of building Jefferson's wall, of separating church and state, did not prevent the legislature from encouraging nondenominational Protestant Christianity, because Virginians believed that religion encouraged the public virtue they regarded as essential for republican government. Heath spelled it out: "Free, voluntary, and general support ... of religious institutions, is absolutely essential to public and private virtue; and without these, Republican government cannot possibly exist."[82] A rising political star, Thomas Walker Gilmer, concurred. Addressing the annual meeting of the Virginia Historical and Philosophical Society in 1837, he expressed the consensus of Virginians. "The great lesson" of history, Gilmer proclaimed, was the central importance of Christianity for "national happiness and glory." "The Christian religion" provided the foundation for all virtue, whether "public or private."[83]

Whether clergy or laity, most Virginians identified the Old Dominion by the mid-nineteenth century as a Christian rather than a secular republic. Christianity had become, in the words of John Holt Rice, "the religion of the nation."[84] Forty years after the Revolution, James Madison wrote that religion was thriving in Virginia and singled out the remarkable revival of the Episcopalians. "The Church for Gentlemen," as one layman proudly described it, was gaining ground steadily throughout the Old Dominion. That proved to the former president "that the law is not necessary to the support of religion."[85] Jefferson's statute, soon to be enshrined in the state's constitution, left individual Virginians free to believe or not believe, worship or not worship, contribute or not contribute as they wished. The voluntary principle had proved its success. Religious belief and practice flourished. Protestant churches of every stripe dotted the towns and countryside, while in the cities Catholic and Jewish communities were also visible and growing. Legislators and judges read Jefferson's statute to approve such religious aids as Sabbath laws and legislative prayers that appeared to benefit all. Civil government supported religion in this fashion because the political culture demanded involvement, not rigid separation, in Virginia and throughout the United States.[86] In effect, Virginia achieved a functional establishment of Protestant Christianity. By the mid-nineteenth century, a fair-minded historian boasted that "in no one of the United States, has Christianity had more vital power than in Virginia."[87]

Richard Cassius Lee Moncure served on the Supreme Court of Appeals for over thirty years and for half of those as its presiding judge. The devout Episcopalian fit the model of a nondenominational evangelical Christian. At the time of his death in 1883, one of his fellow justices called him a "Nestor of the Bench" and praised his broadly tolerant spirit that "recognized in all the Churches the principles of the Christian religion." A simple faith in the Bible formed the foundation of his religious belief. Once when asked what law book would be most useful for an aspiring lawyer, the judge urged him to begin with the Bible. "Read and study that as the foundation of all law and of all jurisprudence of every civilized country."[88]

8

Education

"Christianity Will Go In of Itself"

A few months before Jefferson's death in 1826, William Atkinson, a Petersburg lawyer, sent an anxious letter to another Petersburg lawyer, William Henry Brodnax, urging him to consider the professorship of law at the University of Virginia. Jefferson's choice for that position had been his friend Francis Walker Gilmer, but by early 1826 Gilmer was dying. A Presbyterian elder who would eventually enter the ministry, Atkinson was concerned about the implications for Christianity in this academic position. He wrote to Brodnax in warmly evangelical language: "I hope and believe you have experienced in your heart, the renewing power of the Holy Spirit, & I am sure you would not be ashamed to own before men, him who died to save you." The lawyer viewed the professorship through religious lenses. "The University is destined to exert a powerful influence over the religious and moral, as well as intellectual, character of our country," he wrote. "I think it of great importance, of incalculable importance, that this professorship, if no other, should be given to a pious man."[1]

By the time Jefferson died that summer, Virginia was solidly fixed on an evangelical trajectory. The prolonged discussion over the place of religion in education best illustrates the relationship between church and state in that cultural context. As with Americans today, so also for nineteenth-century Virginians, education represented a core value, the transmission of culture from one generation to the next. The historical setting is crucial. As the century unfolded, the Old Dominion's social and cultural values increasingly demonstrated a profound commitment to evangelical Protestant Christianity. Legal and constitutional development adjusted and kept pace with that transformation. The struggle for boundary definition began in the arena of higher education and then spread to secondary and primary schools after the establishment of the first statewide system of public education following the Civil War.

The College of William and Mary

The College of William and Mary provided the initial battleground. Following the Reverend John Bracken's retirement in 1814, the school received its first lay president, John Augustine Smith. An Episcopalian, Smith proposed the reestablishment of a chair of theology. His major concern was the "irreligious character" of the school, which he argued alienated the state's clergy and hurt student recruitment. But Smith also wanted to re-create the college as a site where once again men could be educated for the Episcopalian ministry as they had been before then governor Jefferson and the future bishop Madison as college president had eliminated theology from the curriculum in 1780. Bishop Moore and the Episcopal conventions in 1815 and 1816 gave their enthusiastic approval to Smith's proposal. The revival of the Episcopal Church would require new cadres of clergy. Possessed of a strong theological library, the historically Episcopalian college was the obvious place to train them and the faculty and the Board of Visitors who oversaw the school's operation appeared benevolent.[2] The state legislature also offered an implicit endorsement. In 1816 it refused to incorporate Union Theological Seminary for the Presbyterians; but the next year when a bill to establish Jefferson's proposed university was brought forward, the assembly's evangelicals flexed their newfound muscles and rejected a rider that would have forbidden "the establishment of any professorship of Theology or Divinity . . . in the University of Virginia."[3]

That opened up possibilities at William and Mary, and in 1819 the Visitors created a new faculty position. Some board members favored naming a professor of theology, but others objected, and they settled finally on a position in history and humanities which Bishop Richard Channing Moore, one of the new Visitors, enthusiastically described as embracing "the history and doctrines of Christianity!"[4] Its first occupant was an Episcopal clergyman, Reuel Keith, who had replaced John Bracken as rector of Bruton Parish Church. At their 1821 convention the Episcopalian leaders named trustees for a "theological school" at Williamsburg with the understanding that the William and Mary faculty would offer free access to their lectures for any students preparing for the ministry.[5] That invitation and the prospect that Episcopalian divinity students would also be using the classrooms and library roused the watchdogs for church-state separation. At issue, however, was not Christianity but denominationalism. "A Dissenting Farmer" initiated a newspaper campaign against the proposed arrangement by attacking such "exclusive patronage of any sect of religion in any public body incorporated by law" as a violation of Virginia's Declaration of Rights and Jefferson's statute. In his view the Visitors managed the school as a public trust and possessed no authority to allocate its resources in such a sectarian fashion.⁶

Expressing "sorrow and surprise" at this reaction, Bishop Moore responded that the proposed professor of theology would be appointed and supported solely by his church's convention. Beyond that, he challenged those who objected to the generosity of the professors and their reluctance to have books "mouldering upon the shelves for want of use" read by "the youth of Virginia."⁷ Through July and well into August, the battle raged in the *Richmond Enquirer*. One advocate suggested that other denominations might also locate their seminaries at the college and take similar advantage of its facilities and faculty, but the "Dissenting Farmer" stood his ground and warned against this "invasion of our equal rights."⁸ He found allies among liberal Episcopalians of Bishop Madison's generation. For example, Dr. Philip Barraud of Norfolk considered Smith's plans a violation of "the Spirit of our Government" and "the *Death Blow* to the venerable and honored Seat of Virginia Learning."⁹

Moore pressed on, nonetheless, fund-raising vigorously for both student scholarships and a professor's maintenance. He wanted the Williamsburg connection to work for his diocese, but it was not to be. As Joseph Cabell observed to a friend, "I suspect the Dissenting Farmer has put an end to the scheme."¹⁰ By early 1822 Keith's position at William and Mary had become untenable. He resigned from the faculty and migrated north to assist in the establishment of what would become the highly successful Virginia Theological Seminary in Alexandria.¹¹ Moore initially opposed this move to Alexandria because it placed the school beyond his oversight as well as that of the diocesan convention, its standing committee, and the trustees the convention had established. By 1824, however, he threw his support behind the new seminary, regarded it "as the nursery of both religious & Episcopal principles," and rejoiced over its graduates whom he was about to ordain.¹² The new seminary lay within the boundaries of the District of Columbia beyond the legal reach of Jefferson's statute. But the religious character of William and Mary did not suffer from Keith's departure. Bishop Moore worked successfully to keep the college, in his words, "subservient to the cause of religion in general, and to the good of the Church of Christ"; that is, Episcopalian. When Smith resigned in 1826, Moore lobbied the governor and others to have William Wilmer, his close clerical confidant, succeed him as college president and professor of moral philosophy. Then when Wilmer died shortly after assuming the presidency, Moore selected Adam Empie, another Episcopal minister, who as president conducted services in the school chapel and served as rector of Bruton Parish.¹³

The University of Virginia

A similar contest occurred at the University of Virginia where the Visitors had elected Thomas Jefferson as the school's first rector. In an 1818 report designed to win legislative support, Jefferson felt obliged to justify the exclusion of a "Professor of Divinity" from the faculty of his proposed university. In the first place, he explained, Virginia's constitution placed "all sects . . . on an equal footing, with the jealousy of the different sects in guarding that equality from encroachment and surprise." His ally James Madison put it more bluntly in a letter to Edward Everett, professor of Greek at Harvard. The new university was no place for "Theological Gladiators" in "Sectarian professorships."[14] Second, the General Assembly's views on religious liberty mandated the separation of church and state. How could he implement that mandate in education? By implicitly defining theology as sectarian, Jefferson eliminated it from consideration, but he did not exclude religion and morality. In his curriculum design a "professor of ethics" would treat "the proofs of the being of a God, the creator, preserver, and supreme ruler of the universe, the author of all the relations of morality," with their "laws and obligation." All dogma, even fundamental Christian doctrines such as the divinity of Jesus Christ, was discarded from his scheme. Instruction would be confined to matters of natural theology that could be known by human reason and those "moral obligations . . . in which all sects agree," together with a study of Hebrew, Greek, and Latin. In Jefferson's mind this would provide a basic religious education "common to all sects" and acceptable to the state's constitution.[15] Sectarian theology was ruled out. Jefferson was arguing that nonsectarian religious education and moral formation taught under the aegis of moral philosophy did not violate the separation of church and state. This resolution of the issue would prove crucial for Virginia's educational praxis even as evangelical educators and public institutions pushed against those boundaries in the nineteenth and early twentieth century.

A major crisis erupted, however, over Jefferson's selection of Thomas Cooper as the university's first professor. The English-born Cooper, who had immigrated to Pennsylvania and become a judge, was the son-in-law of Joseph Priestley and was widely known to hold heterodox religious views. The sage of Monticello might consider him the most brilliant man in America, but Jefferson found his judgment challenged by outraged evangelicals who regarded the appointment as "atheistical." Presbyterian John Holt Rice led the pack. He could not abide the idea that a man who was a "Materialist, a Necessitarian, and . . . Socinian," a person who held in "bitter contempt . . . those who believe in the Divinity and Atonement of our Saviour," should ever "instruct the youth of Virginia!"[16] Rice took his case to the public through the pages of his magazine, and Jefferson lost. In a letter to Cooper in 1822, he poured out his bitterness against the Presbyterians. "Systematical in grasping at an ascendancy over all other sects, they aim, like the Jesuits, at engrossing the education of the country, are hostile to every institution which they do not direct, and jealous at seeing others begin to attend at all to that object." What Jefferson overlooked, however, was his own effort to do precisely that himself: to make the state university, as George Marsden has pointed out, a seedbed for his own brand of sectarianism. What he failed to tell Cooper was that the majority of the Board of Visitors did not support his views. He did not have the votes of the next generation. Much as they admired Jefferson, trustees such as Joseph Carrington Cabell and John Hartwell Cocke agreed with Rice. The evangelical clergy checked Jefferson's plans for the state university through men of Jefferson's own background and socioeconomic class.[17]

Only compromise would save his cherished plans. In a shrewd effort to defuse the idea that his university would be hostile to Christianity, Jefferson piggybacked on a proposal that had appeared in the press during the controversy over William and Mary in 1821. In his annual report the next year, Jefferson suggested that the various denominations install professors of divinity in separate quarters "on the confines" of the university to enable students to combine university training with sectarian theological education. The students might attend religious services with their professors as they wished, either in the professors' lecture rooms or in the soon-to-be-built Rotunda. Though the churches never seized that opportunity, Jefferson's proposal loosened up building funds in the state's assembly.[18]

It is difficult to imagine that the Jefferson who forty years earlier had been instrumental in eliminating the chair of theology from the College of William and Mary really wanted theologians stationed on the fringes of his university. But Virginia's religious context had shifted dramatically. In a letter to Cooper in 1814, he spelled out the strategy he would follow to obtain his university. Though he shared Cooper's opposition to a "professorship of theology," Jefferson recognized that he had to deal with a legislature increasingly guided by evangelical currents. So the political realist wrote his friend: "We cannot always do what is absolutely best. Those with whom we act, entertaining different views, have the power and the right of carrying them into practice. Truth advances, and error recedes step by step only; and to do to our fellow men the most good in our power, we must lead where we can, follow where we cannot, and still go with them, watching always the favorable moment for helping them to another step."[19]

Jefferson also encountered opposition to building the Rotunda, which some tightfisted legislators thought extravagant. So in his 1822 report he repeated his proposal four years earlier that the building would include "rooms for public worship" along with the library, thus making the project more palatable.[20] Musing privately about the compromises he had made to bring the university into existence, Jefferson philosophized about the need to sacrifice one's "pride and prejudices." "No good in life can be obtained pure and unmixed," he insisted. "We must take it as it is offered, alloyed always with some evil."[21] With immense pleasure Jefferson watched his "academical village" finally open for business in March 1825.

Others were not so pleased. Even though they had blocked Thomas Cooper's appointment to the faculty, evangelical clergy and laity expressed alarm at what a Philadelphia minister labeled a "great infidel university" for its exclusion of theology. "Virginia is a Christian County," he exclaimed. "Why should her sons be brought up as heathens?" The future bishop Meade agreed and anguished over the continuing spread of "infidelity" in his native state. He thought that the university should be "imbued with the spirit of Christianity" and proposed to Cocke that the board establish a chair in theology, appoint a chaplain, and require "morning and evening prayers" and "Sunday lectures."[22]

This was not good enough for John Faulcon, the clerk of Surry County. Two years after Jefferson's death, he wrote his friend Cocke that the university had gotten off on the wrong foot: "No Seminary of learning can ever be useful to the Public that is not conducted by Persons of genuine Piety." The "prospect" was "still gloomy," and great changes were needed to put the school on "a Religious course."[23] Meade concurred. When the 1829 Episcopal convention met in Charlottesville, the bishop preached in the university's Rotunda on the importance of prayer and the search for divine wisdom, not merely human. He also urged some curriculum changes: "Let the divine philosophy of the Bible be here studied. Let the morality here taught be the morality of the Bible. Let the Bible, which is the religion of Protestants, be the text-book of first esteem and most constant reference. . . . Let it not be said that nothing is taught contrary to Christianity; that the mind is left free to its own choice." A few years later the bishop reported that his sermon had created an uproar because some had interpreted it as an attack on the university's faculty and Visitors as well as on the memory of Jefferson.[24]

Within little more than a decade, however, the university squarely reflected Virginia's evangelical culture. Students, faculty, and administrators voluntarily contributed to pay the salary of a university chaplain, and clergy from various denominations rotated regular services in the Rotunda. "Mr. Jefferson committed one great error" by "banishing religion" from the University of Virginia, declared the *Southern Literary Messenger* in 1842. But all had now been set right because "the system of Mr. Jefferson has been abandoned" and religion was now regarded as an "essential" element in the life of the school.[25] Presbyterian minister William Holmes McGuffey, editor of the famous series of readers, arrived in 1845 to fill the chair in moral philosophy and on the side instructed prospective ministers in theology. For the next several decades, the distinguished professor of law John Barbee Minor, an Episcopalian vestryman, taught Sunday Bible classes that he clearly expected all his students to attend. The Presbyterian chaplain William White reported proudly in 1841 that more than half of both the faculty and the student body were members of the university's Bible society.[26] Several warm revivals passed through Charlottesville, leaving behind multiple conversions, a missionary society, and the YMCA. By the eve of the Civil War, as the administration selected a site on which to build a chapel, Jefferson's university clearly had adopted an evangelical Protestant character. Should anyone question its religious identity, one of its chaplains assured the world that "Christianity is now established at the University of Virginia."[27]

Developing a Formula at
Randolph-Macon

But granted that by the second quarter of the nineteenth century, Virginians recognized religion's importance in education, what place did it hold in the curriculum? Placing a chaplain on the staff, making provision for Bible study groups, and providing regular religious services for students and faculty were all acceptable; but the academic study of theology, or divinity as it was sometimes called, remained a point of contention. The issue received its first major legislative test when Bishop John Early and other leaders of the Virginia Conference of the Methodist Church sought a charter to establish a college. Virginia already held four institutions of higher education: the College of William and Mary, the University of Virginia, Hampden-Sydney College, and Washington College. The first had become an Episcopalian stronghold, while the last two were controlled by Presbyterians. The Methodists wanted a school that would provide an educational foundation for their ministerial candidates. Although education had not been prized in the early years of Methodism, by the 1820s the church's elders commonly examined ministerial candidates for "full connection" not only on their knowledge of the Bible but also on such subjects as English grammar, philosophy, history, and geography. As the examiners' evaluation sheets make clear, the Methodist leaders needed an institution that would provide a competent literary background for prospective clergymen. In 1825 they publicly proposed to their church members what became Randolph-Macon College.[28]

The incorporation bill for the college provoked vigorous debate when it was introduced in the House of Delegates in January 1830. Suspecting that the

Methodists planned "to establish a Theological Institution," Benjamin Cabell called the measure "a snake in the grass" and proposed tabling it immediately. But William O. Goode, the bill's sponsor, denied that intention. In a long speech extensively reported in the press, James Garland of Nelson County defended the measure. Both he and Goode were among the college's prospective trustees, and Garland disclaimed any desire for a "connexion between church and state." Yet he insisted that "equal security" must be guaranteed "for all our institutions" including religion. Rejecting a strict separationist position, the shrewd lawyer argued instead that government should exercise a benevolent neutrality that benefited all denominations. The maxim should be "Encouragement to all, exclusive privileges to none." He then named the elephant in the room: the real objection to the bill had arisen because the majority of the proposed trustees were Methodists who undoubtedly would select a faculty and college president from among the ranks of their own denomination. Garland, who announced that he was not a Methodist, found no fault in this. Ministers led almost all of the colleges in the United States. Should the assembly exclude clergymen from the school's presidency, he asked, and want only "the irreligious and the infidel" to teach there? Wasn't it to be expected that those who gave their support and financed the new school would determine its leadership?

But what to do about the danger that, in what some regarded as a violation of Jefferson's statute, the state might "squint at Theology"? Conservative Democrat Archibald Atkinson finally cut through the church-state impasse with a proposed amendment: "That nothing herein contained shall be so construed as at any time to authorize the Establishment of a Theological Professorship in the said College." In other words, no school chartered by the state could become a denominational seminary. The House accepted his rider, and the bill passed. Randolph-Macon, named for two individuals who were not Methodists, was to be purely and simply a "literary institution."[29]

But literary did not mean secular. The first president, Methodist minister Stephen Olin, won high praise for his inaugural address, which urged a thoroughly traditional classical education: "The primary object of education should be—the highest development of morals and intellect." In pursuit of that objective, parents need not fear an innovative curriculum, or that religion would be slighted. "Christianity is our birthright," Olin proclaimed. "I see no safety but in the preaching of the cross, and in a clear and unfaltering exhibition of the doctrines and sanctions of christianity." But the flattering review of his address in the *Southern Literary Messenger* also pointed out that the new president did not favor denominational control of "our public seminaries" or the imposition of "sectarian views" on the "faith of the student." The faith taught would be the shared one appropriate to "a christian land."[30]

The resolution of the debate over Randolph-Macon's incorporation established a formula that the legislature would follow for the next decades as more colleges sought state charters. The incorporation acts for such schools as Emory and Henry College in 1839, Richmond College and Bethany College in 1840, Roanoke College in 1853, and Marshall College in 1858 all forbade the establishment of a chair of theology in the college.[31]

Nonsectarian but Christian

During at least the first half of the nineteenth century, the developing concern centered on the distinction between a "private" or unincorporated school or college controlled by a denomination and a "public" one incorporated under the aegis of the state. The issue became more complicated because virtually all the schools in the state insisted that their educational system inculcated Christian principles and values while maintaining a nondenominational character. Closely related to this was the business of financial support. Beginning with their refusal to pass Jefferson's proposed bill "for the more general diffusion of knowledge," Virginia's legislators repeatedly rejected a state-supported system of public education; but at the urging of Governor John Tyler, the General Assembly approved the establishment of the Literary Fund in 1810. This endowment, to be raised from various sources such as escheats, fines, forfeitures, and confiscations, was originally designated for the education of poor children.[32] But as the fund increased and the colleges watched the assembly draw upon it to support Jefferson's proposed university, they recognized its potential as a source of funding for their cash-strapped institutions. The legislature proved reluctant. In 1821 a bill to support Hampden-Sydney with a loan for $10,000 from the Literary Fund failed in the House of Delegates, as did similar attempts in 1823 and 1825.[33] Five years later the school was still trying to get assistance from the state. In an open letter to the assembly, a "Citizen of Richmond" protested against the misrepresentation of Hampden-Sydney as "a sectarian institution" and insisted that it had no "connection" with Union Theological Seminary despite their proximity to each other. As he expressed it, the college taught "the great principles of Christianity . . . divested of the peculiarities of any sect or party."[34]

A religious ethos pervaded all these collegiate institutions, flavored by the denominational style of its faculty and administration. Richmond College was a Baptist institution, the successor to the Virginia Baptist Seminary. When the trustees received the college charter, they accepted the limitation on the formal instruction in theology, but everything else stayed in place including daily religious services that all faculty and students were obliged to attend.

Students preparing for the Baptist ministry supplemented the school's regular curriculum by taking Bible courses off campus.[35] In an 1837 graduation address at William and Mary the lay president Thomas R. Dew emphasized the value of religion, urged "a spirit of devotion and prayer," and praised the Bible as the supreme source for morality and history. It had vanquished "popery" and "infidelity," the two great opponents of Christianity as he embraced it.[36] That same year across the state in Lexington, Presbyterian minister Henry Ruffner, delivering his inaugural address as president of Washington College, emphasized the value of "the Christian religion" in college formation. Philosophy was not enough. "I shall deem it my indispensable duty to teach the Christian religion," he pledged, "to all who may be committed to my charge." Yet Ruffner insisted on a nondenominational approach:

> By the Christian religion, I do not mean the peculiar dogmas of any sect or school of theology. In the religious exercises of this college, we use no sectarian creed, catechism or formulary. We offer up our prayers . . . in terms common to all Christian worshippers. We teach our students to read, and to understand for themselves, the sacred records to which all Protestants resort for instruction; and . . . we avoid the discussion of those theological questions, which unhappily divide our religious community. . . . This College is designed for the education of youth of all Christian denominations. . . . We inquire not into the articles of their creed; we teach them nothing that is peculiar to our own.

Virginia's nineteenth-century educators in state-chartered institutions trod a narrow path. Because Washington College existed to teach the classics and science, including moral science, but was not a theological seminary, Ruffner assured his audience that the curriculum did not include "scholastic theology" or matters of "sectarian bigotry."[37] Yet the 1849 inaugural address of Ruffner's successor, George Junkin, emphasized that a college was essentially a religious institution. Civil institutions belonged to the area of coercive law and were responsible for the "administration of justice," he explained. The church, however, oversaw the "remedial law," which was the "law of love," and "its primary function is *teaching*," which was "the all important function of the Church." Citing legal authorities and the witness of history, Junkin argued, "A college is a religious, and not a civil institution." The sole purpose of granting it a civil charter was a legal one: to enable the school to hold property and conduct its business.[38]

Moreover, despite all the disclaimers, the struggle for denominational control was evident soon after Junkin took office. Though a Presbyterian minister like his predecessor, Junkin lacked Ruffner's tact. When he made changes in the college's daily worship, a small group of students, complaining that they were being forced to become Presbyterians, rebelled by disrupting the services and "drinking and yelling at night." Junkin confronted them, stating flatly that "this College always has been Presby[terian] and always must be."[39]

A few years earlier Lexington physician Alfred Leyburn expressed his concerns to a fellow Presbyterian, Governor James McDowell, that Colonel Francis Smith, superintendent of the newly founded Virginia Military Institute (VMI) located next door to Washington College, was turning that state school into an Episcopalian institution. After the Visitors had rejected Smith's choice of Episcopal minister William Bryant as an instructor on ethics, he brought the clergyman in to lead prayer meetings for the students over the board's objections. In Leyburn's view Smith was set on making VMI "an institution from whence shall flow streams of episcopacy." Parents who were not Episcopalians soon would be keeping their sons from applying, "knowing that . . . at the Institute they will be drilled to the use of the Prayerbook and plyed with every Episcopal influence." The doctor urged the governor to appoint "a Presbyterian" to VMI's governing board.[40]

Concerns about such denominational control surfaced from time to time in legislative discussions of college bills. When the assembly incorporated Emory and Henry College in southwestern Virginia, the 1839 act included the familiar prohibition of "any theological school or professorship"; but it further specified that "a majority" of the trustees could not come from "one religious denomination." Moreover, no one could be disqualified from "any office or trust" in the school or any of the school's "privileges and benefits . . . on account of his religious tenets."[41] Nevertheless, Methodists clearly regarded Randolph-Macon College as their school, and they had the same perspective on Emory and Henry. The press, in fact, identified most of the colleges in Virginia in denominational terms.[42]

The Common Schools and Religion

The university and the colleges catered to the upper classes in Virginia. Below the collegiate level, private schools and academies dotted the landscape for those families who could afford them; but despite elaborate plans and valiant efforts, no state system of publicly funded education existed until after the Civil War. The Literary Fund was designed to provide basic schooling for poor children; but the system did not function effectively, in part because it stigmatized the poor and lacked sufficient money. Meanwhile, private academies and denominational colleges also tapped into it to support their strained budgets.[43] Both in private schools, which educated the majority of white children who achieved literacy, and in county free schools established for poor whites, nonsectarian religious instruction with the Bible as a principal text formed an academic staple.

Despite the repeated urging of governors like David Campbell and James McDowell, a parsimonious legislature consistently refused to fund a statewide system of common schools; and county and urban initiatives were spotty at best.[44] When a few counties in the 1840s opted to establish free schools at their own expense, the assembly insisted that teaching be without denominational bias and texts contain nothing immoral, irreligious, or sectarian in nature.[45] Sectarianism, in particular, proved a great bugaboo. The widespread illiteracy among the white population revealed by the census of 1840 triggered a series of educational conventions but few concrete results. Addressing a meeting in western Virginia, Alexander Campbell expressed a typical antebellum perspective when he asserted that despite "sectarian differences," Virginians shared "a *common* Christianity ... in which all good men of all denominations are agreed; and that these great common principles and views form a common ground on which all christian people can unite, harmonize and co-operate in one great system of moral and christian education."[46]

An optimist like Campbell might expect that this "system" could form the basis of the common schools' education in piety and morality. No less a personage than Archibald Alexander agreed. In an address at Washington College in 1843, the distinguished first professor at Princeton Theological Seminary and former president at Hampden-Sydney College insisted on the indispensable need for religious education in the common schools. He dismissed the charge of sectarianism by advising that the schools should limit themselves to the Bible and those doctrines on which "all protestants" agreed.[47] Not all Christians, however, were satisfied with a vague nonsectarian Christian formation. Their economic standing made parochial or denominational education financially feasible for some Episcopalians and Presbyterians; and during the first half of the nineteenth century, they founded some highly successful schools and academies in Virginia.[48] Yet these could never substitute adequately for the public system that the commonwealth so badly needed.

The "Horace Mann of Virginia"

It took the Civil War to bring a public system of education into existence. The new Underwood Constitution, produced in 1867–68 by a convention dominated by radical Republicans, mandated a statewide system of public education.[49] That document provided for a highly centralized system directed by a board of education consisting of the governor, the attorney general, and a state superintendent of public instruction chosen by the legislature, who within one month of his appointment was to draw up a plan for the school system. The board would appoint local school superintendents for every city and county in the state with the responsibility to implement it.[50] Shortly after the constitution's ratification, the General Assembly in 1870 elected forty-four-year-old William Henry Ruffner to be state superintendent.

It was an inspired choice. Although one refined Virginia woman found Ruffner "very big and awkward" and his manners "peculiar," the background and temperament of the Lexington native made him an excellent fit for the position.[51] He had received both bachelor's and master's degrees from Washington College during his father's presidency there before deciding to study for the ministry, first at Union Theological Seminary near Hampton-Sydney and then at Princeton Theological Seminary under the leading Presbyterian theologians in the United States. At various times in the 1840s, Ruffner also managed his father's salt mines in western Virginia, served as an agent for the American Colonization Society, and worked as a colporteur under commission from the Synod of Virginia selling religious books and tracts in the environs of Lexington. At the age of twenty-five, he accepted the care of a congregation at Charlotte Court House in Southside Virginia; but the young licentiate threw himself into his ministry with such gusto that his health collapsed in a few months, and he had to withdraw from his charge and spend the summer of 1849 recuperating. Somewhat recovered that autumn, Ruffner began a two-year stint as chaplain at the University of Virginia. On the side he also studied moral philosophy with William Holmes McGuffey and sponsored a highly successful lecture series on the "Evidences of Christianity" which he edited and published. The strong friendships he forged in Charlottesville with McGuffey and Minor would prove invaluable twenty years later when he needed advice and support in developing Virginia's public school system.[52] In 1851 Ruffner accepted the pastoral care of Philadelphia's Seventh Presbyterian Church in Penn Square, one of the city's largest churches.[53] One lively Fourth of July sermon in support of the Colonization Society was endorsed by a number of his parishioners; and no doubt buoyed by the reception it received, the young minister advanced into the even broader arena of socioeconomic reconstruction.[54]

He soon became immersed in controversy. Stephen Colwell, a leading Presbyterian layman and Philadelphia financier, had written a blistering indictment of the Protestant clergy for their failure to engage the problems of poverty and injustice in the developing industrial age. Embracing the laissez-faire economics of the wealthy classes who supported them, they gutted the gospel of its central message of charity and ignored the implications of Jesus's teaching for America's social problems. Colwell's book, *New Themes for the Christian Clergy: Creeds without Charity, Theology without Humanity, Protestantism without Chris-*

tianity, created a sensation and provoked a storm of criticism.[55] Ruffner rushed to Colwell's defense in 1853 by writing *Charity and the Clergy: Being a Review, by a Protestant Clergyman, of the "New Themes" Controversy*. In a subtitle elaborating his issues with his ministerial brethren, Ruffner suggestively proposed *Sundry Serious Reflections upon the Religious Press, Theological Seminaries, Ecclesiastical Ambition, Growth of Moderation, Prostitution of the Pulpit, and General Decay of Christianity*. This passionate broadside by a Virginia clergyman not yet thirty years old rankled many in Philadelphia's ecclesiastical establishment who had smarted under Colwell's assault.[56] Undoubtedly they welcomed Ruffner's departure later that year when the young pastor for health reasons returned to the more congenial environment of his native Virginia. His family and friends welcomed him home, and eventually he joined the Lexington Presbytery, preaching occasionally in rural churches in the Shenandoah Valley while primarily engaged in farming and studies in geology. Though opposed to slavery, Ruffner supported the Confederacy after Lincoln asked for troops to suppress the rebellion.[57]

The war's conclusion brought a renewed effort to develop primary schools in Virginia. The Educational Association of Virginia, formed at a teachers' convention in 1863, held its first postwar meeting in the summer of 1866 in Charlottesville. Clergymen, and particularly Presbyterian ministers, were strongly represented, but laymen McGuffey and Minor from the University of Virginia quickly emerged as forceful exponents of "moral and religious education" and insisted on the Bible as a fundamental text in the schools. The 1867 convention with such luminaries as Robert E. Lee in attendance proposed a daily half hour of Bible study for all primary schools. The association also endorsed education for the newly emancipated slaves.[58] Thus when the Underwood Constitution mandated a public school system for the state, significant segments of the educated population already were prepared to support the effort.

Ruffner had not been involved in the association, but he campaigned vigorously for the position of state superintendent and received the important endorsement of Lee. "I'm the man! Between the office & me there is a natural & exact correspondence," he wrote a friend. "I understand the subject; I understand also the present condition of our poor old State: I think my sympathies are right all around." Ruffner's efforts paid off. The editorial in the *Educational Journal of Virginia* announcing his election by the General Assembly noted his "peculiar fitness" for the position, praised the energy with which he began his work, and promised its support.[59] In the ensuing years he would use the *Journal* to sell his program and defang the opposition.

In drawing up his plan for the educational system, Ruffner drew upon an extensive network of friends including Stephen Colwell, McGuffey, and espe-

Portrait of William Henry Ruffner (1824–1908)
by M. Miley & Son, late 19th century. (Virginia
Historical Society, 2006.100.6)

cially John B. Minor. The school legislation passed by the assembly in 1870 established a fixed curriculum; a state board of education specified the textbooks;
and a system of county superintendents and district boards of trustees oversaw
local school operations. But Ruffner faced daunting challenges. Funding the
schools by public taxation and the question of racial integration were immediate, perturbing concerns that threatened the schools' very survival. And negoti-
ating the shoals of church-state controversy in an evangelical culture called for
a delicate hand on the part of the new superintendent.[60]

On the question of religious instruction, the law said nothing. That silence
satisfied some Virginians. Even before Ruffner's election, the *Educational Journal of Virginia* drew upon the Baptists' *Religious Herald* in arguing that parents
rather than "the common schools" were responsible for their children's religious
education. Reviewing the uproar over the classroom use of the Bible in Cincinnati, Ohio, the previous year, the editorial offered a laundry list of objections

to "compulsory" Bible reading, including the danger of "irreligious teachers" who might even be "infidels, open or covert."[61] Presbyterian clergyman Benjamin Mosby Smith, a professor at Hampden-Sydney College, agreed. A long-standing advocate for public free schools, he thought that the government had no business interfering in "man's relationship with his Maker." If the state could "prescribe" Bible reading, Smith pointed out, it could also "proscribe" it, "and if to define the Bible as a reading book, to define *what* Bible, or what translation, or with what aids and comments."[62] Ruffner would adopt the same stance.

Others were outraged, however, by the potential removal of the Bible from the schools. This threat in turn served as a useful weapon for those opposed to public education for other reasons. Denominational schools had won the allegiance of some religious groups even before the war. Though Presbyterians argued bitterly about establishing their own educational system, the Winchester Presbytery had favored it, and ten schools were operating in Virginia by 1870. Episcopalians followed suit. Concerned at least in part that some of their children were attending Catholic schools, the Episcopal diocese of Virginia urged their parishes to establish schools along the lines of the Catholic parochial system. Not to be left behind, the influential Dover Baptist Association in 1867 urged support for "*general* education" and their own Baptist structure of colleges and schools. Though their forebears might have rolled over in their graves, the Baptist leaders insisted that the future "prosperity" of their denomination depended upon a "learned ministry" with "educated men" and "polished and intelligent women" in the pews.[63]

The discussion over religion in public education also surfaced old jealousies. In 1870 the Dover Association begged its adherents "to patronize and build up Baptist schools as a matter of *their own self-respect.*" The association charged that even though Baptists formed one of the two most numerous religious bodies in the commonwealth, they were generally omitted from the governing bodies of state institutions, while members of the old "State church," though much fewer in number, "seem to regard the State and its establishments as still [their] property by right of prescription."[64] It would take five years before Ruffner could win Dover Baptists over to the public school system.

"The Religion of the People"

Meanwhile, advocates of public education, anxious that it not be branded as godless, demanded that the schools provide basic Christian education. In his first *Report* as superintendent, Ruffner addressed this concern. He countered the objection that public schools would be irreligious by arguing that they would reflect the "moral influence" of the neighborhoods in which they were located. He further defended the religious commitment of public school teachers. "Truth and piety," he insisted, "have everything to hope for—nothing to fear—from public free schools."[65] When a local superintendent took it upon himself to ban Bible reading in the schools under his care, Ruffner made his position even more explicit. First in a published letter in 1871 and later in other newspaper articles and writings, Virginia's foremost educator enunciated a policy he called the "Virginia doctrine," claiming that Jefferson had initiated it in his reports on the University of Virginia. While state schools must not teach or sponsor sectarian doctrines or worship, or prefer one denomination over another, yet authorities could permit religious activities such as Bible reading, and teachers could inculcate moral habits and values that were compatible with the local community's desires and sensibilities. In sum, it amounted to local option. Conscience rights must be respected, and no one should be forced to attend religious services or classes.[66]

Ruffner's encouraging words about the value of denominational colleges undoubtedly helped win friends. In his *Report* of 1872, he emphasized that both public and private institutions contributed to a Christian society. "It is a blessed fact," he wrote, "that all our higher institutions are earnestly Christian without any of them being narrow in their spirit." That included both the denominational colleges and the University of Virginia. The former were "valuable as institutions of public education because of their denominational character." But so was the nondenominational school. He then rang the tocsin he would sound repeatedly in the years ahead. "Religiously, colleges, like common schools, will be what the people are. Mr. Jefferson's only educational mistake was in supposing that he was able to construct an institution which could maintain a life of religious indifference in the midst of a Christian people. Had not the University been converted to Christ it would inevitably have perished." Then, returning to the defense of the public schools, he reminded his readers that "Christian people were formerly as uneasy about the religious influence of, and within the University as many of them now are in regard to the same influence in public free schools—forgetting the nature of leaven, of salt and of light!"[67]

A few years later, after a hectic campaign in the Conservative Party caucus that controlled state politics, the General Assembly reelected Ruffner to a second term as superintendent in January 1874.[68] Three months later he resigned from the Presbytery of Lexington and formally withdrew from the ministry. What he called "throat and nervous difficulties" had largely restricted him from the pulpit for over two decades, but he also felt a growing "incongruity" between his secular occupation as superintendent and the vocation of a minister. Though some in the Virginia Synod criticized its decision, the presbytery happily agreed to let Ruffner become simply a lay member of the Lexington Presbyterian Church. As one minister pointed out, "Is not *everybody* convinced that there is stronger evidence that God has called Ruffner to be superintendant of public schools than to be a minister?"[69] But now, for the first time, his school system met both considerable support and formidable opposition from within the church communities.

In the summer of 1875, the Dover Baptist Association in its report on education praised Virginia's "efficient and widely extended public school system" and the "high reputation" of its teachers. The Baptist *Religious Herald* and the Methodist *Christian Advocate* editorialized on behalf of public education, and a cadre of Virginia educators and clergy backed Ruffner's work.[70] Others did not. Robert Lewis Dabney had been a classmate and good friend when he and Ruffner had studied together at Hampden-Sydney. By the mid-1870s Dabney had become a professor at their alma mater and an influential spokesman for Old School Presbyterianism in the South. A staunch postwar defender of slavery and the Confederacy, he was dead set against public education, favoring instead what he called "*the old Virginia plan*" of private schools and academies. Bennett Puryear, a professor at Richmond College, shared his views. At its core their quarrel with public schools was racist: they opposed the education of the newly emancipated African American population. But the two educators also argued that the church-state separation mandated by the Virginia constitution prevented public schools from teaching religion. Public education must consequently become the seedbed of atheism. Their quarrel with Ruffner was splashed across the pages of the Richmond press in the spring and summer of 1876.[71]

Ruminating on his own Presbyterian upbringing, Ruffner wondered whether private schools taught religious truth either. Christian parents, homes, Sunday schools, and churches performed that task, he asserted. But the superintendent hearkened back to Jefferson's plans for moral philosophy at the university. The schools taught "Christian ethics," without teaching sectarianism, Ruffner asserted. The "state may formally teach the recognized morality of the country, and the will of God as the standard and ultimate authority of all morality." Moreover, Virginia law did not forbid religious teaching, nor did Virginia law need to mandate it. "Christianity," he argued, "*will go in of itself*." All public school authorities needed do was "regulate voluntary religious observances" and protect minority rights. As for religious education, "schools maintained by free, popular governments of necessity express and conserve the religion of the people."[72]

Ruffner's opponents were not persuaded. In July 1878 Colonel William Allen, principal of a private school in Maryland, spoke at a meeting of the Educational Association of Virginia. His address detailed the troubles of the times and echoed the complaints of Dabney and Puryear against public education. It was a huge mistake, he argued, to trust public schools. Their need to conform to "American principles" made them "entirely secular," devoid of "religious instruction." As "agencies of an exceedingly variable, uncertain and imperfect ... moral training," they made at best a feeble contribution to the formation of public "virtue" in a community.[73]

Allen's talk was published in the *Educational Journal of Virginia*, along with a response by Ruffner which attacked the Maryland principal's "gloomy negativism." Allen had offered only the "old Bourbon doctrine" of laissez-faire and had given no reasons why public schools could not teach morality. Ruffner argued that private and public school teachers operated on essentially the same basis because they only taught what the parents permitted. Instructing students in religion, he felt, was "a delicate matter, and is rarely done wisely and properly in any school ... and perhaps the fewer stones we throw on this point the better."[74] By the end of the decade, it was clear that the old friendship between Dabney and Ruffner had ended. An article in Ruffner's favorite organ, the *Educational Journal*, spelled it out: "This eminent divine can see no possible way in which any moral or religious ideas can be gotten into the heads of public school children, and he even maintains that morality cannot be taught in public schools. And therefore there is nothing left but the overthrow of the public schools! This is right funny." No byline was needed to indicate Ruffner's authorship.[75] By the time Readjuster politics forced him out of office in 1882, the public school system, though woefully underfunded, was secure in Virginia.[76]

As state superintendent for over a decade, Ruffner set policy and supported the law's silence on questions of religious education and moral formation in the schools. This remanded the issue squarely to the desks of local school authorities, who moved forward along the lines suggested by the state superintendent's written reports and articles in the *Educational Journal*. Character building was encouraged by such popular textbooks as *Moral Maxims. For Schools and Families*. Carrying the endorsements of Ruffner and some of the state's most important political and educational leaders, it announced on the cover that "This Book is used in the Public Free Schools of Virginia" and promised that "SECTARIAN DOCTRINES ARE RIGIDLY EXCLUDED." It aimed instead at "systematic moral instruction," which consisted of a numbered sequence of precepts beginning with "*Love and reverence God, and obey His laws, for this is right*" and closing with a dictum from Stonewall Jackson: "*What is life without honor? Degradation is worse than death.*"

Emphasizing obedience to parents and legitimate authority, the need for personal honesty and integrity, and similar virtues, the text included stirring examples or pithy quotations from such heroes as George Washington, Robert E.

Lee, Daniel Webster, Henry Clay, John C. Calhoun, and John Randolph.[77] For direct religious instruction Virginia public schools overwhelmingly embraced Bible reading together with other nondenominational Christian activities such as hymn singing and the recitation of the Lord's Prayer. In its very first issue in 1892, the *Virginia School Journal* laid out what it considered to be a suitable religious program for beginning the school day. It consisted of a psalm recited alternatively by teacher and students followed by the Lord's Prayer said together. This "religion of the people," as Ruffner styled it, informed public education in various forms on every level until the U.S. Supreme Court intervened in the school prayer cases in the 1960s.[78]

Apart from Ruffner, arguably the person most responsible for introducing these developments in public education was Thomas Jefferson. In proposing a chair in moral philosophy and encouraging voluntary religious services at the university, Jefferson had opened the door for possibilities far beyond his own vision. He had wanted to encompass all sects and so neutralize the opposition to his university. But the exploding evangelical context transformed his educational program of rational religion and moral formation into an expression of the Bible-based Protestant culture that the vast majority of Virginians embraced. This became the staple of the public school system, and its capstone was the nondenominational chapel dedicated near the Rotunda at the University of Virginia in 1890.[79]

In effect, the Old Dominion redefined separation and moved Jefferson's wall out into the midst of Roger Williams's garden. In virtually every area touching church-state life and practice, nineteenth-century Virginians increasingly experienced a culturally contextualized separation. The evangelical churches controlled that dimension of political culture practically from the time the statute was passed. In demanding repeal of the Episcopal Church's charter and the seizure of the church's lands, Baptists had led the fight. In the assemblies and constitutional conventions that restricted clergy from political office for the first two-thirds of the century, evangelicals supplied the votes. In the continuing debates over religious incorporation laws, the clergy opposed one another and repeatedly defeated the movement toward incorporation. It was a clergyman, William Henry Ruffner, who defined separation in public education. From his perspective, fidelity to the Statute for Religious Freedom meant not the absence of religious education and worship in the public schools but freedom from coercion and compulsion. In fairness to Ruffner, he had no other choice if he wanted a public school system. Evangelical Protestants to the core, Virginians would have rejected any other arrangement.

As might be expected, evangelical churches provided public support for community-based nonsectarian expressions of religious belief. But surprisingly, some clergy favored regulating and even restricting the institutions of believing communities. Motives for this latter position were undoubted mixed, but Jefferson was not alone in recognizing the realities of sectarian jealousy and fear. Despite all the claims of separating church and state, Virginia's lived expression of that principle was far different from our own. This underlines the truth of Justice Felix Frankfurter's observation in the 1948 *McCullom* case: "The mere formulation of a relevant Constitutional principle is the beginning of the solution of a problem, not its answer. This is so because the meaning of a spacious conception like that of the separation of Church from State is unfolded as appeal is made to the principle from case to case."[80]

The interpretation of the Virginia statute, of separation of church and state, not only unfolded in Virginia, it changed. Its application, like that of the First Amendment, has been and always will be culturally contextualized. Even Jefferson himself refused to follow rigid principle to its logical, absolute conclusion when it jeopardized higher concerns and values. He would have his university, even if that meant holding religious services in the Rotunda and having divinity schools on the edges of the university. As it turned out, those seminaries never materialized, but the commonwealth's commitment to church-state separation enshrined in its constitution guaranteed that the contest over religion in public education would continue well into the twentieth century.

❧ 9 ❧

Constitution

"A Past That Is Dead and Gone"

As the twentieth century made its debut in Virginia, a convention assembled in Richmond to replace the hated Underwood Constitution of 1868. In his opening address John Goode, the president of the convention, asserted that the document had been the work of "aliens" and "newly emancipated slaves," while the state's natural aristocracy, men who carried the bloodlines of the Old Dominion's first families, had been disfranchised. At the age of seventy-two, Goode was a senior member of the convention. A graduate of the University of Virginia and lifelong Democrat, he had served in the state legislature, the Secession Convention of 1861, the Confederate legislature, and the U.S. House of Representatives before his appointment as solicitor general of the United States in 1885. Goode reflected the mentality of the vast majority of convention delegates when he called black suffrage "a great crime against civilization and Christianity." It had subverted the natural order and thrust into power a people incapable of education or citizenship. Finally, after thirty years a convention of authentic Virginians could undo that mischief by adopting new suffrage provisions similar to those enacted in other southern states: poll taxes, literary tests, and understanding clauses. "The omniscient Ruler of the Universe" had eternally determined the innate inferiority of those who had been slaves, Goode proclaimed; and sometime in the future, when the North came to its senses, the Fifteenth Amendment would be repealed.[1]

Removing the African American population from the voting rolls was the convention's prime objective, but the emphasis placed on the grim tale of disfranchisement has led historians to overlook other aspects of the convention's deliberations. Some of the most contentious issues revolved around the subject of church-state relations. As Episcopalian Goode's maiden speech suggests, references to Christianity, the Bible, and God's design laced the convention debates. One of the members, Richard McIlwaine, a Presbyterian minister and president of Hampden-Sydney College, later praised "the reverence displayed by the members in dealing with sacred things." They acknowledged "the existence of an overruling Providence, who has made himself known in the Bible and in the works of His hands, to whom we owe duty and service." Though he noted that for some, this may have resulted from "good breeding and innate courtesy," he thought that the overall religious atmosphere was "attractive and hopeful." McIlwaine's recollections of the convention's tone reinforce the impressions conveyed by the statistics for church membership in the religious census of 1906, the backgrounds of the delegates, and the printed record. Out of a total state population of 1.8 million in 1900, almost 800,000 Virginians were formal church members, and over half of those were Baptists who limited membership to those baptized as adults. At least two-thirds of the delegates belonged to Protestant churches, and all of them operated within the evangelical religious culture—the beliefs, values, symbols, and practices—that formed the substratum of southern society.[2]

Major religious bodies in Virginia, 1906

Total population (1900)	1,854,184
Total church members	793,546
Total Protestants	761,996
Baptists	415,987
Methodists	200,771
Presbyterians	39,628
Episcopalians	28,487
Disciples of Christ	26,128
Lutherans	15,010
Dunkers	11,524
Christians	8,266
Other	
Roman Catholics	28,700
Jews	915 (heads of families)

Source: U.S. Bureau of the Census, *Special Reports Religion Bodies 1906*, pt. 1, *Summary and General Tables* (Washington, DC, 1910), 278, 280, 365–68.

Religious affiliation of delegates, Constitutional Convention of 1901–2

Total number of delegates	100
Responses to questionnaire	85
Episcopalians	19
Baptists	14
Presbyterians	11
Methodists	7
Christians	3
Lutherans	1
Decline to state	30

Source: John Garland Pollard, "The Members of the Constitutional Convention of 1901–1902: Data for Biographical Sketches," typescript, Virginia Historical Society, Richmond.

In treating issues of church and state, the delegates repeatedly invoked Thomas Jefferson's Statute for Establishing Religious Freedom, but reverence for that text did not produce agreement on its interpretation. During the convention the delegates wrangled over the Virginia statute as it applied to church-state issues on four counts: religious equality, the legal status of churches, public assistance for sectarian institutions, and tax exemptions for churches and parsonages. Even a hundred years later, their fights sound a contemporary ring.

"Christian Forbearance" in Action

When the convention opened in Richmond on June 12, 1901, church-state concerns were already on the minds of some delegates and their constituents across the state. Indeed, the members had scarcely settled into their seats in the State Capitol and begun to exchange pleasantries when John Garland Pollard, a Richmond lawyer, offered a brief amendment to the sixteenth article of Virginia's Declaration of Rights. Regarded as the Magna Carta of conscience rights, the article concluded with the admonition "that it is the mutual duty of all to practice Christian forbearance, love and charity, toward each other." Pollard proposed to erase the word "Christian" from that document. The Baptist son of a Baptist preacher and graduate of two Baptist schools, Richmond College and Columbian University in Washington, Pollard espoused the principle of absolute religious equality. Most Virginians accepted that principle, at least theoretically. He was tampering, however, with the Old Dominion's Bill of Rights, drafted by George Mason, amended by James Madison, and approved in 1776. It possessed icon status.[3]

Pollard's amendment electrified the convention as well as pulpits and press offices across the state. Prematurely gray at twenty-nine, the Richmond delegate was the second youngest member of the convention. The aspiring politician and able young attorney had campaigned actively that spring in the election of delegates to represent his city. During the previous summer he had published a series of articles in a local newspaper comparing Virginia's constitution with those of other states; he had pointedly noted the religious tests for officeholders that existed outside the Old Dominion.[4] Pollard's Baptist heritage and his close study of fundamental laws had attuned his constitutional antennae to the potential for legal discrimination rooted in religious prejudice. But his outspoken stance roused strong opposition, both lay and clerical, from those who would preserve for the Old Dominion a Christian heritage and traditional language against an encroaching pluralism.

John Garland Pollard (1871–1937) from 1901–2 album of Virginia Constitutional Convention by Foster's Photographic Gallery. (Virginia Historical Society, 1992.182)

At issue were the Jews. Pollard defended their cause. In a letter to a Richmond banker, John L. Williams, who had condemned his amendment in the press, the young Democrat argued that a state's "constitution should be purely a secular instrument," without even "a single word" suggesting religious "discrimination." Language that might have been appropriate in 1776 was out of step with the contemporary world. It was unjust, Pollard wrote, "to enjoin upon the Jewish citizen . . . Christian forbearance, love and charity." It breathed a "sectarian" spirit.[5] Some Protestant clergymen disagreed. From the pulpit of Richmond's Trinity Methodist Church, George W. Spooner attacked Pollard's resolution as the work of a "demagogue" who was "evidently catering to Jewish patronage and support." The *Richmond Dispatch* published Spooner's remarks, and Pollard responded by carefully distinguishing between his desire that Virginia be "a Christian State" from any efforts to force the issue by law. In good Baptist form he argued: "True Christianity does not need nor ask any special recognition at the hand of the law. All it wants is a fair field and no favors."[6] After the press published that exchange, an apologetic Spooner quickly wrote Pollard to explain that only his own "emphatic way of speaking" had caused his "harsh language." Pollard quickly grasped the olive branch. "You simply misconstrued my motives," he wrote, "and thought I was attacking the Christian religion, which is dear to us both." In actuality, "the difference between us is not one of aim but of method."[7]

Warm supporting letters commending Pollard's stance on church-state separation poured into his office. Dr. Joseph Eggleston, a Richmond dentist soon to become grand master of the state's Masons, praised the young politician's forthright stance on religious freedom and compared him to Patrick Henry. From his perspective, which other correspondents shared, the whole sorry business just reemphasized the need to keep religion away from the government.[8] Perhaps the most noteworthy epistle came from Edward Nathan Calisch, the rabbi at Beth Ahabah in Richmond and leader of the city's small but significant Jewish community. At the age of twenty-six, Calisch had arrived in Richmond in 1891 to assume the leadership of a highly respected Jewish congregation. An Ohio native educated at Hebrew Union College in Cincinnati under the influence of Rabbi Isaac Mayer Wise, Calisch firmly guided Beth Ahabah into the rapidly expanding Reform tradition. Reform Judaism abandoned many of the traditional Jewish beliefs and practices, emphasized instead its progressive nature, and urged Jews to identify themselves as fully American citizens rather than as outsiders. Broadly interested in interfaith cooperation, Richmond's new rabbi quickly developed excellent relations with clergy from various churches. When Grace Street Baptist Church burned down in the mid-1890s, Calisch offered Beth Ahabah for its worship services, and he did the same for the Grove Avenue Baptist congregation when fire destroyed their church building in 1900. In 1899 an editorial in Richmond's *Evening Leader* praised his contribution to the city's "religious fellowship." As he explained to a reporter from the *Richmond News*, "The highest privilege given to man is to worship God, and the congregation of Beth Ahabah would feel gratified if it could assist. . . . While the forms of faith differ yet Judaism has always taught the brotherhood of man."[9]

Under his leadership over the next half century, Beth Ahabah became a bulwark of Reform Judaism. Calisch strove to Americanize his growing flock of first-generation German immigrants while reaching out to promote interfaith understanding and cooperation.[10] He was already on record in support of strict church-state separation. Writing in the *Virginia School Journal* in 1897, the young rabbi praised the public school system as "the corner-stone of the nation." But at a time when virtually every school in the commonwealth began the day with some combination of prayers, Bible reading, and hymns, he argued against "even the simplest kind of religious exercise." Public education, he insisted, must be "completely and purely secular."[11]

Calisch had been in Richmond to offer the invocation on the second day of the convention, but he was vacationing in Atlantic City when the furor over Pollard's resolution broke in the press in mid-July. Regretting his absence "at this interesting juncture," the rabbi had read the *Dispatch* and thought the "intemperateness" of Spooner and Williams hurt their cause. Whatever the convention ultimately decided, Calisch thought that Pollard had "gained immensely in the esteem of liberal minded and reputable people."[12] A few days later he wrote Pollard again. He was obviously tempted to enter the fray himself. "I would have answered Spooner's latest diatribe," the rabbi huffed, "except for the fact that he has descended to so low a level that I do not care to follow. I would have to go down too far to reach him."[13]

Spooner, the pastor of the "Mother Church of Richmond Methodism," had evidently pulled out all the stops. While other clergy rallied behind his banner, the convention's committee on the preamble and Bill of Rights met to hear witnesses. Methodist and Episcopalian ministers insisted that the Bill of Rights was a venerable document and *Christian* a harmless, even nonsectarian word. The Jews, moreover, were latecomers. They had entered Virginia knowing the terms of the Bill of Rights and therefore had no right to complain. In response, Pollard cogently demolished their arguments, one by one, with the help of M. Ashby Jones, a liberal Baptist minister and an outspoken opponent of racial and religious bigotry. They might have persuaded the committee had not Goode arrived at the last minute and warned that removing "Christian" from the text might jeopardize the whole constitution when the state voted on its ratification.[14]

As Calisch observed, politics, not principle, had carried the day in the committee hearings. Pollard had another opportunity when the committee presented its proposal for the preamble and Bill of Rights on the floor of the convention in September. For his eloquence then, the rabbi later echoed Eggleston and compared Pollard to Patrick Henry. It must have been a heady moment for the young politician when he rose to explain his reasons for offering the amendment. The fundamental issue, he pointed out, was one of "religious equality" for all the commonwealth's citizens. Christians might consider the word *Christian* to be nonsectarian, but it stated a preference that effectively excluded non-Christians. The state should profess no religion and respect the beliefs and consciences of all. In Pollard's view, the whole debate had revealed a significant body of people who regarded Virginia as "legally, a Christian State" in which non-Christians should be tolerated but nothing more. "I do not believe in religious toleration," he proclaimed in words reminiscent of Madison. "I believe in religious liberty—the most sacred form of personal freedom."

What might have been appropriate when Christianity was the only religion in the state no longer belonged in the constitution. The situation now was more pluralistic. Virginia had "a large class of eminently respected, law-abiding and useful citizens who profess another religion." The convention was not a preservation society for "legal relics." The commonwealth's fathers had not written their fundamental law in concrete. "The question should be, not when or by whom this word was placed in the Bill of Rights, but whether to-day it properly belongs there." Opponents had accused Pollard of subverting Christianity. That was, he avowed, the furthest desire of his heart. In words that echoed Baptist petitions from the Revolutionary era, the politician insisted that genuine Christianity did not need state support. Though a single word in the frame of government might seem a trivial matter to some, for Pollard it represented a fundamental principle: the state had no business judging "the virtues of the religions professed by its citizens."

Having given his reasons for the change, he then concluded by explaining why he would not press his amendment. Goode had warned that across the state people were terribly upset by what they perceived as "an attack upon Christianity." Pollard understood their concern. He would not risk the constitution's defeat. He then concluded by explaining that the disfranchisement of African American voters, "a corrupt and ignorant electorate—the great, overshadowing evil we were called here to correct"—took precedence over "religious equality before the law, which should exist in every free State and which should be recognized and freely according to every citizen." Like the great bulk of his fellow white Virginians, Pollard did not appreciate that religious equality and racial equality were of a piece, that prejudice was a seamless garment.[15]

The irony also escaped Calisch. The rabbi applauded Pollard's address as "the only redeeming feature in a convention that is fast slipping into ridicule." The speeches were too long, the progress was too slow, and the argument over "Christian forbearance" stank of the "bigotry" that he had personally experienced even from clergymen. Allowing themselves to be intimidated by "sensational preachers of hysterical women and unreasoning men," the delegates had sacrificed a fundamental "principle of justice upon the altar of political expediency." The rabbi was disgusted.[16] Calisch's judgment may not seem excessively harsh when one considers the speech that followed Pollard's by Joseph Wysor, a Democrat from Southwest Virginia. With the chivalry expected of southern gentlemen, he announced that he would vote to retain "Christian" in the Bill of Rights "because Christianity redeems womanhood, which made us all we are and all we expect to be."

"The Milk in the Cocoanut": Revisiting Incorporation

Pollard was not the only delegate who wished to expunge words from earlier constitutions, and interested parties were observant. Keep church and state separate, one correspondent, Lewis Mason, warned Pollard, and "as far apart in politics as you can." In particular, he was counting on the young delegate's opposition "to incorporation of Church or religious bodies."[17] Indeed, that issue had already surfaced in June. Amid the resolutions submitted to the committee on the legislative department, Alfred Thom, a Norfolk lawyer, had proposed: "That it is against public policy to prohibit the incorporation of churches and religious denominations."[18] This issue's stormy history reached back to the 1840s when Presbyterian minister William Swan Plumer had bested Baptist and Episcopalian advocates of a general incorporation law for churches and religious denominations. The 1851 constitution had inserted a prohibition against such incorporations, and the Reconstruction constitution had maintained that exclusion in 1868. Yet successive assemblies gradually had allowed seminaries and religious agencies to incorporate. In the 1850s the legislature incorporated a great variety of institutions ranging from St. Mary's Female Academy and Orphan Asylum and the English and Hebrew Institute, both located in Norfolk, to Richmond's YMCA.[19] Union Theological Seminary finally received its charter in 1855; but it was restricted to 250 acres, and the value of its endowment could not exceed $250,000, the same limitations the assembly had placed on the Episcopal seminary when it was chartered two years earlier.[20] The Diocesan Missionary Society of Virginia was incorporated for the Episcopal Church in the legislative session of 1874–75, but the rush to incorporate religious organizations did not come until the 1880s when all the major Protestant denominations along with the Catholics sought and received charters for their agencies, charities, and benevolent associations.

Only the prohibition on incorporating churches remained. Thom wanted it expunged from the new constitution. When the legislative committee heard testimony on his resolution, a number of clergymen, mainly Episcopalians and Methodists, urged reasons for church incorporation. Robert P. Kerr, pastor of Richmond's First Presbyterian Church, was absent in New York but wrote a strong letter endorsing the change, which he said all of Richmond's Presbyterian clergy supported. "I have known many churches to lose money bequeathed to them for charitable objects by reason of this defect in our Constitution," he wrote. "The present prohibition is a discrimination against churches. It is strange that men associated together for religious purposes should be the only ones not allowed to form a body corporate."[21] It all seemed plausible, and the first two committee votes heartily supported Thom's resolution. But then it became coupled with a proposal that the new constitution should include a specific limitation on the amount of property that churches could own. This restriction already existed in statutory law, but some wanted definite limits written in constitutional concrete, particularly if churches were allowed to incorporate. Future congressman R. Walton Moore, an Episcopalian lawyer from Fairfax County who chaired the committee, favored this approach.[22]

As the hearings continued, the pro-incorporation forces encountered a formidable foe in Wayland Fuller Dunaway, a Baptist preacher. A graduate of the University of Virginia who had served in the Confederate army and practiced law before entering the ministry in 1870, Dunaway had been elected to the convention from two rural counties in the Northern Neck. Thom's proposal alarmed the minister, and he objected vociferously that incorporated churches might become wealthy and hence corrupt religion, thus reviving fears that had cropped up periodically during the previous century. When Thom rejected the inclusion of a constitutional limit on the amount of property incorporated churches might hold, the committee majority led by Moore and encouraged by Dunaway rescinded its previous support for his incorporation resolution, and it failed its last two votes.[23]

The Norfolk attorney and his committee allies determined to argue their position before the whole convention. That autumn their minority report proposed to replace the statement in the previous constitution that forbade the incorporation of churches with the following substitution: "The General Assembly shall limit by law the extent to which corporations formed for religious purposes shall be permitted to acquire or hold property." The wording represented an attempt to win support from those who feared that incorporated churches might pile up riches. On Friday, October 11, the convention began two full days of debate on the issue. William Robertson, a distinguished lawyer and former judge from Roanoke, spoke persuasively for the minority proposal. The testimony of numerous clergymen had persuaded Robertson that Virginia was out of step with the nation, that baseless fear rather than sound "judgment" drove present policy. He traced the previous opposition to church incorporation to bitter denominational feuds and jealousies that no longer existed. Having read Plumer's 1846 arguments against church incorporation, Robertson thought that the rationale for the minister's attack on the Catholic Church's wealth in the centuries before the Reformation was more rhetorical than reasonable. He also considered it irrelevant. Virginia courts had ruled that church agencies could be incorporated. Why should churches be treated differently? It was time for a change, he argued. In matter-of-fact language Robertson explained what that entailed. Churches ought to have the same legal rights that every corporate organization in the modern world possessed: to own property, to make contracts, to transact business, to sue and be sued, and to be held liable. Although church trustees could now hold legal title to a limited amount of church property, their authority ended there. They could make no binding contracts. To buy, sell, or improve church property, the law made them go to court. What the state currently offered to breweries, jockey clubs, and baseball teams, it refused to churches. Robertson thought this patently nonsensical and unjust, the result of fears and deep-seated "prejudice rather than fact and reason."[24]

Dunaway spoke in opposition. The state could limit church property holdings already, but the heart of the matter or, in the Baptist preacher's odd phrase, "the milk in the cocoanut," lay in the power of incorporating churches. Wrapping himself in the mantle of Jefferson, Madison, and succeeding generations, he praised the sagacity of their church-state arrangements. Knowing that "wealth is power," the founders strove to keep religion out of politics. The convention should not repudiate their work. As Robertson predicted, Dunaway's case rested on his fears for both church and state. "It is now the glory of the churches of Jesus Christ," the minister proclaimed, "that they are different from other associations." Incorporation would secularize and corrupt them with wealth and worldliness. Eventually they would own "a large part of the real and personal property" of Virginia and emerge as rival powers outside the "State's control."

By framing the church-state issue in terms of wealth and power, Dunaway was arguing along the same lines that nineteenth-century European liberals set up against the Catholic Church. In this contest either the state or the church must have mastery. It was a far cry from the American system of church-state separation. But a particular historiography, the Enlightenment critique of the

Wayland Fuller Dunaway (1841–1916) from 1901–2 album of
Virginia Constitutional Convention by Foster's Photographic Gallery. (Virginia Historical Society, 1992.182)

medieval church, grounded his argument. During the "Dark Ages," clerical "coffers" spilled over with income and bequests. Church wealth and power brought the decline of "piety" and the growth of "superstitions." People relied on "external baptism," instead of "justification by faith." Finally, "the Bishop of Rome put his foot upon the neck of the Emperor of Germany." Unlike Robertson who had spoken at length without interruption, Dunaway faced numerous questions and objections from the floor. But nothing deflected him. The fact that forty-three of the other forty-four states now incorporated churches made no difference. Who could tell what evils the future held for them? In his view the present arrangement had served Virginia and the cause of religion well. It should remain in place.[25]

When Dunaway finished, the other clerical member, Presbyterian Richard McIlwaine, spoke briefly in support of his Baptist colleague. In warmly evangelical terms, he pointed out that the church of Jesus Christ needed no "charter" to fulfill its mission. Church "agencies" possessed all the authority they needed to do their work, and incorporation would only hurt the churches. Strict church-state separation, Virginia-style, worked in McIlwaine's view of things. "The State has its sphere. The church has its sphere. The State protects the church in its rights. That is adequately done to-day. We ask no more." McIlwaine sat down to a round of applause, and the convention adjourned for the evening.[26]

The first speaker on Saturday morning was Joseph Stebbins. A Presbyterian businessman and banker from South Boston, close to the North Carolina border, he repeated much of the clerical delegates' arguments. But the essence of his case against church incorporation was that the churches themselves, in terms of their governing officers or bodies, had not requested it. Carter Glass disagreed. A newspaper editor and dairy farmer from Lynchburg, Glass would begin in 1902 a long career in the U.S. House of Representatives and then the Senate. Identifying himself as a Methodist, he informed Stebbins that he knew personally that numerous district conferences of Methodists had asked for the change. The debate then moved into whether church officials had asked for the insertion of the prohibition in the constitution of 1851. Stebbins retreated further back into the comforts of medieval history, ranging from the corruption of the church under Constantine to its purification in the Reformation, and then detailed his concerns for its future "spiritual" welfare. To bolster his case against ecclesiastical wealth, the banker pulled out a copy of France's recently passed "Associations Law" with a map showing the recent growth in church property there that the law was designed to reverse. "My Kingdom is not of this world!" Christ had proclaimed. Separation from the world demanded separation from the state. For Stebbins, wealthy church endowments displayed Christianity's greatest obscenity when believers lounged "in richly upholstered pews listening to one who knows his stipend will be paid, no matter how the crops are or what general business conditions are." Such a church reeked of "spiritual deadness, laxity of morals and putrefaction."[27]

After Stebbins finished his lengthy oration, an irritated Glass rose from his seat. Though unprepared to give a speech, he felt compelled to object. He found much of the debate irrelevant to the issue. Robertson had succinctly spelled out the rationale for change. Amid all the opposition's verbiage, their single argument was that incorporation would make churches "excessively wealthy and . . . worldly." Yet in fact future corporate status would not permit churches to possess any more property than they already could own. The whole business was "a bugbear." In voting on Robertson's resolution, the only real question to consider was whether the churches should conduct their business directly or continue to act by subterfuge through their agencies.[28]

The second day of the incorporation debate was wearying the members, but before Thom could conclude the case for the resolution, a prolonged wrangle erupted over whether Robertson would be willing to amend it and write into the constitution the current statutory limits on church property in Virginia. As tempers rose in the chamber, Joseph Wysor provided comic relief: "Is not a corporation an artificial person without a soul," he queried. When the speaker agreed, Wysor continued: "Is not the church frequently described in the Scriptures as the bride of Christ!" Well then, "What will the bridegroom do when he comes and finds the bride incorporated?" That broke the tension, the delegates laughed and applauded, and Thom rose for his address.

He found himself in an awkward position. The proposal that he championed had not originated with him, or Robertson, or Glass. They had simply responded to the requests of Methodist, Presbyterian, and Episcopalian clergy. But the two ministers at the convention opposed it. While McIlwaine as a college president might not adequately represent Presbyterian pastors, Thom was sure that Dunaway reflected Baptist views. Bluntly accusing the preacher of religious prejudice, Thom slashed away at Dunaway's argument: "At the bottom of it, taking out his medieval history, we have nothing left [but] his medieval sentiment. He comes before this Convention declaring that his fears largely control him, and . . . before the Committee in debate, that he was not only actuated by his fears, but he was actuated by the inherited prejudices of his church." That charge brought Dunaway to his feet. He had never, he said, "admitted that I was influenced by my prejudices." Had he ever done so, he now retracted that confession.

Thom then reviewed the limitations churches faced in managing their affairs. It made no sense for the convention to hamper their work. The references speakers had made to established churches in England and "Roman Catholic countries" were not pertinent to Virginia. Incorporation would not establish the church. Though it changed the "legal relationship," it would not place "the State in the church business any more than the State goes into the railroad business when it incorporates a railroad company." Incorporation, in short, would not create a "union of Church and State." The delegates had been terrified by "mere visions." Thom reassured them, "There is no danger of a great religious octopus coming and eating us up." The real peril lay in yielding to "medieval" ideas that chained Virginia to "a past that is dead and gone." When the vote was taken, however, the past won, and Robertson's resolution failed. The churches remained unincorporated.[29]

"A Great Bugaboo": Funding
Sectarian Charities

When the convention reconvened on Monday, Dunaway switched from opponent to advocate. In June he had sponsored a resolution before the legislative committee "to prevent the appropriation of public funds to sectarian uses," which he now proceeded to urge. The Baptist preacher wanted the new constitution to forbid the General Assembly or any city, county, or government agency from providing land, money, or "personal property . . . to any church or sectarian society, or help to maintain or support any society, association or institution whatever, which is entirely or partly, directly or indirectly, controlled by any church or sectarian society."[30]

Dunaway's concern centered on a fiscal policy in several Virginia cities. A year after the Civil War, at the request of the Sisters of Charity, Richmond's city council had voted an appropriation of $1,000 for St. Joseph's Orphan Asylum. In 1867 the city began assisting St. Paul's Church Home for children, operated by the Episcopalians. Over the next decades city officials voted funds, eliminated property taxes, and provided gas from the city's gasworks for a growing number of Catholic and Protestant charitable institutions: orphan asylums, old people's homes, and hospitals.[31] By 1900 Richmond, the largest city in Virginia, had a population of 85,000, and the city council was partially funding twenty-five private institutions with grants ranging from $100 to $750 at a total cost of $8,674. That comprised 28 percent of the city's charitable budget. Norfolk, half Richmond's size, was assisting both the Protestant Hospital and St. Vincent's Hospital staffed by the Sisters of Charity. Other, smaller cities followed suit.[32]

But public funding of private and church-based charities bothered some Virginians. In a long article published in 1878, the *Baptist Religious Herald* criticized the grants by Richmond's city council to St. Joseph's Orphan Asylum and St. Paul's Church Home. The author insisted:

No religious denomination should receive one cent from the public treasury. . . . Appropriations of property or money to sectarian institutions is at variance with the entire freedom of religious belief and action that is the distinctive characteristic of our governments. To favor any religious denomination or creed is a discrimination forbidden by the spirit of our Constitution and the genius of our institutions. Entire separation of church and state, the right to worship God according to the dictates of conscience, the right to choose one's religion or have no religion at all, if one prefers, have been regarded as fundamental political axioms. To tax a citizen of one faith to support or encourage the tenets and doctrines of a citizen of another faith; to compel me to contribute money, under any pretext, to the support of church or school or Asylum or Home of any denomination, my own or another, is a flagrant wrong.[33]

Virginia's cities ignored the *Herald*'s criticism of their policy. But now the convention offered Baptists an opportunity to press the issue. Charles Fenton James, a Baptist minister, educator, and historian, recently had reminded his confreres of the part Baptists had played in the great contest over church and state during the Revolutionary era. In 1900 the president of Roanoke Female College in Danville published his *Documentary History of the Struggle for Religious Liberty in Virginia*. A decade earlier, James had crossed pens with William Wirt Henry, a Presbyterian, who had given preeminence to the Presbyterian role in winning religious liberty. Now James sought to correct the record with a definitive history. His book paid lavish attention to the Baptist contribution.[34] Undoubtedly Dunaway was familiar with James's work.

While the Baptist argued his case before the legislative committee in the Capitol, the Dover Baptist Association met nearby at the Leigh Street Baptist Church and formulated a petition. Notifying the convention that they represented 14,742 Virginia Baptists, the ministers complained that cities were appropriating public funds for "sectarian institutions." They asked that the new constitution prohibit this "violation of the principle of entire separation of Church and State."[35] The legislative committee, however, voted against the inclusion of Dunaway's resolution in its report to the convention. For three weeks in August, the convention shut down while members escaped from Richmond's summer humidity. Upon their return, they soon faced the heat of public opinion. The minister and his allies had not been idle.

Dunaway's arguments had persuaded five members of the legislative committee that this was a blatant case of church-state separation. When the committee reported to the convention toward the end of August, a minority resolution recommended that the new constitution prohibit any

> appropriation of public funds or personal property or real estate . . . by the General Assembly, or by the authorities of any city, town, county district, or other municipal corporation, to any church or sectarian society, association, or institution of any kind whatever which is entirely or partly, directly or indirectly, controlled by any sectarian society, or make any appropriation for paying for any religious services; nor shall any like appropriation be made to any charitable, industrial, or educational institution which is not owned or controlled by the State, or by such city, town, county district, or other municipal corporation.[36]

As the delegates drifted back into Richmond after summer holidays, they began receiving Baptist petitions from across the state. Over the next month and a half, at least fifteen more Baptist associations followed the Dover Association to support Dunaway's proposal against public funding of church-based institutions. It was an impressive display of denominational solidarity reminiscent of the petition campaign that resulted in the passage of Jefferson's statute. The Methodist clergy joined them. Claiming to express the views of 200,000 Virginia Methodists, Richmond-area ministers wrote the convention that they were "unalterably and emphatically opposed" to the public funding of "sectarian or any institution not owned and controlled by the State."[37]

Throughout the fall and into December, the Junior Order United American Mechanics (JOUAM) added its voice to that of the Baptists and Methodists. Founded in 1853, this whites-only men's association of skilled workers and managers and its women's auxiliary, the Daughters of Liberty, promoted a blend of patriotism, nationalism, and nativism. They advocated nonsectarian Bible reading in the public schools, urged laws restricting immigration, and opposed "any union of Church and State." They regarded Catholics as their chief opponents. In the 1890s the JOUAM established councils in over twenty states and were a growing presence in Virginia's cities and towns. Whenever a new public school opened, they held dedicatory services, presented the principal with a Bible and a flag, and hosted speeches by local ministers. Their official newspaper, the *Virginia Courier*, covered such events and reported in March 1901 that a preacher out in Rockingham County had warned "of the great enemy we have to fight the most, and that is Romanism."[38] As the convention opened, Richmond had fourteen councils of men and seven of women, and the *Virginia Courier* encouraged the Junior Order "to let your delegate know your views and your wishes, for he is but your servant, paid to execute your will." At least a dozen Virginia councils petitioned explicitly against public funding of religiously sponsored institutions.[39]

In October, while the JOUAM state convention met in Richmond, the constitutional convention debated the minority resolution. Two issues worried some delegates at the latter meeting. First, by forbidding appropriations for institutions not fully owned and controlled by the state, the minority proposal would stop the assembly from helping fund the College of William and Mary. Second, it would prevent Richmond, Norfolk, and other cities from aiding charitable institutions that performed essential services. In both cases, if state and local governments had to assume complete responsibility and pay all the bills, public costs would skyrocket. For the rest of that day, the convention discussed amendments to the minority report that might somehow balance church-state separation with the practical need for social services.

Urban delegates controlled the evening debate. Alexander Hamilton from Petersburg and Samuel Meredith from Richmond each offered amendments to the minority report that were designed chiefly to preserve the cities' authority to make grants to charitable institutions. Robertson of Roanoke, who had served on the legislative committee, stated the issue succinctly. The cities were not appropriating money for religious proselytizing but simply helping charities in benevolent work that served people of all faiths and none. A wealthy Catholic woman from New York, the wife of Thomas Fortune Ryan, recently had purchased a Roanoke hospital that had been closed by its previous owners. She proposed opening it "for the benefit of all classes" and religions but wanted help from the city council. Roanoke needed that hospital, Robertson insisted. He saw a golden opportunity slipping away. Because convention delegates disliked Catholics, they were going to tie the hands of the city council. How odd, another delegate observed, that nonbelievers could run a hospital with public assistance but not Catholic or Protestant organizations. In Robertson's view fear, not reason, controlled the convention's decisions on church-state matters. "For God's sake," he implored, "let us stop talking about churches."[40] Thom echoed his concern. Explaining the situation in Norfolk, he pointed out the enormous savings that religiously based institutions provided the cities.

But what Robertson called "a great bugaboo," Dunaway regarded as a matter of "fundamental principle." His resolution had two parts. The first was directed against appropriations for sectarian institutions. The second opposed funding in whole or in part any institution that the state did not completely own and control. Recognizing the great concern over support for the College of William and Mary, Dunaway suggested that each part be treated separately and expressed a personal indifference toward the second. However, any public assistance to a church-related institution helped advance denominational objectives. A religiously owned and operated hospital, orphan asylum, or old people's home "breathed a sectarian atmosphere" and conveyed "denominational doctrines." To allocate tax monies that would benefit the propagation of religious beliefs violated Jefferson's statute and the "American doctrine of the separation of church and state," he insisted.[41]

In stating that the practice of Virginia's cities violated the U.S. Constitution, Dunaway ignored the fact that the Supreme Court had not yet applied the First Amendment's religion clause to the states; it would not do so until the 1940s. More to the point, however, he also overlooked an 1899 decision in which the court had approved the constitutionality of federal support for church-sponsored institutions. The District of Columbia had funded a Catholic hospital's construction of isolation wards to combat contagious diseases. Because the hospital was separately incorporated from the church, served a secular purpose, and opened its services to all, the Supreme Court had ruled in *Bradford v. Roberts* that its religious affiliation did not matter. This case set a precedent for church-state contractual relationships in social welfare.[42]

None of Dunaway's opponents, however, challenged his interpretation of the First Amendment or mentioned *Bradford*. Had he been at the convention, Rabbi Calisch would have sided with Dunaway. At the beginning of the century, a New Jersey judge had refused to allow the testimony of a Chinese non-Christian on the grounds that he could not take a Christian oath. In a newspaper article Calisch castigated that decision and interpreted the First Amendment to state that "Congress, (and consequently any individual state, for no state has powers superior to the United States) shall make no law" concerning religion. It also violated the Fourteenth Amendment, which safeguarded "an equal right to the protection and the benefits of the law." In the same article the rabbi explained the basis for his concern with a reference to the dispute over the wording of the sixteenth article of the Bill of Rights at the Virginia convention: "We Jews are interested in this, both as citizens and as Jews. We have been constantly fighting the purblind fanaticism that is seeking to place sectarian recognition in the constitution, in the public schools and wherever else it can."[43]

As he had done previously in the debate over incorporation, Dunaway played on the fear of precedent. From small beginnings "a great crying evil" might well develop with thousands of dollars diverted into sectarian pockets. The Baptist minister emphasized the Catholic charities in Richmond. The committee on the legislative department had been invited to visit the Little Sisters of the Poor Home for the Aged where fifteen sisters cared for seventy men and sixty-five women. Though the annual city grant of $500 represented a small portion of the total budget for that institution, Dunaway reverted to principle. "Let every man, let every association do good in all possible ways, . . . but then let them not seek a reward for their well-doing by asking for the people's taxes. Cannot we sometimes do good in this world without proclaiming it abroad before the public and going to the public crib to seek a reward for well-doing?" The implication that the sisters received pay for their work infuriated Charles Meredith, a city of Richmond delegate; and Dunaway backpedaled slightly only to repeat his earlier charge, that church-related institutions existed to propagate "sectarian doctrines."[44]

But as the minister rambled across the Virginia landscape citing various institutions that had not requested public support, he tripped. The General Assembly had recently incorporated a Methodist orphanage, and Dunaway averred that the Methodists would not come seeking assistance. That pulled Carter Glass out of his seat. "They have already come," Glass announced. They had asked Lynchburg for thirty-five acres, which the city gave them. Dunaway was surprised but recovered quickly, stating that Lynchburg would receive a "quid pro quo" in terms of business that the asylum would bring to the city. Thus it was purely "a business transaction," which Dunaway would not oppose. Meredith was now roused. "Is not the whole milk in the coaconut the Catholic question?" he asked, repeating the charge of anti-Catholicism against Dunaway that Robertson had made a few days earlier. The Baptist minister "emphatically" denied it and seized the offensive by stressing the popular support the petitions manifested. "I may be in a minority in this Convention, but I am in a great majority of the people of the Commonwealth of Virginia," he warned his fellow delegates. The *Dispatch* called it the "strongest speech" he had yet given.[45]

Meredith responded the next day. The fifty-one-year-old graduate of Richmond College was highly regarded as a brilliant lawyer, eloquent in debate and skilled in cross-examination. Though he would die an Episcopalian, he was not yet a communicant of any church.[46] He had thought from the outset that the whole matter should be left as it presently existed, at the discretion of city governments. His argument rested on the "public purposes" that these charities fulfilled. For the benefit of the delegates, he enumerated in detail the work of each of the private institutions in the capital and contrasted their management "by people who have devoted their lives to the work for the love of God" with "public charities" operated by "paid officials." From a purely financial perspective, if Richmond took over these essential institutions run by religious groups, it would "bankrupt" the city.[47] At the outset of his speech, Meredith had eschewed emotion, but when he described the work of the Little Sisters of the Poor, he attacked Dunaway personally. The Baptist preacher had "dealt most harshly" with these sisters, Meredith said, though they were now taking care of an old Baptist minister. "Consider," the lawyer asked the convention, "when they are attacked, and that denomination is spoken of more harshly by the Baptists than almost any other denomination, that they still hold out their hand, and take up from the place of want and need and suffering a minister of that denomination, and bring him where he can get peace and comfort and rest." Now "they are to be cut off because . . . a spirit of Catholicism . . . permeates the whole institution, which will injure this man, who is needing help and cannot get it elsewhere." Confederate veterans and old people from all over Virginia lived in their home. To support them the sisters "tread the streets of this city, begging for assistance to help them . . . not themselves."[48]

Meredith may have swayed some delegates, but the last word belonged to Robert Turnbull, who had chaired the legislative committee's minority report. A lawyer and former state legislator from Brunswick County, he represented the rural perspective that distinguished the opponents of support for sectarian charities. An Episcopalian, he denied any animosity toward the Catholic Church. But as with other delegates from the countryside, questions raised during his speech showed that Turnbull possessed very little knowledge about the actual operations of institutions like the Norfolk hospitals or the College of William and Mary. Instead, he took refuge in the principle that public funds should only support public institutions and repeatedly raised the fear of future abuses if the private sector received government assistance. Ignoring the urban experience of almost forty years, he warned, "If you ever open the door there is going to be no end of it."[49]

That argument controlled the outcome. By a vote of 33 to 26, the convention voted to prohibit the "appropriation of public funds, or personal property, or real estate" by the legislature or any other governmental authority on any level "to any church or sectarian society, association, or institution." Walton Moore immediately urged a reconsideration of the first vote. Operating on the principle of absolute separation of church and state, the convention had forbidden cities to help the "lovely charities" described by Meredith. Consistency demanded, therefore, that the convention should also end tax exemptions for church property and abolish the Sunday closing laws. The majority was not prepared to go that far. Bending slightly to Moore's position, a heavily amended statement left the state legislature with authority to allow "cities, towns or counties" to assist charitable institutions.[50]

Nothing came of that proviso, however. When the Richmond City Council considered its annual allocation of funds, gas, and water for various charitable agencies, the city attorney advised that they could not act without the General Assembly's permission. A bill was working its way through the state Senate in mid-January 1903. By a lopsided vote, "being satisfied that an emergency exists," it initially proposed that the officials of any city, town, or county could appropriate "public funds, or personal property, or real estate to any charitable institution or association" they deemed worthy of aid. But then the senators reconsidered. They amended the measure by eliminating towns and counties and restricting it to cities of over 40,000 inhabitants, leaving only Richmond and Norfolk. The *Richmond Times* meanwhile protested against raising the church-state issue in a matter of "local self-government." Arguing that the state should respect urban needs, the newspaper characterized Richmond's charitable institutions as nonsectarian "public charities" that accepted all and did "great good in relieving distress" and serving "the poor."[51]

As opposing petitions from the Junior Order of United American Mechanics rolled in to the legislature, the House of Delegates balked at the Senate bill and broadened the measure to include other cities and towns. The Senate, however, rejected those amendments, and the bill failed to pass. It would not be revived. In the next year's biennial report for the city of Richmond, all private institutions had been dropped from the list of charities, and the appropriation for maintaining the almshouse and caring for the poor had jumped appreciably. Religiously based and private charitable agencies, or at least most of them, did not fade away, but the government had imposed a severe disjunction between public and private services. The formal cooperation that had marked the relationship between urban government and private charity in Virginia had ended.[52]

Separating Church and State, Virginia Style

What do these debates and their outcomes tell us about Virginians and their understanding of Jefferson's statute at the beginning of the twentieth century? First, the arguments over church incorporation and the funding of church-related institutions reveal a significant cleavage between urban and rural delegates. In a state where over 80 percent of the population still lived in the countryside or in small villages and towns, the rural element dominated state politics and controlled the convention.[53] Most Virginians did not realize or appreciate the challenges of an increasingly modern society. The complexities of city life with its attendant problems and demand for institutionalized social services escaped them, just as the need for public education, reform of the penal system, and professional care for the retarded and mentally ill had eluded their ancestors.[54] The prevailing mentality remained a "We take care of our own" conservatism. Living tightly circumscribed lives, they lacked exposure to the socioeconomic conditions and ethnoreligious pluralism that increasingly defined Richmond, Norfolk, and, to a lesser degree, the other growing cities in the Old Dominion. Rural Virginians clung to the past with a vengeance and relied on its aphorisms to guide their lives.

Second, the convention rhetoric often reveals the stubborn persistence of classical republican thought within Virginia's governing class. Socially and politically, these men operated in an eighteenth-century world. Their speeches display a profound distrust of the messiness of democracy. Their principal work would be to curtail it as much as possible. Institutions they did not or could not control were suspect. Refusing to incorporate churches not only checked any pretensions the churches might have to an autonomous existence, it deflected a host of potential dangers that only a few recognized as nonexistent. In ominous tones delegates warned of potential conspiracies, of corruption, wealth, and luxury smothering authentic Christianity. The experience of other states, even their own history, meant nothing in the face of their fears for the future. They spoke as men besieged. A century and a quarter had passed since Independence, but the continuities in thought over time are remarkable.

Richard Beeman has documented the expansion of tobacco and slaves into Lunenburg County in that earlier era, with its concomitant commitment to agrarianism and slavery, and asserts that slavery provided "the central point of definition for the Southside's white citizens." This in turn went hand in hand with the perpetuation of an "increasingly oligarchic and archaic . . . social and political system . . . nearly wholly out of step with the pace of American development in the nineteenth century."[55] By the beginning of the twentieth century, racial segregation and disfranchisement replaced slavery, but nothing had really changed in the Virginia mind-set. Most convention delegates in 1901 would have found congenial the libertarian republicanism of John Taylor of Caroline and John Randolph of Roanoke. These men and their confreres of the old Virginia school with their insistence on strict construction, states' rights, and the promotion of agricultural rather than commercial interests shaped the conservative ideology that perdured through the Civil War and into the next century.[56]

Third, this provincial outlook fit neatly with an easily exploited religious prejudice against Catholics, Jews, and any other group that appeared somehow different or strange. Bigotry and intolerance seldom confine themselves to a single object. Pollard's proposal to drop the word *Christian* from the Declaration of Rights laid bare the anti-Jewish sentiment. Urban delegates, notably Robertson and Meredith, perceived a harsh anti-Catholicism that drew upon a particular critique of the medieval church for its justification.[57] The fear, which Dunaway played upon several times, that permitting cities to assist sectarian charities would contribute to the propagation of Catholicism perhaps set some delegates firmly against assistance to any church-based institutions. Disparaging remarks made on the convention floor about Christian Scientists and Mormons offer further examples of bigotry. In sum, the "complex of fears and hates," which Wilbur Cash a few decades later identified as the "savage ideal" in the South, luxuriated in the Old Dominion.[58] This was, after all, the catalyst that assembled the convention to disfranchise voters on the basis of race and class. It embraced religion also.

What then did Jefferson's statute mean for this generation launching the twentieth century in the Old Dominion? Religious freedom, for everyone; religious equality, certainly for Protestants; church-state separation, applied selectively. Even Pollard wanted Virginia identified as a Christian country. No resolutions embodied Rabbi Calisch's perspective by calling for a ban on religious exercises in the public schools. But the elephant in the Capitol was tax exemption for churches. Carter Glass raised the issue when Dunaway was railing against incorporation. Corporations and individuals paid taxes; churches did not. Glass thought such "paternalism" should be eliminated. Incorporate the churches and tax them. That would eliminate the dangers of excessive ecclesiastical wealth. But Dunaway saw no need to change Virginia's historic practice.[59]

When the convention debated tax policy in the spring of 1902, nearly everyone professed a desire to end exemptions for churches but then retreated behind the argument that the people would not stand for it. As attention shifted to the clergymen's homes, the rural-urban split surfaced once again. A delegate from a farm county proposed an amendment to exempt parsonages. In the countryside, he pointed out, one parson often served a number of small churches, people struggled financially to support that minister, and a parsonage tax would fall on them. Urban delegates countered that city churches often had no parsonages and so would not share in any tax exemption. How was there equality in that? As the discussion concluded, Dunaway spoke for exempting both churches and parsonages. The convention's foremost exponent of church-state separation now argued for an accommodation as he drew ever more imprecise lines. "It is not the part of a secular government to support religion," he avowed; but "secular government" needed "religion, in a certain sense, which, if not maintained and fostered, is still recognized and looked favorably upon by the government." That justified tax exemptions for churches. Parsonages should also be exempted, he continued, because "they are along the same line." Dunaway then followed with a long encomium on the importance of religion to society and the need for government to foster it. Indeed, he concluded, "the very civilization of the Commonwealth is built upon the religion of Jesus Christ."[60]

Few if any of the delegates would have disagreed with the principled preacher. For Virginians, as for most Americans of that day, church-state separation was contextualized by the overwhelming consensus that they were a Christian people. The Old Dominion was committed both to Jefferson's statute and to Protestant Christianity. It had been for over a century. Few people then, or for decades to come, considered such commitments to be incompatible.

Bible

"To Lift Humanity"

In *Engle v. Vitale* in 1962 and then the following year in *Abington School District v. Schempp*, the U.S. Supreme Court banned prayer in the public schools. In support of those decisions, the majority of the justices advocated a strict separationist interpretation of the establishment clause of the First Amendment.[1] These school prayer decisions rank among the most controversial in our national history, and half a century later the argument continues.[2] It may never end. The effort to strip religious formation from public education deeply offended the cultural values of millions of Americans. As Justice William O. Douglas—much to his later chagrin—once stated, "We are a religious people whose institutions presuppose belief in a Supreme Being."[3] From the inception of the common or public school, religious exercises and school textbooks expressive of a Protestant culture were taken for granted across the country.[4] Because of their Protestant form and style, Catholics objected. In the nineteenth century they asked, however, not for a wall of separation in the public schools but for a separate system with a share of the common fund to teach their own religious beliefs and values in their own parochial schools.[5] Few nineteenth-century voices argued for a strict separation of church and state in public education, except in Virginia.

Indeed, even before they enshrined Jefferson's statute in the constitution of 1829, Virginians claimed that by virtue of the statute and its apotheosis as the sole determinant of the church-state relationship, they had separated church and state.[6] Yet as evangelical Protestantism swept the state in the nineteenth century, the wall of separation gradually displayed its porous character. Before the Civil War the legislature reversed itself and began to charter seminaries and church-related schools, permitted churches to own a limited amount of land, and returned chaplains to the assembly. Then the Reconstruction constitution allowed preachers to sit in the legislature, and by the 1880s church agencies and institutions were being incorporated throughout the state. The place of religion in public elementary and secondary education remained controversial, however, and may be viewed as part of an even larger concern for moral reform that marked the first three decades of the twentieth century.[7] The subject fits nicely as a three-act play, or more realistically, as a series of three major battles in an almost thirty years' war of intermittent skirmishes and pitched fighting.

To illuminate the ensuing contest, something must be said first about the lay of the land in the second half of the nineteenth century. A few counties maintained free schools for poor children before the Civil War, but most education was private, and privately paid for. Virtually all schools included religious exercises and especially Bible reading in the daily order, and state laws insisted that any religious instruction in tax-supported institutions be nonsectarian.[8] After the war William Henry Ruffner for almost a dozen years negotiated ever so delicately the treacherous straits between the supporters and opponents of public education. The debate was fundamentally about whether Virginians would have access to free public schools, but the issue of religious instruction and formation preoccupied both sides. For Protestant Virginians the Bible provided a crucial text that shaped their outlook on life and the world around them. To exclude it from their schools would have set up an intolerable disjunction between their religious culture and their political and social lives. Yet Jefferson's statute also possessed quasi-religious status as a powerful symbol of religious liberty and conscience rights. Public education opponents insisted that its language in the state's constitution forbade any religious education in the schools.

Ruffner proposed an alternative reading of Jefferson's work. The statute forbade compulsion, so nothing concerning religion should be said in school law or regulations. In essence, the superintendent advocated a policy of silence that allowed local communities, individual schools, and especially the teachers to decide the matter themselves. "Christianity," he argued, "will go in of itself." The law's only function was to protect the "rights of minorities" by guaranteeing that religious exercises be entirely "voluntary." What Ruffner did, in anthropologist Clifford Geertz's terms, was to recognize the power of "religion as a cultural system." Geertz pointed to the power of religious symbols "to synthesize a people's ethos . . . and their world view—the picture they have of the way things in sheer actuality are, their most comprehensive ideas of order. In religious belief and practice, a group's ethos is rendered intellectually reasonable by being shown to represent a way of life adapted to the actual state of affairs the world view describes."[9] Ruffner's approach worked. Very informally but pervasively Virginians introduced what he termed "the religion of the people" into their public schools.[10] The very first issue of the *Virginia School Journal* in 1892 suggested a sample exercise for opening the school day. Teacher and students would alternate in reciting a psalm and then say the Lord's Prayer together.[11]

Such proposals did not pass unchallenged, however. Apart from those who preached what Ruffner derided as "the good old Bourbon doctrine" of completely private education—a system designed only for children of prosperous white families—some few voices articulated a different vision for the public schools. In the state capital Rabbi Edward Nathan Calisch of Congregation Beth Ahabah vigorously opposed Ruffner's perspective. Echoing his mentor, Rabbi Isaac Wise, Calisch viewed the public school as integral to the process of Americanization and foundational to the Republic. In an article he wrote for the *Virginia School Journal* in 1897 entitled "The Democracy of the Public Schools," the rabbi laid out his vision for public education. Calisch argued that for the schools to perform their primary task of education, they must be "essentially *public* schools . . . under public and secular control." Because they

Edward Nathan Calisch (1865–1946). (Beth Ahabah
Museum and Archives, Richmond, VA)

were designed for children of all faiths and supported by the entire populace, public schools should not introduce "even the simplest kind of religious exercise." Catholics had established their own schools, Calisch noted regretfully, because the religious instruction in public schools violated their beliefs. Other parents left their children in public education but "denied, contradicted and even ridiculed" the religious instruction the teachers offered, thus setting home and school, parents and teachers in opposition. No religious teaching or formation in the schools could satisfy all.

Church and state in America, he argued, had developed happily along parallel but separate paths. The division between them should not be broken down in public education. Religion belonged at home and in church or synagogue, not the schoolhouse. But all the children belonged in the public schools, and the whole community should give public education its moral as well as material support. In language that anticipated the thought of John Dewey, the rabbi praised the public schools as America's laboratories of democracy, offering to each new generation a level playing field with "equal opportunity" and without class distinctions. In his view the public school system was excellent, and he criticized an "aristocracy" that preferred "private institutes" and "academies" which set up class distinctions and differences among children at their most impressionable age.[12]

"The Great Protestant Pulpit of Virginia"

Calisch's piece represented a preliminary shot in a war about Bible reading that soon engulfed Virginia. Though it would be fought out state by state, the conflict was national, as John Kilgo, president of Trinity College in North Carolina, demonstrated in the spring of 1904. The bishops of the Methodist Episcopal Church, South, had sent Kilgo as a "fraternal delegate" to the General Conference of the Methodist Episcopal Church in Los Angeles. Kilgo's lengthy address to the northern and western portion of what had once been one denomination enumerated the serious issues confronting supporters of a Christian America in the new century. Among them "the school question" sounded alarm bells. He blamed Jefferson for introducing from France an infidelity that divorced religion from education. Now secularists were appealing to the U.S. Constitution and church-state separation to banish the Bible from the nation's classrooms and to eliminate religious exercises and instruction. "Orthodox" believers had just as much right to exert their influence on behalf of the country's welfare. "It is a national shame," Kilgo thundered, "to make American Christians the vassals of American infidels." The battle was joined, and the issue defined: "whether this nation shall be a Christian nation or a pagan nation."[13]

Kilgo may have had in mind a recent decision by the Nebraska Supreme Court that forbade Bible reading in the public schools when the teacher had a sectarian purpose in mind.[14]

In Virginia, Protestant clergymen in the Richmond area had organized a ministerial union to discuss matters of common interest. It provided the first battlefield. At a December meeting in 1903, Thomas Semmes, a highly respected Episcopal rector, presented a paper on "The Bible and the Public Schools." Referring to a New York newspaper editorial, the minister decried the contemporary assault on basic biblical teaching about the prophets, miracles, the Incarnation, and the Virgin Birth. He wanted the Bible not only read but taught in public schools. As the Richmond *News Leader* reported that afternoon, Semmes's paper provoked a "Spicy Debate" when two Baptist ministers challenged him on church-state grounds.[15] One of them, a senior pastor in the city, James B. Hawthorne, a decade earlier had denounced the American Protective Association for its nativism and anti-Catholicism. Hawthorne elaborated on his objections to Semmes's proposal at the next union gathering in January. Then on the following Sunday in a sermon that made front-page headlines, he reviewed the history of Virginia's struggle for religious liberty and charged the Episcopal minister with advocating an establishment of religion in violation of Virginia's constitution.[16]

The newspaper noted that numerous state legislators in the congregation paid close attention to the preacher's words. Their interest was no doubt related to a bill they were about to discuss during the current assembly session. James Cannon Jr., the future Methodist bishop who was already emerging as a major political and religious figure in Virginia, had helped draft a proposal to establish and fund public high schools in every county in the state. As the new editor of the *Baltimore and Richmond Christian Advocate*, he enthusiastically promised that "the great Protestant pulpit of Virginia can do more than any other one agency to arouse our people to their duty and their opportunity."[17] Though Cannon's bill did not become law for another two years, any expansion of the public school system inevitably resurrected the issue of religion in the schools. At the outset confusion reigned supreme over the terms of the argument. Gradually during the next month and a half, four alternative positions emerged: one of advocacy and three in opposition.[18]

In support of religion in the schools, Episcopal, Methodist, and Presbyterian ministers and writers urged varied combinations of Bible reading, religious instruction, and prayer in the schools. For example, Robert Strange, rector of St. Paul's Episcopal Church in downtown Richmond, argued for a half-hour daily service on the grounds that morality depended upon religion. He proposed that classes open with the recitation of the Lord's Prayer, the Apostles'

Creed, and the Ten Commandments. For the next fifteen minutes, the teacher should then read the Bible, without commentary. Those who objected to this regimen, including "the Hebrew," might keep their children at home until these exercises concluded. But such Christian instruction was essential for the "many children who are taught nothing at home and who do not go to church or Sunday school."[19]

Russell Cecil, pastor of Second Presbyterian Church, agreed that Bible reading and school prayer represented obvious values to be preserved and enhanced. But he also attacked the larger separationist argument on both practical and theoretical grounds. Accepting that viewpoint meant abolishing a range of current practices from military chaplaincies to prayers before legislative sessions. More important, because both state and church were founded by God and were necessarily interdependent, "an absolute and perfect separation of church and State" was both impossible and undesirable. An editorial in the *Central Presbyterian* agreed and detailed the concerns. While acknowledging that church-state separation was essential to individual rights and the "security and progress of true religion," it distinguished between the church and religion. The state's only responsibility for the church—"the organized religious life of any people"—was to protect its right to exist. But the government could not be separated from religion because the well-being and security of any state depended upon the moral values that religion taught. If the state took responsibility for education, it must necessarily include the Bible in the curriculum in order "that the fundamental character of the people shall not be ignored." People who objected to the scriptures being read in the schools could withdraw their children from that particular exercise.[20]

All the advocates of public school religious instruction offered panegyrics to the Bible as the best source of moral formation as well as other education. Perhaps Methodist minister H. E. Johnson was the most enthusiastic: "Is not Moses as really a historian as Macauly, or Luke as truly as Livy?" Another Methodist writer thought a nondenominational anthology along the lines of the "Jefferson Bible" should be published "as a text-book," though not everything in the good book was deemed appropriate for students' ears. Certain psalms and Solomon's Song of Songs should be sliced out, together with passages that lent themselves to controversy between the churches. Semmes agreed. He thought it critically important that the various denominations concur on a "'School Bible' containing the essential principles of religion and truth."[21]

Among the three forces opposing Semmes's proposal, the ultraconservative *Times-Dispatch* assumed the most regressive posture. In tones reminiscent of the old Virginia Bourbon leaders who had vigorously opposed Ruffner's entire educational program, this widely read newspaper considered the public school system "Socialistic" and "dangerous." Hence its editors warned against giving public schools any further responsibility beyond providing a basic education for the poor.[22] Perhaps these conservatives feared most that investing the public school system with the task of religious instruction might win them the kind of support that contemporary advocates of public secondary education needed.

The Baptist opposition was larger and more vocal. Initially it confused many people, including some Baptists. Richmond's *News Leader* editorialized against Hawthorne as if he had proposed excluding the Bible entirely and questioned the Baptist minister's consistency on the grounds that he absolutized religious liberty while supporting Sunday laws that offended Seventh-day Adventists and Jews. Frantic letters to the press expressed grave misgivings over his program to rid the classroom of the scriptures. But he had not opposed Bible reading. He only objected to placing it in the curriculum and expecting the teachers to become instructors in religion. Yet even some Baptists, always fiercely independent, also parted company with the Richmond preacher.[23]

The Baptists' *Religious Herald* attempted to correct the misunderstanding by pointing out that it had no objection to the common practice by which Virginia teachers read from the Bible before classes began and encouraged the pupils to "sing a cheerful hymn." The argument was whether "the teacher would be commissioned as an instructor in religious matters." The Baptist newspaper opposed "this new departure," while simultaneously questioning the charge that public schools were "godless."[24] Richmond's Baptist clergy also reinforced Hawthorne's position on voluntary Bible reading. "Mere reading without comment is not teaching," argued M. Ashby Jones, but teaching the Bible was teaching religion and hence was prohibited on church-state grounds. Jones also pointed out the problems inherent in state certification of religion teachers. Maintaining freedom of conscience in a pluralistic society was a huge challenge. In yet another Sunday sermon, the pastor of Grace Street Baptist Church, Dr. Charles Gardner, stated bluntly, "I do not believe the State is a suitable agency to teach religion."[25]

Rabbi Calisch would have certainly agreed, but he represented a third, quite different position. Though his brief published statement ignored the fact that the First Amendment at that time applied only to the federal government, not the states, it anticipated the interpretation of the federal Constitution that the U.S. Supreme Court adopted decades later: "The Constitution of the United States, and, consequently, of each State, provides that no appropriation shall be made for the maintenance or support of any form of religious belief. The reading of the Bible is a violation of the Constitution, when done in any institution, supported by public moneys. It is the first step toward the union of church and State, whose separation is the necessary condition of our republic's welfare and individual freedom." Unlike his fellow clergymen, Calisch insisted that any religious Bible reading in the public schools violated Jefferson's statute. The following summer in the *American Israelite*, he elaborated on his argument and urged his fellow Jews to support Jefferson's perspective, citing his letter to the Danbury Baptist Association. Church-state separation, Calisch wrote, is "the one great fundamental principle, whose insistence is the safeguard of our national ideals, and whose violation is the mother of innumerable evils."[26] No one else in the debate staked out so sweeping a position.

Because the Old Dominion's Protestant ministry remained divided, Semmes's proposal went nowhere.[27] Virginians eventually got their public high schools, but Bible reading, hymns, and prayers in schools stayed as Ruffner originally envisioned them: a matter of local option. Writing in 1911 in the *Virginia Journal of Education*, Willis Jenkins, the superintendent of schools in Newport News, argued that while church-state separation characterized higher civilizations, such a policy did not secularize the schools. Christian values and standards marked the educational environment and defined its objectives, including a broadly tolerant spirit that valued "the brotherhood of man" and respected the diversity of religious beliefs. "This is a Christian country," Jenkins wrote, but the formation of men and women of Christian character did not require a specific religious content in the instruction. "We read the Bible, we sing Christian songs, we recite the Lord's Prayer. . . . May the day never come when the public schools will want to do more."[28] The effort to do something more in the form of mandating scriptural reading touched off Virginia's second campaign for the Bible.

Trying to Avoid "National Apostasy"

When the city of Richmond opened its first public schools in 1869, the Bible was one of its required texts. In 1892 the Richmond schools attempted to develop "a more systematic course of moral training," but Bible reading remained a classroom staple until the city's school board decided to make scripture reading optional at the discretion of the teacher. Then, as the second semester opened in January 1913, the school board passed a resolution asking principals and teachers to begin each day with biblical selections from either the Hebrew or Christian scriptures. As that resolution was widely understood, Bible reading would now become compulsory in the capital's schools.[29]

According to the local Baptist press, the school board's action left Richmond "all agog."[30] On the following Friday evening in a sermon at Beth Ahabah, Rabbi Calisch protested strenuously. While acquitting the board of bad intentions, he argued that their action violated church-state separation and "the rights of the minority." Advocates of Bible reading had asserted that parents could always withdraw their children if they found it objectionable. But the rabbi fingered the problem that later Supreme Courts would find persuasive: "What right has any one to subject any child in the public schools to embarrassment and to humiliation in thus marking it off and separating it from its school fellows?" Insisting that "the public school is the very heart of our democracy" and "the citadel of republican principles," Calisch appealed to "the sense of fair play and of justice" in Virginia and cited the state's history of religious freedom, Madison's writings, and Jefferson's statute. He told his congregation that he expected the support of Baptists and others; but even if no one else objected to the board's resolution, "we cannot silently and supinely permit this encroachment upon our constitutional rights as citizens, or upon our religious convictions as Jews."[31]

The rabbi's protest made front-page headlines on Saturday. On Sunday morning some Protestant preachers used their sermons to defend the board's action. At the Seventh Street Christian Church, the Reverend Hugh David Cathcart Maclachlan, one of Richmond's most progressive pastors, respected highly for his ecumenical outreach, likened the abandonment of the Bible to "a species of national apostasy." Morality, religion, and literature—indeed, "the welfare of the nation"—demanded that the scriptures be read to the next generations. This could be done in a nonsectarian fashion by simply reading the text without interpretation. The minister concluded his sermon, which was extensively quoted in Monday's press, by invoking the maxim "The safety of the people is the supreme law." In his view, "Judged by that standard, the Bible is the one essential book which we as a nation must never cease to reverence and love."[32]

The city's Methodist ministers, claiming to represent over 10,000 adherents in Richmond, also endorsed the board's resolution. The Bible taught those qualities crucial for republican citizenship urged by articles fifteen and sixteen of Virginia's own Declaration of Rights; namely, "justice, moderation, temperance, frugality and virtue" along with "Christian forbearance, love and charity." Reading the scripture, therefore, would instill "a spirit of patriotism" in the children.[33] In the Methodist *Christian Advocate*, editor James Cannon suggested that those who opposed the resolution were free to move elsewhere, a position that Robert Pitt, editor of the Baptist newspaper, the *Religious Herald*, found incredible as he reminded his readers in mid-February of the treatment Baptists had experienced in the Revolutionary era.[34]

As the initial congratulations poured in to the school board's offices, Calisch stood virtually alone. And he stood by his principled beliefs. He made no effort to placate his opponents or soften the impact of his words. In a sermon prepared for a service on the eve of the feast of the Atonement, the rabbi spoke about various kinds of hypocrisy, including those "sects and societies who are trying to insist upon their Bible being read in the public schools, who wish to regulate the curricula of schools and colleges and institutions of learning, to bar the teaching of any thought or theory they do not believe in." Under the guise of religion, they operated as political pressure groups to impose their views upon the rest of society. For the twenty years he had served in Virginia, Calisch had maintained a consistent position on the school question: the educational system should be open to all and free of any religious instruction, exercises, or bias. What was appropriate to the home and the place of worship did not belong in schools that were open to all regardless of religious affiliation or no affiliation.[35]

Calisch remained in isolation until the following Sunday when George White McDaniel mounted his pulpit at First Baptist Church and strenuously supported the rabbi's stance. Born in Texas and educated at Baylor University, the dynamic preacher had served two Texas churches before accepting a call to Richmond's premier Baptist pulpit in 1905. McDaniel objected to the board's resolution on church-state grounds. His sermon, published in Monday's *Times-Dispatch*, pointed out the violation of Virginia's Bill of Rights and Jefferson's statute in paying teachers out of state funds and compelling them to read the Bible. Echoing Calisch, McDaniel also made a plea for minority rights. The next day the rabbi thanked the minister warmly. "It is what I would have expected of you," he wrote, "that a voice such as yours should be lifted up in the cause of justice and freedom of conscience."[36]

Calisch thought McDaniel's sermon would cause people to think twice about the issues at stake, and he was confident that their views would prevail. But the two men were swimming against the tide. Endorsements for the board's action poured in from the Federation of Mothers' Clubs of Richmond, the Bible Society of Virginia, the Ministerial Association of the Disciples of Christ, the Episcopal clergy, Bible classes in Episcopal, Methodist, and Baptist churches, and various civic organizations.[37] Later that month some two thousand members of the Junior Order of United American Mechanics and the Daughters of Liberty celebrated Washington's Birthday at the city auditorium with speeches supporting the board's resolution. The press reported that a "pleasing feature" of the evening was a "tableau, struck by two little girls and one boy, carrying the Bible and a large American flag," which the presiding officer proclaimed "the two fundamentals of our civilization."[38]

Though the *Religious Herald* supported McDaniel's views, not all Baptist ministers followed suit. His most notable challenger was Beverly Lacy Hoge of Emmanuel Baptist. An elderly man—he was seventy-six to McDaniel's thirty-

George White McDaniel (1875–1927). (Virginia Baptist
Historical Society, University of Richmond)

seven—from a venerated Virginia family of Baptist preachers, Hoge wanted
the Bible read in the schools as a textbook for history, literature, and morality. The Baptist Ministers' Conference of Richmond initially sat on the fence
because of another concern. At issue was the exact meaning of the word "requested" in the board's resolution. Was this an order, or did it actually leave
Bible reading as it had been before, up to the teacher?[39]

Meanwhile, an undaunted Calisch lined up further support and asked the
school board for a special session to discuss objections to its resolution. At a
crowded evening meeting on March 6, Henry Robinson Pollard, Richmond's
city attorney and a Baptist layman, introduced the four speakers: McDaniel,
Calisch, Pitt of the *Religious Herald*, and Samuel Weatherby, a Unitarian minister. In a formal statement to the board, the Richmond Baptist Ministers' Con-

ference, two Baptist churches, and Congregation Beth Ahabah protested that the board, as a state agency, had exceeded its legitimate authority in mandating religious services in the schools. They asked the board "to reconsider and rescind the resolution." At the end of the meeting, however, more commendations were read into the board's minutes, principally from Methodist and Presbyterian ministers' associations. Still more individuals, churches, and organizations registered approval at the board's regular meetings in March and April. So it did not retract its resolution; Calisch and McDaniel lacked the votes.[40] Meanwhile, in the *Christian Advocate*, editor James Cannon expressed amazement that fear of a church-state "Union" had brought forth such an unlikely alliance as "a Jewish rabbi, a Unitarian preacher, and some Baptist clergymen," when a much greater danger, the "invasion of the Roman Catholic Church," presented itself. Protestants should unite against that threat instead of working to prevent "the reading of God's Word—the reading of which is the surest hope of continued religious liberty."[41]

But simple daily scripture readings did not satisfy the more zealous advocates of the religious education movement that was gathering steam in Virginia and across the nation in the second decade of the twentieth century.[42] From its perspective, the survival of democracy required moral citizens, yet the church-state roadblock inevitably stymied efforts to incorporate religious education into the public school curriculum. Religious educators offered different theoretical answers to the problem while various states and cities experimented widely. Some including Calisch favored teaching the Bible as a work of literature, which McDaniel abhorred as trivializing the word of God.[43] Others thought it possible to find in the scriptures elements of a common faith which the public schools could then teach.[44] Yet another group argued that teachers were more important than the disciplines they taught, that the right methodology and proper example could transform any subject, even mathematics or physical education, into religious education.[45]

Like some other states, Virginia attempted yet another alternative: offering public high school credit for optional courses in the Bible. Under the direction of the state board of education in 1916, a committee chaired by William M. Forrest, professor of biblical history and literature at the University of Virginia, and composed of seven religious leaders and educators including Rabbi Calisch and a Catholic priest drew up syllabi for three courses, two in the Hebrew scriptures and one in the Christian scriptures. Though syllabi and exams were limited to biblical history and literature, teachers were free "to bring out moral and spiritual applications" if they wished. The board did not prescribe requirements for the instructors. They might be clergymen, public school or Sunday school teachers, or someone specially hired by the churches. Classes were held in church buildings, private homes, or anywhere outside the public schools; but the tests were given with the ordinary exams in each school, and the state reviewed the grades. The program grew steadily from one class with twenty-seven students in the first year, 1916–17, to forty classes with 933 students in 1923–24. Yet even then it reached only a fraction of Virginia's high school students.[46] And fewer than 10 percent of the white student population went on to high school.

"Mixed Up in Politics"

But if the campaign for the Bible and religion in the public schools seemed to falter in the second decade of the twentieth century, at least some of its supporters had achieved a signal triumph on another evangelical front: Prohibition. For James Cannon Jr. rum presented an even bigger threat than Rome. In the second decade of the twentieth century, as the leader of the Anti-Saloon League and then a newly minted bishop of the Methodist Episcopal Church, Cannon became a national figure. He reached the apogee of his influence in Virginia in 1916 when a statewide referendum endorsed Prohibition, and the General Assembly passed the Mapp Act outlawing the sale of intoxicating beverages. It was a signal triumph for evangelical clergy like Cannon who had helped draft the legislation and McDaniel who had lent his voice at Prohibition rallies. Within three years the country would launch the "noble experiment" with the passage of the Eighteenth Amendment and then agonize for the next decade over its enforcement.[47]

Prohibition created warm alliances between evangelical preachers and politicians who actively sought their endorsement. Such cozy relationships suggested to a "wet" newspaper like the *Times-Dispatch* that an "ecclesiastical despotism" was in the making.[48] McDaniel clearly relished his political involvement. Among the Old Dominion's political leaders, he counted Governor E. Lee Trinkle, U.S. Senator Claude A. Swanson, and state Senator Harry Flood Byrd as his friends.[49] Prohibition enforcement—"this great moral issue," as the Baptist pastor styled it—drove McDaniel's dislike for Governor Westmoreland Davis and his support for Trinkle in the 1921 gubernatorial primary.[50] And with Swanson in particular he developed strong political ties. The clergyman wrote the victor after Swanson had defeated Davis in the Senate primary election: "I rejoice with you over your signal and well-deserved victory. It was the most complete triumph I ever witnessed. . . . I hope you have eliminated from public life a petifog and demagogue."[51] For their part, politicians like Trinkle enthusiastically embraced the rhetoric and political causes of evangelical Protestantism. A recently obscure state senator from southwestern Virginia, Trinkle defeated an able and popular congressman from Lexington for the Democratic Party nomination in 1921, leading a South Carolina journalist to pun, "Trinkle, Trinkle, Little Star, How we wonder who you are."

Trinkle had stars on his mind, too. In his fulsomely pious "Christmas Message" for 1923 delivered "by invitation" at Frederick Chenault's Broad Street Methodist Church, Governor Trinkle retold the story of the Star of Bethlehem and the three wise men, blended Christianity with the founding of Virginia and America, and concluded with a gubernatorial blessing: "May the grace of God, which passeth all understanding abide with America, with Virginia and with the world. And may the torch of truth, lit by the gospels and made perfect in Christ, still lead us on to higher and to better things."[52] Jefferson must have spun in his grave.

The "dry" crusade was only the best-known effort for the moral reform of the state and nation. There were numerous others, and the price the Virginia clergy paid was their personal injection into politics. Some relished the combat it afforded. Cannon regularly occupied a seat on the floor of the legislature during the debates over the Mapp Act, a practice that other clergy also adopted for their pet causes. Not all legislators were happy with such clerical preferment in the assembly. In 1930 an outraged delegate from Norfolk finally demanded the House enforce its rules regarding lobbyists and eject Chenault, the feisty pastor of Broad Street Methodist Church, for campaigning on the floor against changes he had proposed in the state's boxing statutes.[53] Cannon had a tough hide that enabled him to engage in conflicts that daunted others, but not all clergy enjoyed the rough and tumble of politics. John Vines, pastor of First Baptist Church in Roanoke, came to Richmond to lobby for the antigambling bill in 1924. After strenuous efforts, the measure finally passed the House, but the Senate provoked an even tougher fight. Vines wrote afterwards that the committee chairman "seemed called of God or the devil to do all in his power to becloud and intimidate or question every man who dared speak against gambling." He left the capital convinced that some lawmakers were "consecrated to the ruin of law." The more astute McDaniel, however, shepherded an alternative bill through the Senate and later wrote Vines about the difficulties of dealing with such political questions: "One who had watched the Legislature through the years knows that there are many slips and tricks and that scarcely anything can be taken for granted."[54]

It was not always clear what role government should play in dealing with the "moral questions" that preoccupied the evangelical clergy and their lay allies. The issue of censorship, for example, intensified with the arrival of motion pictures. Thomas Dixon, author of *The Clansman*, on which D. W. Griffith based *The Birth of a Nation*, was "deeply grieved" when Virginia passed a censorship bill. "The country is hell bent and hell bound in its futile reform legislation," the former Baptist minister complained to Samuel Adams, a state legislator. "Virginia rebelled against George III and put 'Sic Semper Tyrannis' in their crest for less than your bill has done to the authors of Virginia." Adams passed Dixon's letter along to McDaniel, congratulating him on a "dressing down" he had afforded Dixon and the leadership he had provided in the "moving Picture Censorship fight." The minister in reply praised Adams as "a force for righteousness in the Legislature" and asked his help in combating criticism he had received from the *Roanoke World News*.[55] Outraged by "nude illustrations" advertising plays, the *Methodist* urged the "secular press" to change their policies: "If Venus comes to town, let her be shown in a decent garb or cut her out."[56]

The list of concerns grew throughout the decade. Worried about the rising divorce rate in the mid-1920s, the Board of Temperance and Social Reform for the Virginia Conference of Methodist clergymen condemned "the use of methods or instruments" of "contraception" as "one of the greatest moral dangers now threatening the human race." The board "heartily" urged the state's assembly to pass a law "to prevent the manufacture, sale or use of such instruments."[57] But if birth control distressed some clergy, forced sterilization did not. In the flush of progressive reform, the Baptist General Association of Virginia in 1913 passed a resolution that marriage should be restricted to those who were "mentally and physically fit" in order to "strengthen the home as a bulwark of morals and health." Writing to Walter Russell Bowie, the youthful liberal rector of St. Paul's Episcopal Church in Richmond, McDaniel averred that it was insufficient for ministers simply to refuse to marry couples who failed to meet this requirement; he wanted such "wise legislation" written into law.[58]

Urged on by Governor Trinkle, the 1924 legislature overwhelmingly passed two bills: the Racial Integrity Act forbidding interracial marriages and an act "for the sexual sterilization of inmates of State institutions" who suffered from conditions such as retardation, epilepsy, and mental illness. That law had the active support of Methodist minister Joseph Mastin, the outstanding leader in the reform of Virginia's public welfare system and author of *Mental Defectives in Virginia*. No religious opposition to the eugenics movement surfaced in Virginia as the Old Dominion led the way right behind California in the number of sterilizations.[59]

Sunday closing laws were another regular matter of contention before the assembly. Luther Jenkins, a Richmond businessman and member of McDaniel's First Baptist Church, wondered "how 'blue' our laws should be" and thought the issue would provoke "continual fights" in the legislature. He found the whole thing tedious. Jenkins would happily turn such arguments over to the clergy as well as the women who were "electioneering and working around the polls."

Religious composition of Richmond, Virginia, in 1924

Richmond population, 1924: 188,000		
Racial composition, 1924: 67% white; 30% African American; 3% other		
Denomination	No. of churches	No. of members
Baptist	29	22,724
Methodist	26	15,276
Presbyterian	24	11,000
Episcopal	26	7,808
Disciples of Christ	8	3,184
Catholic	11	10,000+[a]
Jewish	4 synagogues	Not stated

Source: "Town and City Church Questionnaire," 1924, George McDaniel Papers, Virginia Baptist Historical Society, University of Richmond.

[a] In addition there is a record of 10 Catholic schools, 53 teachers, and approximately 1,905 students.

Richmond's "foreign element" wanted the Sunday laws altered, but the Baptist businessman thought it a mistake to permit the cities to do whatever they wanted and expressed his opposition to various legislators. He liked the comfortable old Virginia system with the "Sundays we have always enjoyed in Richmond."[60] For the clergy that meant enforcing the Sunday ban on professional baseball and keeping the golf courses and public athletic fields closed. When an effort was made in 1926 to permit such activities after two o'clock on Sunday afternoon, a bevy of ministers appeared before a Senate committee to oppose any change in the law. The Reverend William S. Sullivan, editor of the *Presbyterian of the South* in Richmond and a representative of the Lord's Day Alliance, denounced the very idea that "the State" would "barter away the morals of its young people." This was but an opening wedge for "Sunday movies." Methodist minister Thomas Reeves of Norfolk and Portsmouth repeated Jenkins's change that this effort came from a "foreign element" in those cities. "We can't have the old Sabbath and also a new one," he warned. "We must choose between the two."[61]

Some laity shared the clergy's perspective. For example, Delegate Samuel Adams angrily disapproved of proposals that would allow Jews and Seventh-day

Adventists to work on Sunday or "the loafing and dissipated" to "play baseball, or any other game they please." This was an issue that a city council could resolve. Norfolk, perhaps because of its ethnic mix, supported an "open Sunday" policy; but when Mayor John Bright vetoed that idea for Richmond, Adams was delighted. We must "hold things together," the Halifax County legislator advised McDaniel, "until people get back to the old paths, from which they seem to have been switched during the World War."[62]

McDaniel trod a fine line. As the most important Baptist minister in the state, he was continually asked for his advice on such matters by both clergy and laity and called to testify before legislative committees on a range of social issues including divorce, censorship, and Prohibition enforcement.[63] But while maintaining a consistent witness to the benefits of Prohibition and supporting Sunday closing laws and movie censorship, he knew his limitations. In 1926 a Baptist pastor wrote to ask his support for a bill pending in the legislature that would forbid fishing on Sunday. During the summer months young people came out "for fishing and frolicking." He complained this was "demoralizing" the younger members of his flock. Another correspondent explained that "car loads" arrived with "whiskey and other drink, and spend the day in fishing and carousing." Their activities had spawned a whole new Sunday enterprise. Moreover, "the women strip almost to the skin and go in bathing in public with men." The young males were flocking on Sundays "just to see these naked women," and it was devastating their "morals."[64] McDaniel promised to do what he could, but he held out little hope for the bill. The city pastor was not as alarmed as his confreres in rural Virginia. He had a robust affection for the next generation. When asked for his view of social dancing, he replied that he thought "some ministers destroy their influence with young people by Puritanical views." He saw no problem with dancing, had gone to dances himself when he was growing up, and thought it had not harmed him. "Dancing with young people," wrote the genial minister, "is like measles with children—they have it and get over it." And he concluded with this warning: "I know some preachers who have absolutely destroyed their ability to win young people because of narrowness. You mustn't be little."[65]

McDaniel was also a leader in social outreach. When some in Richmond objected to the care of delinquent girls in a private home, he, Maclachlan, and some others went to the assembly for help. The Baptist minister recognized the difficulties he faced with conservative politicians concerned that their constituents' neighborhoods might be sheltering the wrong sort of people. As McDaniel wrote a fellow pastor and close friend in Kentucky, "When you get mixed up with politics the result is uncertain and often unsatisfactory." It turned out happily, however, when the state assumed responsibility for the home.[66] Writing in 1922 to the preacher and writer A. C. Dixon, with whom he was about to exchange pulpits, McDaniel described his own congregation while tactfully advising fundamentalism's major spokesman to avoid the religious controversies that preoccupied the 1920s: "You will find our people sound in the faith—with little interest in questions of evolution and eschatology. They love the gospel that warms the Christian heart, inspires to higher living, incites to Christian service, and that saves lost souls." It was an apt summation of the evangelical minister that McDaniel embodied and the reason that the Southern Baptist Convention chose him as its president in 1924.[67]

"Moral and Religious Instruction"

That year he had a tough fight with members of the General Assembly over an antigambling bill. In that contest, however, he could draw upon the support of groups like the Women's Law Enforcement League. Writing in approval of a sermon the preacher had given against slot machines, a leader in that organization offered McDaniel its services. "We are banded together to wage war against every kind of vice," she wrote, "and we intend to work without limitation to lift humanity."[68]

Lifting humanity in evangelical America invariably involved the Bible. Amid the various moral crusades of the era, the push for compulsory Bible reading in the public schools gained new force across Virginia. In early March 1924 the lower house of the assembly overwhelmingly passed, 83 to 5, a bill to require the daily reading of five verses of the King James version of the scriptures. If a teacher or school administrator should ignore or prevent such reading, anyone could bring disciplinary charges to the local school board. Though the single Jewish member in the House, Israel Brown of Norfolk, and a few other delegates warned that the measure violated Jefferson's statute as embedded in the state constitution, its advocates argued that the Bible's moral teaching had universal applicability. Teachers were explicitly forbidden to add their own comments, and children whose parents objected would be excused.[69]

In support of the bill, the *Virginia Journal of Education* that month carried a brief article entitled "Moral and Religious Instruction in the Public Schools," by Herman Harrell Horne. A distinguished professor of the history and philosophy of education at New York University, Horne was an exponent of an idealist philosophy in opposition to John Dewey's pragmatism. His numerous books advocating Christian education included *Jesus: The Master Teacher*. In his *Virginia Journal* article, Professor Horne distinguished between "education," which "appeals to the emotions and will, as well as the intellect," and "instruction," which "appeals to the intellect." The public school should provide religious education in the forms of Bible reading, "common prayer," and "hymns of worship." But religious instruction or communicating "religious ideas in instructional form" was inappropriate. "The American public school excludes the letter of religious instruction," he argued, "but makes room for the spirit of religious education." Indeed, the latter was essential because democracy and Christianity were mutually supportive. "Democracy is the right of each to the best. Christianity is the right to become children of God. So democracy is Christianity in social relationships and Christianity is democracy in religion."[70]

McDaniel had been traveling in the Northeast when the Bible bill passed the House of Delegates in 1924. Until then, his major concern that session had been an antigambling measure that he had helped guide through the assembly. During the decade since the fight over the Richmond School Board's resolution, the Baptist preacher had grown in statute not only in Virginia but throughout the United States as a vocal advocate for enforcing Prohibition, strengthening the Sunday laws, and general moral reform. In February the Kilgrapp of the local Ku Klux Klan commended his efforts to "clean up" the city and pledged him the "hearty support" of a thousand Richmond Knights. His Baptist brethren appreciated his leadership, as a Portsmouth minister wrote him in early 1925, "not only in denominational affairs, but in moral reforms in our native state."[71]

Now the Baptist leader disappointed some of his evangelical friends as he swung into action against the Bible bill. He would need all the help he could summon to defeat or postpone it in the Senate. Writing in the *Religious Herald*, he argued the case for church-state separation based on the right to religious freedom, which he claimed as "a Baptist trophy." Baptists had been divided during the Richmond School Board fight, and the opposition he faced now was even more formidable. In April a Baptist preacher out in Wheeling, West Virginia, complimented McDaniel on his courageous stand and observed that sentiment there was running fifty to one against him.[72] When the Senate deferred action on the bill in 1924, the issue moved out of the assembly and provoked statewide controversy. In Harry Byrd's campaign for governor the next year, his opponent attacked his vote against the Bible bill in the state Senate.[73] Since the assembly met only every other year, 1926 would be definitive.

All through 1925 the Bible forces gathered strength. The trial of John Scopes in Tennessee over the teaching of evolution reinforced their anxieties and strengthened their resolve. Presbyterians, Episcopalians, and especially Methodists were vocal supporters, with the last group urging that the Bible should be taught and not just read in the public schools. How else to protect the next generation from the teaching of evolution?[74] Writing in the *Virginia Journal of Education*, the head of the English department at Petersburg High School reported the results of a questionnaire on biblical knowledge drawn up by the

Virginia Sunday School Association. Seventy Petersburg seniors had taken the exam. Appalled by their ignorance, he urged that public schools should teach the Bible and get over "the great bugaboo" and "terror" of violating separation of church and state. The teachers could explain the scripture's literary and ethical dimensions, he proposed, without dabbling in denominational doctrines.[75]

The state's educational establishment agreed. In December the *Virginia Journal* advertised *Old Testament Readings for Schools*, included a poem entitled "The Indwelling God" by the well-known Unitarian minister Frederick Lucian Hosmer, and published the "Suggestions" of Principal Lindsay Crawley to the teachers in his Appomattox schools. They included: "Require attendance of all pupils for physical training and worship."[76] That month the Methodist Conference press for the Danville District criticized the Virginia Baptist Convention for failing to support Bible reading in Virginia's public schools. "Its exclusion is by no means helpful to the Christian children of our State," the *Methodist* warned. Indeed, the pervasive threat of "modernism" demanded the Bible. When the local Baptist pastor pointed out that the concern was the word *compulsory*, the *Methodist* fired back that compulsion was not such a bad thing "if it be necessary to secure the reading of the Bible to the school children of our State."[77]

"Religion Is a Voluntary Act"

After his election as president of the Southern Baptist Convention in 1924, McDaniel initially felt constrained to take a less public stance in the upcoming battle over the Bible; and his mantle descended upon Robert Pitt, a close friend and ally and the longtime editor of the *Religious Herald*. Baptist unity was of paramount importance, but not all the pastors were of one mind on the issue. Pitt was concerned. Together with two other ministers, he selected a committee of thirty-six members, one from each of the twenty-nine district associations of Baptists in the state plus a few at-large delegates. On behalf of the General Association of Virginia Baptists, they would present a memorial at the next session of the legislature. Respecting McDaniel's reluctance to become involved publicly, Pitt enlisted Martha Scarborough McDaniel to serve in place of her husband.[78]

But the Old Dominion's leading Baptist preacher could not remain silent for long. In a Sunday sermon on January 31, 1926, he characterized the supporters of the Bible bill as "Sincere, But Wrong" in thinking that such a law would help the progress of Christianity. "Religion is a voluntary act," he insisted, "or it is not religion." McDaniel also coached Pitt on strategy, suggesting that his committee identify influential individuals, Baptists and non-Baptists, in each senator's district and ask them to put pressure on their representatives. He thought the bill should fail in committee before reaching a vote in either the House or the Senate. Writing to another minister, he urged him to contact a friend in the Senate who had supported the bill in 1924. McDaniel thought Rabbi Calisch had somehow offended the senator during the 1924 committee hearings. But from the Baptist leader's perspective, the Jewish opposition was only incidental; he was concerned about "the principle" at stake.[79]

Harry Byrd began his term as Virginia's governor on February 1, 1926. A few days later, after Senator John May Parsons, a Methodist from Grayson County in the rural Southwest, introduced Bill No. 138 "to provide for the reading of the King James Version of the Holy Bible in the public free schools," Pitt's committee presented the Baptist memorial that John Garland Pollard had drafted. The former delegate to the constitutional convention of 1901–2 and former attorney general was now the director and a professor at the William and Mary School of Law.[80] In eight carefully crafted paragraphs, the petition reviewed the multiple ways in which the Bible bill violated Virginia's constitutional guarantees of religious freedom embodied in the sixteenth article of the Declaration of Rights and Jefferson's statute. Echoing James Madison's *Memorial and Remonstrance* and the many petitions their Baptist predecessors had submitted during the fight over general assessment in 1784 and 1785, Pollard's work insisted that religion did not need "the strong arm of the law." The conclusion asked the legislature "to adhere to the doctrine, peculiarly bound up with the history of this Commonwealth, which completely separates church and state, which refused to exercise force in the realm of religion, and which places all religions on a plane of absolute equality before the law."[81]

The battle was now joined. Letters to the editor of the *Times-Dispatch* argued either that the state desperately needed the moral tone that Bible reading in the public schools would promote or, alternatively, that the bill represented "the first logical step to a State church."[82] The *Times-Dispatch* and the *News Leader* and most of the secular press eventually opposed the bill. Meanwhile, Senator Parsons reported that he had never had such an influx of mail and calls from all sorts of groups and individuals supporting it.[83] The issue came to a climax at a crowded hearing before a Senate committee on February 25, 1926. George E. Booker, presiding elder of the Methodist district and former Richmond pastor, commanded the advocacy forces and expressed his horror that such a complete "Fundamentalist" as McDaniel should be found on the other side. Pitt represented the Baptist committee. McDaniel, after rebutting the arguments of Booker and his team, spoke against the measure in forceful, sometimes colloquial, terms. While urging all present to study the scriptures daily, he pointed to the principles of religious freedom and equality at stake, the blessings conferred by the church-state separation required by Jefferson's statute, and the potential the bill had for harming both teachers and students. Immediately after hearing the speakers, the Senate committee in executive session voted 10 to 4 to postpone the bill indefinitely.[84]

The "Noble Principle"

Rabbi Calisch also had spoken in opposition, but his presence and contribution were scarcely noticed in the press. The past few years had been a difficult period for the rabbi and his congregation in Richmond. Decreased attendance at Sabbath services had finally forced the question of whether to hold a service on Sunday. After some agonizing, Calisch had agreed with his congregation's affirmative vote in the hopes that this "departure" from Jewish practice would "bring these people back—that their interest in the faith would be revived."[85] It was difficult to buck the tide in the Bible Belt.

Ignoring Calisch's consistent position, the *Times-Dispatch* hailed "the Baptist church in Virginia" and singled out Pitt and McDaniel. Congratulations poured into the preacher's home from Baptists and non-Baptists alike, and newspapers such as the *Baltimore Sun* and the *Columbus Enquirer* republished his Senate committee address.[86] But what some admirers missed, and McDaniel promptly corrected, was that he had not opposed Bible reading in the schools but "*compulsory* reading . . . in the public schools or anywhere else." So long as it was "voluntary," the community was "homogeneous," and no one's "conscience" was violated, McDaniel had no objection to the Virginia practice.[87] It would continue, as Ruffner had anticipated, along with prayers and hymn singing in the state's public schools and elsewhere across the nation until the 1960s. In this respect, McDaniel's position was not so far removed from the views of his Protestant opponents who thought the Bible and prayers belonged in the schoolhouse, along with the flag and the Pledge of Allegiance. But his victory in the legislature reinforced the policy that Ruffner had articulated fifty years earlier for reconciling two of Virginia's most powerful symbols: the Bible and Jefferson's statute.

Calisch would object, but his was a lonely voice in an evangelical Protestant culture. Speaking at a bicentennial celebration of George Washington's birthday in 1932, the rabbi forcefully condemned "the fundamentalist mind," which he claimed dominated "all organized religion." By insisting on "sectarian religious instruction" and forbidding the teaching of evolution, it controlled the nation's public schools. Fundamentalism brought the Bible into the classroom either by law or by the "connivance of local authorities." The United States needed to reclaim the "noble principle of the separation of church and state." Two years later, writing in the *Times-Dispatch*, Calisch noted that while the U.S. Constitution enshrined that principle, it was "often honored in the breach."[88] Elsewhere he called the efforts to take religion into the schools "purblind fanaticism."[89]

But such efforts continued unabated. By 1938 sixteen counties in Virginia had so-called released-time programs in which teachers selected by the local clergy came into the classroom during the school day for a course entitled "Adventures in Christian Living." When the *Virginia Journal of Education* presented a forum on such instruction, the head of the Virginia Education Association asked the rabbi for his views. They had not changed in forty years. Calling the schools "the cradles of our American Democracy," Calisch decried the violation of church-state separation. Classes in Protestant Christianity resulted in "differences, dissension and disunity," among the students, produced "an atmosphere of class distinctions," and discriminated against the minority faiths. Religious training belonged at "home and church," not in the public schools. A few weeks after Pearl Harbor, the Richmond school superintendent called on Calisch for his opinions of a released-time program as well as the opening school exercises in one of the elementary schools that included the Lord's Prayer. In his response the rabbi tactfully pointed out the constitutional issue at stake in teaching religion in the schools. He could tolerate the informal "custom" of a prayer at the beginning of the school day or the reading of a psalm or a selection from the Sermon on the Mount only because no official policy authorized or directed it.[90] The rabbi knew that the evangelicals controlled the politics in both Richmond and the state.

The "Dark Cloud" of "Romanism"

Catholics discovered that reality a decade earlier when Bishop Cannon and the "political parsons," as Senator Carter Glass referred to them, enjoyed their last hurrah at the defeat of Al Smith in the presidential election of 1928.[91] Being both "wet" and Catholic was too much to overcome for the four-term governor of New York. To even the most tolerant of Protestant preachers in Virginia, Catholics had been a suspect breed for decades. In the spring of 1917, McDaniel preached a sermon on "The Methods of Romanism" that was widely disseminated and fanned fears of Catholicism's influence in government.[92] "Romanism is certainly a dark cloud that overhangs our fair America," wrote an appreciative correspondent in mid-July.[93] That cloud became a thunderstorm in the 1920s. Individuals like Cannon and groups like the Junior Order of Mechanics and the Ku Klux Klan warned regularly about the danger of Catholicism to American liberties, but so few Catholics existed in Virginia that it hardly seemed worthwhile to get much bothered about their presence. Then in 1925 John Michael Purcell, a Roman Catholic, won the Democratic primary for the office of state treasurer, and tocsins sounded. Never before in the history of Virginia had a Catholic appeared on a statewide ballot. Thanks to the Klan, Purcell had a much closer race than the other Democrats on the ticket headed by Byrd. That election identified religion as an issue in Virginia and forecast problems for Al Smith, the leading contender for the 1928 Democratic nomination.[94]

Fears of a Roman takeover intensified when the Catholics held a massive Eucharistic Congress in Chicago in the summer of 1926. Ever alert to the mixing of church and state, McDaniel preached a sermon attacking the "Obeisance" paid to the papal delegation by New York City's mayor and New York State's governor and wrote several essays for the religious press warning against the errors of Catholicism.[95] As Al Smith's candidacy became imminent, the Baptist pastor publicly criticized the Catholic politician in a letter to the editor of the *Atlanta Constitution* for "his stand on prohibition, his inexperience in national and international affairs," his association with Tammany Hall, but especially "his publicly demonstrated devotions to a foreign potentate who claims temporal power over all the rulers of the earth." McDaniel found the idea of "a dual allegiance . . . insufferable in the presidency of the United States."[96] As the country geared up for that election, McDaniel wrote an essay for the *Western Recorder*, the official newspaper of Kentucky Baptists, citing papal statements and Catholic textbooks and pointing out the "preponderance" of Catholics already working in the federal government.[97]

Many Protestants shared the pastor's concerns. But what was most striking about the 1928 election in Virginia was not the opposition Smith encountered from Protestant pastors or his eventual loss to Hoover but the strong support the nominee received from Democratic officeholders and politicians across the state. In stinging terms Pollard blistered Bishop Cannon, while Senators Swanson and Glass and especially Governor Byrd reminded Virginians of Jefferson's statute and the tradition of religious liberty in the Old Dominion.[98] The election rhetoric underlined that history, and the tradition embedded in the statute had become a legacy. Whether honored or violated, Jefferson's work remained. In the coming decades the U.S. Supreme Court would broaden that legacy from Virginia to the United States as it interpreted the First Amendment.

EPILOGUE

In applying the Statute for Establishing Religious Freedom, nineteenth-century Virginians anticipated the U.S. Supreme Court and seized on Jefferson's metaphor of a "wall of separation" to explain their own efforts to keep government and religion apart. By the Civil War, however, even a casual observer could see that the gentry used the statute's language to bolster their continuing control over the church, an overweening lay authority analogous to that enjoyed by their forefathers throughout the colonial period. Constructing a wall in antebellum Virginia invariably discriminated against the churches.

In the name of strict separation, Virginia's government withheld those neutral aids the churches needed to function as independent, autonomous entities in society. By refusing to recognize in law the existence of either the churches or their agencies and denying them corporate status, the assembly denied civil equality to those persons and groups and discriminated against them precisely on the basis of religion. From the churches' perspective, this policy obstructed their efforts and ability to raise funds, construct buildings, establish institutions, maintain works of charity, educate their clergy and adherents, and carry out missionary activities. Ironically, in light of the common perception that Jefferson's statute guaranteed "full religious freedom and separation of church and state," churches and religious groups were less free in the Old Dominion than anywhere else in the Union.

Thus in its application the statute penalized communal religious life and practice. Some of this changed after the Civil War as ever so gradually the church-state relationship evolved in a Protestant evangelical context. The constitutional convention of 1901 provided a stunning example. Baptist preacher-delegate Wayland Dunaway almost single-handed turned back the movement to permit the incorporation of churches by speaking long and eloquently against any public support for sectarian institutions and in favor of the strictest separation. But when the issue of taxing churches and parsonages came to the floor, he backpedaled vigorously. Tax exemptions should remain. The welfare of the commonwealth depended upon religion, so the government, he argued, should recognize it and support it.[1]

Most Virginians then and many Americans today would agree. The expanding culture of evangelical Protestantism made this development possible by embracing Jefferson's statute for the freedom it provided to mold a Christian America. Superintendent Ruffner's policy of accommodating prayer in the public schools embodied that change. It ensured the survival of the public schools in Virginia because it allowed the religious symbols of a Protestant society entry into the classroom. Simultaneously, he found a way to reconcile that policy with Jefferson's statute by making all religious exercises purely voluntary on the part of teachers, administrators, and students. In the twentieth century, despite challenges from the left, represented by Rabbi Calisch, and the right, represented most forcefully by the Methodists, Ruffner's policy survived because of the leadership of pastor McDaniel and editor Pitt in the Baptist community. They best represented the commitment to religion as a voluntary enterprise in public education and without legal prescription. This worked best, as McDaniel recognized, when applied in a religiously homogeneous community that respected the consciences of those who dissented.[2]

For the public schools, however, the U.S. Supreme Court's rulings in the *Engle* and *Abington* cases in 1962 settled the issue, at least until the rise of the Religious Right in American politics. Twenty years after the school prayer cases, the Southern Baptist Convention in a dramatic reversal of their traditional policy became the first religious body to endorse a school prayer amendment to the U.S. Constitution.[3] Then twenty years later Jerry Falwell, the pastor of Thomas Road Baptist Church in Lynchburg, asked a federal court to overturn Virginia's ban on church incorporation and the limitation the state imposed on church property ownership. Remarkably, the American Civil Liberties Union of Virginia, which on more than one occasion had been the object of Falwell's wrath, joined the Baptist preacher in the suit. In the 2002 case of *Falwell v. Miller*, a federal judge applied the free exercise clause of the First Amendment, which under the Fourteenth Amendment now applied to the states, in determining that the church could be incorporated. Later that year a ruling by the state's attorney general eliminated Virginia's church property limitations for incorporated churches. Thus two state laws urged by Virginia Baptists at the beginning of the nineteenth century were overturned at the behest of their spiritual heirs two hundred years later.[4]

We count religious freedom among our most prized legacies from the founding era. Like the founders, we also recognize the important benefits the religious faith of our people confers on our republic, paradoxically because church and state are separated. Where precisely to place Jefferson's wall or to draw Madison's line has always been the tricky part. In either state or church, the devil is in the details.

Notes

AA	*Acts of the General Assembly of Virginia*
ANTS	Franklin Trask Library, Andover Newton Theological School, Newton Centre, MA
Assn.	Association
BOL	Bishop of London
Boyd	Boyd, Julian P., ed. *The Papers of Thomas Jefferson.* 38 vols. to date. Princeton, NJ, 1950–.
BRCA	*Baltimore and Richmond Christian Advocate*
Brock	Brock Collection, Henry E. Huntington Library, San Marino, CA
Brydon	Brydon, George MacLaren. *Virginia's Mother Church and the Political Conditions under Which She Grew.* 2 vols. Richmond, 1948–52.
Com.	Committee
Conv.	Convention
DAB	*Dictionary of American Biography.* Ed. Allen Johnson et al. 22 vols. New York, 1928–58.
DB	Deed Book
DLC	Library of Congress, Washington, DC
DU	Rare Book, Manuscript, and Special Collections Library, Duke University, Durham, NC
DVB	*Dictionary of Virginia Biography* Ed. John Kneebone et al. 3 vols. to date. Richmond, 1998–.
EJ	*Executive Journals of the Council of Colonial Virginia.* Ed. H. R. McIlwaine and Wilmer L. Hall. 6 vols. Richmond, 1925–66.
EJV	*Educational Journal of Virginia*
Foote	William Henry Foote. *Sketches of Virginia, Historical and Biographical. First Series.* 1850. New ed. Richmond, 1966. *Second Series.* 2d ed. rev. Philadelphia, 1856. All references are to the *First Series* unless otherwise noted.
Gen.	General
GWM	George White McDaniel
Hawks	Francis L. Hawks. *Contributions to the Ecclesiastical History of the United States of America.* Vol. 1. *A Narrative of Events Connected with the Rise*

and Progress of the Protestant Episcopal Church in Virginia. App. *Journals of the Conventions of the Protestant Episcopal Church in Virginia from 1785 to 1835.* 2 vols. New York, 1836–39.

HEH   Henry E. Huntington Library, San Marino, CA

Hening   Hening, William Waller, ed. *The Statutes at Large, being a Collection of All the Laws of Virginia, from the First Session of the Legislature in the Year 1619.* 13 vols. Richmond, 1809–23.

HMPEC   *Historical Magazine of the Protestant Episcopal Church*

Hutchinson   Hutchinson, William, et al., eds. *The Papers of James Madison.* 17 vols. Chicago, 1962–91.

JAH   *Journal of American History*

JER   *Journal of the Early Republic*

JHBV   *Journal of the House of Burgesses of Virginia*

JHDV   *Journal of the House of Delegates of Virginia*

JPH   *Journal of Presbyterian History*

JSH   *Journal of Southern History*

JSV   *Journal of the Senate of Virginia*

LP   Legislative Petitions, RG 78, LVA

LVA   Library of Virginia, Richmond

Min(s).   Minute(s)

NL   *News Leader* (Richmond)

OB   Order Book

Perry   Perry, William Stevens, ed. *Historical Collections Relating to the American Colonial Church.* Vol. 1. *Virginia.* Hartford, CT, 1870.

Pet(s).   Petition(s)

PHS   Pennsylvania Historical Society, Philadelphia

RE   *Richmond Enquirer*

RG   Record Group

RH   *Religious Herald*

RHB   Rough House Bills, Resolutions, etc., LVA

RMC   McGraw-Page Library, Randolph-Macon College, Ashland, VA

RSCB   Richmond City School Board

SHC   Southern Historical Collection, University of North Carolina, Chapel Hill

Shepherd   Shepherd, Samuel, ed. *The Statutes at Large of Virginia, from October Session 1792 to December Session 1806, inclusive, being a Continuation of Hening.* 3 vols. Richmond, 1835–36.

SLM   *Southern Literary Messenger*

TCP   Tucker-Coleman Papers, WMC

T-D   *Times-Dispatch* (Richmond)

UPS   William Smith Morton Library, Union Presbyterian Seminary, Richmond

UVA	Albert H. Small Special Collections Library, University of Virginia, Charlottesville
VBHS	Virginia Baptist Historical Society, University of Richmond
VBR	*Virginia Baptist Register*
VHS	Virginia Historical Society, Richmond
VMHB	*Virginia Magazine of History and Biography*
VSJ	*Virginia School Journal*
VTS	Bishop Payne Library, Virginia Theological Seminary, Alexandria
WMC	Earl Gregg Swem Library, the College of William and Mary, Williamsburg, VA
WMQ	*William and Mary Quarterly*

INTRODUCTION

1. Jefferson to the Danbury Baptist Assn., 1 Jan. 1802, in Boyd, 36:258. Dreisbach, *Jefferson and the Wall of Separation,* is the definitive account of the background and context for this letter.

2. The text of the statute is in Boyd, 2:545–53. For its impact and place in the development of religious freedom, see, e.g., Peterson and Vaughan, *Virginia Statute;* Robert S. Alley, ed., *The Supreme Court on Church and State* (New York, 1988); Noonan, *Lustre of Our Country.*

3. For Jefferson's use of establishment language in a new context, see Hamburger, *Separation.*

4. Madison to Robert Walsh, 2 Mar. 1819, in Hunt, *Writings of Madison* 8:432. Writing to an Episcopalian clergyman in a more moderate vein, Madison referred to a "line of separation, between the rights of Religion, & the Civil authority," but the operative word here and throughout his writings was *separation* (Madison to Jasper Adams, Sept. 1833, in Dreisbach, *Religion and Politics,* 120).

5. John F. Wilson, "The Founding Era (1774–1797) and the Constitutional Provision for Religion," in Davis, *Oxford Handbook,* 24.

6. *Reynolds v. United States,* 98 U.S. 145 (1878); Drakeman, *Church, State, and Original Intent,* 2–4, 21–73.

7. William G. McLoughlin, *New England Dissent: The Baptists and the Separation of Church and State, 1630–1833,* 2 vols. (Cambridge, MA, 1971), provides the most complete account. For the states more generally, see Thomas J. Curry, *The First Freedoms: Church and State in America to the Passage of the First Amendment* (New York, 1986).

8. Joseph Story to Jasper Adams, 14 May 1833, in Dreisbach, *Religion and Politics,* 115–17. For Story, see R. Kent Newmeyer, *Supreme Court Justice Joseph Story* (Chapel Hill, 1985), and Sekulow, *Witnessing Their Faith,* 21–39.

9. *Everson v. Board of Education of the Township of Ewing,* 330 U.S. 1, 18, 33 (1947). Drakeman offers an extensive critique of *Everson* in *Church, State, and Original Intent,* 74–148. In his dissent in *Wallace v. Jaffree,* Chief Justice William Rehnquist charged

that the "'wall of separation between church and State' is a metaphor based on bad history, a metaphor which has proved useless as a guide to judging. It should be frankly and explicitly abandoned" (*Wallace v. Jaffree*, 472 U.S. 38, 107 [1985]).

10. For an early expression of this perspective in a legislative debate and its overwhelming acceptance, see *JHDV*, 2 Feb. 1827, 132–33.

11. *Cantwell v. Connecticut*, 310 U.S. 296 (1940).

12. Harry N. Scheiber urged the integration of legal and constitutional study within a social history context in "American Constitutional History and the New Legal History: Complementary Themes in Two Modes," *JAH* 68 (1981): 337–50; for this reading of texts, see Joan W. Scott, "The Evidence of Experience," *Critical Inquiry* 17 (1991): 773–97. For the interpretive history of the First Amendment, see, e.g., Thomas J. Curry, *Farewell to Christendom: The Future of Church and State in America* (Oxford, 2001); Drakeman, *Church, State, and Original Intent*; Witte and Nichols, *Religion and the American Constitutional Experiment*.

13. Eckenrode, *Separation of Church and State*.

14. Bell, *Church, State, and Education*.

15. Buckley, *Church and State*; Isaac, *Transformation of Virginia*.

16. For an example of the first, see William Lee Miller, *The First Liberty: Religion and the American Republic* (New York, 1996); and for the second, Ragosta, *Wellspring of Liberty*.

17. Green, *Second Disestablishment*. For a similar periodization in constitutional development, see Gordon, *Spirit of the Law*, 4–14. Green focuses on the second period, while Gordon analyzes the third.

18. Green, *Bible, School, and Constitution*.

19. Hamburger, *Separation*, 191–251.

1. ESTABLISHMENT

1. Patrick Henry to William Dawson, 13 Feb. 1744/45, Patrick Henry to William Dawson, 8 June 1747, in "Letters of Patrick Henry," quotes at 261, 273.

2. Chamberlayne, *Vestry Book of St. Paul's Parish*, 147, 148, 150, 157–58, 160, 183, 196.

3. Nelson, *Blessed Company*.

4. Worrall, *Friendly Virginians*, 3–11, 16–17. Kenneth Carroll argues that Harris had preached in Maryland but not in Virginia, and he regards Thomas Thurston and Joan Coale as the first Quakers in the colony (Carroll, "Robert Pleasants on Quakerism," 7n10). The most inclusive enumeration of early Virginia Quaker meetings is Hinshaw, *American Quaker Genealogy*, vol. 6.

5. McIlwaine, *Mins.*, 506. For Virginia Quakers and their encounters with the civil authorities in this period, see Bond, *Damned Souls in a Tobacco Colony*, 160–74.

6. What non-Quakers found objectionable, they persecuted. See, e.g., *Declaration of Sufferings*, 30–31.

7. Carroll, "Quakers on the Eastern Shore"; [Tyler], "Major Edmund Chisman," 91.

8. Hening, 1:532–33. For one Quaker's eloquent response to this persecution, see Billings, "A Quaker in Seventeenth-Century Virginia," 127–40.

9. William Berkeley to Richard Conquest, 8 Aug. 1660, in Billings, *Papers of Berkeley*, 127; Hening, 2:48.

10. McIlwaine, *Mins.*, 492; Hening, 2:180–83; Billings, *Sir William Berkeley*, 185, 188.

11. Worrall, *Friendly Virginians*, 32. Jordan had already suffered fines and imprisonment in 1661 (Putnam, *Early Quaker Records*, 49). For the law's effect in another county, see Robert Armistead Stewart, "Excerpts from the Charles City County Records (1665–1666)," *VMHB* 42 (1934): 341–44.

12. Worrall, *Friendly Virginians*, 61–63.

13. "Order suppressing Quakers in Nansemond County," 10 June 1675, in Billings, *Papers of Berkeley*, 472; [Fox], *Journal* 2:167 (quote), 170.

14. Hinshaw, *American Quaker Genealogy* 6:23. See also Nicholson, "Correspondence," 156, 168–72.

15. For a similar experience in New England, see Jonathan M. Chu, *Neighbors, Friends, or Madmen: The Puritan Adjustment to Quakerism in Seventeenth-Century Massachusetts Bay* (Westport, CT, 1985).

16. Larabee, *Royal Instructions* 2:495.

17. Gee and Hardy, *Documents*, 641–44. This was first published in April 1687 and a year later republished in almost identical language. For James's policy and the reaction in England, see Murphy, *Conscience and Community*, 134–42.

18. *EJ*, 21 Oct. 1687, 2 Feb. 168[8], 1:85, 89. For the text of the final address, see "Address to James II," in Billings, *Papers of Howard*, 364.

19. *EJ*, 27 Feb., 26 Apr. 1689, 3 June 1690, 1:101, 106, 113; Billings, *Virginia's Viceroy*, 88–89, 91–92.

20. The act is reprinted in Douglas, *English Historical Documents* 8:400–403 (quote at 403). The excerpted words in article 20 are: "the Church hath power to decree rites or ceremonies, and authority in controversies of faith" (ibid., 403). The word *toleration* does not occur in the title or the text of the law. For the English background, see Nicholas Tyacke, "The 'Rise of Puritanism' and the Legalizing of Dissent, 1571–1718," in Grell et al., *From Persecution to Toleration*, 17–49; Murphy, *Conscience and Community*, 157–61.

21. *EJ*, 20 Feb., 7 Mar. 169[1], 27 Jan. 169[2], 31 May 1699, 1:160–61, 167, 214, 441; Douglas, *English Historical Documents*, 402–3; Henrico Co. Order (& Wills) Book, 1 Apr. 1691, 358. For Nicholson's approach to religion and government, see Webb, "Strange Career of Nicholson," and esp. Hardwick, "Narratives of Villainy and Virtue."

22. *EJ*, 29 Apr. 1699, 1:427. For Makemie, see Foote, 40–53; Smylie, "Francis Makemie."

23. Hening, 3:171. This exception was also made explicit by a parenthetic phrase in an act that was part of the 1705 revisal of the laws. See ibid., 360.

24. *EJ*, 21 June 1699, 1:456.

25. *EJ*, 16 Nov., 19 Dec. 1699, 27 Aug. 1703, 2:27, 37, 336.

26. Butler, *Huguenots in America*, 220; Gundersen, "The Huguenot Church at Manakin."

27. For the Baptist preacher, see *Journal of Thomas Story*, 165.

28. Brydon, 2:83–93, 98–104; Eisenberg, *Lutheran Church in Virginia*; Brunk, *Mennonites in Virginia*.

29. Manarin and Dowdey, *History of Henrico County*, 66; Crawshaw, "Letters from Virginia Quakers," 93.

30. *Journal of Thomas Story*, 155, 158.

31. *EJ*, 31 Jan. 171[2], 3:299.

32. Worrall, *Friendly Virginians*, 92, 105.

33. *Journal of Thomas Story*, 387, 388. Nicholson's friendly attitude toward the Quakers may have been guided by his quarrel with Anglican commissary James Blair. See Parke Rouse Jr., *James Blair of Virginia* (Chapel Hill, 1971).

34. *EJ*, 13 Nov. 1717, 3:611; "Queries to be Answered," Perry, 257.

35. Jones, *Present State of Virginia*, 83.

36. Putnam, *Early Quaker Records*, 49; Carroll, "Robert Pleasants on Quakerism," 8; Douglas, *English Historical Documents* 8:402.

37. *Journal of Thomas Story*, 387.

38. *Va. Gaz.*, 17 Nov. 1738; Carroll, "Robert Pleasants on Quakerism," 8–9; Hening, 6:88–90. At least one Anglican clergyman exempted the Quakers in his parish from the levy for his salary. See Frederick B. Tolles, "A Conscientious Parson: The Reverend William Davis and the Quakers," *VMHB* 51 (1951): 359–61.

39. Douglas, *English Historical Documents* 8:152; Hening 3:298.

40. *EJ*, 10 May 1722, 4:13; Worrall, *Friendly Virginians*, 114. See also Hinshaw, *American Quaker Genealogy* 6:30.

41. *EJ*, 27 Oct. 1727, 4:150; Worrall, *Friendly Virginians*, 111–12. For a later petition requesting exemption from all military service, see *JHBV*, 26 Apr. 1757, 436.

42. *EJ*, 16 Apr. 1745, 5:170.

43. "Mr. [Alexander] Forbes' 'Account of the State of the Church,'" 21 July 1724, Anthony Gavin to Bishop of London, 5 Aug. 1738, in Perry, 1:333, 360; Gragg, *Migration in Early America*, 99n18.

44. *EJ*, 27 Apr. 1724, 4 May 1725, 4:65, 86.

45. Foote, 98–105 (quote at 104).

46. Hofstra, "'The Extension of His Majesties Dominions.'"

47. Bidwell, "The Morris Reading-Houses," 7–8, 14–15, 24, 44, 65–71; Foote, 119–29; Alexander, *Biographical Sketches*, 196–99. See also Mulder, "Converting the New Light."

48. *Va. Gaz.*, 3 Oct., 21 Dec. 1739; James Blair to the Bishop of London, in Perry, 1:364. For a superb history of this movement of which Whitefield was a part, see Mark A. Noll, *The Rise of Evangelicalism: The Age of Edwards, Whitefield, and the Wesleys* (Downers Grove, IL, 2003). For Whitefield, see Frank Lambert, *"Pedlar in Divinity": George Whitefield and the Transatlantic Revivals, 1737–1770* (Princeton, NJ, 1994).

49. Trinterud, *Forming an American Tradition*, 86–121.

50. Foote, 132–35; Patrick Henry to William Dawson, 13 Feb. 1744/45, in "Letters of Patrick Henry," 261, 263.

51. Foote, 123–24, 135–38. For the governor's change, see Burk, *History of Virginia* 3:119–21.

52. Foote, 138–41.

53. Alexander, *Biographical Sketches*, 201–2; Patrick Henry to William Dawson, 14 Oct. 1745, in "Letters of Patrick Henry," 267.

54. Miller, *Memoir of Rodgers*, 49; *EJ* 5:227–28, 490.

55. Alexander, *Biographical Sketches*, 202; Foote, 160; Davies, *State of Religion*, quote at 19.

56. Patrick Henry to William Dawson, 8 June 1747, in "Letters of Patrick Henry," 272, 273.

57. Pilcher, *Samuel Davies*, 13–18; Foote, 160–65 (quote at 162).

58. This account is in Miller, *Memoir of Rodgers*, 54, and is repeated in Foote, 166. Samuel Miller (1769–1850) was a founder and the first professor of church history at Princeton Theological Seminary. He published his *Memoir of Rodgers* in 1813, the year the school opened.

59. Miller, *Memoir of Rodgers*, 50–51.

60. Davies, *State of Religion*, 21–23 (quote at 23).

61. Foote, 169–70; Davies, *State of Religion*, 42.

62. William Dawson to BOL, 27 July 1750, in Perry, 1:366.

63. Samuel Davies to Doddridge, 2 Oct. 1750, ibid., 368–71.

64. BOL to Doddridge, 11 May 1751, ibid., 371–73. See also Foote, 177.

65. Doddridge to BOL, 14 May 1751, in Perry, 1:374–77.

66. William Dawson to BOL, 16 Aug. 1751, and Address to Burgesses, ibid., 379–83.

67. Dinwiddie to BOL, 5 June 1752, ibid., 393–96; Davies, *State of Religion*, 44; Foote, 184–88 (quote at 188).

68. Foote, 208; William Dawson to BOL, [1752], in Perry, 1:384.

69. Davies to Avery, 21 May 1752, in Foote, 207–11 (quote at 209).

70. Avery to Davies, [1752], ibid., 212–13.

71. Davies presented Ryder's opinion, but it appeared to overlook the fact that dissenting clergy had applied for an amendment in the Toleration Act, approved in 1712, which granted them permission "to preach occasionally" in counties other than the one for which they had received a license. This law understood them to be assigned to a local congregation in a particular county (Thomas Dawson to BOL, 23 July 1753, in Perry, 1:407).

72. Davies, *State of Religion*, quotes at 4, 5, 6. Davies sent this publication to his dissenter contacts in England as part of his campaign to enlist their support in obtaining more licensed preaching stations (Davies to Avery, 21 May 1752, in Foote, 210). For Bellamy, see Mark Valeri, *Law and Providence in Joseph Bellamy's New England: The Origins of the New Divinity in Revolutionary America* (New York, 1994).

73. Samuel Davies, *Faithful Minister*, quotes at 5, 9, 102.

74. William Dawson to the BOL, [1752], in Perry, 1:384. See also Hockman, "'Hellish and Malicious Incendiaries.'"

75. Thomas Dawson to the BOL, 23 July 1753, in Perry, 1:405–7.

76. For a thoughtful treatment of dissenters, see Nelson, *Blessed Company*, 282–89.

77. See the returns of almost thirty ministers to the bishop's questionnaire in 1727 in Perry, 1:261–334.

78. "Fairfax Co. List of Titheables." For Green, see Henriques, "Lawrence Washington versus Charles Green."

79. For Carlyle, see Frank E. Grizzard, *George Washington: A Biographical Companion* (Santa Barbara, CA, 2002), 43–45; for Colville, see Donald A. Wise, "Colonel John Colville, 18th Century Gentleman," *Historical Society of Fairfax Yearbook* 16 (1980): 94–103.

80. For the Catholic position in England during this period, see Gordon Rupp, *Religion in England, 1688–1791* (Oxford, 1986), 180–203; John Bossy, "English Catholics after 1688," in Grell et al., *From Persecution to Toleration*, 369–87.

81. *EJ* 5:484–85.

82. "Fairfax Co. List of Titheables." For Catholics in neighboring Stafford Co., see Steiner, "The Catholic Brents."

83. "Fairfax Co. List of Titheables."

84. See, e.g., *EJ*, 24 Apr. 1753, 5:421.

85. Pilcher, *Samuel Davies Abroad*, 79, 82–83, 85, 134 (quotes at 79). The dissenter committee did not impress Davies (ibid., 134).

86. Nath[nie]l Sheffield to Davies, 5 Feb. 1755, in Foote, 296–97.

87. "Journal of the Proceedings," in Perry, 1:416.

88. Samuel Davies, "Religion and Patriotism the Constituents of Good Soldiers" and "The Curse of Cowardice," *Sermons* 3:41–62, 84–99 (quotes at 42, 43); Pilcher, *Samuel Davies*, 164–68.

89. Foote, 284; Rachal, "Mins. of Hanover Presbytery," 54.

90. Rachal, "Mins. of Hanover Presbytery," 60–62 (quotes at 61). Presbyterianism became the established Church of Scotland in 1690 following the Glorious Revolution. See Stewart J. Brown and Michael Fry, eds., *Scotland in the Age of the Disruption* (Edinburgh, 1993); Andrew Herron, *Kirk by Divine Right: Church and State—Peaceful Coexistence* (Edinburgh, 1985). For Davies's conviction that he belonged to the established Church of Scotland, see Davies to Bp. Sherlock, 10 Jan. 1752, in Foote, 202–3.

91. Rachal, "Mins. of Hanover Presbytery," 165.

92. John Leland and David Currie to Thomas Dawson, 12 Apr. 1758, Edwin Conway to Thomas Dawson, 3 Mar. 1758, Dawson Papers, DLC. For Conway, see "Conway, Edwin," *DVB* 3:412–13.

93. *EJ*, 14 Dec. 1757, 19–20, 25 May, 13 June, 4, 12 Oct. 1758, 19–20 Jan. 1759, 6:75, 91–94, 95–96, 110, 112 (quote), 124–29, 140; Rachal, "Mins. of Hanover Presbytery," 70, 71, 164. See also Frederick V. Mills, "The Society in Scotland for Propagating Christian Knowledge in British North America, 1730–1775," *Church History* 63 (1994): 15–30.

94. "Journal of Gordon," 11:99.

95. Davies, "The Apostolic Valediction," *Sermons* 3:478–93 (quotes at 485, 488, 489).

96. "Journal of Gordon," 11:107.

97. Ibid., 110. For further discussion of Gordon and dissenters on vestries, see Nelson, *Blessed Company*, 287–88.

98. "Journal of Gordon," 11:199.

99. Ibid., 12:4, 5.

2. TOLERATION

1. *JHBV*, 1 Feb. 1727/28, 4. For Gooch, see Flippin, *William Gooch*. Actually, he was a lieutenant governor. The governor was the earl of Albemarle, William Anne von Keppel, who remained in England.

2. *JHBV*, 14 Feb. 1727/28, 20.

3. Robert Carter Nicholas to [Samuel] Henley, *Va. Gaz.* Supplement (PD), 20 May 1773. For vestry-clergy conflict, see Gundersen, "Myth of the Independent Vestry."

4. Gov. Dinwiddie to BOL, 29 Jan. 1753, Thomas Dawson to BOL, 23 July 1753, in Perry, 1:401–2, 406–7. See also Hening, 6:90.

5. Maury, *To Christians of every Denomination*, 31.

6. Francis Fauquier to the Lords Commissioners of Trade, 1 Dec. 1759, *JHB*, 282. The operative 1748 law on clerical salaries is in Hening, 6:88–90.

7. Hening, 6:369–70.

8. For his argument, see Isaac, *Transformation of Virginia*, 144–57, and "Religion and Authority." For the Parson's Cause, see Morton, *Colonial Virginia* 2:751–818.

9. Hening 9:568–69 (quote at 569).

10. Clergy of Virginia to BOL, 29 Nov. 1755, 25 Feb. 1756, in Perry 1:434–46.

11. Hening, 7:240–41.

12. The size of this convention and the percentage of attendees favoring the petition are matters of dispute. There were at that time at least seventy clergy in Virginia ("A List," 10 June 1755, in Perry, 1:429–31). Commissary William Robinson later recalled that thirty-five ministers had attended the convention (he erroneously gave sixty as the total clergymen for Virginia) and that all but one approved sending Camm to London (Robinson to BOL, 20 Nov. 1760, ibid., 466). But Landon Carter claimed that only "one third" of the colony's ministers were present and of that number just a "bare majority" approved the "cruel Censure on the Legislature" ([Carter], *Letter to the Right Reverend*, 56). Richard Bland agreed in his published letter that only a "small part of the Clergy" had been involved ([Bland], *Letter to the Clergy*, 3). Subsequently, Bland stated that twenty-five ministers had been present, of whom "perhaps" fifteen endorsed Camm's mission ([Bland], *Colonel Dismounted*, 11, 13). Camm attacked these figures without offering any concrete alternatives. See [Camm], *Critical Remarks*, 9.

Rhys Isaac uses the Robinson figure of thirty-five clergymen present and omits Carter's and Bland's estimates. According to Isaac, Carter and Bland were "doughty anticlericals" ("Religion and Authority," 16, 17). J. Jefferson Looney uses these same figures in his entry on "Camm, John," *DVB* 2:538–41.

13. But the Privy Council failed to repeal them explicitly or to make them null and

void from their passage, which Camm had requested while he was in London ("Petition of the Clergy," in Perry, 1:487–88). For the importance of this issue of repeal, see Robinson to BOL, 17 Aug. 1764, ibid., 494–99; Tate, "Coming of the Revolution," 328–29.

14. Giberne, *Duty of Living Peaceably*, 9, 16. Giberne had arrived in Virginia in 1759 and was rector at Hanover Parish in King George County when he preached this sermon. He became rector of Lunenburg Parish in Richmond County in 1762 (Nelson, *Blessed Company*, 173–78, 310; Isaac, *Landon Carter's Uneasy Kingdom*, 249–53, 259–61, 385–86). Isaac incorrectly places Giberne in Virginia for the first time in 1762. For his efforts to ingratiate himself, see Giberne to BOL, 31 Aug. 1764, in Perry, 1:501–3. For the commissary's enmity toward him, see Robinson to BOL, 6 June 1766, ibid., 522.

15. [Carter], *Letter to the Right Reverend*, 56. For Camm, see Homer D. Kemp, "To Raise a Flame and Live in It," in Lemay, *Essays in Early Virginia Literature*, 165–80.

16. Richard Bland, *Letter to the Clergy*, 3, 19. Isaac's charge of anticlericalism seems particularly inappropriate for Bland. A staunch churchman, he served as a lay reader in his parish church ([Bland], *Colonel Dismounted*, 15). For Bland, see Brent Tarter, "Bland, Richard," *DVB* 3:10–13.

17. Camm, *Single and Distinct View*, 42. For accounts of this interview, see Robinson to BOL, 20 Nov. 1760, [Robinson] to BOL, [1763], in Perry, 1:464, 476.

18. For the lively exchange between Camm and Josiah Royle, the Williamsburg printer, see the appendix in Camm, *Single and Distinct View*, 45–51. Camm's exile from power was not permanent. He served as president of the College of William and Mary from 1771 to 1777, and in 1771 he became the commissary and a member of the council.

19. Camm, *Single and Distinct View*, 36.

20. James Maury to John Camm, 12 Dec. 1763, in Ann Maury, *Memoirs*, 420, 422–23 (first quote at 423); [James Maury], "Narrative of the Determination of a Suit," Boucher Papers, box 2, folder 1; Robinson to BOL, 17 Aug. 1764, in Perry, 1:489–501 (second and third quote at 497). Camm published Maury's account of the trial in [Camm], *Colonel Reconnoitred*, 23. For Henry's role in the Parson's Cause, see Meade, *Patrick Henry*, 114–38.

After the Stamp Act Crisis, Maury endorsed Henry's views on what the minister called "this detestable Act" (Maury to John Fontaine, 31 Dec. 1765, in Ann Maury, *Memoirs*, 424–31 [quote at 431]).

21. For Davies's oratory, see Pilcher, *Samuel Davies*, 54–85. For his impact on Henry, see Meade, *Patrick Henry*, 71–74.

22. Isaac, "Religion and Authority."

23. For the testimony of his widow and children, see Hawks, *Contributions* 1:100–101.

24. "Statement of Spencer Roane," in Morgan, *Patrick Henry*, 444.

25. *JHBV*, 26, 27 Apr. 1757, 436, 439; Brock, *Pioneers of the Peaceable Kingdom*, 42–44.

26. *JHBV*, 28, 31 Mar. 1767; Hening, 8:242–43. For the operation of this law in one Quaker community, see Society of Friends, Richmond Monthly Meeting, Record Book, 249, 257, 261–62.

27. Roger Atkinson to Samuel Pleasants, 1 Oct. 1774, "Letters of Roger Atkinson,

1769–1776," *VMHB* 15 (1908): 856. See also Robert Pleasants to Esteemed Friend, 22 [Feb.] 1774, "Letters of Robert Pleasants," 108; Carroll, "Robert Pleasants on Quakerism," 3–16; Peter V. Bergstrom, "Atkinson, Roger," *DVB* 1:241–43.

28. "To Norborne Berkeley," *Va. Gaz.* (PD), 24 Nov. 1768.

29. *JHBV*, 14, 17 Nov. 1769, 101, 104, 256, 267.

30. For the earliest Baptist history, see Edwards, "History of Baptists in Virginia." Other early histories of Virginia Baptists include Fristoe, *History of Ketocton Association*, 5–11; Burkitt and Read, *History of Kehukee Association*, 28–40; Benedict, *General History* 2:24–26, 33–36, 53–58; and esp. Semple, *Baptists in Virginia*. The standard modern study is Alley, *Baptists in Virginia*. But see also Spangler, *Virginians Reborn*; Najar, *Evangelizing the South*. A helpful guide to the enormous variety of early Virginia Baptists is Gardner, "Virginia Baptist Statistics."

31. James Maury to Jonathan Boucher, 14 Feb. [17]69, Boucher Papers, box 2, folder 3; Boucher, *View of the Causes*, 100.

32. James Maury to Jonathan Boucher, 29 Aug. 1768, Boucher Papers, box 2, folder 3.

33. Semple, *Baptists in Virginia*, 29–30; John Blair to ?, 16 July 1768, ibid., 30–31. For the confusion over the Toleration Act's application in Virginia, see Foote, 174–200.

34. *JHBV*, 1770–73, 26 May, 1 June 1770, 20, 40. For Baptist hagiography, see Little, *Imprisoned Preachers*.

35. Robert Carter Nicholas to [Samuel] Henley, *Va. Gaz.* Supplement (PD), 20 May 1773.

36. South Quay [Baptist] Church, 7 Jan. 1777; Antioch Baptist Church, 17 July 1773 (first quote); Broad Run Baptist Church, 27 July 1778. For a fine summation of Baptist development, see Spangler, "Becoming Baptists." An example of Anglican-Baptist conflict is in Little, *Imprisoned Preachers*, 78–81.

37. Isaac, *Transformation of Virginia*, 171–72. For this development in a particular congregation before the Revolution, see Broad Run Baptist Church, Min. Book. For a black preacher, see Burkitt and Read, *History of Kehukee Association*, 258–60. Spangler argues that slaves who joined Baptist churches after the Revolution were "second-class members" ("Becoming Baptists," 258–63). Examples of church covenants may be found in Lumpkin, "Early Virginia Baptist Covenants."

38. Little, *Imprisoned Preachers*, 48, 49; Semple, *Baptists in Virginia*, 30.

39. Andrew Glassell to Anne Wiatt, 23 May 1774, Wiatt Papers. For Glassell, see Hayden, *Virginia Genealogies*, 5–7.

40. Andrew Glassell to Francis Wiatt, 3 Dec. 1773, Wiatt Papers.

41. Chesterfield Co. OB 4, 4 Jan. 1771, 486; Chesterfield Co. OB 5, 5 June 1772, 4 June, 6 Aug., 3 Sept. 1773, 4 Feb. 1774, 109, 280–81, 306, 322, 400. For Cary, see Brent Tarter, "Cary, Archibald," *DVB* 3:101–3.

42. Taylor, *Virginia Baptist Ministers*, 57–58.

43. Ireland, *Life of Ireland*, 165–67, 178.

44. Caroline Co. OB, 12 May, 10 June, 10 Nov. 1768, 12 May, 9 Nov., 15 Dec. 1769, 13 June, 11 July, 11 Aug., 14 Nov. 1771, 122, 152, 211, 242, 255, 372; Caroline Co. Min. Book, 1770–73, 10 Sept. 1772, 12 Mar., 12 Aug., 11 Nov. 1773, 107, 198, 355, 423.

45. Little, *Imprisoned Preachers*, 470–80.

46. Maury, *To Christians of every Denomination*, 3.

47. James Maury to [Thomas Dawson], 6 Oct. 1755, Dawson Papers.

48. Maury, *To Christians of every Denomination*, 33, 37, 42.

49. *Va. Gaz.* [PD], 20 Feb. 1772.

50. Maury to Dawson, 6 Oct. 1755, in "Letters to Patrick Henry, . . . Maury," 278.

51. *JHBV*, 7, 11 Nov. 1769, 228, 252; "A Real Layman," *Va. Gaz.* (PD), 20 June 1771.

52. "To the Clergy of Virginia," *Va. Gaz.* (Rind), 9 May 1771. For the controversy, see Isaac, *Transformation of Virginia*, 183–204; Bridenbaugh, *Mitre and Sceptre*; Brydon, 2:347–59. The most recent research is summarized in Rhoden, *Revolutionary Anglicanism*, 37–63. See also Mills, "The Colonial Anglican Episcopate."

53. "Protest against the *Proceedings*," *Va. Gaz.* (PD), 6 June 1771; ibid. (Rind), 18 July 1771.

54. Ibid. (PD), 17 Sept. 1771, 16 Jan. 1772. No record of this meeting, if it was held, has been located.

55. Gwatkin, *Letter to the Clergy*, postscript.

56. Philanthropos Americanus, *Va. Gaz.* (PD), 20 Feb. 1772.

57. See Pilcher, "The Pamphlet War" and "Virginia Newspapers."

58. Semple, *Baptists in Virginia*, 41; Foote, 317–18. For these Baptist petitions, see *JHBV*, 12, 22, 24, 27 Feb., 14 Mar. 1772, 160–61, 162–63, 185–86, 188, 194, 197, 245.

59. Act of Toleration Engrossed by the Va. House of Burgesses, Mar. 1772, Colonial Papers, box 149, published as "Bill for extending the Benefit of the several Acts of Toleration," *Va. Gaz.* (Rind), 26 Mar. 1772; Robert Carter Nicholas, "To Hoadleianus," *Va. Gaz.* (Rind), 8 June 1773.

60. Henley, *Distinct Claims of Government and Religion*; "To the Reverend Mr. Henley," *Va. Gaz.* Supplement (PD), 20 May 1773.

61. Robert Carter Nicholas to [Samuel Henley], Henley to Nicholas, *Va. Gaz.* (PD), 3 June 1773; Nicholas to Samuel, ibid., 24 Feb. 1774. When the vestry voted for a new rector in 1773, they chose John Bracken over Henley, much to the latter's dismay. For a full treatment of this contest, see Isaac, *Transformation of Virginia*, 209–40.

62. *Va. Gaz.* (PD), 10 Mar. 1774.

63. [Hoadleianus] to A. W., *Va. Gaz.* (Rind), 5 Mar. 1772. For Nicholas's mature reflections, see "To the Rev. Mr. Henley," ibid. (PD), 20 May 1773.

64. Robert Carter Nicholas to "Hoadleianus," ibid. (Rind), 10 June 1773.

65. Ibid., 20 Feb. 1772. This opinion that only the General Court had authority to license dissenting clergymen and their meetinghouses was much more restrictive, and contrary to the council's decision of 1725 that had vested this power in the county courts (*EJ* 4:81, 86.) Brydon states incorrectly that the 1725 decision "fixed the custom of the colony for the remainder of the colonial period" (1:259).

66. Randolph, *History of Virginia*, 179; Semple, *Baptists in Virginia*, 41.

67. "Statement of Spencer Roane," in Morgan, *Patrick Henry*, 440.

68. Semple, *Baptists in Virginia*, 87. The marriage law was finally changed in 1784 (Buckley, *Church and State*, 111).

69. Henry, *Patrick Henry* 1:112–16 (quotes at 112, 114, 115, 116).

70. *JHBV*, 27 Feb., 17 Mar. 1772, 194, 197, 249; *Va. Gaz.* [Rind], 26 Mar. 1772.

71. "To the Rev. Samuel Henley," *Va. Gaz.* Supplement (PD), 20 May 1773.

72. The best treatment of this is in Nelson, *Blessed Company*, 145–51.

73. William Dawson to BOL, 15 July 1751, in Perry, 1:377–78. For one layman's praise of Blair's methods in church-state matters, see Carter, *Letter to the Right Reverend*, 17–18.

74. William Dawson to BOL, 15 July 1751, Thomas Dawson to BOL, 11 Mar. 1754, in Perry, 1:378, 410. For this sensational trial, see Henriques, "Major Washington versus Reverend Green."

75. The reason for this failure is not clear.

76. *EJ*, 19, 20 May 1757, 6:47–48; Thomas Dawson to BOL, 9 July 1757, Dinwiddie to BOL, 12 Sept. 1754, in Perry, 1:451–53, 454–55. See also Rankin, "The General Court"; Gundersen, *Anglican Ministry*, 123–42.

77. John Camm, "An Answer to . . . Samuel Henley," *Va. Gaz.* (PD), 13 June 1771. For a particularly scandalous case, see Nelson, *Blessed Company*, 152–55.

78. *EJ*, 12 Apr. 1771, 1:400. See the exchange between Thomas Nelson as council president and the earl of Hillsborough in the Fulham Papers, 41:348–350, cited in Nelson, *Blessed Company*, 401n50.

79. John Camm, "Answer to Henley," *Va. Gaz.* (PD), 13 June 1771; John Camm, "To the Rev. Gwatkin," ibid., 15 Aug. 1771.

80. John Camm, "Answer to Henley," ibid., 13 June 1771.

81. *JHBV*, 25 Feb., 27 Mar., 7 Apr. 1772, 188–89, 275, 304.

82. *EJ*, 20 Apr. 1774, 6:556. For Morton, see Weis, *Colonial Clergy*, 110.

83. Bland, *Letter to the Clergy*. Although opposed to the introduction of episcopacy into Virginia, Bland was an orthodox, devout Anglican. See his letter in the *Va. Gaz.* (PD), 10 Mar. 1774. Like so many colonial Anglicans, he saw no need for bishops. See also Clinton Rossiter, *Six Characters in Search of a Republic*, pt. 2 of *Seedtime of the Republic*, rev. ed. (New York, 1964), 169–71.

84. [Henley], *Candid Refutation*, 70–71.

85. Madison, *Oration*, 10–11.

86. Hutchinson, 1:106. For Madison's religious thought, see Rodney A. Grunes, "James Madison and Religious Freedom," in *James Madison: Philosopher, Founder, and Statesman*, ed. John R. Vile et al. (Athens, OH, 2008), 105–32.

87. *JHBV*, 12, 16 May 1774, 72, 102 (quote).

88. *JHBV*, 17 May 1774, 103; Bedford Co., Colonial Papers, Pets., RG 1.

89. *JHBV*, 5 June 1775, 189 (first quote); Presbytery of Hanover, Colonial Papers, Pets., RG 1 (second and third quotes).

90. *JHBV*, 12, 13 June 1775, 217, 225.

91. LP, Misc. Pet., 16 Aug. 1775; Van Screeven, *Revolutionary Virginia*, 14, 16 Aug. 1775, 3:441–42, 450–51 (quote at 451). For Henry's role, see ibid., 453n3.

92. Mays, *Letters of Pendleton* 1:180. For this declaration, see Dreisbach, "Mason's Pursuit of Religious Liberty."

93. Henry to Adams, 20 May 1776, in Taylor, *Papers of Adams* 4:201; Randolph, *History of Virginia*, 254.

94. Hutchinson, 1:174. For the final text, see Hening, 9:111–12.

95. Randolph, *History of Virginia*, 179.

96. Hutchinson, 1:174–75; Brant, *James Madison* 1:247, 430n16.

3. STATUTE

1. *Va. Gaz.*, 11 Oct. 1776; *JHDV*, 11 Oct. 1776, 7; LP, Prince Edward Co., 11 Oct. 1776.

2. LP, Misc. Pet. ("Ten-thousand Names"), 16 Oct. 1776, Albemarle Co., 22 Oct. 1776, Misc. Pet. (Hanover Presbytery), 24 Oct. 1776, Berkeley Co., 25 Oct. 1776, and Augusta Co., 9 Nov. 1776. See also Ragosta, "Fighting for Freedom."

3. Jefferson, *Autobiography*, in Koch and Peden, *Writings of Thomas Jefferson*, 41. Jefferson's draft resolutions for the church's disestablishment and his notes for this debate are in Boyd, 1:525–58. For a fuller description of the activities of this session, see Buckley, *Church and State*, 21–37.

4. LP, Misc. Pet., 8 Nov. 1776; *Va. Gaz.* (Purdie), 6 Dec. 1776. The Methodists also supported the established church's position. They would not become an independent denomination until 1784. See *JHDV*, 28 Oct. 1776, 30.

5. *JHDV*, 23, 30 Nov., 5, 9 Dec. 1776, 69, 76, 83, 89–90; Hening, 9:164–67.

6. LP, Essex Co., 22 Oct. 1779.

7. Alexander Balmain to John Balmain, 8 May 1783, Balmain Memorandum Book.

8. *Va. Gaz.* (Purdie), 5 June 1778; *Va. Independent Chronicle*, 17 Sept. 1788; *Va. Gaz. or the American Adver.*, 14 June 1786; *Va. Journal and Alexandria Adver.*, 8 Nov. 1787. Examples of subscription papers may be found in Farnham Parish, VA, Misc. MSS, DLC; Upper Parish Vestry Book, Nansemond Co., 11 Oct. 1785, 258; St. George's Parish Vestry Book, Accomack Co., 20 Aug. 1785, 117; Lexington Parish Vestry Book, Amherst Co., 14 Dec. 1789, 25.

9. Boyd, 2:6–8 (quote at 6); St. Anne's Parish Vestry Book, Albemarle Co.; Meade, *Old Churches* 2:48–50; LP, Albemarle Co. (Pet. of Charles Clay), 14 Oct. 1779, Fluvanna Co., 4 June, 25 Oct, 24 Nov. 1779; Hening, 10:112–13. Clay evidently thought of leaving the parish in 1779. See Jefferson's "Testimonial for Charles Clay," [15 Aug. 1779], in Boyd, 3:67. For his biography, see John K. Nelson, "Clay, Charles," *DVB* 3:279–81.

10. Accomack Co. OB, 1777–80, 27 May (quote), 1 July, 25 Aug. 1778, 88, 99, 185; Little, *Imprisoned Preachers*, 470–80; Whitelaw, *Virginia's Eastern Shore* 1:123. For his biography, see John S. Moore, "Baker, Elijah," *DVB* 1:289–90.

11. Noonan, *Lustre of Our Country*, 75. For Jefferson's use of establishment language, see Hamburger, *Church and State*, 146–47.

12. Boyd, 2:545–47 (quotes at 545, 546).

13. Buckley, *Church and State*, 56–59.

14. For this growing acceptance of religious pluralism, see Beneke, *Beyond Toleration*.

15. Madison to Ezra Stiles, 27 Aug. 1780, in Dexter, *Diary of Stiles* 2:446. At the

time Madison seriously considered resigning from the ministry (Rev. James Madison to James Madison Jr., 11 Jan. 1781, in Hutchinson, 2:294).

16. The best exposition of Jefferson's personal religion and its development is Eugene R. Sheridan's Introduction in Adams, *Jefferson's Extracts*, which has been slightly revised and published as Sheridan, *Jefferson and Religion* ([Charlottesville], 1998). Also helpful are Edwin S. Gaustad, *Sworn on the Altar of God: A Religious Biography of Thomas Jefferson* (Grand Rapids, MI, 1996), and Charles B. Sanford, *The Religious Life of Thomas Jefferson* (Charlottesville, 1984). Jefferson may also be considered the architect of American civil religion. See Thomas E. Buckley, S.J., "The Political Theology of Thomas Jefferson," in Peterson and Vaughan, *Virginia Statute of Religious Freedom*, 75–108.

17. LP, Misc. Pet., 24 Oct. 1776.

18. Ibid., 3 June 1782. See also LP, Amelia Co., 12 May 1780, Spotsylvania Co., 5 June 1780, Charlotte Co., 8 Nov. 1780 (second quote), Prince Edward Co., 22 Nov. 1781, Misc. Pet., 3 June 1782 (first quote), Essex Co., 30 May 1783, Amelia Co., 21 May 1783. The restrictions surrounding marriage remained a major irritant, however. See Buckley, *Church and State*, 66–68.

19. Hutchinson, 1:174. This argument first appears in the memorial from the Presbytery of Hanover, 24 Oct. 1776, LP; but a Baptist association used it specifically against the vestries in 1782 (LP, Misc. Pet., 3 June 1782).

20. Daniel Dreisbach points out that Jefferson included in the revised code a bill to secure to the Episcopal Church the church property that would become the major target of Baptists after 1785 (Dreisbach, "A New Perspective").

21. [Maury], "Narrative of a Suit"; Maury to Camm, in Ann Maury, *Memoirs*, 423; Henry, *Patrick Henry* 1:112.

22. Boorstin, *Lost World of Jefferson*, 194–203.

23. [Braxton], *Address to the Convention*, 6, 15.

24. Henry to Adams, 20 May 1776, in Taylor, *Papers of Adams* 4:201. For an important discussion of the meaning of virtue in the late colonial period, see Jack P. Greene, "The Concept of Virtue in Late Colonial British America," in *Imperatives, Behaviors, and Identities: Essays in Early American Cultural History* (Charlottesville, 1992).

25. Van Screeven, *Revolutionary Virginia* 7:450; Randolph, *History of Virginia*, 254.

26. See Shain, *Myth of American Individualism*, 122.

27. "Statement of Spencer Roane," in Morgan, *Patrick Henry*, 452; Patrick Henry to Archibald Blair, 8 Jan. 1799, in Tyler, *Patrick Henry*, 409–10.

28. Henry, *Patrick Henry* 1:81–82.

29. Jefferson to Peter Carr, 10 Aug. 1787, in Boyd, 12:15. See also Jefferson to Thomas Law, 13 June 1814, in Adams, *Jefferson's Extracts*, 355–58.

30. Jefferson to Martha Jefferson, 11 Dec. 1783, in Boyd, 6:380.

31. "A Bill for the More General Diffusion of Knowledge" (quotes on 527), Jefferson to George Wythe, 13 Aug. 1786, in Boyd, 2:526–35, 10:244. See also Eugene R. Sheridan, "Liberty and Virtue," in Gilreath, *Thomas Jefferson*, 242–63.

32. Rutland, *Papers of Mason* 2:553. For the text of the bill as passed, see Hening,

2:553. In his autobiography Jefferson mistakenly wrote that in 1779 "the question against a general assessment was finally carried, and the establishment of the Anglican church entirely put down" (42). For the legislative sessions in 1779, see Buckley, *Church and State*, 21–62.

33. For this troublesome period in Jefferson's life, see Kranish, *Flight from Monticello*, 252–301. The call to investigate his conduct as governor created a lasting hatred for Patrick Henry. See also Henry Mayer and James M. Elson, *Patrick Henry and Thomas Jefferson* (Brookneal, VA, 1997).

34. Jefferson, *Notes on Virginia*, 159, 160.

35. Rutland, *Papers of Mason* 2:769–74 (quote at 770); Wood, *Creation of the American Republic*, 65–70, 117–18, 427–28.

36. Jenyns, *Evidence of the Christian Religion*, 50, 98–99 (quote), 109–13, 175–79; "Statement of Samuel Meredith," in Morgan, *Patrick Henry*, 423; "Winston's Memoir of Patrick Henry," undated folder in Henry Papers. For Butler, see David Brown, "Butler and Deism," in *Joseph Butler's Moral and Religious Thought: Tercentenary Essays*, ed. Christopher Cunliffe (Oxford, 1992), 1–35. For Doddridge, see Malcolm Deacon, *Philip Doddridge of Northampton* (Northampton, UK, 1980), and the essays in G. F. Nuttall, *Philip Doddridge, 1702–51: His Contribution to English Religion* (London, 1951).

37. Henry's interest in books would appear to belie Jefferson's remark that Henry "was the laziest man in reading I ever knew" (Jefferson, *Autobiography*, 10). See Hayes, *Mind of a Patriot*.

38. Schopf, *Travels* 2:62–63 (quote at 62).

39. For Griffith, see the articles by Sydnor.

40. For these letters and Meade's comments, see Meade, *Old Churches* 2:264–67.

41. David Griffith to William White, 26 July 1784, White Papers.

42. See LP, Misc. Pet., 4 June 1784.

43. A bill "for incorporating the clergy of the Protestant Episcopal Church," 1 June 1784, RHB, box 8, June 1784. For the clergy's petition, see LP, 4 June 1784. It details the disadvantages the Episcopal Church faced as a result of its establishment.

44. Madison to Jefferson, 3 July 1784, in Boyd, 7:360–61. Madison's sentiments were not unique, nor were they limited to Virginia Episcopalians. Gov. William Paca of Maryland voiced similar sentiments after the Episcopal clergy in that state met to nominate a bishop (William Paca to Joseph Reed, 12 Sept. 1783, typescript in Misc. Letters, Prot. Epis. Church, Va. (Diocese) Papers, sec. 1).

45. Samuel Shield to David Griffith, 20 Dec. 1784, Griffith Papers. For the text of this act, see Hening, 11:532–37.

46. Madison to Jefferson, 9 Jan. 1785, in Boyd, 7:594. For a similar letter to his father, see Madison to James Madison Sr., 6 Jan. 1785, in Hutchinson, 8:217.

47. Madison to Jefferson, 3 July 1784, in Boyd, 7:360–61; *JHDV*, 17 Nov. 1784, 27.

48. LP, Misc. Pet., 12 Nov. 1784.

49. LP, Lunenburg Co., 8 Nov. 1783, Amherst Co., 27 Nov. 1783 (quote).

50. Rainbolt, "'Religious Liberty' in Maryland"; Underwood, *Constitution of South Carolina* 3:63–71; Wright, "Piety, Morality, and the Commonwealth."

51. "To the Legislature of Va.," *Va. Gaz. or American Adver.*, 8 Nov. 1783; "To the Printer of the Va. Gaz.," ibid., 31 July 1784.

52. Miller, *Revolutionary College*, 124–25; *Va. Gaz.*, 30 Nov. 1782.

53. Mins. of Hanover Presbytery, 28 Oct. 1784, transcript, 326–27; LP, Misc. Pet., 12 Nov. 1784, Dinwiddie Co., 1 Dec. 1784, Surry Co., 1 Dec. 1784.

54. "A Bill Establishing a Provision for Teachers of the Christian Religion," *Va. Journal and Alexandria Adver.*, 17 Mar. 1785. For Henry's role, see Madison to Jefferson, 9 Jan. 1785, in Boyd, 7:594–95.

55. For Lee's position, see Richard Henry Lee to James Madison, 26 Nov. 1785, in Hutchinson, 8:149–50. For the politics of this session, see Buckley, *Church and State*, 89–112.

56. LP, Misc. Pet., 2 Nov. 1785.

57. See, e.g., James, *Documentary History*, and Little, *Imprisoned Preachers*.

58. Semple, *Baptists in Virginia*, 69–71; Fristoe, *History of the Ketocton Association*, 60–61. The four Separate Baptist associations in Virginia were the Orange, the Lower (also called Dover), the Middle, and the Upper (also called Strawberry). For Baptist activity throughout this period, see also Buckley, *Church and State*, 38–91 and passim.

59. LP, Buckingham Co., 27 Oct. 1785.

60. *Va. Gaz. and Weekly Adver.*, 6 Nov. 1784.

61. Sources for early Methodist history are abundant. Esp. helpful are Baker, *From Wesley to Asbury*; William A. Williams, *The Garden of American Methodism: The Delmarva Peninsula, 1769–1820* (Wilmington, DE, 1984); Russell E. Richey, *Early American Methodism* (Bloomington, IN, 1991). More recent studies include Wigger, *Taking Heaven by Storm* and *American Saint*; Cynthia Lynn Lyerly, *Methodism and the Southern Mind, 1770–1810* (New York, 1998); Andrews, *Methodists and Revolutionary America*. For Virginia Methodism, see William W. Bennett, *Memorials of Methodism in Virginia: From its Introduction into the State, in the Year 1772, to the Year 1829* (Richmond, 1870); William Warren Sweet, *Virginia Methodism: A History* (Richmond, 1955); Gewehr, *Great Awakening in Virginia*, 138–66.

62. *Va. Gaz.* (PD), 30 July 1772; Thrift, *Memoir of Jesse Lee*, 6–7.

63. Bangs, *Freeborn Garrettson*, 110; Archibald McRobert to [Devereux Jarratt], 13 July 1780, in Clark, *Journal of Asbury* 3:24; Jarratt, *Life*; Gewehr, *Great Awakening*, 141–48; Clark, *Journal of Asbury* 1:414.

64. William Warren Sweet, *Religion on the American Frontier, 1783–1840*, vol. 4, *The Methodists: A Collection of Source Materials* (Chicago, 1946), 31–50; Wigger, *Taking Heaven by Storm*, 80–102. For membership statistics, see *Mins. of the Annual Conferences*, 6–7.

65. LP, Misc. Pet., 28 Oct. 1776.

66. Asbury to Wesley, 3 Sept. 1780, in Clark, *Journal of Asbury* 3:35. For this controversy, see Bucke, *American Methodism*, 1:176–80, 189–95. For Asbury's contribution, see esp. Wigger, *American Saint*.

67. Asbury to John Wesley, 20 Sept. 1783, in Clark, *Journal of Asbury* 3:31.

68. Asbury to John Wesley, 8 May 1780, ibid., 1:349; Bucke, *American Methodism* 1:186–87, 195–96.

69. Hughes, "Methodist Christmas Conference"; Baker, *From Wesley to Asbury*, 148–53, 163–76; Bucke, *American Methodism* 1:213–32; Wigger, *American Saint*, 139–48.

70. For the evolution of Methodist polity, see Kirby, Richey, and Rowe, *Methodists*, 1–161.

71. Asbury to George Shadford, Aug. 1783, in Clark, *Journal of Asbury* 3:29; Coke, *Extracts of the Journals*, 39.

72. Asbury to Ezekiel Cooper, 16 Nov. 1789, in Clark, *Journal of Asbury* 3:76. They did not possess that many churches anyway, and though here and there some circuit riders would soon begin to dismount, mainly because of ill health or family matters, the itinerant preacher remained the desired model for ministry. In the 1788 Conference Minutes a new classification of preachers appears for the first time: those who have "a partial location on account of their families." Six names were listed. By 1790 the minutes list eight preachers as "under a location through weakness of body or family concerns." This number grew to fourteen by 1792 and twenty-eight by 1794 (*Mins. of Methodist Conferences* 1:30, 36, 45, 54).

73. LP, Misc. Pet., 28 Oct. 1776; Thomas Coke, sermon, 1 Mar. 1785, Methodist Episcopal Church, South, Papers.

74. Hawks, app., *Conv. of 1785*, 3–11. For Griffith's role, see Page Notebook.

75. *Va. Gaz. and Weekly Adver.*, 6 Nov. 1784; Hawks, app., *Conv. of 1785*, 6. For the New York meeting and its resolutions, see Loveland, *Critical Years*, 90–92, but she misconstrues the objections of the 1785 Virginia convention.

76. Page Notebook; Page to Tucker, 7 May 1785, Tucker-Coleman Papers, box 10.

77. Sheild to Griffith, 20 Dec. 1784, Griffith Papers. John Page Jr. would also be a delegate to the Episcopal convention.

78. Page Notebook; White, *Memoirs*, 118.

79. Page Notebook; Hawks, app., *Conv. of 1785*, 7.

80. Hawks, app., *Conv. of 1785*, 8–11 (quotes at 10 and 9).

81. Ibid., 11; Page to Jefferson, 23 Aug. 1784, in Boyd, 8:426 (Page noted, however, that Andrews had left the ministry shortly after the convention to keep from "starving"); Edmund Randolph to Madison, 17 July 1785, in Hutchinson, 8:324.

82. Thomas B. Chandler to William Samuel Johnson, 28 Dec. 1785, in Beardsley, *Life of Johnson*, 370.

83. Hawks, app., *Conv. of 1785*, 6; William Nelson Jr. to William Short, 17 July 1785, Short Papers; LP, Misc. Pet., 2 Nov. 1785; Madison to Jefferson, 20 Aug. 1785, in Boyd, 8:415.

84. Hawks, app., *Conv. of 1785*, 5.

85. For the legislative history of the statute's passage, see Buckley, *Church and State*, 74–165.

86. John Page, "On the Opposition of the Legislature of Virginia to a general Assessment in support of Religion," Page, [*Poems*]. I am grateful to Margaret Cook for bringing these verses to my attention.

87. John Marshall to William B. Sprague, 22 July 1828, in Johnson, *Papers of Marshall* 11:168.

88. For the religious breakdown in the 1784–85 and 1785–86 assemblies, see Buckley, *Church and State*, app. 2, 192–200.

89. Hawks, app., *Conv. of 1786*, 16–17; [Madison], *Sermon Preached Before the Convention*, 3. A dozen years later Madison reversed himself. In the convention of 1799, he proposed that the issue of a general assessment be reconsidered "by every friend to virtue and genuine republicanism" (Madison, "Address to a Convention" in Hawks, app., *Conv. of 1799*, 83).

90. [Swanwick], *Considerations on an Act*, iii, 24; Swanwick to Griffith, 3 Nov. 1786, Randolph Family Papers.

4. PROPERTY

1. Hutchinson, 8:474 (first quote); Boyd, 10:244, 604 (second quote).

2. LP, Henrico Co., 31 Oct. 1786, Louisa Co., 31 Oct. 1786, Misc. Pet. (Baptist General Committee), 1 Nov. 1786.

3. Semple, *Baptists in Virginia*, 69–71; LP, Chesterfield Co., 24 Nov. 1786.

4. The most comprehensive treatment of this article is in Howard, *Commentaries on the Constitution* 1:77–81. The Baptist petitions, in quoting the article, always omitted the second half of the text, which continued: "which, not being descendible (neither ought the offices) of Magistrate, Legislator, or Judge (to be hereditary)." The article did not apply to the established church but to hereditary offices, such as those obtained in Great Britain.

5. LP, Albemarle Co., 24 Nov. 1786. The petition also named their delegates: Col. George Nicholas and John Nicholas, brothers and friends of Thomas Jefferson. They and their brother, Wilson Cary Nicholas, were sons of Robert Carter Nicholas and Episcopalians.

6. Neither Hanover nor Lexington presbyteries mentioned the incorporation issue in their minutes for 1786 (Hanover Presbytery, Records, 1786–1814; Lexington Presbytery, Mins., 1786–92. Only one memorial came from the largely Presbyterian counties across the Blue Ridge (LP, Rockbridge Co., 2 Nov. 1786), and none from Prince Edward County, the Presbyterians' Piedmont stronghold.

Hanover and Lexington Presbyterians, together with the newly created Abingdon Presbytery in southwest Virginia and North Carolina and the Transylvania Presbytery in the Kentucky district, became the new Synod of Virginia. Two years later all the American synods finalized their union as one church by adopting the Form of Government and established a General Assembly as the central governing body for all Presbyterians in the United States (Hanover Presbytery, Records, 28–30 Mar. [1786], 329–35; copy of Motions from the Hanover Presbytery, 28 Mar. 1786, Graham Letters and Papers; Trinterud, *American Tradition*, 279–308).

7. David Griffith to William White, 20 Oct. 1786, White Papers.

8. Conway, *Omitted Chapters*, 164.

9. LP, Stafford and King George Cos., 24 Nov. 1786, Elizabeth City Co., 4 Dec. 1786, Caroline Co., 4 Dec. 1786.

10. Meade, *Old Churches* 2:87. County petitions also made the same point. See, e.g., LP, Amelia Co., 8 Nov. 1784. For Leland's importance as an advocate for religious freedom, see Butterfield, "Elder John Leland."

11. LP, Elizabeth City Co., 4 Dec. 1786.

12. "A bill to empower certain societies to hold lands," RHB, box 10, session of 1786–87.

13. LP, Misc. Pet. (Standing Committee of P.E. Church), 5 Dec. 1786; Madison to Jefferson, 15 Feb. 1787, in Boyd, 11:424. Madison and Page, along with Zachariah Johnson, a Presbyterian leader, served on the ten-member drafting committee (*JHDV*, 23 Dec. 1786, 120).

14. Hening, 12:266–67; David Griffith to William White, 28 Apr. 1787, White Papers; Hawks, app., *Conv. of 1787*, 18–25.

15. LP, Augusta Co., 31 Oct. 1787; *JHDV*, 4 Dec. 1787, 82; Semple, *Baptists in Virginia*, 74. See also Benjamin Johnston to James Madison, 19 Jan. 1789, in Hutchinson, 11:424.

16. Hawks, app., *Conv. of 1786*, 12; Madison, *A Sermon, 1786*, 8, 10; Page Notebook. For the General Convention, see Loveland, *Critical Years*, 152–58. For Griffith's troubles, see Griffith to White, 4 July 1787, 12 June, 9 July, 27 Nov. 1788, 10 Feb., 30 Apr. 1789, White Papers; Hawks, app., *Convs. of 1789 and 1790*, 26, 30, 31; Perry, *Gen. Convs.*, 73.

17. Coke, *Journals*, 70, 109; Thrift, *Memoir of Jesse Lee*, 94–95; William Spencer Diary, 25 Dec. 1789, 21. For this revival, see Boles, *Great Revival*, 7–8; Gewehr, *Great Awakening*, 166–86. For Methodism, see Wigger, *Taking Heaven by Storm*; Andrews, *Methodists and Revolutionary America*.

18. Thomas Haskin Journal, 1 Jan. 1785; *Mins. of Methodist Conferences*, 38–39; Jarrett to Edward Droomgo[o]le, 22 Mar. 1788, Droomgoole Papers; Asbury to Jasper Winscom, 15 Aug. 1788, in Clark, *Journal of Asbury* 3:64; White, *Memoirs*, 195–96, 208–9, 211–12; Coke to White, 24 Apr. 1791, ibid., 408–12.

19. Edward Graham to George Baxter, 11 Jan. 1811, Grigsby Papers; Foote, 413–29; Hill, *Autobiographical Sketches*, 12, 113; Gewehr, *Great Awakening*, 177–85.

20. Bayard, *Travels*, 87.

21. Lexington Presbytery, Mins., vol. 1, 1786–92, 25 Oct. 1787, 27 Oct. 1790, 20, 67; Synod of Va., Records, 24 Oct. 1789, 1:14. For the burdens imposed by the insistence on an educated clergy, see Trinterud, *American Tradition*, 264–68. Though Hanover Presbytery sometimes yielded on the issue of a classical education, it held firm on theological formation (Hanover Presbytery, Records, 1786–1814, 16, 19 Oct. 1789, 18–19, 21).

22. Semple, *Baptists in Virginia*, 73–74; Robert Carter to Asa Hunt, 26 Dec. 1787, Carter Papers, Amer. Antiq. Soc. The two Regular Baptist associations were the Ketocton and Kehukee, which was partly located in North Carolina. The Southside Virginia section of the Kehukee became the Virginia Portsmouth Association in 1791. Several other associations such as the Redstone and Salisbury had some churches in Virginia but were based in other states.

23. Semple, *Baptists in Virginia*, 12–23, 59–63, 403–11; James B. Taylor, "John Waller," in Sprague, *Annals* 6:113–17.

24. Semple, *Baptists in Virginia*, 75. Asplund's *Register* for 1790 lists all the Baptist associations in America, with explanatory notes stating whether or not each association subscribed to the Philadelphia Confession (48–53).

Contrary to what Semple (*Baptists in Virginia*, 92) and others have written, the General Association did not dissolve in 1783. It continued to function and deal with questions submitted for advice. At its last meeting in Oct. 1788, it recommended that the General Association and the General Committee be composed of both clerical and lay members. Then it decided to discontinue the General Association and set the date for the next General Committee meeting ("Abstract of the Minutes of a General Association held at Upper Essex, May 1787," "Minutes of General Association held at Burruss's Meeting House in Caroline County, 3 Oct. 1788," Misc. MSS, VBHS).

Some ministers wanted a national union of Baptists. Asa Hunt, a minister from Middleborough, MA, traveled in Virginia for two months in late 1787 to promote "a Union and Intercourse" among all the Baptist churches in the new nation. Occasional letters were exchanged, but no union took place at this time (Robert Carter to Asa Hunt, 26 Dec. 1787, Carter Papers, Amer. Antiq. Soc.; Hunt to Carter, 12 Aug. 1788, Carter Papers, DLC).

25. Burkitt and Read, *History of the Kehukee Assn.*, xvi.

26. Associational Letter, Morattico Baptist Church, to Baptist Assn. meeting at Arias in Westmoreland Co., 5 Oct. 1787, Carter Papers, VBHS.

27. Gen. Com. to Several Baptist Assns. in the Northern States, 8 Mar. 1788, Warren Assn. Papers; Asa Hunt to Isaac Backus, 7 Nov. 1787, Backus Papers; Greene, *Writings of Leland*, 115. To trace the growth in just one church, see Robert Carter to Frances Carter, 10 July 1788, to Asa Hunt, 26 Dec. 1787, and to Lewis Richards, 2 Aug. 1788, Carter Papers, Amer. Antiq. Soc.

28. Norwood, *Methodist Discipline*, 122–25; Greene, *Writings of Leland*, 115.

29. Backus to William Rogers, 21 Oct. 1789, to [(?) Backus], 9 Mar. 1879, Backus Papers; McLoughlin, *Diary of Backus* 3:1273; Backus to John Rippon, 19 Aug. 1791, Backus Papers. For a summary of his views on church-state relations, see McLoughlin, "Isaac Backus and Separation."

30. Asplund, *Annual Register*, 32; Greene, *Writings of Leland*, 117.

31. Semple, *Baptists in Virginia*, 77; Madison to Eve, 2 Jan. 1789, Benjamin Johnson to Madison, 19 Jan. 1789, John Leland to Madison, ca. 15 Feb. 1789, in Hutchinson, 11:405, 424, 442–43. Both Madison and his opponent, James Monroe, had voted against the sale of the church property, so that could not have been the major issue for the Baptists, though Monroe apparently had promised to support the Baptist cause only to reverse himself in the legislature.

32. Joseph Herndon to [James] Stephenson, 8 Apr. 1787, typescript, Herndon Letters; clergy lists for before and after the Revolution are in Brydon, 2:608–12. See also two helpful dissertations: Lohrenz, "The Virginia Clergy," and Dresbeck, "The Epis-

copalian Clergy." For a detailed account of the politics of the glebe issue, see Buckley, "Evangelicals Triumphant."

33. The other petitions that year favoring the sale came from Buckingham, Chesterfield, Cumberland, and Orange Cos. (LP, 6, 17 Oct., 20 Nov. 1787). They were also signed by Baptist clergy in these areas. The names and church locations of the Virginia Baptist ministers and preachers are listed by county in Asplund, *Annual Register*, 24–32.

34. LP, Cumberland Co., 6 Nov., Spotsylvania Co., 10, 22 Nov. 1787. The next year the vestry hired Hugh Corran Boggs, a newly ordained minister who served as rector of Berkeley Parish until his death in 1828 (Brydon, "A List of Clergy").

35. *Va. Independent Chronicle*, 17 Sept. 1788; St. John's Vestry Book, Richmond, 25 Apr. 1791. See also advertisements for vacant parishes in *Va. Gaz., and General Adver.*, 21 Dec. 1791, 19 Dec. 1792. Along with newspaper advertisements for clergymen and parish vestry books, the personal property and land tax records at the Library of Virginia indicate the worth of this property.

36. Eckenrode (*Church and State in Virginia*) treats it as a postscript to the passage of Jefferson's statute, rather than as an important incident in its own right. Political historians have mistakenly attributed the repeal of the glebe laws to party politics and to the intervention of James Madison, though there is no evidence that Madison became involved or that Republican-Federalist rivalries caused the final result. See, e.g., Beeman, *Old Dominion*, 93–95, 198–99; Risjord, *Chesapeake Politics*, 487–89.

37. LP, 14 Nov. 1789. This year the committee appeared united in its opposition to the Episcopal Church's continued title to the property. A factor was probably the bill passed by the previous assembly reconfirming to the newly constituted trustees of the Protestant Episcopal Church all the powers formerly held by the vestries. Whenever the legislature seemed to be assisting the Episcopalians, the General Committee reacted viscerally (Hening, 12:705–6).

38. Madison to Jefferson, 17 Oct. 1788, in Boyd, 14:19.

39. *JHDV*, 27 Nov., 9 Dec. 1789, 83–84, 113. The vote was 69 to 58.

40. Judging from the number of ministers' signatures, the petitions must have circulated at church meetings, and most were well subscribed (LP, 30 Oct.–15 Nov. 1790). *JHDV*, 19 Nov. 1790, 73–74; Roanoke Baptist Assn., Records, June 1790.

41. LP, Misc. Pet., 10 Oct. 1792; *JHDV*, 8, 17 Dec. 1792, 177, 192; a "bill authorizing the sale of glebe lands," 17 Dec. 1792, RHB, session of Oct. 1792. The vote to reject the drafted bill was not recorded.

42. LP, 25 Nov. 1794; *JHDV*, 28 Nov. 1794, 48–49; Thomas Evans to John Cropper, 30 Nov. 1794, John Cropper Papers.

43. Five identical petitions carried 327 signatures, including those of several Baptist ministers (LP, 15 Nov. 1794). The last Episcopal minister had been William Peasley who had served throughout the Revolution and either died or retired in 1787. No vestry appears to have been elected after 1785 (Brydon, "A List of the Clergy," 425). Hawks, app., *Conv. of 1794*, 66.

44. *JHDV*, 22, 27, 28 Nov., 1, 2 Dec. 1794, 30, 45, 47–48, 54, 57. The text is in Shepherd, 1:311. The final House vote was 68 to 58. Seventeen delegates who voted against the Baptist petition to repeal the glebe laws approved the sale of Tillotson glebe. Sixteen others either abstained or were absent. In contrast, only three votes shifted on the other side, and only eight delegates were absent or abstained.

45. Hening, 12:627, 720; Hawks, app., *Conv. of 1790*, 31, 33. This convention, for the first time, also authorized parish trustees to sell a glebe if they judged it beneficial (ibid., 31). Hening, 13:189–91.

46. LP, 4 Oct. 1792; *JHDV*, 4, 24, 25, 29 Oct., 30 Nov., 1 Dec. 1792, 10, 73, 75, 85, 154, 156; Hening, 13:555–56. Confusion over jurisdiction continued throughout these years. The assembly received requests to approve the sale of church property, while some parish vestries, acting upon previous laws and the church canons, bypassed the assembly and sought approval from the convention (Hawks, app., *Conv. of 1793* and *1796*, 59, 68).

47. LP, Halifax Co., 16 Nov. 1795. The others were from Powhatan Co. (Southam Parish), Powhatan and Chesterfield Cos. (King William Parish), 24 Nov. 1795. More than 1,000 names are on these petitions, including those of at least nine Baptist preachers, two of whom, Ruben Pickett and George Smith, were members of the General Committee. Lest the legislature miss the point, they counted the names in each column and put the grand total at the end. The Louisa Co. petition is only in *JHDV*, 17 Nov. 1795, 22–23.

48. LP, Halifax Co., 17 Nov., Powhatan Co., Powhatan and Chesterfield Cos., 24 Nov. 1795. These contained about 200 signatures.

49. *JHDV*, 27 Nov. 1795, 47–48. The vote was 63 to 70.

50. Hawks, app., *Conv. of 1796*, 67–69; LP, 17, 22 Nov. 1796; *JHDV*, 17, 22 Nov., 14 Dec. 1796, 23, 35, 77. The Episcopalian petition argued that the parishes had originally received the property not from the legislature, which had only directed that land be set aside for the church's use, but by a parish purchase or private gifts. For Andrews's background, see Daphne Gentry, "Andrews, Robert," *DVB* 1:167–68.

51. *JHDV*, 14, 23 Dec. 1796, 77–79, 96. The third resolution was amended to permit a majority of the people of the parish to decide how the money would be used (ibid., 95).

52. Barrow to Backus, 27 Jan. 1797, Backus Papers. Barrow was a leader in the Portsmouth Association and General Committee (Taylor, *Lives of Baptist Ministers*, 161–63; Fredrika J. Teute, "Barrow, David," *DVB* 1:371–72).

53. Augustine Smith, an incumbent, won the election. He had been challenged by John West who argued that the Court of Appeals should settle the glebe issue (*Columbian Mirror and Alexandria Gaz.*, 23 Mar., 4, 18 Apr. 1797). The results reported in April showed Roger West, 155; Aug. J. Smith, 127; and John C. Hunter, 79. Smith's victory, however, may not necessarily indicate voter agreement with his views on the glebes. In the assembly West would vote against the Baptist position and Smith would vote for it. For one participant's comments on the involvement of state politics in national affairs that year, see John Marshall to Charles Lee, 20 Apr. 1797, in Johnson, *Papers of Marshall* 3:70–71.

54. Only one county petition called for repeal (LP, Fauquier Co., 9, 20 Dec. 1797).

55. Mays, *Letters of Pendleton* 2:638–46. For Pendleton's work on behalf of his church in 1776, see Mays, *Edmund Pendleton* 2:129, 133–37.

56. Pendleton to [Bishop James Madison], 25 Sept. 1797, in Mays, *Letters of Pendleton* 2:642. Only two petitions opposed repeal that year: one in Pendleton's handwriting from his parish in Caroline Co. and the other from neighboring Spotsylvania Co. (LP, 18 Dec. 1797).

57. Hawks, app., *Conv. of 1797*, 69–72. The manuscript opinion of Bushrod Washington is in the Hook Papers. Randolph's part in the controversy is ably told in Reardon, *Edmund Randolph*, 348–53. The five-member committee included Ludwell Lee from the state Senate and Robert Andrews, James Breckinridge, John Page, and George K. Taylor from the House of Delegates.

58. For a detailed breakdown of the composition of these assemblies, see Buckley, "Evangelicals Triumphant," 50–53.

59. For the printed version of the bill with handwritten amendments, see RHB, 21 Jan. 1798, box 16, Jan. 1798; *JHDV*, 2, 4, 5, 8, 13, 15 Jan. 1798, 73, 78, 80, 85, 94, 96. Spencer, [printed letter concerning action of the General Assembly], 15 Jan. 1798, VHS.

60. *JHDV*, 20, 22 Jan. 1798, 105–6, 108; Strawberry Baptist Assn., May 1798, 101; *JHDV*, 15 Dec. 1798, 12, 21, 23, 25 Jan. 1799, 24, 84, 86, 97, 98, 100; Miller, *Senate Journal, 1798–99*, 23, 24 Jan., 96–97, 100–101. The text of the bill is in Shepherd, 2:149.

61. Hawks, app., *Conv. of 1799*, 73, 74.

62. *JHDV*, 4, 9, 17, 20, 21, 24, 25 Dec. 1799, 3, 6, 13 Jan. 1800, 8, 19, 29, 33, 35, 38, 40, 50, 52, 83. The three parishes were in Hardy, Prince William, and Louisa Cos. John Hooker Reynolds was rector of Hardy Parish (1796–1804), and Thomas Harrison was rector of Dettingen Parish (1798–1810) in Prince William Co. (Brydon, "A List of Clergy," 406, 415, 428, 432).

63. LP, Halifax Co., 17, 19 Dec. 1799.

64. Brydon, "List of Clergy," 406–7; Antrim Parish Vestry Book, Halifax Co., 201–4; LP, Halifax Co., 19 Dec. 1799.

65. *JHDV*, 16, 21 Jan. 1800, 89, 96; *JHDV*, 5, 30 Dec. 1800, 3 Jan. 1801, 10, 48, 51; William Brockenbrough to Joseph C. Cabell, 18 June 1801, box 2, Cabell Family Papers; *JHDV*, 9, 17, 22 Dec. 1801, 8, 23, 35. For Brockenbrough, see F. Thornton Miller, "Brockenbrough, William," *DVB* 2:255–56.

66. *JHDV*, session of 1801–2. The draft texts and amendments are in "A Bill concerning the Glebe Lands and Churches of this Commonwealth," 11 Dec. 1801, RHB, box 20, Dec. 1801. The final text is in Shepherd, 2:314–16. The central issues in debate are discussed in Nicholas Faulcon to John Hartwell Cocke, 17 Jan. 1802, Cocke Papers, no. 640, and William Brockenbrough to Spencer Roane, 5 Sept. [1803], Roane-Harrison-Williams Papers.

67. *Mins. of the Baptist Gen. Com., 1790*, 8; Henry Toler to Isaac Backus, May 1795, Backus Papers; "Address to the Public," *Columbian Mirror and Alexandria Gaz.*, 23 June 1795.

68. Leland, *Storke at the Branch*, 19; LP, 24 Nov. 1795, 5 Nov. 1789, Richmond Co., 30

Oct. 1790. For other expressions of this drive for equality, see LP, 20 Nov. 1787, 14 Aug., 30 Oct. 1790.

69. Beeman, *Old Dominion and New Nation*, 119–37, 140–44; Risjord, *Chesapeake Politics*, 424–60; Burruss's Baptist Church to Goshen Assn., Sept. 1795, Misc. MSS, VBHS; *Mins. of the Goshen Baptist Assn., 1795*, 5; Elisha Purrington to Isaac Backus, 31 Mar. 1797, Backus Papers.

70. LP, Misc. Pet., 17 Nov. 1795; Fristoe, *History of the Ketocton Assn.*, 90.

71. Madison to Jefferson, 21 Jan. 1798, in Hutchinson, 17:69.

72. LP, Augusta Co., 31 Oct. 1787; *Mins. of the Baptist Gen. Com., 1790*, 4–8; Hanover Presbytery, Records, 10 July 1790, 1 Aug., 29 Oct. 1791, 12 May, 28, 30 July 1792, 29, 45, 50, 56, 58, 59.

73. *JHDV*, 14, 27, 28, 30 Nov., 1, 3 Dec. 1789, 59, 86, 88, 89–90, 92, 98; LP, Berkeley Co., 13 Nov. 1790, Alexandria Town, 16 Nov. 1790; Hening, 13:85, 174–75.

74. *Mins. of the Baptist Gen. Com., 1790*, 6, 7; *Mins. of Methodist Conferences*, 34–35; *Mins. of the Baptist Gen. Com., 1791*, 6. For Methodist refusal to cooperate with the Baptists, see LP, Amelia Co., 4 Nov. 1790, Lunenburg Co., 19 Nov. 1790. For Ashbury's reflections on the Petersburg meeting, see Clark, *Journal of Asbury* 1:642. O'Kelly, an influential minister in Southside Virginia, was opposing Asbury's authority. He would soon break with the church and organize the Republican Methodists. See Kilgore, *James O'Kelly Schism*.

75. White, *Memoirs*, 195–96; Coke to White, 24 Apr. 1791, ibid., 408–12.

76. LP, Prince Edward Co., 4 Oct. 1792; Edmund Pendleton to [Bishop James Madison], 25 Sept. 1797, in Mays, *Letters of Pendleton* 2:642; *Va. Argus*, 17 Oct. 1797.

77. LP, Amelia Co., 4 Nov. 1790.

78. See, e.g., *Mins. of the Ketocton Assn.*, 18 Aug. 1792, 4; Strawberry Baptist Assn., Records, Oct. 1792, 50–51.

79. *Mins. of the Baptist Gen. Com., 1790*, 8, *1793*, 4, and *1799*, 4.

80. LP, Lunenburg Co., 19 Nov. 1790; Ireland, *Life of Ireland*, 182; *Va. Argus*, 17 Oct. 1797.

81. Asplund's *Register* lists all the Baptist ministers and licensed preachers in Virginia in 1790 by county. Checking their names against the personal property and land tax records for 1790 in the Library of Virginia, I located 198 (74%) of the 267 men listed for Virginia. Of these, 135 (68%) owned one or more slaves above the age of 12. The landholdings of 119 ministers averaged 406 acres.

82. Edmund Pendleton to James Madison, 6 Oct. 1788, in Hutchinson, 17:530; Bishop Madison to William White, 19 Dec. 1790, White Papers; Meade, *Old Churches* 1:50.

83. William Price to Edward Payne, 20 Dec. 1787, to Luke Allen, 23 Dec. 1787, in Coe, "Price's Priceless Penn," 12–13.

84. "An Address to the Public," *Columbian Mirror and Alexandria Gaz.*," 23 June 1795; LP, Misc. Pet., 17 Nov. 1795.

85. A "bill authorizing the sale of glebe lands," 17 Dec. 1792, RHB, box 14, session of Oct. 1792; LP, Chesterfield Co., 13 Nov. 1790, Richmond Co., 30 Oct. 1790.

86. Meade, *Old Churches* 1:16, 412; Edmund Pendleton to James Madison, 30 July

1801, in Brugger, *Papers of Madison* 1:487. For Bishop Madison's concerns over the clergy, see Madison to William Peachy, 1 Aug. 1794, in Meade, *Old Churches* 2:175.

87. Jarratt, *Life*, 123; Jarratt to Archibald McRobert, 11 Jan. 1800, Gratz Coll.; *Va. Argus*, 17 Oct. 1797; Eleazar Clay to Isaac Backus, 23 May 1795, William Brown to Backus, 20 Feb. 1797, George Smith to Backus, 15 Mar. 1797, Backus Papers.

88. "Viator," *Va. Gaz. and Gen. Adver.*, 22 Mar. 1797; Channing, *Memoir of Channing* 1:126.

89. For the statistics, see Buckley, "Evangelicals Triumphant," 52, 64. For an example of one Episcopalian's reasoning in favor of the glebe sale, see Meade, *Old Churches* 1:187–88.

90. Madison to White, 19 Dec. 1790, White Papers. The best study of Madison is Crowe, "Madison and the Republic of Virtue." See also the sketch by G. MacLaren Brydon in *DAB* 12:182–84.

91. "The Petersburg Monitor," *Va. Gaz. and Petersburg Intelligencer*, 14 Dec. 1786. For the conflict over a Virginia episcopate before the Revolution, see Brydon, 2:341–59, and Bridenbaugh, *Mitre and Sceptre*, 316–32.

92. *Richmond and Manchester Adver.*, 20 Aug. 1795; John Tyler to St. George Tucker, 10 July 1795, Tyler Papers.

93. Madison to White, 12 July, 19 Dec. 1790, White Papers. For his public statements, see Hawks, app., *Conv. of 1791, 1793*, and *1799*, 37–45, 55–59, 78–83. For his private correspondence, see, e.g., his letters to Henry Tazewell in 1795–98 (Madison Papers, DU). Despite the pressure the church was under in Virginia during this time, Madison does not mention church problems to Tazewell, a devout Episcopalian. In fact, he defended the legislature against Tazewell's criticism. Of the 1797 session the bishop wrote, "I cannot however accord with all your observation upon the last House of Delegates. Their Conduct ought to be exposed in Defense of pure and genuine Republicanism" (3 Feb. 1798, ibid.).

94. Hawks, app., *Conv. of 1799*, 81; Joseph C. Cabell to David Watson, 4 Mar. 1798, Watson Papers. For a more sympathetic view of Madison at William and Mary in this era, see Godson, *College of William and Mary* 1:195–98; Baker, *Richmond Theater Fire*, 154–58.

95. Madison's last report of a visitation was made to the 1796 convention (Hawks, App., *Conv. of 1796*, 68). He attended the General Conventions of 1792 and 1795 but absented himself thereafter (Perry, *Gen. Convs.* 1:161, 199).

96. James Madison, *Address to the Church*, in Hawks, app., 78–83 (quotes at 78, 79, 81, 83).

97. Ibid., 71; Bishop Madison to James Madison, 9 Jan. 1800, in Hutchinson, 17:353; Perry, *Gen. Convs.* 1:381; *Protestant Episcopal Church, House of Bishops*, 8, 9. For Bishop Meade's defense of his predecessor, see *Old Churches* 1:28–29.

98. Bishop Madison to James Madison, 12 Nov. 1794, 23 Feb. 1801, in Hutchinson, 15:374, 17:472–73; David Meade to Judge [Joseph] Prentis, 30 Apr. 1798, Charles K. Mallory to Joseph Prentis Jr., 25 Aug. 1803, box 8, Webb-Prentis Papers. The Columbia presidency had been vacant since the summer of 1800 and was only filled in May 1801

by the election of another Episcopal clergyman, Charles H. Wharton, of New Jersey ([Brander Matthews et al.], *A History of Columbia University, 1754–1904* [New York, 1904], 81–82).

99. James Madison to George Logan, 16 Dec. 1802, Logan Papers; Jefferson to Madison, 13, 17 Sept. 1802, in Brugger, *Papers of Madison* 3:578, 588; Crowe, "Madison and the Republic of Virtue," 61. For the bishop's distinctive blend of politics and religion, see "Bishop Madison's Prayer," *RE*, 6 June 1807; Madison to Jefferson, 11 Feb. 1800, in Boyd, 31:364–65.

100. Hawks, app., *Convs. of 1799,* and *1805,* 73, 79, 85.

101. Absalom Waller to Isaac Backus, 24 Apr. 1799, Backus Papers.

102. David Watson to Joseph C. Cabell, 4 Dec. 1801, Cabell Family Papers, no. 38–111, box 2.

103. LP, Caroline Co., 8 Dec. 1804; Shepherd, 3:156–57. Eighty-eight signatures accompanied Waugh's petition, including that of John Taylor of Caroline. For similar cases, see ibid., 214–15, 409–10.

104. E.g., Shepherd, 3:391–95, 427–28, 432.

105. LP, Albemarle Co., 7 Dec. 1803; "A bill appropriating certain funds toward repairing the Churches in the Parish of St. Ann," RHB, [1804], box 20; LP, Surry Co., 12 Dec. 1809, King and Queen Co., 7 Dec. 1811, Richmond Co., 3 Dec. 1812, Williamsburg, 8 Dec. 1831. In the session of 1812–13, a bill "concerning churches, church plate and property" made it through one reading before it was rejected (RHB, box 27).

106. "Communication," *Va. Gaz. and Gen. Adver.*, 11 Dec. 1802; "Mrs. M'Knight versus Bishop Courtney," *Recorder*, 22 Dec. 1802; Fred Anderson, "Courtney, John," *DVB* 3:487–88. For Blair's Federalism, see [John D. Blair], "Senex" articles in Blair Papers, Brock.

107. See, e.g., *JHDV*, 5 Dec. 1809, 10, 18 Dec. 1817, 36, 20 Dec. 1827, 53, 16 Dec. 1829, 22.

5. LITIGATION

1. Elizabeth McCroskey to St. George Tucker, 9 May 1803, box 23, TCP; Hungars Parish Vestry Book, Northampton Co., 1812–1937. McCroskey's DD appears in a 1789 list of clergy in *Journals of the Gen. Convs.*, 159. For Tucker's early career, see Cullen, *St. George Tucker.*

2. Henry St. George Tucker to St. George Tucker, 18 May 1795, box 19, Elizabeth McCroskey to St. George Tucker, 2, 27 June 1803, box 23, TCP. Each General Court judge also served on a district court that met in April or May. The General Court met in Richmond in June. For Tucker's judicial duties and his edition of Blackstone, see Cullen, *St. George Tucker,* 80–82, 159–63. The gravestone inscription with a marginal note identifying Tucker as the composer is in Mackey and Perry, *Vestry Book of Hungar's Parish,* 95–96. This is a published version of the first vestry book, no. 23606 (photostat), LVA.

3. Thomas Davis to St. George Tucker, 26 Oct 1801, box 22, 27 July 1803, box 23, TCP.

For a description of Hungars glebe, see *Va. Gaz. and Gen. Adver.*, 3 Aug. 1803, and Whitelaw, *Virginia's Eastern Shore* 1:426, 431–34.

4. Charlton's will is copied in Hungars Parish Vestry Book, Northampton Co., ii; Elizabeth McCroskey to St. George Tucker, 14 Dec. 1803, box 24, TCP. See also Stitt, "Will of Stephen Charlton."

5. Elizabeth McCroskey to St. George Tucker, [3 Dec. 1803], box 24, TCP. For Gardiner, see Meade, *Old Churches* 1:259; Brydon, "A List of Clergy," 431; Elizabeth McCroskey to St. George Tucker, 14 Dec. 1803, box 24, TCP. Thomas Davis succeeded Gardiner as rector in 1808.

6. Elizabeth McCroskey to St. George Tucker, 22 Nov., 23 Dec. 1803, 16 Jan. 1804, box 24, TCP. For the ferry house, see Whitelaw, *Virginia's Eastern Shore* 1:299–300. Peter Bowdoin, Elizabeth's brother, owned it. She later moved to a house in Williamsburg where she died in 1812 (Memorandum of money found in the House of Mrs. McCroskey the day after death, 11 Nov. 1812, TCP, box 32).

7. Elizabeth McCroskey to St. George Tucker, 16 Jan. 1804, box 24, TCP.

8. The text of this bill is quoted in the *Richmond Examiner*, 23 May 1804, as editor Thomas Ritchie began a series of articles reporting the court debate on *Turpin v. Lockett*.

9. The best account of the first trial before the Supreme Court of Appeals is in Mays, *Edmund Pendleton* 2:337–45. William Brockenbrough to Spencer Roane, 5 Sept. [1803], Roane-Harrison-Williams Papers. For a near contemporary's Episcopalian perspective, see Hawks, *Contributions* 1:238–39. For a Presbyterian defense of the law and the court's decision composed a few years later, see Robert R. Howison, *History of Virginia* 2:394–405. See also Nelson, *Study of Judicial Review*, 47–50.

10. James Semple to St. George Tucker, 13 Dec. 1803, St. George Tucker to Semple, 16 Dec. 1803, George Tucker to St. George Tucker, 18 Dec. 1803, John Minor to St. George Tucker, 6 Jan. 1804, box 24, TCP; St. George Tucker, *Blackstone's Commentaries* 2:104–18 (quote at 117); Cullen, *St. George Tucker*, 174–77.

11. *RE*, 9 May 1804; Burwell Bassett to St. George Tucker, 6 Jan. 1804, box 24, TCP.

12. *Turpin v. Lockett* contains the published text with Tucker's decision on pp. 128–57. His original manuscript text is located in Va. Court of Appeals, April Term, 1804, folder 8, TCP. In what follows, I quote from Tucker's manuscript text which while practically identical with the printed text contains emphases that were not reproduced in Call's *Virginia Reports*.

13. Pendleton's decision does not appear in Mays's edition of his papers, but his views may be gauged by his "Proposed Memorial concerning the Glebe Lands of the Episcopal Church," 25 Sept. 1797, in Mays, *Papers of Pendleton* 2:637–42.

14. Tucker, Decision, 11–12.

15. Ibid., 16, 17, 21.

16. Ibid., 21–22, 27.

17. *Mins. of the Middle District Assn., 1804*, 4. Both men would purchase pews in the Monumental Church a decade later. See Fisher, *History of Monumental Church*, 35, 37.

18. Hawks, app., *Conv. of 1804*, 83–87 (quotes at 83 and 85); *RE*, 14 May 1805.

19. *Journals of the Gen. Convs.*, 276; Meade, *A Brief Review*, 7. Bishop Madison repeatedly summoned conventions that apparently never met, probably for lack of a quorum. For his announcements of these meetings, see, e.g., *RE*, 10 Apr. 1807; *Va. Gaz.*, 31 Mar. 1809; *Va. Argus*, 5 Apr. 1810; *RE*, 16 Apr. 1811.

20. Hawks, *Contributions* 1:250–51. For an appreciation of Moore written shortly after his death, see Norwood, "Sketch of Bishop Moore." See also Godson, "Bishop Richard Channing Moore."

21. The Virginia portion of the District of Columbia remained within the Episcopal diocese of Virginia and was retroceded to Virginia in 1846. Today that includes the city of Alexandria and Arlington County.

22. Lee, *Lee of Virginia*, 374–75; Hawks, app., *Conv. of 1813*, 90; J. H. Hobart to Edmund J. Lee, 18 Dec. 1813, Richard Channing Moore to Lee, 23 Oct. 1817, Moore Letterbook A, box 39; Moore to Lee, 17 Feb. 1814, Meade Papers, box 1, folder 1.

23. *Terrett v. Taylor*, quotes at 50–51 and 52. Further litigation before the U.S. Supreme Court over this glebe reaffirmed the decision in *Terrett* and determined that the vestry of Christ Church, Alexandria, was the successor vestry to that of Fairfax Parish. See *Mason v. Muncaster*.

A separate intrachurch dispute arose in the 1820s when St. Paul's Parish in Alexandria thought it was entitled to part of Fairfax glebe. For Moore's diplomacy in this conflict, see Moore to John Marshall, 2 Apr. 1824, to [Edmund J. Lee], [6? Apr. 1824], and to Oliver Norris, 6 Apr. 1824, Moore Letterbook E.

24. *Young v. Pollock*, 517n; *Claughton v. Macnaughton*, 513–18; Meade, *Old Churches*, 276–77.

25. Inventory of Shelburne Parish, 10 May 1785, Loudoun Co. Will Book C, 139; Worsley, *Old St. James*, 3–5. The appeal to the U.S. Supreme Court was not made. By the time the decision was finally rendered in Virginia's Supreme Court of Appeals, three of the four vestrymen were dead, and the last one had lost interest.

26. Moore to Thomas Jackson, 9 Jan. 1829, Moore Letterbook K. For Moore's concern over his clergy's financial problems, see Moore to Meade, 30 Dec. 1822, Moore Letterbook B.

27. *Selden v. Overseers*.

28. Henry St. George Tucker, *Opinion of Chancellor Tucker*, 5. Tucker republished this opinion in *Commentaries on the Laws of Virginia* 2:app.

29. *Opinion of Chancellor Tucker*, 8, 9, 11, 12.

30. See, e.g., "Indenture from Joseph Dodson to William Stams and Trustees of the Baptist Church on Barker's Branch," 23 Sept. 1765, Fauquier Co. DB 2, 368.

31. For the practice in Albemarle County, Jefferson's home, see chap. 6, n. 87.

32. *Opinion of Chancellor Tucker*, 12, 16. This negative judgment on European religious history became increasingly popular during the nineteenth century. See S. J. Barnett, *Idol Temples and Crafty Priests: The Origins of Enlightenment Anticlericalism* (New York, 1999).

33. [Lee], *Selden and Others*, 1. Lee may also have written "*The Pamphlet*," or *Thoughts on High Church Principles, and the Probable Connection between Church and State, by A*

Layman (Lynchburg, 1830). This responded to an 1829 pamphlet of Presbyterian minister John Holt Rice.

34. [Lee], *Selden and Others*, 2–7 (quotes at 6, 7).

35. Ibid., quotes at 26, 25, 41, 42, 43.

36. *Selden v. Overseers*, quotes at 140. Other frictions remained over such issues such as the use of the churches. For one such argument between Episcopalians and Methodists involving Yeocomico Church, see LP, Westmoreland Co., 3 Jan. 1844,; *JHDV*, 3, 22 Jan. 1844, 70, III; David McComas to William N. Ward, 20 Jan. 1844, in Meade, *Old Churches* 2:153–54.

37. Hening, II:532–37, 12:266–67; Shepherd, 2:149. For early examples of incorporation requests rejected by the assembly, see petitions of the Episcopal vestry of Antrim Parish (Halifax Co., 22 Dec. 1803) and the Fincastle Presbyterian congregation (Botetourt Co., 19 Dec. 1805), LP. About 1799 the Methodist congregation in Norfolk had drawn up an incorporation petition, but apparently they never formally submitted it to the assembly. It does not appear in the legislative journals (LP, Norfolk Borough, [1799?]).

38. *Terrett v. Taylor*, quotes at 50–51, 52, and 49.

39. Hoge, "Life of Moses Hoge," 198–202, Hoge Papers,; Synod of Va., Mins., 29 Oct. 1814, 14, 16, Oct. 1815, 50, 87, 91–92; LP, Prince Edward Co., 7 Dec. 1815. Presbyterian awareness of the objections to church incorporations can be found in John Holt Rice's *Va. Rel. Mag.* 3 (1807), 210–II, and Foote, *Second Series*, 332–33. The management of the seminary fund had originally been committed to Hampden-Sydney College's board of trustees (Rice, *Duties of a Minister*, 20). But the synod wanted more direct control over the seminary, and the college's board included non-Presbyterians.

40. John Holt Rice to William Wirt, 21 Dec. 1815, 3, 31 Jan. 1816, Rice Papers; *RE*, 27 Jan., 3, 5, 13 Feb. 1816; Rice, *Illustration*, 13, 52, 54. See also Benjamin Rice to William McPheeters, 5 Apr. 1816, typescript, Rice Papers.

For a discussion of what William G. McLoughlin called "incorporated voluntaryism" in other states, see his "Role of Religion in the Revolution"; Kauper and Ellis, "Religious Corporations and the Law," 1505–27; Dignan, *A History of the Legal Incorporation*, 54–66.

41. Hanover Presbytery, Mins., 23 Oct. 1826, 30 Apr. 1827, 241–46, 293; *Mins. of the Gen. Assembly, 1826*, 30–31; *Mins. of the Gen. Assembly, 1827*, 126–27. A precedent for this move had been set in the previous decade when the Virginia Synod placed the tract, mission, and Bible societies under the Presbyterian General Assembly's Board of Missions (Synod of Va., Mins., 28 Oct. 1816, 143).

42. Hoge, "Life of Moses Hoge," 210; Scervant Jones to the People of York Co., 4 Mar. 1824, Brand Papers; Howison, *History of Va.* 2:492–93; *Selden v. Overseers*, 138–39.

43. Keiley, *History of the Catholic Church*, 8; *Gallego's Executors v. Attorney Gen.*, quotes at 477, 478. For Gallego, see Hall, *Portraits in the VHS*, 89. The Marshall decision is in *Baptist Assn. v. Hart's Executors*.

44. LP, Loudoun Co., 17 Dec. 1833. The petition file also contains Butcher's will,

dated 12 Sept 1769 and proved 9 Mar. 1778. *JHDV*, 17, 30 Dec. 1833, 54, 72. A few years earlier the assembly had rejected a bill appointing trustees in a similar situation (see "A Bill appointing trustees to hold a piece of land belong to the Baptist Church at Occoquan," Jan. 1830, RHB, box 45; *JHDV*, 16, 29, Jan. 1830, 91, 116).

45. *AA*, 1841–42, ch. 102, "An Act concerning conveyances or devises of places of public worship," 60–61.

46. LP, Northampton Co., 29 Jan. 1838. A counterpetition by the ministry and vestry of Hungars Parish claimed the validity of their title on the basis of a law of February 1745 permitting the vestry to purchase some land. This law had never been repealed. For the legal complications in this case, see Stitt, "The Will of Stephen Charlton."

47. LP, Misc. Pet., 3 Jan. 1840; *JHDV*, 3 Jan.–4 Mar. 1840; ibid., 15 Dec. 1841, 29. Established by the colonial clergy in 1755, the Episcopalian fund was managed by the diocesan treasurer. For the problems this created, see Hawks, app., *Conv. of 1835*, 322, and *1839*, 14; *Rich. Whig and Public Adver.*, 14 Jan. 1842. The assembly turned down the Methodist society by a vote of 26 to 89. The text of the proposed bill was printed ibid., 12 Feb. 1842. The early development of the corporation in the United States is traced by Pauline Maier, "The Revolutionary Origins of the American Corporation," *WMQ*, 3d ser., 50 (1993): 51–84.

48. Hawks, app., *Conv. of 1843*, 11, 12; *JHDV*, 14 Jan. 1844, 95; Hawks, app., *Conv. of 1844*, 12, 13; LP, Spotsylvania Co., 21 Dec. 1844.

49. LP, King and Queen Co., 13 Dec. 1844. Identical or supportive petitions came from at least seven other counties as well as Fredericksburg, Lynchburg, and Richmond (*JHDV*, 3 Dec. 1844–25 Jan. 1845).

50. Eli Ball et al., *Appeal to the Legislature of Va.*, 3, 9, 10.

51. White, *Southern Presbyterian Leaders*, 286–92.

52. For the Old School–New School division, see Parker, *United Synod of the South*; Smith, "Role of the South in the Presbyterian Schism." For the separation in the Richmond congregation, see Foote, *Second Series*, 546; Thompson, *Presbyterians in the South* 1:406.

53. Synod of Va., Mins., Oct. 17–19, 21, 1844, 177–78, 182–83, 187–89, 202; William S. Plumer to Speaker of the House of Delegates, 17 Dec. 1844, in LP, Richmond City, 17 Dec. 1844; *RE*, 11 Nov. 1844; *Rich. Whig and Public Adver.*, 24 Dec. 1844. For Plumer's early opposition to incorporation, see *Watchman of the South*, 20 Jan. 1842, 4 Sept. 1844. A firsthand account of the dispute over incorporation may be found in Howison, *Hist. of Va.* 2:484, 494–97. Howison had been a Presbyterian minister, but had left the ministry for health reasons in 1845, and then practiced law in Richmond (Bryson, "Robert Reid Howison," 113).

54. *Mins. of the Va. Baptist Gen. Meeting of Correspondence*, 1822, 3; *Mins. of the Eighth Annual Meeting of the Gen. Asso.*, 16; *Proceedings of the Ninth Annual Meeting of the Gen. Asso.*, 21; *Proceedings of the Tenth Annual Meeting of the Gen. Asso.*, 9–11; *Proceedings of the Twenty-First Annual Meeting of the Gen. Asso.*, 13, 18, 26, 36.

55. LP, Richmond City, 4 Jan. 1845. See "To the Gen. Assembly of Virginia," in *Rich.*

Whig and Public Adver., 10 Jan. 1845. For a Presbyterian response, see "The position of the Synod of Virginia," ibid. A history of the Baptist appeal is recounted by Eli Ball, "To the Editors of the Whig," ibid., 7 Jan. 1845.

56. James B. Taylor to the Chairman of the Com. for the Courts of Justice, 4 Jan. 1845, in LP, Richmond City, 19 Dec. 1845.

57. LP, Franklin Co., 10 Dec. 1844. See also a similar petition from the Dunkard or Old German Baptists (LP, Franklin Co., 13 Dec. 1844). An excellent study of the Old School Baptists is Wyatt-Brown, "Antimission Movement in the Jacksonian South."

58. "A Member of the Synod" defended the synod's opposition to the incorporation bill in *Rich. Whig and Public Adver.*, 24 Dec. 1844, 10, 17, 21 Jan., 4, 7 Mar., 25 Apr. 1845. Various authors attacked the synod's position and defended the proposed act. See, e.g., articles, ibid., by "A Listener" (17 Dec. 1844, 14 Jan., 14 Feb. [2 parts], 18 Mar. 1845), "Equal Rights" (3 Jan., 18 Feb. 1845), "Sydney" (4, 7 Feb. 1845), "One of the Memorialists" (14 Feb., 18 Mar. 1845), and "A Citizen of Prince Edward" (11 Feb., 11 Apr., 27 May 1845). The newspaper itself editorialized in favor of the bill in "The Position of the Synod of Virginia," 24 Dec. 1844.

59. Hawks, app., *Conv. of 1845*, 11; P[eyton] Harrison to Henry St. George Tucker, 9 Dec. 1844, Tucker Family Papers, Brock, box 9 (48); *Proceedings of the Twenty-Second Annual Meeting of the Baptist Gen. Asso., 1845*, 4, 7; LP, Misc. Pet., 3 Feb. 1846, and Richmond City, 11 Dec. 1845.

60. Howison, *Hist. of Va.* 2:494–95; "Rev. Wm S. Plumer's Challenge," *Rich. Whig and Public Adver.*, 13 Dec. 1844; *Watchman of the South*, 21 Nov. 1844.

61. Macfarland, *Argument in Reply to Plumer*, 30. For Macfarland's biography, see Gaines, *Biographical Register of Members*, 53–54.

62. Plumer, *Substance of an Argument*, 5, 10. Meade's address had been extremely critical of the colonial church (Meade, *Brief Review of the Episcopal Church*).

63. Macfarland, *Argument in Reply to Plumer*, 10, 28, 30, 35.

64. R[obert] E[den] Scott to Christian B. Scott, 9 Jan. 1846, VHS; Moses Drury Hoge Journal, 9, 30 Jan. 1846, Brock, box 170.

65. Plumer, *Substance of an Argument*, 43. For an earlier example of Methodist opposition, see the account from the *Rich. Christian Advocate* in *Watchman of the South*, 2 Jan. 1845. Macfarland, *Argument in Reply to Plumer*, 33; *JHDV*, 23 Feb. 1846, 193.

66. LP, Amherst Co., 27 Nov. 1783. Ironically, this was the identity the supporters of religious taxation had urged upon the legislature, which that body supposedly rejected by the passage of Jefferson's statute.

67. *Proceedings of the Twenty-Third Annual Meeting of the Baptist Gen. Asso.*, 5; LP, Clarke Co., 16 Jan. 1847; *JHDV*, 16, 28 Jan., 8 Mar. 1847, 88, 111, 183; LP, Franklin Co., 15 Jan. 1848. See also the Baptist appeal "To the Citizens of Virginia," *Rich. Whig and Public Adver.*, 24, 27 Aug. 1847. Meanwhile, the Episcopalians tried other methods for securing bequests. See Hawks, app., *Conv. of 1846*, 15–17.

68. *JHDV*, 14 Feb., 1 Mar. 1848, 250, 299; *Rich. Whig and Public Adver.*, 20 Feb. 1849, 4.

69. LP, Misc. Pet., 28 Jan. 1850; *JHDV*, 28 Jan., 4 Feb., 12, 18 Mar. 1850, 188–89, 214,

386, 422. Although Meade reported to the 1850 church convention that the fund "had been, and perhaps still is, in some jeopardy," it evidently remained secure. The assets had been under the control of three trustees since 1839, and the system seems to have functioned effectively even without legal incorporation (Hawks, app., *Conv. of 1850*, 44, *1839*, 14, and *1851*, 35).

70. *AA, 1851–1852*, 332; *AA, 1853–1854*, ch. 107, "Act incorporating the Protestant Episcopal Theological seminary and high school in Virginia," 65. In both cases it limited the amount of land to 250 acres and endowment to $250,000.

71. *Seaburn's Ex'or v. Seaburn*, 423–33 (quote at 432). For Moncure, see Christian, "Hon. R. C. L. Moncure," 714.

72. Hawks, app., *Conv. of 1846*, 14; Plumer, *Substance of an Argument*, 43–45; Philip Barraud to St. George Tucker, 3 Sept. 1827, TCP. See also John Grammar Jr. to William H. Brodnax, 17 Jan. 1826, Brodnax Papers.

73. Hanley, *Beyond a Christian Commonwealth*. See also Daniel Walker Howe, "Religion and Politics in the Antebellum North," in Noll, *Religion and Politics*, 132; Conser, *Church and Confession*, 290–91, 322.

74. Plumer, *Substance of an Argument*, 48, 46, 12; LP, Franklin Co. (Pig River Assn.), 15 Jan. 1848, Franklin Co. (Old School Baptists), 10 Dec. 1844, Franklin Co. (New River Assn.), 15 Jan. 1848, Pittsylvania Co. (Mayo Assn.), 15 Jan. 1848.

75. Rice, *Historical and Philosophical Considerations of Religion*, 59. For the importance of nativism in religious politics, see Robert P. Swierenga, "Ethnoreligious Political Behavior in the Mid-Nineteenth Century: Voting, Values, Cultures," in Noll, *Religion and American Politics*, 146–71.

76. *Rich. Whig and Public Adver.*, 14 Jan. 1842.

77. Robert Young Conrad to Elizabeth Powell Conrad, 11 Dec. 1843, Conrad Papers.

78. Plumer, *Substance of an Argument*, 51. His views were not unique. In the 1840s the Virginia Synod regularly scheduled a "sermon on Popery" for its annual gathering (*Rich. Whig and Public Adver.*, 26 Oct. 1847).

79. See, e.g., the report of the legislative debate in *Rich. Whig and Public Adver.*, 14 Jan. 1842.

80. *Journal of the House of Representatives*, 6 June 1809, 18 Jan. 1810, 36, 180; *Annals of Congress*, pt. 2, 11th Cong., 2d Sess., 24 Jan., 2, 9, 16 Feb. 1810, 1300, 1368, 1402, 1411; pt. 3, 11th Cong., 3d Sess., 20 Dec. 1810, 26, 28 Jan. 1811, 454, 828, 832. The text of the act "for incorporating the Protestant Episcopal Church in the town of Alexandria, in the District of Columbia" and Madison's veto message are in *American State Papers*, Class X: Misc., 2:152–54. In the Library of Congress's microfilm edition of the James Madison Papers (ser. 1, reel 13), there is the text of "A bill concerning the Protestant Episcopal Church in the town of Alexandria and District of Columbia." In contrast to the act passed by Congress, this bill simply specified the church's property and assigned its legal title and management to the church's vestrymen and their successors. It concluded: "that nothing in this Act shall be construed as in any manner establishing the said Church or the religion thereof." Though not in Madison's handwriting, this may have been proposed as an alternative to the congressional bill.

A week later Madison vetoed another act that granted preemption rights to a tract of federal land to a Baptist church in Mississippi. He argued that such government support for a religious group violated the establishment clause (*American State Papers* 2:154). See Rutland, *Presidency of James Madison*, 77–78.

81. *Annals of Congress*, pt. 3, 11th Cong., 3d Sess., 23 Feb. 1811, 995–98; Rice to Wirt, 3 Jan. 1816, Rice Papers.

82. Fleet, "Madison's 'Detached Memoranda,'" 556, 557. For an analysis, see Leo Pfeffer, "Madison's 'Detached Memoranda': Then and Now," in Peterson and Vaughan, *Virginia Statute for Religious Freedom*, 283–312. Neither Fleet nor Pfeffer refers to the Virginia controversy over church incorporation. Madison expressed similar concerns in a private letter; see Madison to Jasper Adams, 1832, in Hunt, *Writings of Madison* 9:484–88.

83. *JHDV*, 15 Dec. 1841, 11, 24 Jan., 3 Feb. 1842, 29, 72, 96, 116. For the Virginia courts, see *Seaburn's Executor v. Seaburn*, 15 Grattan (56 Va.) 423 (1859); *Kelly v. Love's Administrator*, 20 Grattan (61 Va.) 124 (1870); *Moore v. Perkins*, 169 Va. 175, 192 S.E. 806 (1937). For similar fears voiced in legislative debate, see *Rich. Whig and Public Adver.*, 14 Jan. 1842.

84. LP, Misc. Pet., 3 Jan. 1840, King and Queen Co., 17 Dec. 1844, Richmond City, 4 Jan. 1845. See also the Episcopalians' petition in LP, Richmond City, 11 Dec. 1845, and Clarke Co., 16 Jan. 1847. During this same period various denominations including the Baptists were also seeking state funds to support their colleges. See Daniel, "Genesis of Richmond College," 147–48.

85. Howe, "Religion and Politics," in Noll, *Religion and American Politics*, 135; Bertram Wyatt-Brown, "Religion and the 'Civilizing Process' in the Early South, 1600–1860," ibid., 172–95. Although they generally ignore church-state relations, a multitude of studies have documented the control that conservative planters maintained over Virginia politics during the first half of the nineteenth century. See, e.g., Dickson D. Bruce Jr., *The Rhetoric of Conservatism: The Virginia Convention of 1829–30 and the Conservative Tradition of the South* (San Marino, CA, 1982); Jordan, *Political Leadership*, 205–24; Malone, "Fate of Revolutionary Republicanism"; Sutton, *Revolution to Secession*, 103–21.

86. LP, Greenbrier Co., 8 Dec. 1847; Plumer, *Substance of an Argument*, 45; LP, Richmond City, 20 Feb. 1846, Misc. Pet., 28 Jan. 1850. See also the article by "Presbyteros" in *RE*, 13 Feb. 1816.

87. Rice, "Mutual Relations of Church and State," Rice Papers.

88. *Seaburn's Executor v. Seaburn*, 15 Grattan (56 Va.) 423 (1859). This disability continued into the twentieth century. See *Kelly v. Love's Administrator*, 20 Grattan (61 Va.) 124 (1870); *Fifield v. Van Wyck's Executor*, 94 Va. 557 (1897); *Moore v. Perkins*, 169 Va. 175, 192 S.E. 806 (1937).

89. See Howard's brief discussion of the incorporation restriction in Virginia's constitution (*Commentaries on the Constitution* 1:546).

90. See, e.g., LP, Richmond Co., 17 Mar. 1838; *AA, 1837–1838*, ch. 298, "An Act concerning the parishes of Farnham and Lunenburg," 218. Nor did the assembly accept the invitation offered by the Methodists in Yeocomico Parish to clarify the ambiguities left

from the 1802 law (LP, Westmoreland Co., 3 Jan. 1844; *JHDV*, 22 Jan. 1844, 111; David McComas to William N. Ward, 20 Jan. 1844; Meade, *Old Churches* 2:153–54).

91. *AA, 1841–1842*, ch. 202, "An Act authorizing commissioners to convey a certain tract," ch. 203, "An Act authorizing the sale and conveyance of a tract of land," ch. 204, "An Act authorizing a sale of a part of the lot belonging to the Episcopal church," 151–52; *AA, 1843–1844*, ch. 133, "An Act authorizing a sale of a portion of a lot in the town of Morgantown belonging to a church," 105; *AA, 1849–1850*, ch. 298, "An Act releasing to the trustees of St. Paul's church," 220–21.

92. E.g., see *JHDV*, 19, 25 Jan., 5 Feb. 1839, 41, 54, 86.

93. LP, Wythe Co., 9 Dec. 1845, 10 Jan. 1846; *JHDV*, 9, 12, 13, 17 Dec. 1845, 10, 21 Jan., 7 Feb. 1846, 31, 37, 40, 42, 45, 83, 101, 140; *AA, 1850–1851*, ch. 272, "An Act to authorize a sale of a part of the tract of land in Wythe county belonging to the Lutheran and German Reformed church," 190; LP, Monongalia Co., 11 Jan., 31 Dec. 1844; *JHDV*, 31 Dec. 1844, 2, 4 Jan. 1845; *AA, 1843–1844*, ch. 133, "An Act authorizing a sale of a portion of a lot in the town of Morgantown belonging to a church," 105; LP, Berkeley Co., 25 Jan., 18 Feb. 1850, 9 Jan. 1851, 16 Mar. 1853; *JHDV*, 21 Mar. 1850, 451, 18, 19 Dec. 1850, 8 Jan. 1851, 100, 105, 144; LP, Richmond City, 29 Dec. 1846; *AA, 1846–1847*, ch. 76, "An Act concerning suits against trustees of religious congregations," 66.

94. LP, Page Co., 3 Feb. 1851; *JHDV*, 3 Feb. 1851–6 Mar. 1852; *AA, 1851–1852*, ch. 99, "An Act to authorize the circuit courts to direct the sale of church property," 80. See also *AA, 1855–1856*, ch. 37, "An Act to re-enact and amend the lst section of an act entitled an act to authorize the circuit court to direct the sale of church property," 34. For examples of continuing petitions and legislative activity, see LP, Elizabeth City Co., 20 Jan. 1854, Craig Co., 19 Feb. 1854, Shenandoah Co., 15 Jan. 1858; *AA, 1853–1854*, ch. 205, "An Act authorizing the trustees of the Methodist Episcopal Church in Winchester to sell and convey certain property belonging to the said church," 130–31.

6. CULTURE

1. John Campbell to David Campbell, 27 Dec. 1811, Campbell Papers.

2. For similar reactions, see Robert Gamble to James Breckinridge, 27 Dec. 1811, Breckinridge Papers; John Randolph to [Gabriella Harvie Randolph] Brockenbrough, 31 Dec. 1811, Randolph-Tucker Papers, Brock, box 6. For a compilation of newspaper accounts of the event, see *Full Account of the Burning of the Richmond Theatre, on the Night of December 26, 1811* (Richmond, 1858). For a detailed history, see Baker, *Richmond Theater Fire*. See also Tyler-McGraw, *At the Falls*, 82–85; Shockley, *Richmond Stage*, 360–82.

3. Maxwell, *Oration Commemorative of John Holt Rice*, 11; Joseph Marx to Littleton W. Tazewell, 28 Dec. 1811, Tazewell Papers.

4. [John D. Blair], "A Sermon Occasioned by the Dreadful Calamity with which the City of Richmond was Visited on the Night of the 26th of Dec. 1811," Blair Papers; *RE*, 2 Jan. 1812. For Blair, see Maurice Duke, "Blair, John Durburrow," *DVB* 1:546–47.

5. Hoge, *Sermons*, 363–74 (quotes at 363, 373); James Muir, *Ten Sermons* (Alexandria, 1812).

6. Alexander, *Discourse*, 18.

7. *RE*, 9, 14 Jan. 1812.

8. William B. Giles to Wilson Cary Nicholas, 1 Jan. 1812, Wilson Cary Nicholas Papers, box 9.

9. Alexander, *Discourse*, quotes at 20, 21, 22. That summer he left his pastorate to become the first professor of Princeton Theological Seminary. See Mark A. Noll, "Alexander, Archibald," *DVB* 1:54–56. For a critique of Alexander's perspective, see Baker, *Richmond Theater Fire*, 86, 89, 145–46.

10. Joseph C. Cabell to David Watson, 4 Mar. 1798, Watson Papers; Blair, "For I am not ashamed of the Gospel of Christ," Uncataloged Sermons, Blair Papers, box 46. For Cabell, see Lynn A. Nelson, "Cabell, Joseph Carrington," *DVB* 2:488–90.

11. *Va. Gaz. and Gen. Adver.*, 22 Mar. 1797. See also Hoge, "Life of Moses Hoge"; La Rochefoucauld, *Travels* 2:104.

12. Davis, *Travels*, 306–7; David Barrow to Backus, 27 Jan. 1797, Samuel Davies Brame to Backus, 25 Jan. 1797, William Brown to Backus, 20 Feb. 1797, Backus Papers. See Luke 5:5.

13. William Brown to Backus, 25 Dec. 1798, Backus Papers; [Madison], *Discourse*, 5; Wirt, *Letters of the British Spy*, 203; Hanover Presbytery, Mins., 11 Apr. 1807, 213–24 (quotes at 214). See also "On Infidelity," *Va. Religious Magazine* 1 (31 May 1805): 129–32. By this time the Second Great Awakening was already in full swing in Virginia, but the Episcopalians and Presbyterians did not reap the same immediate results enjoyed by the Baptists and Methodists.

14. "Address from the Synod," Synod of Va., Mins., 27 Oct. 1814, 53–65.

15. Meade, *Old Churches* 1:29. See also David L. Holmes, "The Decline and Revival of the Church in Virginia," in Cleaveland et al., *Up from Independence.*

16. Stith Mead to John Kobler, 15 May [1795], Mead Letterbook, 158; Gen. Com. in Va. to Warren Assn., 9 Mar. 1788, Warren Assn. Papers.

17. For this movement, see esp. Robert T. Handy, *A Christian America: Protestant Hopes and Historical Realities*, 2d ed. (New York, 1984); Nathan O. Hatch, *The Democratization of American Christianity* (New Haven, 1989); Wigger, *Taking Heaven by Storm.*

For an attack on Jefferson's statute as a successful attempt "to degrade Christianity to a level with the creed of Mecca" and "a design to heap dishonour upon the faith of Christians," see Hawks, *Contributions* 1:178.

18. Among the most important studies for the revivals in the South are Donald G. Mathews, *Religion in the Old South* (Chicago, 1977); Robert M. Calhoun, *Evangelicals and Conservatives in the Early South, 1740–1861* (Columbia, SC, 1988); Christine Leigh Heyrman, *Southern Cross: The Beginnings of the Bible Belt* (New York, 1997).

19. *Va. Argus*, 2, 6 Apr. 1802 (quote at 6 Apr.).

20. Drury Lacy to Ashbel Green, 6 Oct. 1804, Gratz Coll. See Bruce, *They All Sang Hallelujah*; Wigger, *Taking Heaven by Storm*; David Hempton, *Methodism: Empire of the Spirit* (New York, 2005).

21. Jacob Grigg to Backus, 18 June 1801, Backus Papers; Baptist Church (Richmond), Letter to Dover Assn., 2 Oct. 1801, Clergymen's Collection, box 119, Brock.

22. Synod of Va. Mins., 1 Oct. 1801, 4 Oct. 1802, 2:65, 109.

23. Lexington Presbytery, Mins., 8 Nov. 1804, 151–52; Wilson, "A Brief Biographical Sketch." For a Baptist critic, see William Brame to Backus, [Feb. 1806], Backus Papers.

24. "An act for the effectual suppression of vice, and punishing the disturbers of religious worship, and Sabbath Breakers," *Revised Code, 1819,* 554–56; *JHDV,* 19 Jan. 1820, 127.

25. S. Hubard to Edmund Hubard, 4 Aug. 1825, Hubard Papers; [John Durburrow Blair] to [Samuel] Pleasants, 24 Oct. 1806, Blair Papers, box 45. For similar views by another Virginia Presbyterian minister, see Drury Lacy to Moses Waddel, 26 Jan. 1803, Letterbook, Waddel Papers.

26. Dover Baptist Assn., Records, 1809, 11.

27. For the changing environment at camp meetings, compare *RE,* 22 Aug. 1804, with "Communication," *Va. Argus,* 21 July 1809; "Camp-Meeting," *RE,* 9 June 1812. See also "On a Camp Meeting," 13 Aug. 1822, Peyton Family Papers; Stith Mead, "The Jubilee Meeting," *Virginian,* 10 Aug. 1824. For a persuasive interpretation, see Schneider, *Way of the Cross.*

28. *RE,* 16 Oct. 1810; S. Hubard to Edmund Hubard, 4 Aug. 1825, Hubard Papers.

29. Mary Pocahontas Bolling to Susan Hubard, 21 Mar. 1815, Hubard Papers; "Meeting of the General Committee, 1815," 8, VBHS. For examples of newspaper coverage, see *Va. Argus,* 23 Oct. 1810; "Methodist Conference," ibid., 6 Feb. 1812; *Virginian,* 25 May 1826.

30. Baker, *Richmond Theater Fire,* 159–66; "Notes taken from the Council Records regarding the burning of the Theatre on the site now occupied by the Monumental Church" (photocopies), Drinard Papers; List of Subscribers [1810?], Carrington Papers. For early church records, see Fisher, *Monumental Church.* For Buchanan, see Maurice Duke, "Buchanan, John," *DVB* 2:368–69.

31. Rice to Benjamin Grigsby, 2 Jan. 1807, Rice Papers; N. B. Tucker to St. George Tucker, 9 Feb. 1812, TCP.

32. Benjamin Rice to William McPheeters, 28 Jan. 1811, 28 Dec. 1813, Rice Papers.

33. At the instigation of Archbishop John Carroll of Baltimore, Catholics formed a congregation in Richmond in 1812. See, e.g., the announcements in *RE,* 29 Feb. 1812; *Va. Argus,* 17 Sept. 1812.

34. Thomas H. Drew to Thomas H. Ellis, 8 June 1868, in Fisher, *Monumental Church,* 175–77; John Holt Rice to Archibald Alexander, 14 May 1812, in Maxwell, *Memoir of Rice,* 79; Hanover Presbytery, Mins., 8 May 1813, 326–27; *Va. Argus,* 7 May 1812. See also Hoge, *Portraiture of Four Pastors,* 6–7. In 1815 Blair resumed services in the Capitol (*RE,* 25 Feb. 1815). Both Rice brothers would later serve as moderators of the Presbyterian General Assembly.

35. Hawks, app., *Conv. of 1813,* 90. For Bracken, see St. George Tucker to Joseph C. Cabell, 3 Mar. 1813, Bryan Family Papers, no. 3400, box 2; Daphne Gentry, "Bracken, John," *DVB* 2:179–80.

36. Wilmer to Moore, 27 Jan. 1813, Meade to Moore, 4 Mar. 1813, in Henshaw, *Memoir of Moore*, 121. See also Brown, "Richard Channing Moore"; Godson, "Bishop Richard Channing Moore"; Waukechon, "The Forgotten Evangelicals," 201–36.

37. James Madison to William Meade, 10 Oct. 1810, in Meade, *Old Churches* 1:28; Moore to Wilmer, 19 Feb. 1814, Moore Letterbook A.

38. Wilmer, *A Sermon, Delivered in the Monumental Church*, 8; Meade, *Old Churches* 1:58; Hawks, app., *Conv. of 1814*, 92; *RE*, 23 May 1814; John Jay to John Marshall, 7 June 1814, in Johnson, *Papers of Marshall* 8:51. For Moore's reception in Virginia, see his address to the 1815 convention in *Va. Argus*, 3 June 1815.

39. Burr Powell to Catherine Powell, 23 Nov. 1814, Holmes Papers; Meade, *Old Churches* 2:217; Brown, "Richard Channing Moore."

40. Moore to Rev. Mr. Cook, 26 Aug. 1824, Moore Letterbook F; Moore to Meade, 8 Dec. 1828, Moore Letterbook K. On the importance of observing the liturgical rubrics, see Moore to Nicholas H. Cobb, 1 Jan. 1825, to Franklin G. Smith, 1 Jan. 1825, Moore Letterbook G.

41. [Wirt et al.], *Old Bachelor*, 209.

42. Louisa Holmes (later Cocke) Diary, 2, 14, 16 (quote), 20 (quote) Oct., [1816], 8 Nov. 1819 (quote), Cocke Papers, no. 640, box 10; John Campbell to Elizabeth Campbell, 10 Nov. 1816, Virginia T. J. Campbell to Lavina Kelly, 15 Mar. 1838, Campbell Papers. As Virginia noted in her letter, she did not know any Methodists in Richmond, and "the members of that church are of the lower classes." When she later married a clergyman, her uncle David Campbell was not pleased (David Campbell to [his nephew], 20 Oct. 1849, ibid.).

43. *RE*, 13 May 1817.

44. Hawks, app., *Conv. of 1822*, 162,; *Virginian*, 24 Sept. 1822.

45. Hawks, app., *Conv. of 1826*, 194, "Pastoral Address," ibid., *1827*, 196; *Virginian*, 25 May, 4 Sept. 1826.

46. See Moore to F. Campbell, 7 June 1824, to Bishop Kemp, 5 Nov. 1824, Moore Letterbook F. See also Goodwin, *History of the Theological Seminary* 1:120–55; Booty, *Mission and Ministry*.

47. *Va. Religious Magazine* 1 (1804): vi, vii. For the later impact, see Nord, "Evangelical Origins of Mass Media."

48. *Christian Monitor* 1 (8 July 1815): 3. Rice published a "Prospectus" for his periodical in *Va. Argus*, 25 Feb 1815.

49. "Sunday Schools," *Christian Monitor* 2 (10 May 1817): 276; "The Sunday School," *Virginian*, 11 July 1836; "Thoughts on Sunday Schools, and Sunday School Books," *SLM* 4 (1838): 224–27. See also Boylan, *Sunday School*.

50. John N. Gordon to John H. Cocke, 5 July 1819, Cocke Papers, no. 640, box 14.

51. *Va. Argus*, 17 June 1813; *RE*, 22 June 1813.

52. *Va. Argus*, 28 June, 8 Sept. 1813.

53. Ibid., 19 Mar., 16 Apr. 1814; Hanover Presbytery, Mins., 16 Oct. 1813, 336; Synod of Va., Mins., 27 Oct. 1814, 4:63–64.

54. LP, Richmond City, 16 Dec. 1813; "Annual Report," *RE*, 7 June 1820; *Eleventh Annual Report*, 9.

55. Synod of Va., Mins., 20 Oct. 1817, 4:177–78 (quote at 177).

56. "Meeting of the Baptist Gen. Meeting, 1817," 8; Dover Baptist Assn., Records, 11 Oct. 1819, 6; Va. Portsmouth Assn., Records, 1822, 5.

57. Mathews, "The Second Great Awakening."

58. [Philip] Barraud to St. George Tucker, 3 Sept. 1816, 3 Sept. 1827, Cocke Papers, no. 640, box 34; Heron, *Address*, 3–5, 12.

59. John Early Diary, [16] Jan., 10 May [1814], 135, 140; Hill, *Ministerial Parity*; *Virginian*, 11, 15, 18 (quote), 25, 29 Oct. 1822. For other examples of competition, see John Campbell to David Campbell, 30 July 1821, Campbell Papers; William Hill to John Mason, 8 May 1816, to John Holt Rice, 20 Sept. 1830, Gratz Coll.; [Hill] to [?], 5 Nov. 1817, Hill Papers.

60. Stith Mead to William Mead, 12 June 1793, Mead Letterbook, 24.

61. Hanover Presbytery, Mins., 4 Apr. 1791, 37–38. Not all the ministers were convinced that dancing was immoral, however, and both Hanover and Lexington presbyteries wrestled with dissent over this stricture despite its inclusion in the catechism (Hanover Presbytery, Mins., 26 July 1793, 72; Lexington Presbytery, Mins., 11 Apr., 18 Oct. 1798, 8, 9 May, 16 Oct. 1799, 123–24, 137, 148, 149, 165–66).

62. See, e.g., Dover Baptist Assn., Records, 12 Oct. 1801, 8, 13 Oct. 1806, 4, 1814, 13–32; Goshen Assn., Records, 1822, 10; Va. Portsmouth Assn., Records, 1807, 8–11 (quote at 8), 1810, 8.

63. Clark, *Journal of Asbury* 3:59, 89; John Early Diary, 5, 6 Aug., 26; [Harlow], *Richmond Alarm*, 105.

64. *Va. Argus*, 25 Feb. 1815.

65. Rice to Archibald Alexander, 14 May 1812, in Maxwell, *Memoir of Rice*, 86–87; "The Theatre Again," *Christian Monitor* 2 (16 Aug. 1817): 393–98 (quotes at 396, 397); "On Innocent Amusements," ibid., 2 (2 Aug. 1817): 378–80. For other examples from this period, see Va. Religious Tract Soc., *Lawful Amusements* (Harrisonburg, VA, 1813).

66. Hawks, app., *Conv. of 1815*, 97, 102, and *1816*, 105; *RE*, 29 May 1816. See also Baker, *Richmond Theater Fire*, 228–29. That year St. George's had 90 communicants and the Monumental Church had 120, making them among the most prosperous in the diocese (Hawks, app., *Conv. of 1816*, 107).

67. Hawks, app., *Conv. of 1817*, 115, 117; Moore to Edmund J. Lee, 23 Oct. 1817, Moore Letterbook A. The list of those who purchased pews at the original sale is in Fisher, *Monumental Church*, 34–38; the theater's original stockholders are listed in Shockley, "The Proprietors of Richmond's New Theatre," 303. A few years later John Holt Rice encountered Wirt in Washington and found him very friendly, but when Rice told him that he wished "to own him as a brother," Wirt "sighed, and looked as solemn as a preacher, and said he was a great sinner" (John Holt Rice to Anne L. Rice, 8 May 1820, Rice Papers). See also Baker, *Richmond Theater Fire*, 228–31; Waukechon, "Forgotten Evangelicals," 259–62.

68. Hawks, app., *Conv. of 1818*, 126–27; *RE*, 28 May 1818.

69. Meade, *Old Churches* 1:22–23 (quote at 23). Meade adopted Addison's perspective.

70. *RE*, 2 June 1818.

71. *RE*, 9, 16 June 1818.

72. *RE*, 19 June 1818.

73. *RE*, 23 June 1818.

74. "A Friend to the Church" and "To The Reverend Doctor Moore," *RE*, 26 June 1818.

75. "Cyprian," *RE*, 30 June 1818.

76. Standing Committee to Richard Channing Moore, 3 Aug. 1818, in Biddulph, *Inconsistency of Conformity*, app., 46–53 (quotes at 46, 50, 51).

77. "To the Protestant Episcopal Convention," *RE*, 7 May 1819.

78. So the press noted at the conclusion of the convention (*RE*, 21 May 1819).

79. Frances Amanda Taliaferro to Hester Eliza Van Bibber, 28 Aug. 1820, copy, VHS; John D. Blair to [John Holt Rice], 30 Nov. 1821, Blair Papers, box 45.

80. *RE*, 23 June 1818.

81. For these lists and figures, see Fisher, *Monumental Church*, 104–8, 190–93, 207–8.

82. Peyton, *Augusta County*, app., 378–79; Fisher, *Monumental Church*, 106, 207, 208; C. M. Steele, "Chapman Johnson," *VMHB* 35 (1927): 161–74, 246–57.

83. Charles W. Andrews, Circular to his Congregation, 1 Apr. 1844, Andrews Papers. As the various responses make clear, Andrews used this form throughout the 1840s at Trinity Parish in Shepherdstown, VA. For Andrews, see Marie Tyler-McGraw, "Andrews, Charles Wesley," *DVB* 1:163–64. Waukechon argues that "women did not have to redefine themselves to the same extent men did when they accepted evangelicalism." He also points to the impact of an 1836 canon that required all members of a diocesan convention to be full communicants in the church. Admission to communion required the approval of a clergyman, thus giving the clergy a leverage in church polity that they had never known before in Virginia ("Forgotten Evangelicals," 36, 298–308).

84. Jefferson to Benjamin Waterhouse, 26 June 1822, in Ford, *Works of Jefferson* 12:243. For the Unitarian efforts and failure in the South, see Gohdes, "The Unitarian Church in the Ante-bellum South." For a contemporary view of the limitations of the Unitarian perspective for most Americans, see Grund, *Americans*, 281–88.

85. Noll, *American Evangelical Christianity*, provides a useful overview of this aspect of Christianity. See also Howe, *What Hath God Wrought*, 164–97.

86. Jefferson to Thomas Cooper, 2 Nov. 1822, in Ford, *Works of Jefferson* 12:271; Jefferson to Michael Megear, 29 May 1823, in Lipscomb and Bergh, *Writings of Jefferson* 15:434; LP, Albemarle Co., 8 Dec. 1815. Speece is quoted in Bennett, *Methodism in Charlottesville*, 9.

87. Jefferson to Thomas Cooper, 2 Nov. 1822, in Ford, *Works of Jefferson* 12:271. The transfer of property to trustees to build churches for the various denominations is found in the counties' deed books. See, e.g., Albemarle Co.: DB 6 (1772–76), 190–91; DB 12 (1795–98), 10–11; DB 15 (1804–7), 172; DB 16 (1807–9), 375; DB 25 (1824–26),

280–81, 416–18; DB 26 (1826–27), 46, 381; DB 27 (1827–29), 192–93, 331–32; DB 29 (1830–32), 394–95; DB 30 (1832–33), 73–75, 196–97, 429–30; DB 31 (1833–34), 203, 216, 398–400, 491–92; DB 32 (1834–35), 8–9, 529–31; DB 33 (1835–36), 83–86, 383–86; DB 34 (1836–37), 53–55; DB 35 (1837–38), 367–70; DB 38 (1840–41), 34–35, 115–16, 261–63, 493–94; DB 39 (1841–42), 152–53, 158–59, 173–74, 363–64; DB 40 (1842–43), 35–36. For a similar explosion of church building in Richmond, see Baker, *Richmond Theater Fire*, 213–14.

88. John Holt Rice to Samuel Miller, 2 Jan. 1828, Miller Papers, box 11.

89. Kennedy to Elizabeth Gray, 19 Aug. 1828, quoted in Charles H. Bohner, "*Swallow Barn*: John P. Kennedy's Chronicle of Virginia Society," *VMHB* 68 (1960): 320; Royall, *Black Book* 2:201.

90. Royall, *Mrs. Royall's Southern Tour*, 43, 44, 86, 111.

91. Nathaniel Beverley Tucker, "Sermon on the death of Adams and Jefferson," Bryan Family Papers, box 2. For Tucker's religious beliefs at this stage in his life, see Brugger, *Beverley Tucker*, 67–72.

92. Thomas, "Reasonable Revivalism." For Randolph's explanation of his conversion, see his letter of 1818 in "Mss of John Randolph," *SLM* 2 (1836): 462–63. See also Jennifer R. Loux, "Cocke, John Hartwell," *DVB* 3:330–32.

93. For reflections upon the value of such organizations for the social capital they create, see Jean Bethke Elshtain, *Democracy on Trial* (New York, 1995); Robert D. Putnam, *Bowling Alone: The Collapse and Revival of American Community* (New York, 2000). Sutton offers a perspective on the problems that the elite faced in "Nostalgia, Pessimism, and Malaise," as does Kierner in "Dark and Dense Cloud."

94. For a contrary view, see William Meade to John Hartwell Cocke, 29 May 1827, Cocke Papers, no. 640. He wrote: "I think upon my native state, rent as it is by religious parties, deeply infected still with infidelity, the great mass of the people even if professing Christianity denying the efficacy of religious education; when I know the entire dependence of the university [of Virginia] upon the legislature, and the entire dependence of that upon an ignorant, prejudiced, irreligious, a bigotted multitude, which would never consent to any wholesome measures . . . ." For Meade, see Holmes, "William Meade."

7. POLITICS

1. Heinemann et al., *Old Dominion*, 171–74; Sutton, *Revolution to Secession*; Shade, *Democratizing the Old Dominion*, 50–77.

2. Sutton, "Virginia Constitutional Convention," 167.

3. *Debates of the Conv.*, 25 Nov. 1829, 459–60; for Brodnax, see Alison Goodyear Freehling, "Brodnax, William Henry," *DVB* 2:257–58; for Campbell, see David Edwin Harrell Jr., "Campbell, Alexander," ibid., 550–53, and Moorhouse, "Campbell and the Virginia Constitutional Convention." Campbell would later change his views on seminary education and found Bethany College in 1840.

4. *Debates of the Conv.*, 21 Dec. 1829, 708–9.

5. William Graham to Zachariah Johnson, 3 Nov. 1787, Fleming Papers; Madison to George Eve, 2 Jan. 1789, Benjamin Johnson to Madison, 19 Jan. 1789, John Leland to Madison, ca. 15 Feb. 1789, in Hutchinson, 11:405, 424, 442–43.

6. Madison to Henry Tazewell, 4 Feb. 1798, [Bishop] Madison Papers; Bishop Madison to Jefferson, 16 Dec. 1801, in Boyd, 36:126–27; Crowe, "The War of 'Pure Republicanism'"; Blair, Independence Day Address, [4 July 1798], Blair Papers, box 45. See also the attack on William Hill for his sermon decrying the conduct of the federal government during the War of 1812 (Winchester Presbytery, Mins., 16 Dec., 290–91).

7. Ephraim Abell to Backus, 20 Apr. 1799, Backus Papers; "Address of the Baptist Gen. Meeting of Correspondence," *RE*, 27 Jan. 1809.

8. Boyd, 1:382. E.g., the constitution of 1851 stated that "no minister of the Gospel or priest of any religious denomination . . . shall be capable of being elected a member of either house of assembly" (*AA, 1851–1852*, art. 4, ch. 7, 328). Some resigned their clerical duties to stand for office. See, e.g., Thomas Mann Randolph to James Madison, 28 Dec. 1799, in Hutchinson, 17:296–97. See also Frederic S. Le Clercq, "Disqualification of Clergy for Civil Office," *Memphis State University Law Review* 7 (1977): 555–614; Loveland, *Southern Evangelicals*, 113–19; William M. Hogue, "The Civil Disability of Ministers of Religion in State Constitutions," *Journal of Church and State* 36 (1994): 329–55.

9. *JHDV*, 1 Nov. 1777, 9; Lohrenz, "The Virginia Clergy," 274.

10. "Madison's Observations" and Jefferson to Chastellux, 2 Sept. 1785, in Boyd, 6:311, 8:470. Writing to a Baptist preacher, Jefferson reversed himself after the clergy, in his view, "seem to have relinquished all pretension to privilege" (Jefferson to Jeremiah Moore, 14 Aug. 1800, in Boyd, 32:102–3). But see Hamburger, *Separation of Church and State*, 147–55.

11. Thomas [Crump] Mead to Frederick Carper, 31 May 1822, Misc. MSS, DLC. For this sentiment elsewhere in the early republic, see Hamburger, *Separation of Church and State*, 130–43, 181–89.

12. *JHDV*, 2 Feb. 1827, 132, 133, 8 Jan. 1830, 72. Some preachers were wise enough to refuse to stand for election. See Edward Folkes, "To the Freeholders of the County Charles-City," *RE*, 6 Apr. 1816. Others publicly supported their exclusion from civil and political offices. See, e.g., Rice, *Historical and Philosophical Considerations*, 87. The 1870 constitution dropped the disqualification of ministers from political office (Thorpe, *Federal and State Constitutions* 7:3884). Two clergymen were among the active postwar political leaders: Southern Unionist James W. Hunnicutt was a radical Republican candidate for Congress, and Noval Wilson was a member of the Conservative minority at the convention that drafted the first postwar constitution. Even more significant, perhaps, was the selection by the General Assembly in 1870 of Presbyterian minister William Henry Ruffner to be Virginia's first superintendent of public education, a position in which he served for twelve years (Maddex, *Virginia Conservatives*, 49–50, 57, 60, 80, 206–7).

13. *Journal, Acts and Proceedings*, 7 Dec. 1829, 68–69.

14. *Debates of the Conv.*, 456–57.

15. Henry St. George Tucker, *Commentaries on the Laws*, 10–11.

16. *Debates of the Conv.*, 26 Nov. 1829, 457.

17. Ibid., 457–59.

18. Ibid., 21 Dec. 1829, 706–7.

19. Gatewood, "Diary of Thomas Green," 300, 310.

20. Edwin Steele Duncan to John James Allen, 29 Oct. 1829, Allen Papers; Hugh Blair Grigsby Diary, 31 Oct. 1829, 166, Grigsby Papers; Grigsby to John N. Tazewell, 31 Oct. 1829, Tazewell Papers, box 12.

21. John Campbell to David Campbell, 30 July 1821, David Campbell to Mary Campbell, 29 May 1825, Campbell Papers. For these Virginia politicians, see Norma Taylor Mitchell, "Campbell, John," *DVB* 2:572–73, and "Campbell, David," ibid., 560–63.

22. David Campbell to Virginia T. P. Campbell, 27 July 1834, Campbell Papers.

23. David Campbell to Mary Campbell, 1 May 1837, ibid.

24. David Campbell to Margaret T. C. Campbell, 20 Nov. 1838, ibid. When another niece married a minister, he liked the man but disapproved of his occupation because it did not offer enough security and independence (David Campbell [to his nephew], 20 Oct. 1849, ibid.).

25. "Politico Religionism," *SLM* 3 (1838): 549.

26. Philip Barraud to St. George Tucker, 10 Feb. 1821, TCP; "Dr. Plumer's Challenge to Controversialists" and "Plumerisms" in *Rich. Whig and Public Adver.*, 22 Nov. 1844; R[obert] E[den] Scott to Christian B. Scott, 9 Jan. 1846, VHS; Carwardine, *Evangelicals and Politics*, 22–43.

27. John Early to Elizabeth Early, 25 Apr. 1832, Eleazar Early to John Early, 12 July 1833, Thomas L. Robinson to John Early, 6 Feb. 1851, Early Papers.

28. *Rich. Whig and Public Adver.*, 19, 22 Nov. 1844. For religion as an issue in this election, see Carwardine, *Evangelicals and Politics*, 80–89.

29. Jordan Diary, 157; Plumer, *Substance of an Argument*, 5. See also Plumer, "Political Clergymen," *Watchman of the South*, 30 July 1840; Loveland, *Southern Evangelicals*, 111–13, 119–20.

30. Meade to the *Protestant Churchman*, [ca. 1850s], Meade Papers, box 2, folder 2.

31. Grund, *Americans*, 289–91 (quote at 290). For Grund, see Holman Hamilton and James L. Courthamel, "Man for Both Parties: Francis J. Grund as a Political Chameleon," *Pa. Mag. of Hist. and Bio.* 97 (1973): 465–84.

32. Grund, *Americans*, 294–95, 297.

33. Ibid., 286–87.

34. LP, Misc. Pet. (Hanover Presbytery), 12 Nov. 1784, Powhatan Co. (Baptist Pet.), 3 Nov. 1785.

35. LP, Botetourt Co., 14 Nov. 1789; see also Misc. Pet., 12 Nov. 1795. For the Sabbath laws and Jefferson's role in composing them, see Dreisbach, "A New Perspective on Jefferson's Views" and "Jefferson and Bills Number 82–86."

36. *JHDV*, 27, 29 Dec. 1798, 45, 53; John D. Blair to [John Holt] Rice, 30 Nov. 1821, Blair Papers. For the united front put up by the churches against theaters, see "The

Theatre Again," *Christian Monitor* 2 (16 Aug. 1817): 393–98; for a defense of plays and theatrical performance and an evangelical rejoinder, see *Virginian*, 13, 19 Aug., 17 Sept. 1822. See also Patricia Click, *Spirit of the Times: Amusements in Nineteenth-Century Baltimore, Norfolk, and Richmond* (Charlottesville, 1989); Faye E. Dudden, *Women in the American Theatre: Actresses and Audiences, 1790–1870* (New Haven, 1994); Richard Butsch, "Bowery B'hoys and Matinee Ladies: The Re-Gendering of Nineteenth-Century American Theater Audiences," *American Quarterly* 46 (Sept. 1994): 374–405.

37. *Epitome of the Times*, 16 Apr. 1798; William H. Cabell to Joseph C. Cabell, 16 Dec. 1802, Cabell Papers, box 2; Bayard, *Travels*, 51. For the colonial period, see T. H. Breen, "Horses and Gentlemen: The Cultural Significance of Gambling among the Gentry of Virginia," *WMQ*, 3d ser., 34 (1977): 239–57.

38. La Rochefoucauld, *Travels* 2:39–40, 114; "Unlawful Gaming," *RE*, 2 Jan. 1806; "Cards," *Rich. and Manchester Adver.*, 13 June 1795; Bourne, "Cursory Remarks on the United States," 29–30; Weld, *Travels*, 109.

39. Announcement of race in Randolph-Tucker Papers; Briggs Diary.

40. The 1792 law against gambling is in Shepherd, 1:106–10. For examples of later proposals, see "A Bill to amend the Act intitled An Act to prevent unlawful Gaming," 1797 sess., box 16, "A bill more effectually to prevent excessive Gaming," 1801 sess., box 18, "A Bill to Amend the Act intitled 'An Act to Amend the several Acts heretofore made to prevent unlawful gaming,'" 1811 sess., box 25, "To amend An Act to reduce into one, the several Acts to prevent unlawful gaming," 1811 sess., box 26, RHB. See also Fabian, *Card Sharps, Dream Books*, 12–23.

41. "A Bill to amend the several acts heretofore to prevent unlawful gaming," 1815 sess., box 30, RHB.

42. A summary "act for the effectual suppression of vice," etc., is in the *Revised Code*, 554–56.

43. John Y. Mason to William H. Brodnax, 3 Feb. 1826, Brodnax Papers; "Thoughts on Lotteries," Feb. 1826, in Ford, *Works of Jefferson* 12:435–50; Malone, *Jefferson* 6:473–82, 488, 495–96, 511. For a contemporary view that Jefferson's family, led by his grandson and executor Thomas Jefferson Randolph, pushed for the lottery that some thought unnecessary, see David Campbell to James Campbell, 19 Mar. 1827, Campbell Papers.

For legislative efforts to toughen the laws against lotteries, see "A Bill to amend the 27th Section of an Act entitled 'An Act to reduce into one the several Acts and parts of Acts to prevent unlawful gaming,'" 1822 sess., box 39, RHB; "The Lottery Bill," *Virginian*, 20 Feb. 1824; "Lottery Law," ibid., 14 July 1825.

44. "Agricultural Society of Virginia," *RE*, 17 Dec. 1818. For Taylor's emphasis on moral principles, see Eugene Tenbroeck Mudge, *The Social Philosophy of John Taylor of Caroline: A Study in Jeffersonian Democracy* (New York, 1939), 19–26. See also Shalhope, *John Taylor of Caroline*, 179–80; LP, Randolph Co., 10 Dec. 1824.

45. David Campbell to Mary Campbell, 9 Jan. 1823, Campbell Papers.

46. Appomattox Baptist Assn., Records, 1827, 5. The press published the Baptist objections in full (*Virginian*, 4 Oct. 1827). For earlier examples of Baptist opposition to lotteries, see Va. Portsmouth Assn., Mins., 28 May 1792, [p. 3]; Goshen Baptist Assn.,

Mins., 18 Oct. 1807, 4. For Methodist objections, see Va. Conference, Feb. 1806. The early history of lotteries in America is recounted in John Samuel Ezell, *Fortune's Merry Wheel: The Lottery in America* (Cambridge, MA, 1960).

47. Weld, *Travels*, 206; Singleton, *Letters*, 66, 71.

48. See, e.g., Columbia Baptist Assn., Records, 1828, 8–9.

49. John Hartwell Cocke to William Meade, June 1846, Huntington MSS. In this mammoth letter Cocke traced the development of the Prohibition movement in Virginia from temperance to total abstinence. For Cocke, see Jennifer R. Loux, "Cocke, John Hartwell," *DVB* 3:330–32. For the progress of the temperance movement, see Lucian Minor, "The Temperance Reformation in Virginia," *SLM* 16 (1850): 427–30; Charles Chilton Pearson and J. Edwin Hendricks, *Liquor and Anti-Liquor in Virginia, 1619–1919* (Durham, NC, 1967), 36–58.

50. See, e.g., the articles on "Drunkenness" in *Va. Argus*, 10 May 1815, and the essay by "Franklin" in *RE*, 11 Jan. 1816.

51. "Camp Meeting," *Va. Argus*, 16 Apr. 1812. Mead later announced that the encampment had been a huge success ("Camp-Meeting," *RE*, 9 June 1812).

52. *JHDV*, 19 Jan. 1820, 127; a bill "to amend an Act entitled, 'An Act for the effectual suppression of vice, and punishing the disturbers of religious Worship and Sabbath breaking,'" 1819 sess., box 35, RHB.

53. Dover Baptist Assn., Records, 1820, 5–6; Columbia Baptist Assn., Records, 1820, 6; LP, Fairfax Co., 6 Dec. 1820, Prince William Co., 6 Dec. 1820, Northumberland Co. (Dover Baptist Assn.), 8, 19 Dec. 1820; "A bill more effectually to suppress vice, and to punish the disturbers of Religious Worship," 1820 sess., box 36, RHB.

54. LP, Misc. Pet., 11 Dec. 1824, Accomack Co., 15 Dec. 1825, Misc. Pet. (Methodist Episcopal Church), 22 Dec. 1828.

55. LP, Buckingham Co. (Methodist Episcopal Church), 23 Jan. 1829; for later examples, see Stafford Co. (Methodist Episcopal Church), 11 Mar. 1837; Mathews Co. (Dover Baptist Assn.), 11 Jan. 1838; Culpeper Co., 18 Dec. 1841, 26 Jan. 1846; *JHDV*, 1838–39 sess., Harrison Co., 16 Feb. 1839, Harrison and Monongalia Cos., 19 Feb. 1839, Rockingham Co., 20 Feb. 1839, Preston Co., 20 Feb. 1839, 106, 111, 112, 113, 134.

56. *JHDV*, 1837–38 sess., 40, 289; 1848–49 sess., 93; 1850–51 sess., 164, 303.

57. *RE*, 15 Jan. 1805.

58. Levy, *First Emancipator*. Carter converted to the Baptist faith and later became a Swedenborgian.

59. LP, Richmond City, 3 Dec. 1823.

60. Scervant Jones to the People of York Co., 4 Mar. 1826, Brand Papers, sec. 6. For the development of the First African Baptist Church in Richmond, see Janet Duitsman Cornelius, *Slave Missions and the Black Church in the Antebellum South* (Columbia, SC, 1999), 114–17.

61. LP, Petersburg City, 8 Jan. 1839.

62. For this development, see Douglas Ambrose, "Of Stations and Relations: Pro-slavery Christianity in Early National Virginia," in *Religion and the Antebellum Debate over Slavery*, ed. John R. McKivigan and Mitchell Snay (Athens, GA, 1998), 35–67; and

esp. Charles F. Irons, *The Origins of Proslavery Christianity: White and Black Evangelicals in Colonial and Antebellum Virginia* (Chapel Hill, 2008).

63. Sutton, "Virginia Constitutional Convention," 157, 160–61.

64. John Campbell to David Campbell, 19 Jan. 1826, Campbell Papers.

65. "The Influence of Morals on the Happiness of Man, and the Stability of Social Institutions," *SLM* 4 (1838): 148.

66. Buckley, "*The Great Catastrophe.*"

67. Minor, *Institutes* 1:265.

68. Synod of Va., Mins., 28 Sept. 1791, 76–77, 25 Sept. 1793, 105, 24 Sept. 1794, 127; *Christian Monitor* 2 (16 Aug. 1817): 399.

69. Heron, *Address to the Assn.*, 6–8 (quotes at 7).

70. LP, Richmond City, 20 Feb. 1846. For the background to Virginia's Sabbath legislature, see Dreisbach, "Jefferson and Bills Number 82–86," 190–94.

71. Plumer, *Substance of an Argument*, 10–11. For contrasting perspectives on church-state relations in this period, see the exchange in Justus E. Moore, *The Warning of Thomas Jefferson: or a brief exposition of the dangers to be apprehended to our civil and religious liberties, from presbyterianism* (Philadelphia, 1844), and *The Pope and the Presbyterians: a Review of the Warning of Jefferson Respecting the Dangers to be Apprehended to our Civil and Religious Liberties from Presbyterianism. By an American Citizen* (Philadelphia, 1845).

72. LP, Richmond City, 20 Feb. 1846; Berman, *Richmond's Jewry*, 156–62. For an earlier non-Jewish protest against coerced Sabbath observance also rejected by the assembly, see LP, Patrick Co., 2 Jan. 1840, 6 Dec. 1843. For Jewish reaction to Sunday closing laws in the nineteenth century, see Borden, *Jews, Turks, and Infidels*, 103–28.

73. Earlier in the session a Sabbath convention had met in Richmond and invited the legislators to attend the sessions (*JHDV*, 16 Dec. 1845, 43). Plumer published the proceedings as well as the convention's "Address to the People of Virginia" which requested changing court days from Mondays so that people would not have to travel on Sunday (*Watchman and Observer*, 25 Dec. 1845).

74. LP, Richmond City, 8 Mar. 1848; *JHDV*, 18 Mar. 1848, 369; *Code of Virginia*, 1849, ch. 196, "Of Offences Against Morality and Decency," 741. But see also *AA*, 1861–62, ch. 77, "An Act to prevent certain violations of the Sabbath," 93–94, which penalized hunting on Sunday without exempting those who kept Saturday as a day of rest.

75. *AA*, 1846–1847, 7–8; ibid., no. 24, "Resolution permitting the erection of a chapel upon a part of the public ground attached to the armory," 242. It was "removable at the pleasure of the legislature or the executive of state."

76. *JHDV*, 15 May 1783, 7; Edmund Randolph to James Madison, 15 May 1783, in Hutchison, 7:45–46. The House selected the Rev. Benjamin F. Blagrove, an Episcopalian.

77. Fred Anderson, "Courtney, John," *DVB* 3:487–88; White, *Open Door*, 30–37; Maurice Duke, "Blair, John Durburrow," *DVB* 2:546–47. For the press controversy, see *Va. Gaz. and Gen. Adver.*, 11, 18 Dec. 1802; "Mrs. M'Knight versus Bishop Courtney," *Recorder*, 22 Dec. 1802.

78. In his "Simplex" articles," Federalist Blair had earlier attacked the Virginia legislators for their protest against the Alien and Sedition Acts (Blair Papers).

79. *RE*, 7 Dec. 1849. For Claiborne, see Emily J. Salmon, "Claiborne, Nathaniel Charles," *DVB* 3:251–52.

80. *JHDV*, 19, 20 Dec. 1848, 91, 94–95, 4 Dec. 1849, 31. A list of the clergymen is in the index of the *AA, 1848–1849*, 473, and *AA, 1849–1850*, 524. For Madison's disapproval of legislative chaplains, see Fleet, "Madison's 'Detached Memoranda,'" 558–59. See also Stokes, *Church and State* 3:140–41. For examples of earlier debates over chaplains in Virginia, see *JHDV*, 5 Dec. 1809, 10, 18 Dec. 1817, 36, 16 Dec. 1829, 22; *RE*, 7 Dec. 1809.

81. Maxwell, *Oration Commemorative of Rice*, 24.

82. James E. Heath, "Lecture Delivered before the Richmond Lyceum," *SLM* 4 (1838): 705–11. For the significance of this periodical and Heath's role in it, see Robert D. Jacobs, "Campaign for a Southern Literature: The Southern Literary Messenger," *Southern Literary Journal* 2 (1969): 66–98.

83. Gilmer, "Address, Delivered before the Virginia Historical and Philosophical Society," *SLM* 3 (1837): 97–102. For a similar viewpoint, see George Tucker, "A Discourse on the Progress of Philosophy, and its Influence on the Intellectual and Moral Character of Man," *SLM* 1 (1835): 405–21.

84. Rice, *Character and Conduct of the Presbyterian Church*, 52.

85. Philip Barraud to St. George Tucker, 3 Sept. 1827, TCP; Madison to Edward Everett, 19 Mar. 1823, Everett Papers. See also Madison to Robert Walsh, 2 Mar. 1819, in Hunt, *Writings of Madison* 8:430–32; Richard Channing Moore to Thomas Jackson, 8 Jan. 1829, Moore Letterbook K; Tucker, *Life of Jefferson* 1:101.

86. Carwardine, *Evangelicals and Politics*, 17–22.

87. Howison, *Hist. of Va.* 2:478, 479.

88. Joseph Christian, "Hon. R. C. L. Moncure," *Virginia Law Journal* 6 (1883): 708–15 (quotes at 711, 714).

8. EDUCATION

1. W[illiam] M[ayo] Atkinson to Gen. William H. Brodnax, 1 Feb. 1826, Brodnax Papers. For Atkinson, see John T. Kneebone, "Atkinson, William Mayo," *DVB* 1:244–46.

2. Hawks, app., *Conv. of 1815*, 98, *Conv. of 1816*, 108; Joseph C. Cabell to John H. Cocke, 21 Nov. 1821, Cabell Papers, box 14.

3. *JHDV*, 2 Jan., 1 Feb. 1816, 88, 153, 18 Feb. 1817, 214; Alexander Balmain to Charles Dabney, 6 Nov. 1818, Dabney Papers.

4. Cabell to Cocke, 21 Nov. 1821, Cabell Papers, box 14; Richard Channing Moore to John H. Cocke, 15 July 1819, Cocke Papers, no. 640.

5. Hawks, app., *Conv. of 1821*, 149; "Literary and Religious Intelligence," *RE*, 1 June 1821.

6. "To the Public of Virginia," *RE*, 27 July 1821.

7. Richard Channing Moore, "To the Editors of the *Enquirer*," *RE*, 31 July 1821.

8. *RE*, 7 Aug. 1821. See also *RE*, 14, 17, 21 Aug. 1821.

9. Philip Barraud to St. George Tucker, 1 Aug. 1821, TCP, box 39.

10. Richard Channing Moore to Philander Chase, 7 Feb. 1822, to [James] Montgomery, 20 July 1822, Moore Letterbook A; Cabell to Cocke, 21 Nov. 1821, Cocke Papers, no. 640.

11. Richard Channing Moore to William Meade, 19 Jan. 1822, Meade Papers; Moore to Philander Chase, 7 Feb. 1822, to Rev. Mr. Montgomery, 20 July 1822, Moore Letterbook A.

12. Richard Channing Moore to William Meade, 23 Aug., 18 Sept. 1823, Meade Papers; Moore to Bishop Ravenscroft, 1 Aug. 1823, Moore Letterbook D; Moore to Ravenscroft, 5 Nov. 1823, ibid., E; Moore to Mr. F. Campbell, 7 June 1824, to Ravenscroft, 30 June 1824, to Bishop Kemp, 5 Nov. 1824 (quote), ibid., F. For the rapid development of the seminary, see Hawks, app., *Conv. of 1822*, 154, 157, *Conv. of 1823*, 164, *Conv. of 1824*, 171–74, *Conv. of 1825*, 179–82.

13. LP, Pet. of Robert Anderson, Williamsburg City, 8 Dec. 1831. See also Richard Channing Moore to William Wilmer, 8 Aug. 1826, to James Garnett, 21 Aug. 1826, to William Meade, 24 Aug. 1826 (quote), to Adam Empie, 26 Aug., 22 Sept. 1827, Moore Letterbook H; George Junkin to Francis McFarland, 11 Jan. 1848, MS Coll. no. 100.

14. Madison to Edward Everett, 19 Mar. 1823, Everett Papers.

15. *JHDV*, 8 Dec. 1818, 14; Thomas Jefferson to Charles Sigourney, 15 Aug. 1824, photocopy, Jefferson Papers. See also David Wallace Bratt, "Southern Souls and State Schools: Religion and Public Higher Education in the Southeast, 1776–1900," PhD diss., Yale University, 1999.

16. Conrad Speece to John Holt Rice, 17 July 1820, Gratz Coll.; Rice to John Hartwell Cocke, 6 Jan. 1820, Cocke Papers, no. 640. Rice regarded the Socinians as "the worst of heresies" and feared their influence in the South, particularly in the schools. See Rice to William Hill, 26 Jan. 1821, Hill Papers; Rice to William McPheeters, 22 Mar. 1821, typescript, Rice Papers.

17. Jefferson to Cooper, 2 Nov. 1822, in Ford, *Works of Jefferson* 12:271; Joseph C. Cabell to John Hartwell Cocke, 6 Mar. 1819, Cabell Papers, box 13; Malone, *Public Life of Thomas Cooper*, 234–46; Healey, *Jefferson on Religion*, 231–45; Swift, "Jefferson, Rice, and Education"; Marsden, *Soul of the American University*, 68–78. For Presbyterian higher education, see Miller, *Revolutionary College*; for Cabell, see Lynn A. Nelson, "Cabell, Joseph Carrington," *DVB* 2:488–90.

18. Jefferson, "Report . . . to the Pres. and Dirs. of the Lit. Fund," 7 Oct. 1822, *JHDV*, 1822 sess., app,, 3, 4. After Jefferson's death his grandson-in-law objected forcefully to placing seminaries on university land on grounds of church-state separation. See Nicholas Trist to James Madison, 6 May 1827, Trist Papers.

19. Jefferson to Cooper, 7 Oct. 1814, in Lipscomb and Bergh, *Jefferson's Writings* 14:199–202.

20. Jefferson, "Report . . . to the Pres. and Dirs. of the Lit. Fund," 7 Oct. 1822, *JHDV*, 1822 sess., app,, 3, 4; Joseph C. Cabell to Jefferson, 6 Mar. 1822, 3 Feb. 1823, in Cabell, *Early History of the University*, 248, 273.

21. Jefferson to Charles Sigourney, 15 Aug. 1824, Jefferson Papers, ser. 10.

22. [Rev.] George W. Ridgely to John H. Cocke, 11 July 1827, William Meade to Cocke, 29 May 1827, Cocke Papers, no. 640. See also W. M. Atkinson to William H. Brodnax, 1 Feb 1826, Brodnax Papers.

23. John Faulcon to John H. Cocke, 16 Aug. 1828, Cocke Papers, no. 640.

24. Meade, *Old Churches* 2:54–56.

25. [Benjamin Blake Minor], "The University of Virginia," *SLM* 8 (1842): 53.

26. William S. White to James McDowell, 3 Mar. 1841, McDowell Papers. For McGuffey's impact on American education, see Westerhoff, *McGuffey and His Readers.*

27. [Benjamin Blake Minor], "The University of Virginia," *SLM* 8 (1842): 50–54; Howison, *Hist. of Va.* 2:426; [Ruffner], *Lectures on Christianity,* vii–x (quote at x); Bell, *Church, State, and Education,* 384–90.

28. Report of the Examining Committee, Course of Study, 1822, Examination for admission into full connection, 24 Feb. 1825, and *Address, To the Members and Friends of the Methodist Episcopal Church,* Early Papers. At the time of the school's founding, Early was the presiding elder for the Meherrin District of the Methodist Episcopal Church, which included much of Southside Virginia (*Mins. of the Annual Conferences,* 21). See also Schweiger, *Gospel Working Up,* 60–63.

29. *JHDV,* 22 Jan 1830, 100; *RE,* 23 Jan. (article and editorial), 30 Jan. ("Speech of Mr. Garland") 1830; *Rich. Whig,* 23 Jan. 1830; "Act to incorporate the trustees of Randolph Macon College," RMC. See also Scanlon, *Randolph-Macon,* ch. 1.

30. Stephen Olin, "Inaugural Address," *SLM* 1 (1835): 15–16; Scanlon, *Randolph-Macon,* 51–57.

31. *AA,* 1839, ch. 184, 135–36; *AA,* 1839–40, chs. 115, 116, 92–95, 95–97; *AA,* 1852–54, ch. 344, 238–39; *AA,* 1857–58, ch. 35, 212–13.

32. Maddox, *Free School Idea,* 42–75. For a summation of the several acts establishing the Literary Fund, see Pres. and Dirs. of the Lit. Fund to Joseph C. Cabell, 29 June 1811, Cabell Papers, box 8. For Tyler's concern, see his letter to the General Assembly in which he made an impassioned plea for education and its connection with public virtue and republicanism (*JHDV,* 4 Dec. 1809, 8). The other major proposal in the first quarter of the century came from Charles Fenton Mercer. See Egerton, *Charles Fenton Mercer,* 116–28.

33. "Bill Concerning Hampden Sydney College," RHB, box 38; *JHDV,* 2, 12 Jan., 6, 23 Feb. 1822, 97, 117, 168, 197, 17 Feb. 1823, 201–2, 15 Dec. 1825, 30; LP, Prince Edward Co., 15 Dec. 1825.

34. *RE,* 19 Jan. 1839.

35. Daniel, "Genesis of Richmond College."

36. Thomas R. Dew, "Baccalaureate Address," *SLM* 3 (1837): 401–6 (quotes at 405).

37. Henry Ruffner, *Inaugural Address,* 8–10.

38. Junkin, *Christianity the Patron of Literature.*

39. George Junkin to Francis McFarland, 11 Jan. 1848, MS Coll. no. 100.

40. A[lfred] Leyburn to James McDowell, 31 Jan. 1843, McDowell Papers; for Bryant and Smith, see Meade, *Old Churches* 2:66.

41. *AA, 1839*, ch. 184, 136.

42. See, e.g., L. C. Garland to John Early, Feb. 1840, 13 Mar. 1841, Early Papers, RMC; "College Convention in Virginia," *SLM* 10 (1844): 121.

43. Pres. and Dir. of the Lit. Fund to Joseph C. Cabell, 29 June 1811, Cabell Papers, box 8; Heatwole, *History of Education*, 100–136. The county commissioners' annual reports detailing the problems may be found in *JHDV*, 1820–60, doc. no. 4, sec. L.

44. Knight, *Documentary History* 5:45–79. For governors' messages, see "Extracts from Gubernatorial Messages," Cabell Papers, box 1. For a withering critique of Virginia's lapses in education, see Dunn, *Dominion of Memories*, 61–84.

45. "Books in Use," *JHDV*, 1841–42, doc. no. 4, 40; for typical laws requiring that tax-supported schools have only nonsectarian religious teaching, see *AA, 1846–47*, chs. 32 and 33, 29–37; *AA, 1847–48*, chs. 98 and 101, 64–70, 71–77.

46. "Address of the Educational Convention, Held at Clarksburg, Sept. 8, 1841," *JHDV*, 1841–42, doc. no. 7, 18; Alexander Campbell, "An Address . . . on the subject of Primary or Common Schools, September 8, 1841," ibid., 36; Howard, *Popular Education in Virginia*, 2. For the politics of education, see Shade, *Democratizing the Old Dominion*, 184–86, 188–89.

47. Alexander, *Address Before the Alumni Association*, 17.

48. See, e.g., "Rep. of the Com. on Denominational Schools to the Synod of Virginia," *Watchman and Observer*, 4 Nov. 1847, 45. See also Taylor, *Secondary Education*; Seymour, *From Sunday School to Church School*.

49. Lowe, *Republicans and Reconstruction*, 138–39.

50. Pulliam, *Constitutional Convs. of Va.*, 138.

51. Sally Campbell Preston McDowell to John Miller, 14 June 1855, in Buckley, *Courtship Letters*, 157, 269.

52. The best source for Ruffner's life is Fraser, "William Henry Ruffner."

53. Fox, "William Henry Ruffner," 124–25.

54. William Henry Ruffner, *Africa's Redemption*.

55. Morgan, "Stephen Colwell." In the original 1851 publication, the author had been anonymous. Colwell revised it under his own name the following year (Colwell, *New Themes for the Protestant Clergy*). For an attack on Colwell's work, see, e.g., [Stephen Austin Allibone], *A Review, by a Layman, of a Work Entitled "New Themes for the Protestant Clergy"* etc. (Philadelphia, 1852).

56. [Ruffner], *Charity and the Clergy*; Fraser, "William Henry Ruffner," 217–37.

57. Fox, "William Henry Ruffner," 126.

58. *Mins. of the Educational Assn.*, 7–8, 13; *Reports and Other Papers*.

59. Ruffner to William Brown, 22 Dec. 1869, P[eter] T. Penick to W[illiam] Brown, 11 Nov. 1875, *Central Presbyterian*, Correspondence; Robert E. Lee to A. Leyburn, 5 Feb. 1870, Lee Letterbook; "Educational Intelligence," *EJV* 1 (1870): 201–2.

60. Fraser, "William Henry Ruffner." Fraser does not mention the church-state issue in this article. For Minor's important assistance in drafting the school bill and then implementing it, see his letters to Ruffner of 25 Mar., 3, 9, 21 May, 7 Sept., 14, 19 Oct. 1870, 28 Feb. 1872, 21 Nov. 1877, Ruffner Papers.

61. "The Bible in Public Schools," *EJV* 1 (1870): 88–91.

62. Smith, "Common School Education in the United States," quote at 328. For his antebellum proposal of a public school system in Virginia, see Francis R. Flournoy, *Benjamin Mosby Smith, 1811–1893* (Richmond, 1947). For an Episcopalian clergyman's concurrence, see [William F. Gardner], "Religious Education of Virginia Schools: A Report Read at the Meeting of the Educational Association of Virginia, at Winchester, Va., July, 1871," *EJV* 2 (1871): 364–67.

63. Sherrill, *Presbyterian Parochial Schools*, 82; for Episcopalian activity, see Dashill, *A Digest of the Proceedings*, 129, 304–9, 311, 327–28; *Mins. of the Dover Baptist Assn., 1867*, 8–9.

64. *Mins. of the Dover Baptist Assn., 1870*, 5.

65. *Report of the Superintendent of Public Instruction*, 28 Mar. 1870, doc. 6, 4.

66. William Henry Ruffner to R. L. Carne, 21 Feb. 1871, *EJV* 2 (1871): 197. See William Henry Ruffner, "Religion in the Public Schools," *EJV* 5 (1874): 258–62; "Moral Instruction in Schools," *EJV* 6 (1874): 6–10; "Moral Instruction in Lower Schools," *EJV* 6 (Oct. 1875): 525–28; "The Moral Element in Primary Education," *EJV* 7 (Oct. 1876): 528–35. See also Bell, *Church, State, and Education*, 425–39.

67. [Ruffner], *Virginia School Report*, 105–6.

68. Fraser, "William Henry Ruffner," 357–64.

69. Ruffner to Members of Lexington Presbytery, 11 Apr. 1874, Lexington Presbytery, Records, book 16, 1873–80, reel 11; Thomas Enoch, "Speech on the Ruffner Case," [1875], 1–8, 16, and P[eter] T. Penick to W[illiam] Brown, 11 Nov. 1875, *Central Presbyterian*, Correspondence, box 182.

70. *Mins. of the Dover Baptist Assn., 1875*, 8; Pearson, "William Henry Ruffner," 21.

71. Johnson, *Life and Letters of Dabney*, 396–400 (quote at 397); Puryear, *Public School*, 30–32. For the extended newspaper exchange between Dabney and Ruffner, see *RE*, 5, 6, 8, 12, 13, 20, 22, 26 Apr., 6, 10, 17, 24, 28 May, 2 June, 21, 29 July 1876. For Dabney's negative view of African American participation in the Presbyterian Church, see his essay "Ecclesiastical Equality of Negroes," in Robert L. Dabney, *Discussions: Evangelical and Theological* (London, 1891; rept. 1967), 199–217.

72. Ruffner, *Public Free School System*, 31, 32.

73. Allen, "Address," 491, 492.

74. [Ruffner], "Remarks."

75. [Ruffner], "Christianity in the Public Schools," 450.

76. Moger, *Virginia*, 239–41.

77. Baldwin, *Moral Maxims*, 1, 3, [5], 16. For religious teaching in the public schools of this era, see Adams, *Free School System*, 146–59.

78. "Exercises for Opening School," *Va. School Journal* 1 (1892): 9. For a summary judgment, see the editorial, ibid., 8 (1899): 4. For Bible reading and general Christian education in public school textbooks, see Johnson and Yost, *Separation of Church and State*, 33–73; Westerhoff, *McGuffey and His Readers*; Elson, *Guardians of Tradition*.

79. Bruce, *University of Va.* 4:177–80.

80. *McCollum v. Board of Education*, 333 U.S. 203 (1948).

9. CONSTITUTION

1. Goode, *Recollections*, 208–9. Goode's memoir is an excellent, if chilling, source for white attitudes toward race in the early twentieth-century South. The standard history of the convention is McDanel, *Virginia Conv. of 1901–2*. See also Moger, *Virginia*, 181–202; Holt, "Virginia Constitutional Conv." and "Virginia's Constitutional Conv. of 1901–2." For Goode, see Brenaman, *Va. Convs.*, 99. The best study of southern disfranchisement is J. Morgan Kousser, *The Shaping of Southern Politics: Suffrage Restriction and the Establishment of the One Party South, 1880–1910* (New Haven, 1974). For the process in Virginia, see ibid., 171–81.

2. McIlwaine, *Memories*, 364. For the religious background of the delegates, see table 2. At this time even people who were not formal church members by baptism and/or admission to communion regularly attended religious services. For the importance of religion for culture, see Clifford Geertz, "Religion as a Cultural System," in *The Interpretation of Cultures Selected Essays* (New York, 1996), 89–90. For a critique of Geertz, see Daniel L. Pals, *Seven Theories of Religion* (New York, 1996), 233–67. See also David Hackett Fischer, *Albion's Seed: Four British Folkways in America* (New York, 1989), 795.

3. [John Garland Pollard] to John Thompson Brown, 12 June 1902, Pollard Papers, box 6, folder 155; Hening, 9:111–12. For its passage, see Buckley, *Church and State*, 17–19.

4. Unidentified newspaper clipping [Apr. 1901], Pollard Papers; "State Constitutions Compared," *Times*, 22 July 1900. For Pollard's background and political career, see Hopewell, "An Outsider Looking In."

5. Pollard to John L. Williams, 12 July 1901, Pollard Papers.

6. "A Warm Reply by Mr. Pollard," *Richmond Evening Leader* [1901], and Louis C. Phillips to Pollard, 19 July 1901, ibid.

7. George W. Spooner to Pollard, [19 June 1901], Pollard to Spooner, 19 June 1901, ibid.

8. J. W. Eggleston to Pollard, 17 July 1901, ibid.; for Eggleston's background, see Tyler, *Men of Mark* 3:119–21.

9. "Rabbi's Offer," *Richmond News*, 22 Oct. 1900; editorial in *Evening Leader*, 5 May 1899; Charles O. Saville to Calisch, 2 Feb. 1896, Calisch Papers, box 2. For the Richmond Jewish community and Calisch's religious views and social involvement, see Berman, *Richmond's Jewry*, 206–75.

10. Berman, *Richmond's Jewry*, 241–50; Shepherd, *Avenues of Faith*, 45, 202–5; Berman, "Edward Nathan Calisch."

11. Calisch, "Democracy of the Public Schools," *VSJ* 6 (1897): 152, 153.

12. Calisch to Pollard, 19 July 1901, Pollard Papers. See also J. Manning Dunaway to Pollard, 20 July 1901, A. Leo Obedorfer to Pollard, 20 July 1901, ibid.

13. Calisch to Pollard, 22 July 1901, ibid.

14. "It is Now Decided," *Richmond Dispatch*, 20 July 1901; Hugh V. Campbell to Pollard, 20 July 1901, Calisch to Pollard, 22 July 1901, Pollard Papers. For Trinity Methodist, see Shepherd, *Avenues of Faith*, 41; for M. Ashby Jones, ibid., 219, 220, 261, 294. The

convention ultimately "proclaimed" the constitution rather than submit it for ratification by the state's voters.

15. 1901 Conv., *Proceedings*, 328–30.

16. Calisch to Pollard, 18 Sept. 1901, Pollard Papers; 1901 Conv., *Proceedings*, 330.

17. Lewis F. Mason to Pollard, 19 July 1901, Pollard Papers.

18. 1901 Conv., Mins. of Com. on Legislation, 21 June 1901, 14–15.

19. *AA, 1852*, ch. 262, 184–85; *AA, 1852–53*, ch. 356, 247–48; *AA, 1855–56*, ch. 315, 224–25.

20. *AA, 1855–56*, ch. 277, 190–91; *AA, 1853–54*, ch. 107, 65–66.

21. [Robert P. Kerr to Alfred P. Thom], quoted in 1901 Conv., *Proceedings*, 776; 1901 Conv., Mins. of Com. on Legislation, 21 July 1901, 107.

22. 1901 Conv., Mins. of Com. on Legislation, Res., 23 July 1901, 16–17, Mins., 21, 30 July 1901, 107, 108; 1901 Conv., *Proceedings*, 761–62, 774. Moore would later serve as a counselor of the State Department; see Brenaman, *Va. Convs.*, 101.

23. 1901 Conv., *Proceedings*, 761–62. For Dunaway, see *RH*, 6 July 1916; *Rich. Times*, 12 June 1916. For this concern from an important Presbyterian clergyman, see [Dabney], "Ecclesiastical Accumulations of Wealth."

24. 1901 Conv., *Proceedings*, 733–44 (quotes at 733, 734, 738, 744). For Robertson's life, see Staples, "William Gordon Robertson."

25. 1901 Conv., *Proceedings*, 744–55 (quotes at 744, 750, 751, 753, 754). For the background to this historical interpretation of the medieval church, see S. J. Barnett, *Idol Temples and Crafty Priests: The Origins of Enlightenment Anticlericalism* (New York, 1999).

26. 1901 Conv., *Proceedings*, 755–59 (quotes at 755, 756, 759).

27. Ibid., 759–67 (quotes at 766, 767). For Stebbins, see Tyler, *Encyclopedia* 4:380–84; for Glass, see Rixey Smith and Norman Beasley, *Carter Glass: A Biography* (New York, 1939); Harold Wilson, "The Role of Carter Glass in the Disfranchisement of the Virginia Negro," *Historian* 32 (1969): 69–82. For French policy, see Andrew C. Gould, *Origins of Liberal Dominance: State, Church, and Party in Nineteenth-Century Europe* (Ann Arbor, 1999).

28. 1901 Conv., *Proceedings*, 767–71 (quotes at 767, 768, 771).

29. Ibid., 771–82 (quotes at 775–76, 778, 779, 781).

30. 1901 Conv., Mins. of Com. on Legislation, 28 June 1901, 16–17; 1901 Conv., *Resolutions, Ordinances and Petitions*.

31. Richmond, "Journal of Common Council," 12 Nov. 1866, 29 Jan., 11 Nov., 30 Dec. 1867, 5 Jan., 14 Dec. 1868, 29 Dec. 1869, 10 Jan., 16, 30 May, 7 June 1870, 18, 50, 51, 184, 207–8, 283, 346, 502, 536, 618, 620, 626; *Constitution of St. Paul's Church Home*, 4; *After One Hundred Years*, 9–13; Fogarty, *Commonwealth Catholicism*, 164–76, 230–31; Richmond, *Annual Reports*, 160; Lower, *Sheltering Arms Hospital*, 73; "Retreat for the Sick"; "Sheltering Arms Hospital, 1894–1914." For an unusual antebellum tribute to the Sisters of Charity, see "Old Maids," *SLM* 3 (1837): 473–74.

32. Audriot, *Population Abstract*, 690–91; Richmond, *Resolutions and Ordinances*, 140; 1901 Conv., *Proceedings*, 796.

33. *RH*, 27 May 1878.

34. The controversy is reprinted in James, *Documentary History*, app., 241–55. For Henry's reply, see Henry, *Presbyterian Church and Religious Liberty*.

35. *Mins. of the Dover Baptist Assn.*, 1901, 25.

36. *RH*, 5 Sept. 1901.

37. 1901 Conv., Mins. of Com. on Legislation, 2, 18, 21 July 1901, 102, 106, 107; 1901 Conv., *Journal*, 22, 30, 31 Aug., 2, 3, 4, 5, 10, 11, 13, 23 Sept., 7 Oct. 1901, 148, 149, 150, 151, 152, 153, 155, 158, 161, 163, 166, 181, 198; "Resolved, That the Methodist ministers . . . ," 31 Aug. 1901, in 1901 Conv., *Resolutions, Ordinances and Petitions*.

38. "Declaration of Principles," *Va. Courier*, 1 June 1896; "A Big Day in the Valley," ibid., 1 Mar. 1901; Kimball, *Life and Labor*.

39. *Rich. and Manchester City Directory*, 1901, 1321; *Va. Courier*, 15 Aug. 1901; *Rich. Dispatch*, 13 Oct. 1901; 1901 Conv., *Journal*, 23, 24, 26, 27 Sept., 1, 2, 3, 4, 11 Oct., 8, 9 Nov., 3 Dec. 1901, 181, 183, 185, 186, 190, 192, 193, 195, 204, 231, 233, 258.

40. 1901 Conv., *Proceedings*, 794.

41. Ibid., 793, 795, 797, 801.

42. *Bradford v. Roberts*, 175 U.S. 291 (1899); Nichols, *Uneasy Alliance*, 216–17.

43. (E[dward] N[athan] C[alisch], "An Unrighteous Decision," unidentified newspaper clipping, unnumbered Misc. Box, Calisch Papers.

44. 1901 Conv., *Proceedings*, 803.

45. Ibid., 805, 806; "Yesterday's Proceedings," *Rich. Dispatch*, 16 Oct. 1901.

46. Lamb, "Charles V. Meredith"; 1901 Conv., *Proceedings*, 812.

47. 901 Conv., *Proceedings*, 806, 807.

48. Ibid., 808, 809.

49. Ibid., 815; for Turnbull, see Brenaman, *Va. Convs.*, 103.

50. 1901 Conv., *Proceedings*, 815, 816, 818. The final vote was 42 to 15. As Dunaway had suggested, the second part of the resolution, which banned aid to institutions not completely owned by the government, went down to defeat, 24 to 30.

51. Richmond, Board of Alderman Journal, 9 Dec. 1902, 15 Jan. 1903, 145, 158–58; "A Bill to Authorize . . . Appropriations to Charitable institutions or associations," bill 155, RHB, 1902–4, box 62; *JSV*, 14, 15 Jan. 1903, 158, 162; "Local Charities," *Rich. Times*, 16 Jan. 1903.

52. *JHDV*, 15 Jan., 2, 3 Feb., 3, 4, 10, 11, 13, 17 Mar. 1903, 198, 271, 176, 409, 419, 452, 460, 477, 491; *JSV*, 16 Mar. 1903, 336. For the involvement of Protestant churches in social work after 1902, see Shepherd, *Avenues of Faith*, 137–67. See also Arthur W. James, *Virginia's Social Awakening: The Contribution of Dr. Mastin and the Board of Charities and Corrections* (Richmond, 1942).

53. In 1900 the urban population of Virginia numbered 340,000 out of 1.85 million people, or 18 percent (U.S. Bureau of the Census, *Historical Statistics*, 36). For a fine discussion of rural-urban relationships, see "Urban-Rural Relations in Old Virginia" in Goldfield, *Region, Race, and Cities*, 69–86.

54. Dain, *Disordered Minds*, and Keve, *History of Corrections*, are useful studies. A definitive history of the struggle for public education in Virginia remains to be writ-

ten, but see J. L. Blair Buck, *The Development of Public Schools in Virginia, 1607–1952* (Richmond, 1952); Barbara J. Griffin, "Thomas Ritchie and the Founding of the Richmond Lancasterian School," *VMHB* 86 (1978): 447–60; Douglas R. Egerton, "To the Tombs of the Capulets: Charles Fenton Mercer and Public Education in Virginia, 1816–1817," *VMHB* 93 (1985): 155–74; Thomas C. Hunt, "Popular Education in Nineteenth-Century Virginia: The Efforts of Charles Fenton Mercer," *Paedagogica Historica* 21 (1981): 337–46, and "Henry Ruffner and the Struggle for Public Schools in Antebellum Virginia," *American Presbyterians* 64 (1986): 18–26; Hellenbrand, "The Unfinished Revolution."

55. Beeman, *Evolution of the Southern Backcountry*, 218, 225, 226.

56. See Shalhope, *John Taylor of Caroline*; Dawidoff, *Education of John Randolph*. For the decline of Jefferson's influence in Virginia, see Cunningham, *In Pursuit of Reason*, 348; Jordan, *Political Leadership*, 205–24; Malone, "Fate of Revolutionary Republicanism."

57. For Richmond's prejudice against Jews and Catholics in the early twentieth century, see Shepherd, *Avenues of Faith*, 204–5, 206–11. For Protestant-Jewish relations in the South, see "Jews, Blacks, and Southern Whites," in Goldfield, *Region, Race, and Cities*, 145–62.

58. 1901 Conv., *Proceedings*, 2683, 2686; Cash, *Mind of the South*, 341–43.

59. 1901 Conv., *Proceedings*, 751. See also ibid., 792.

60. Ibid., 2687–92 (quotes at 2692). For religious tax exemption, see Witte and Nichols, *Religion and the American Constitutional Experiment*, 185–215.

10. BIBLE

1. *Engel v. Vitale*, 370 U.S. 421 (1962); *Abington School District v. Schempp*, 374 U.S. 203 (1963). The latter included the Maryland case of *Murray v. Curlett*.

2. For the immediate furor, see *New York Times*, 2 July 1962; *Los Angeles Times*, 2 July 1962; "The Court Decision," *Newsweek*, 9 July 1962, 43–45; "The Supreme Court," *Time*, 6 July 1962, 7–9; "Uproar over School Prayer," *U.S. News and World Report*, 9 July 1962, 42–44; Stedman, *Religion and Politics*; Lowry, *To Pray or Not to Pray*.

3. *Zorach v. Clausen*, 343 U.S. 306 (1952) at 313.

4. For Bible reading and general Christian education in public school textbooks, see Johnson and Yost, *Separation of Church and State*, 33–73; Elson, *Guardians of Tradition*; Westerhoff, *McGuffey and His Readers*.

5. Jorgenson, *State and the Non-Public School*.

6. E.g., see *JHDV*, 2 Feb. 1827, 132–33.

7. Bell, *Church, State, and Education*, is the only substantive study. For an overview of the issue of religion in the public schools, see Michaelsen, *Piety*. For the intriguing argument that school religion was unimportant and essentially innocuous in forming young minds, see Moore, "What Children Did Not Learn in School."

8. "Books in Use at the Common Schools in 1840," *JHDV*, 1841–42, doc. no. 4, 40.

For typical antebellum laws requiring tax-supported schools to have only nonsectarian religious teaching, see *AA, 1846–47,* chs. 32 and 33, 29–37; *AA, 1847–48,* chs. 98 and 101, 64–70, 71–77.

9. Geertz, "Religion as a Cultural System," 89–90.

10. Ruffner, *Public Free School System,* 31, 32; *Report of the Superintendent.* For more of the Bible controversy, see Smith, "Merits and Defects."

11. "Exercises," *VSJ* 1 (1892): 9.

12. Calisch, "Democracy," 152. By urging "secular control" Calisch may have been referring to the numerous school districts in Virginia where clergymen served as superintendents and school board members. For Wise's views on religion in public education, see Michaelsen, *Piety,* 31, 200. For an overview of Jewish thought with primary source documents, see Sarna and Dalin, *American Jewish Experience.*

There are similarities between Calisch's position and the views espoused in the next century by John Dewey. Dewey thought of the work of the public school as "religious," by which he meant exposing students to all that is ennobling in human experience; but he opposed teaching religion or holding religious exercises. See, e.g., Dewey, "Religion and Our Schools," *Hibbert Journal* 6 (1908): 796–809; *Democracy and Education* (New York, 1916); and *A Common Faith* (New Haven, 1934). For a kindred perspective, see Nicholas Butler Murray, *The Building of the Nation* (New York, 1916).

13. John Kilgo, "Address," *BRCA,* 24 May 1904, 5. For an overview, see also Michaelsen, *Piety,* 168–69.

14. State ex rel. *Freeman v. Scheve,* 65 Neb. 853, 91 N.W. 846 (1902), judgment adhered to 65 Neb. 876, 93 N.W. 169 (1903). For the Nebraska decision in the Virginia religious press, see *Central Presbyterian,* 6 Jan. 1904. For the larger context of this decision, see Thomas James, "Rights of Conscience and State School Systems in Nineteenth-Century America," in *Toward a Usable Past: Liberty under State Constitutions,* ed. Paul Finkelman and Stephen E. Gottlieb (Athens, GA, 1991), 117–47. Ellwood P. Cubberley, *Changing Conceptions of Education* (New York, 1909), is a useful contemporary source.

15. "Should Teach Bible in Public Schools," *NL,* 14 Dec. 1903, 1. For Semmes, see Shepherd, *Avenues of Faith,* 142–43.

16. "Bible in the Schools will be Discussed," *NL,* 9 Jan. 1904; "Public Schools Should Teach No Religion," *NL,* 18 Jan. 1904. In two long letters to the editor, Semmes first detailed all the arguments against his proposal and then defended his position more fully ("More About Teaching Bible in Public Schools," *NL,* 13 Jan. 1904; "Shall the Bible Be Banished?" *NL,* 5 Feb. 1904). For Hawthorne's career, see Taylor, *Va. Baptist Ministers,* 5th ser., 253–67.

17. Hohner, *Prohibition and Politics,* 58; Dabney, *Dry Messiah,* 24; "Large Sum for Schools," *T-D,* 24 Jan. 1904; *BRCA,* 4 Aug. 1904.

18. Virtually every religious group was represented in the discussion except the Roman Catholics. Numerically tiny in Virginia, they maintained their own schools. In the midst of the controversy, Bishop Augustine Van de Vyver of Richmond urged "Loyalty to Church and State" and said nothing about the Bible controversy. See "Lays All

Blame on Protestants," *NL*, 11 Feb. 1904; "Immense Crowd Attends Vespers," *NL*, 15 Feb. 1904.

19. "Inculcate Religion," *T-D*, 31 Jan. 1904.

20. "Religious Services," *T-D*, 31 Jan. 1904; "State and Education," *Central Presbyterian*, 3 Feb. 1904.

21. "Let Us Keep Step," *T-D*, 31 Jan. 1904; "The Bible in the Public Schools," *BRCA*, 4 Feb. 1904; "Shall the Bible Be Banished?" *NL*, 5 Feb. 1904. For the efforts of the Religious Educational Association to formulate a common Bible, see "All Sorts," *RH*, 24 Mar. 1904.

22. "Public School System," *T-D*, 23 Jan. 1904.

23. "Bible in the Schools," *NL*, 21 Jan. 1904; "Religious Liberty," *NL*, 23 Jan. 1904. For examples of the misunderstanding, see "Favors Bible," *NL*, 11 Jan. 1904; "The People want the Bible," *NL*, 21 Jan.1904; "The Bible in the Schools," *NL*, 25 Jan. 1904. For Baptist opposition to Hawthorne, see "Bible in the Public Schools," *RH*, 19 Feb. 1904.

24. "A Vexed Question," *RH*, 28 Jan. 1904.

25. "Read but not Teach," *T-D*, 31 Jan. 1904; "Says It Violates the Golden Rule," *NL*, 9 Feb. 1904. The *Religious Herald* continued to publish articles against biblical instruction in the public schools for the next two months. See, e.g., "Creed for Public Schools," 4 Feb. 1904; "A Word More on a Current Question," 18 Feb. 1904; "Multitudinous Protestantism and the Public Schools," 18 Feb. 1904; "Bible in the Public Schools," 3 Mar. 1904; "All Sorts and All Sizes," 24 Mar. 1904.

26. "Violates Constitution," *T-D*, 31 Jan. 1904; Calisch, "What the American Jew Stands For," in *Three Score*, 71.

27. "Bible in the Schools," *T-D*, 7 Feb. 1904.

28. "Religious Instruction,'" *VJE* 4 (1911): 633–34.

29. Deierhoi, "Mini-History of Richmond Public Schools," 278, 295, 305; School Board Mins., 27 Jan. 1913, 249–50, in Richmond Public Schools, Records; "Bible in City Schools," *T-D*, 28 Jan. 1913; *Forty-Fourth Annual Report*, 40–41. For the confusion over the board's intentions, see "Shall the State Control?" in *RH*, 27 Feb. 1913.

30. "Greatest in the Kingdom," *RH*, 6 Feb. 1913.

31. "Dr. Calisch on Bible in School," *T-D*, 1 Feb. 1913.

32. "Folk Need Bible in City Schools," *T-D*, 3 Feb., 1913; for Maclachlan, see Shepherd, *Avenues of Faith*, 12–13. Calisch would lead the honorary pallbearers at the minister's funeral in 1929.

33. "Conference Notes and News," *BRCA*, 13 Feb. 1913.

34. "An Old Issue Revived," *RH*, 16 Feb. 1913.

35. Calisch, "Hypocrisies," in *Three Score*, 93. Calisch's position was all the more difficult because it opposed Richmond Jewry's efforts to blend into the southern scene. See Berman, "Rabbi Calisch and the Debate over Zionism," 304–5.

36. "Bible in Schools," *T-D*, 10 Feb. 1913; Calisch to GWM, 11 Feb 1913, McDaniel Papers.

37. "Mothers Endorse Bible Reading," *NL*, 7 Feb. 1913; "Bible Reading in Schools,"

NL, 11 Feb. 1913; "Bible in Public Schools," *NL*, 11 Feb. 1913; School Board Mins., 20 Feb. 1913, in Richmond Public Schools, Records, 259.

38. *NL*, 22 Feb. 1913.

39. "Old Issue Revived," *RH*, 16 Feb. 1913; "Mr. Hoge Wants Bible in School," *TD*, 17 Feb. 1913; "Shall the State Control?" *RH*, 27 Feb. 1913.

40. C. P. Walford to Edward N. "Calish," 21 Feb. 1913, Calisch Papers, box 3; School Board Mins., 20 Feb, 6 Mar. 1913, in Richmond Public Schools, Records, 259, 260–61; "Religion and the State," *RH*, 13 Mar. 1913. The letters of commendation included one from the Men's Bible Class of Broaddus Memorial Church (School Board Mins., 20 Mar., 23 Apr. 1913, in Richmond Public Schools, Records, 267, 288; *Forty-Fourth Annual Report*, 41. Richmond's First Unitarian Church had voted against participating, and Weatherby, a minister from another congregation, represented only himself (Alexander T. Bowser to Calisch, 23 Feb. 1913, Calisch Papers, box 3).

41. "Bible in the Public Schools," *BRCA*, 13 Mar. 1913. For Cannon's concern that Catholics were preventing Bible reading in the public schools of New Orleans, see "Where the Spirit and Power of Rome Hold Sway," *BRCA*, 18 Sept. 1913.

42. For a contemporary overview, see Athearn, *Religious Education*.

43. Wood and Grant, *Bible as Literature*; Courtney, *Literary Man's Bible*; Humphries, "Literary Study of the Bible." For Calisch, see "Bible Knowledge," [1901], unidentified newspaper clipping in Calisch Papers, Misc. Box; for GWM's views, see "Fight Grows," *T-D*, 10 Feb. 1913.

44. See, e.g., Rugh, *Moral Training*; O'Donnell, *Creed and Curriculum*.

45. H. W. Holmes, "New Forces in Religious Education," 213. This school of thought is strongly represented in *Religious Education*. See, e.g., E. O. Sisson, "An Unused Opportunity for Religion in Public Schools," 6 (1911): 78–83; J. W. Jenks, "Values in the Social Science," 6 (1911): 369–74; C. J. Keyser, "The Spiritual Significance of Mathematics," 6 (1911): 374–84; John M. Coulter, "The Making of Religious Citizens Through Biology, 8 (1913): 420–24; Edward L. Nichols, "Physical Science and Religious Citizenship," 8 (1913): 424–25.

46. Athearn, *Religious Education*, 88 (quote); Forrest, *Bible Classes for High School Pupils*, 5–7; *Official Syllabus*.

47. Hohner, *Prohibition and Politics*, 72–125; Shepherd, *Avenues of Faith*, 104–15.

48. Editorial, *T-D*, 20 Feb. 1916.

49. GWM's correspondence with political figures is extensive. See, e.g., E. Lee Trinkle to GWM, 4 Jan., 7 Feb., 10 Mar., 15 Aug. 1921, GWM to Trinkle (endorsement of his candidacy), 7 Jan. 1921, to Claude A. Swanson, 11 Jan. 1921, 8 Feb., 2 Aug. 1922, 10 Mar. 1924, Swanson to GWM, 12 Jan., 28 Sept., 14 Oct. 1921, 10 Feb., 8 Aug. 1922, 15 Mar. 1924, Harry F. Byrd to GWM, 9 Mar. 1926, McDaniel Papers.

50. GWM to Pollard, 25 Jan. 1921, to W. R. Barksdale, 25 Jan. 1921, ibid.

51. GWM to Claude A. Swanson, 2 Aug. 1922, ibid. See also GWM to Swanson, 11 Jan. 1921, 8 Feb. 1922, 10 Mar. 1924, ibid. For this election, see Pulley, *Old Virginia Restored*, 175.

52. "Governor Lee Trinkle's Christmas Message," *Methodist* 31 (Jan. 1924): 3. I am indebted to Brent Tarter for the Trinkle story.

53. Hohner, *Prohibition and Politics*, 84; Shepherd, *Avenues of Faith*, 49.

54. John F. Vines to GWM, 1 Mar. 1924, GWM to Vines, 10 Mar. 1924, McDaniel Papers.

55. Samuel L. Adams to GWM, 15 Mar. 1922, with enclosure Tom Dixon to Mr. Adams, 14 Mar. 1922, ibid.

56. "Suppress Them," *Methodist*, Mar. 1924.

57. *Va. Conference Annual*, 111.

58. GWM to Walter Russell Bowie, 29 Nov. 1913, McDaniel Papers. For Bowie, see Shepherd, *Avenues of Faith*, 267–73.

59. *JHDV*, 27, 29 Feb., 8 Mar. 1924, 498, 509, 578, 772 (the vote in the House of Delegates was 75 to 2). Dorr, *Segregation's Science*, offers a detailed and chilling account of Virginia's role in the eugenics movement. The best study of the court case is Lombardo, *Three Generations*. For the broader context, see Harry Bruinius, *Better for All the World: The Secret History of Forced Sterilization and America's Quest for Racial Purity* (New York, 2006). For Mastin's involvement, see Lombardo, *Three Generations*, 73–74; Shepherd, *Avenues of Faith*, 149–51.

60. Luther Howard Jenkins to John K. Branch, 14 Feb. 1920, to Gordon Shephard, 17 Feb. 1920, to GWM, 5 Mar. 1920, McDaniel Papers.

61. "Churches Make Fight on Sunday Law Changes," *T-D*, 7 Feb. 1926.

62. Samuel L. Adams to GWM, 16 July 1926, McDaniel Papers.

63. E. B. Jackson to GWM, 9 Feb. 1922, GWM to E. P. Alldredge, 8 Mar. 1922, ibid.

64. R. T. Hayes to GWM, 12 Jan. 1926, C. W. Hudson to GWM, 2 Jan. 1926, ibid.

65. [GWM] to Norfleet Gardiner, 26 Feb. 1916, ibid. See also [GWM] to F. G. Noffsinger, 15 Jan. 1916, ibid.

66. Shepherd, *Avenues of Faith*, 120; GWM to E. E. Bomar, 30 Dec. 1913, McDaniel Papers.

67. GWM to A. C. Dixon, 28 Mar. 1922, McDaniel Papers.

68. Mrs. P. H. Ellett to GWM, 18 Dec. 1924, ibid.

69. *JHDV*, 3 Mar. 1924, 607; "House Passes School Bible Bill by Big Vote," *T-D*, 4 Mar. 1924; "Delegates Say Bible Education As Important As Shakespeare," *NL*, 4 Mar. 1924.

70. Horne, "Moral and Religious Instruction." For Horne, see Eugene Dunlap, "The Religious Implications of Herman Harrell Horne's Educational Philosophy," MA thesis, Pacific School of Religion, 1954.

71. W. P. Edwards to GWM, 23 Feb. 1924, H. F. Jones to GWM, 12 Jan. 1925, McDaniel Papers. For his gracious response to the Klan leader, see GWM to W. P. Edwards, 13 Mar. 1924, McDaniel Papers. For his political activities on behalf of social reform, see GWM to E. B. Alldredge, 8 Mar. 1922, ibid.

72. "The Bible and the Public Schools," *RH*, 20 Mar. 1924; I. T. Jacobs to GWM, 8 Apr. [1924], McDaniel Papers. See also Pollard to GWM, 20 Mar. 1924, ibid.

73. E. R. Combs to GWM, 11 July 1925, McDaniel Papers; *JSV,* 4, 7, 8 Mar. 1924, 612, 733, 822. The Senate voted against suspending the rules and considering the bill out of its order by 21 to 12. For events in a neighboring state, see William B. Gatewood Jr., *Preachers, Pedagogues, and Politicians: The Evolution Controversy in North Carolina* (Chapel Hill, 1966).

74. Editorial, *Presbyterian of the South,* 29 Oct. 1924; Report of the Bible Society Board, in *Va. Conference Annual,* 1925, 112. See also Edward J. Larson, *Summer for the Gods: The Scopes Trial and America's Continuing Debate over Science and Religion* (Cambridge, MA, 1997).

75. H. Augustus Miller Jr., "The Bible and the School," *VJE* 19 (Nov. 1925): 94–96.

76. "Principal [Lindsay] Crawley's Suggestions to the Teachers of the Appomattox Schools," *VJE* 19 (1925): 139.

77. "Bible in School," *Methodist,* Dec. 1925, 1; "Reading the Bible in Schools," ibid., Jan. 1926, 1.

78. GWM to E. R. Combs, 15 July 1925, R. H. Pitt to GWM, 22 Sept., [Nov.?] 1925, McDaniel Papers. For the division among Baptists, see also "Scotched, if not Killed," *RH,* 4 Mar. 1926. For the method of committee selection, see "Playing Fair," *RH,* 18 Mar. 1926.

79. "Declares Church Can Stand Alone," *T-D,* 1 Feb. 1926; GWM to R. H. Pitt, 8 Feb. 1926, to T. Ryland Sanford, 12 Feb. 1926, McDaniel Papers.

80. For Pollard's authorship, see *NL,* 23 Feb. 1926.

81. *JSV,* 4 Feb. 1926, 153; "A Memorial by the Baptist General Association," *RH,* 18 Feb. 1926; "Religious Liberty Strongly Urged by State Baptists," *T-D,* 7 Feb. 1926.

82. "Bible in the Schools," *T-D,* 7 Feb. 1926; "The Bible Bill," *T-D,* 14 Feb. 1926. See also "Bible and the Schools," *T-D,* 19 Feb. 1926; "The Bible Bill," *T-D,* 22 Feb. 1926.

83. "Dangerous Tendencies," *T-D,* 25 Feb. 1926; "Scotched, if not Killed," *RH,* 4 Mar. 1926; "Legislative Gossip in and Around the Lobbies," *T-D,* 13 Feb. 1926.

84. "Bill for Compulsory Bible Reading is Killed," *T-D,* 26 Feb. 1926; "Address" of GWM before legislative committee, [25 Feb. 1926], carbon copy, McDaniel Papers; "Scotched, if not Killed," *RH,* 4 Mar. 1926.

85. "Calisch Hopes Sunday Services Helps Many," *NL,* 1 Mar. 1924.

86. Calisch was mentioned as "a Jewish rabbi" in "Playing Fair," *RH,* 18 Mar. 1926. "Thanks to the Baptist Church," *T-D,* 27 Feb. 1926; Amos B. Cooke to GWM, 25 Feb. 1926, McDaniel Papers. See also Joseph H. Chitwood to GWM, 26 Feb. 1926, Robert S. Shriver to GWM, 3 Mar. 1926, Matthew Page Andrews to GWM, 4 Mar. 1926, GWM to Wolf Cohn, 8 Mar. 1926, Elizabeth Fry Kirren to GWM, 16 Mar. 1926, W. B. Swaney to GWM, 21 Apr. 1926, Wm. F. Montavon to GWM, 10 May 1926, McDaniel Papers.

87. GWM to M. F. Godfrey, 12 Mar. 1926, McDaniel Papers.

88. "Fundamentalism versus Religious Freedom," Calisch Papers, box 6; "Rabbi Discusses Religion's Role in Next Conflict," *T-D,* 25 Feb. 1934. In this same piece he also supported ending church exemption from taxes.

89. "An Unrighteous Decision," signed letter published in an unidentified newspaper, Calisch Papers, Misc. Box.

90. [Isadore Franzblau to Abraham N. Franzblau], 13 Dec. 1938, Francis S. Chase to Calisch, 4 Sept. 1941, Calisch to Chase, 9 Sept. 1941, Jesse H. Binford to Calisch, 26 Dec. 1941, Edward N. Calisch to Binford, 31 Jan. 1941, Calisch Papers, box 3. Calisch would be vindicated by *McCollum v. Bd. of Ed.*, 333 U.S. 203 (1948).

91. Heinemann, *Harry Byrd*, 90–94 (quote at 94).

92. J. P. H. Crismond to GWM, 17 Mar. 1917, McDaniel Papers. For an extraordinary instance of anti-Catholicism in the South at this time, see Sharon Davies, *Road Rising: A True Tale of Love, Race, and Religion in America* (Oxford, 2010).

93. E. E. Cook to GWM, 23 July 1917, McDaniel Papers.

94. Kneebone, "'It Must Be a Hoax,'"; Chalmers, *Hooded Americanism*, 232–34.

95. GWM to Ed Charity, 26 June 1926, McDaniel Papers; see also GWM to W. W. Booker, 24 June 1926, J. F. Love to GWM, 17 July 1926, ibid.

96. GWM to the editor, *Atlanta Constitution*, 20 Dec. 1926, ibid. He wrote a similar letter to the editor of the *New York Times* on 31 Dec. 1926.

97. G .W. Paschal to GWM, 17 July 1927, McDaniel Papers.

98. James R. Sweeney, "Rum, Romanism, and Virginia Democrats"; Hopewell, "John Garland Pollard," 135–43.

EPILOGUE

1. Conv. of 1901, *Proceedings* 2:2687–92.

2. But see Bruce J. Dierenfield, "Secular Schools? Religious Practices in New York and Virginia Public Schools since World War II," *Journal of Policy History* 4 (1992): 361–88; Warren A. Nord and Charles C. Haynes, *Taking Religion Seriously across the Curriculum*, Assn. of Curriculum Supervision and Development (Alexandria, VA, [1998?]).

3. Gordon, *Spirit of the Law*, 90–91. I am grateful to Professor Gordon for bringing this to my attention. See also Ronnie Prevost, "SBC Resolutions Regarding Religious Liberty and the Separation of Church and State (1940–1997): A Fundamental Shift," *Baptist History and Heritage* 34 (1999): 73; Charles McDaniel, "The Decline of the Separation Principle in the Baptist Tradition of Religious Liberty," *Journal of Church and State* 50 (2008): 413–30.

4. *Falwell v. Miller*, 203 F. Supp. 2d 624 (W.D. Va. 2002); Smillie, *Falwell Inc.*, 137–43.

Bibliography

MANUSCRIPT SOURCES

"An Act to incorporate the trustees of Randolph Macon College," RMC.
John James Allen Papers, 1820–51, photocopy, VHS.
Charles Wesley Andrews Papers, DU.
Isaac Backus Papers, ANTS.
Alexander Balmain Memorandum Book, WMC.
John Durburrow Blair Papers, box 45, Brock.
Jonathan Boucher Papers, WMC.
Bourne, George. "Cursory Remarks on the United States of America, 1802." Type-
    script, DLC.
John P. Branch Historical Papers, RMC.
Benjamin Brand Papers, VHS.
Breckinridge Family Papers, VHS.
William H. Brodnax Papers, LVA.
Bryan Family Papers, no. 3400, UVA.
Cabell Family Papers, no. 38-III, UVA.
Edward N. Calisch Papers, Beth Ahabah Archives, Richmond.
Campbell Family Papers, DU.
Edward Carrington Papers, 1784–1810, VHS.
Robert Carter Papers, 1772–93, American Antiquarian Society, Worcester, MA.
Robert Carter Papers, DLC.
Robert Carter Papers, VBHS.
Central Presbyterian, Correspondence, 1868–73, box 181; 1874–78, box 182, Brock.
Cocke Family Papers, no. 1480, UVA.
John Hartwell Cocke Papers, 1725–1931, no. 640, UVA.
Colonial Papers, LVA.
Holmes Conrad Papers, 1794–1859, VHS.
John Cropper Papers, VHS.
Charles William Dabney Papers, no. 1412, SHC.
William and Thomas Dawson Papers, 1721–75, DLC.
Deierhoi, William H., et al. "A Mini-History of the Richmond Public Schools,
    1869–1992." Typescript, RCSB.
Drinard Papers, VHS.
Edward Droomgoole Papers, SHC.

Bishop John Early Diary, VHS.
Bishop John Early Papers, RMC.
Edward Everett Papers, 1675–1910, microfilm, Massachusetts Historical Society, Boston.
"Fairfax County List of Titheables for 1749," comp. Charles Green, DLC.
William Fleming Papers, LVA.
William Graham Letters and Papers, 1783–1885, DU.
Gratz Collection, PHS.
David Griffith Papers, VHS.
Hugh Blair Grigsby Papers, 1745–1944, VHS.
Thomas Haskins Journal, 1782–85, DLC.
Patrick Henry Papers, 1776–1818, DLC.
Joseph Herndon Letters, UVA.
William Hill Papers, UPS.
Moses Drury Hoge Journal, Brock.
Moses Hoge Papers, DLC.
James Lewis Hook Papers, 1796–1832, LVA.
Hubard Family Papers, SHC.
Huntington Manuscripts, HEH.
Thomas Jefferson Papers, ser. 10, DLC.
William M. Jordan Diary, 1852, 31 Jan.–31 May 1857, DU.
Robert Edward Lee Letterbook, 29 Nov.1866–2 Sept.1870, photocopy, VHS.
Legislative Petitions, RG 78, LVA.
Logan Papers, PHS.
James Madison Papers, microfilm, DLC.
[Bishop] James Madison Papers, DU.
George White McDaniel Papers, VBHS.
James McDowell Papers, SHC.
Stith Mead Letterbook, VHS.
William Meade Papers, WMC.
Methodist Episcopal Church, South, Papers, DU.
Samuel Miller Papers, Princeton University Library, Princeton, NJ.
Misc. Manuscripts, DLC.
Richard Channing Moore Letterbooks, photocopy, VTS.
MS Collection no. 100, Washington and Lee University Library, Lexington, VA.
Wilson Cary Nicholas Papers, no. 2343, UVA.
John Page Notebook, typescript, WMC.
Peyton Family Papers, 1770–1913, VHS.
John Garland Pollard Papers, WMC.
Randolph Family Papers, 1786–1970, VHS.
Randolph-Tucker Papers, box 7, Brock.
Retreat for the Sick, broadside, VHS.
John Holt Rice Papers, UPS.
Roane-Harrison-Williams Papers, VHS.

William Henry Ruffner Papers, no. 2533-a, box 1, Educational Material (all photostats), UVA.

R[obert] E[den] Scott to Christian B. Scott, 9 Jan. 1846, Letter, VHS.

"Sheltering Arms Hospital, 1894–1914," summary notes from Minutes, typescript, VHS.

William Short Papers, DLC.

William Spencer Diary, 1789–90, VHS.

Tazewell Family Papers, LVA.

Nicholas Philip Trist Papers, 1791–1836, VHS.

Tucker Family Papers, Brock.

Tucker-Coleman Papers, WMC.

John Tyler Papers, microfilm, DLC.

Moses Waddel Papers, DLC.

Warren Association Papers, ANTS.

David Watson Papers, DLC.

William White Papers, Church Historical Society, Austin, TX.

William Wiatt Papers, 1747–85, WMC.

Wilson, Samuel B. "A Brief Biographical Sketch of Samuel B. Wilson Written by Himself." Typescript, UPS.

GOVERNMENT DOCUMENTS, PUBLISHED AND UNPUBLISHED
American State Papers

City of Richmond. *Annual Reports of the City Departments of Richmond, Va. for the Year ending January 31st, 1873*. Richmond, 1873.

———. Board of Alderman Journal, 1902–3, Archives, Richmond Public Library.

———. *Certain Resolutions and Ordinances of the Council of the City of Richmond for the Years Commencing with . . . 1898, and ending with . . . 1900*. Richmond, 1900.

———. Journal of Common Council, VSL.

———. Richmond City School Board. *Forty-Fourth Annual Report of the Superintendent of the Public Schools of the City of Richmond for the Scholastic Year Ending June 30, 1913*. Richmond, 1914.

———. Richmond Public Schools, Records, May 1911–Jan. 1914, RCSB.

Hening, William Waller, ed. *The Statutes at Large, being a Collection of All the Laws of Virginia, from the First Session of the Legislature in the Year 1619*. 13 vols. Richmond, 1809–23.

Minutes of the Educational Association of Virginia, Assembled in University Hall, Charlottesville, Va., Tuesday, July 17th, 1866. Richmond, 1866.

Report of the Superintendent of Public Instruction, 28 March 1870, document no. 6, 4, in Circulars, LVA.

Reports and Other Papers Delivered Before the Educational Association of Virginia, at its Anniversary in Lynchburg, July, 1867. N.p., n.d.

Revised Code of the Laws of Virginia: Being a Collection of All Such Acts of the General

Assembly, of a Public and Permanent Nature as are now in Force, . . . 1819. Richmond, 1819.

Shepherd, Samuel, ed. *The Statutes at Large of Virginia, from October Session 1792 to December Session 1806, inclusive, being a Continuation of Hening*. 3 vols. Richmond, 1835–36.

U.S. Bureau of the Census. *Historical Statistics of the United States*. Washington, DC, 1976.

U.S. Congress. *Annals of Congress*.

——. *Journal of the House of Representatives*.

Virginia Colony. *Executive Journals of the Council of Colonial Virginia*. Ed. H. R. McIlwaine and Wilmer L. Hall. 6 vols. Richmond, 1925–66.

——. *Journals of the House of Burgesses of Virginia*.

——. *Minutes of the Council and Gen. Court of Colonial Virginia*. Ed. H. R. McIlwaine. 2d ed. Richmond, 1979.

Virginia Convention of 1829–30. *Journal, Acts and Proceedings, of a General Convention of the Commonwealth of Virginia, Assembled in Richmond*. Richmond, 1829.

——. *Proceedings and Debates of the Virginia State Convention of 1829–30*. Richmond, 1830.

Virginia Convention of 1901–2. *Journal of the Constitutional Convention of Virginia. Held in the City of Richmond, Beginning June 12th, 1901*. Richmond, 1901[–2].

——. *Minutes of Committee on Legislation, LVA*.

——. *Report of the Proceedings and Debates of the Constitutional Convention, State of Virginia. Held in the City of Richmond, June 12, 1901 to June 26, 1902*. Richmond, 1906.

——. *Resolutions, Ordinances and Petitions* [submitted to the Constitutional Convention of Virginia in 1901–2]. [Richmond, 1901].

Virginia General Assembly. *Acts of the General Assembly*.

——. *Journal of the Senate of Virginia: Session of 1798/99*. Ed. Cynthia A. Miller. Richmond, 1977.

——. *Journals of the House of Delegates of Virginia*.

——. *Journals of the Senate of Virginia*.

——. *Rough House Bills, Resolutions, etc., Virginia Gen. Assembly, LVA*.

CHURCH RECORDS, PUBLISHED AND UNPUBLISHED

Abstract of the Minutes of a General Association held at Upper Essex, May 1787, Misc. MSS, VBHS.

Address, To the Members and Friends of the Methodist Episcopal Church. 13 Jan. 1825. John Early Papers, RMC.

Antioch Baptist Church, Records, 1772–1837, photocopy, VBHS.

Antrim Parish Vestry Book, Halifax Co., photostat, LVA.

Appomattox Baptist Association, Records, VBHS.

Broad Run Baptist Church Minute Book, 1762–1873, Fauquier Co., photostat, LVA.
———, Records, 1762–1872, photostat, VBHS.
Chamberlayne, C. G., ed. *The Vestry Book of St. Paul's Parish, Hanover County, Virginia, 1706–1786.* Richmond, 1940.
Columbia Baptist Association, Minutes, 1820, LVA.
Constitution and Rules and Regulations of St. Paul's Church Home, Richmond, Va. Richmond, 1870.
Dover Baptist Association, Records, VBHS.
Farnham Parish, VA, Misc. MSS, DLC.
Goshen Association, Minutes, LVA.
Hanover Presbytery, Minutes, transcript, VHS.
———, Records, UPS.
Hungars Parish Vestry Book, Northampton Co., 1812–1937, photostat, no. 24265, LVA.
Journal of the Convention of the Protestant Episcopal Church in the Diocese of Virginia, Which Assembled in the Borough of Norfolk, on the 15th of May, 1839. Richmond, 1839.
Journal of the Convention of the Protestant Episcopal Church in the Diocese of Virginia, Held in Monumental Church, Richmond, Virginia, on the 17th of May, 1843. Alexandria, 1843.
Journal of a Convention of the Protestant Episcopal Church in the Diocese of Virginia, Held in St. Paul's Church, Lynchburg, Campbell County, Virginia, on the 15th of May, 1844. Richmond, 1844.
Journal of the Convention of the Protestant Episcopal Church in the Diocese of Virginia, Held in St. George's Church, Fredericksburg, Virginia, on the 21st of May, 1845. Richmond, 1845.
Journal of the Convention of the Protestant Episcopal Church in the Diocese of Virginia, Held in St. Paul's Church, Petersburg, Virginia, on the 20th of May, 1846. Lynchburg, 1846.
Journal of the Fifty-Fifth Annual Convention of the Protestant Episcopal Church in Virginia; Held in St. Paul's Church, Alexandria, On the 15th, 16th, 17th, and 18th of May, 1850. And Constitutions and Canons of the Diocese of Virginia. Baltimore, 1850.
Journal of the Fifty-Sixth Annual Convention of the Protestant Episcopal Church in Virginia; Held in Trinity Church, Staunton, On the 21th, 22th, 23th, and 24th of May, 1851; And Constitutions and Canons of the Diocese of Virginia. Washington, DC, 1851.
Journals of the General Conventions of the Protestant Episcopal Church in the United States of America; from the Year 1784 to the Year 1814. Philadelphia, 1817.
Lexington Parish Vestry Book, Amherst Co., VHS.
Lexington Presbytery, Minutes, UPS.
———, Records, microfilm, UPS.
Mackey, Howard, and Candy McMahan Perry, eds. *Vestry Book of Hungar's Parish, Northampton County, Virginia, 1757–1875.* Camden, ME, 1997.
"Meeting of the Baptist Gen. Meeting, 1817," VBHS.
Minutes of the Annual Conferences of the Methodist Episcopal Church. Vol. 1. 1773–1830. New York, 1840.

Minutes of the Baptist General Committee, at their Yearly Meeting, Held in the City of Richmond, May 8th, 1790. Richmond: T. Nicolson, 1790.

Minutes of the Baptist General Committee, Held at Nickols' Meeting-House, in the County of Goochland, May 1791. Richmond, [1791].

Minutes of the Baptist General Committee, Holden at Muddy-Creek Meeting-House, Powhatan County, Virginia. Richmond, 1793.

Minutes of the Baptist General Committee Held at Waller's Meeting-House in Spotsylvania County, May 1799. Richmond, 1799.

Minutes of the Baptist Middle District Association holden at Rice's Meeting House, in Prince-Edward County, the second Saturday in October, 1804. Richmond, 1804.

Minutes of the Eighth Annual Meeting of the General Association of Virginia, for Missionary Purposes, Held at Lynchburg, Va. June 4–7, 1831: with the Annual Report, and a List of Ordained and Licensed Preachers. Richmond, 1831.

Minutes of the Eighty-Fourth Annual Meeting of the Dover Baptist Association, held at Walnut Grove Church, Hanover Co., September 10–12, 1867. Richmond, 1867.

Minutes of the LXXXVII Annual Session of the Dover Baptist Association, held with the Goochland Church, Goochland County, Virginia, July 19–21, 1870. Richmond, 1870.

Minutes of the General Assembly of the Presbyterian Church in the United States of America with an Appendix, A.D. 1826. Philadelphia, 1826–27.

Minutes of General Association held at Burrus's Meeting House in Caroline County, 3 Oct. 1788, Misc. MSS, VBHS.

Minutes of the Goshen Baptist Association Holden at Glensoe's Meeting House, N. Fork, Pamunkey, in Orange County, 1795. Richmond, 1795.

Minutes of the Ketocton Baptist Association, Held at Long-Branch, in Fauquier County, August 1792. N.p., n.d.

Minutes of the Ninety Second Annual Session of the Dover Baptist Association, held with the Hopeful Baptist Church, Hanover Co., Va., July 9th, 10th and 11th, 1875. Richmond, 1875.

Minutes of the 118th Annual Session of the Dover Baptist Association, held with the Leigh-Street Baptist Church, of Richmond, Virginia, July 23, 24, 25, 1901. Richmond, 1901.

Minutes of the Virginia Baptist General Meeting of Correspondence, Held at the first Baptist meeting-house in the City of Richmond, June 1st, 2d and 3d, 1822. Richmond, 1822.

Perry, William Stevens, ed. *Historical Collections Relating to the American Colonial Church.* Vol. 1. *Virginia.* Hartford, CT, 1870.

———, ed. *Journals of the General Conventions of the Protestant Episcopal Church in the United States of America from A.D. 1795 to A.D. 1853, Inclusive.* [Claremont, NH, 1874].

Proceedings of the Ninth Annual Meeting of the General Association of Virginia. N.p., 1832.

Proceedings of the Tenth Annual Meeting of the General Association of Virginia; Held at the First Baptist Church, in the City of Richmond, on Saturday, June 1st, 1833. N.p., 1833.

Proceedings of the Twenty-First Annual Meeting of the Baptist General Association of Virginia, Assembly at Richmond, Virginia, June 1–4, 1844. N.p., 1844.

Proceedings of the Twenty-Second Annual Meeting of the Baptist General Association of Virginia, Assembled at Lynchburg, Virginia, May 31st, 1845. N.p., 1845.

Proceedings of the Twenty-Third Annual Meeting of the Baptist General Association of Virginia, Assembled at Richmond, Virginia, June 5–10, 1846. N.p., 1846.

Protestant Episcopal Church in the U.S.A. House of Bishops. *A Pastoral Letter to the Members.* Charleston, SC, 1808.

———, Virginia (Diocese), Papers, 1709–1972, VHS.

Rachel, William M. E., ed. "Early Minutes of Hanover Presbytery." *VMHB* 63 (1955): 53–75, 161–85.

Roanoke Baptist Association, Records, 1789–1831, photostat, VBHS.

Society of Friends, Richmond Monthly Meeting, Record Book, 1739–73, photostat, LVA.

South Quay [Baptist] Church, Records, 1775–1827, photostat, VBHS.

St. Anne's Parish Vestry Book, Albemarle Co., LVA.

St. George's Parish Vestry Book, Accomack Co., LVA.

St. John's Church Vestry Book, Richmond, 1785–1887, VHS.

Strawberry Baptist Association, Records, 1787–1822, photostat, VBHS.

Synod of Virginia, Minutes, UPS.

Upper Parish Vestry Book, Nansemond Co., 1743–93, photostat, LVA.

The Virginia Conference Annual Containing the Journal of Proceedings of the One Hundred and Forty-Third Session of the Virginia Annual Conference of the Methodist Episcopal Church, South Held at Richmond, Virginia October 14–21, 1925. Norfolk, 1925.

Virginia Portsmouth Association, Records, VBHS.

Virginia United Methodist Conference Archives, Glen Allen, VA.

Winchester Presbytery, Minutes, UPS.

COUNTY RECORDS

Accomack Co. Order Book, 1777–80, microfilm, LVA.

Albemarle Co. Deed Books, 1772–1841, microfilm, LVA.

Bedford Co., Colonial Papers, Petitions, RG 1, LVA.

Caroline Co. Order Book, 1767–70, microfilm, LVA.

———. Order Book, 1770–72, microfilm, LVA.

———. Minute Book, 1770–73, microfilm, LVA.

Chesterfield Co. Order Book 4, 1767–71, microfilm, LVA.

———. Order Book 5, 1771–74, microfilm, LVA.

Henrico Co. Order (and Wills) Book, 1678–93, microfilm, LVA.

Loudoun Co. Will Book C, microfilm, LVA.

PRINTED PRIMARY SOURCES

Adams, Dickenson W., ed. *Jefferson's Extracts from the Gospels: "The Philosophy of Jesus" and "The Life and Morals of Jesus."* Princeton, NJ, 1983.

Alexander, Archibald. *Address Delivered Before the Alumni Association of Washington College, Virginia, on Commencement Day, June 29th, 1843.* Lexington, 1843.

———. *A Discourse Occasioned by the burning of the theatre in the city of Richmond, Virginia, on the twenty-sixth of December, 1811.* Philadelphia, 1812.

Allen, William. "Address." *EJV* 9 (1878): 483–98.

Asplund, John. *The Annual Register of the Baptist Denominations in North America, to the First of November 1790.* Southampton County, VA, 1791.

Baldwin, C[ornelius] C. *Moral Maxims. For Schools & Families.* 3d ed. Petersburg, 1876.

Ball, Eli, J. C. Stiles, William I. Waller, and George Woodbridge. *An Appeal to the Legislature of Virginia, by the Friends of Literary, Benevolent, and Religious Associations in Virginia, for the passage of a law authorizing them to Receive and Hold Bequests.* Richmond, 1844.

Bangs, Nathan. *The Life of the Rev. Freeborn Garrettson: Compiled from his Printed and Manuscript Journals, and Other Authentic Documents.* New York, 1839.

Bayard, Ferdinand-Marie. *Travels of a Frenchman in Maryland and Virginia with a Description of Philadelphia and Baltimore in 1791, or Travels in the Interior of the United States, in Bath, Winchester, in the Valley of the Shenandoah, etc., during the Summer of 1791.* Trans. and ed. Ben C. McCary. Ann Arbor, 1950.

Beardsley, E. Edwards. *Life and Correspondence of Samuel Johnson.* New York, 1874.

Biddulph, Thomas Tregenna. *The Inconsistency of Conformity to this World with a Profession of Christianity.* Georgetown, DC, [1818?].

Billings, Warren M., ed. *The Papers of Francis Howard, Baron Howard of Effingham, 1643–1695.* Richmond, 1989.

———. *The Papers of Sir William Berkeley, 1605–1677.* Richmond, 2007.

———. "A Quaker in Seventeenth-Century Virginia: Four Remonstrances by George Wilson." *WMQ*, 3d ser., 33 (1976): 127–40.

Bland, Richard. *The Colonel Dismounted: or The Rector Vindicated. In a Letter Addressed to His Reverence: Containing a Dissertation upon the Constitution of the Colony.* Williamsburg, 1764.

———. *A Letter to the Clergy of Virginia.* Williamsburg, 1760.

Boucher, Jonathan. *A View of the Causes and Consequences of the American Revolution: In Thirteen Discourses, Preached in North American between the Years 1768 and 1775.* Rept. New York, 1967.

Boyd, Julian P., ed. *The Papers of Thomas Jefferson.* 38 vols. to date. Princeton, NJ, 1950–.

Braxton, Carter. *An Address to the Convention of the Colony and Ancient Dominion of Virginia; on the Subject of Government in Gen., and recommending a particular Form to their Consideration.* Philadelphia, 1776.

Brugger, Robert J., et al., eds. *The Papers of James Madison: Secretary of State Series.* 9 vols. to date. Charlottesville, 1986–.

Buckley, Thomas E., S.J., ed. *"If You Love That Lady Don't Marry Her": The Courtship Letters of Sally McDowell and John Miller, 1854–1856.* Columbia, MO, 2000.

Burk, John. *The History of Virginia: from its First Settlement to the Present Day.* 4 vols. Petersburg, 1804–16.

Cabell, Nathaniel F., ed. *Early History of the University of Virginia as Contained in the Letters of Thomas Jefferson and Joseph C. Cabell.* Richmond, 1856.

Calisch, Edward Nathan. *Three Score and Twenty: Selected Addresses and Sermons.* Richmond, 1945.

Camm, John. *The Colonel Reconnoitred.* [Williamsburg], 1764.

———. *Critical Remarks on a Letter Ascribed to Common Sense Containing an Attempt to Prove that the Said Letter is an Imposition on Common Sense. With a Dissertation on Drowsiness, as the Cruel Cause of that Imposition.* Williamsburg, 1765.

———. *A Single and Distinct View of the Act, Vulgarly Entitled, the Two-penny Act: Containing An Account of It's Beneficial and Wholesome Effects in York-Hampton Parish, in Which is Exhibited a Specimen of Col. Landon Carter's Justice and Charity, as well as of Col. Richard Bland's Salus Populi.* Annapolis, MD, 1763.

Carroll, Kenneth L. "Robert Pleasants on Quakerism: Some Account of the First Settlement of Friends in Virginia." *VMHB* 86 (1978): 3–16.

[Carter, Landon]. *A Letter to the Right Reverend Father in God The Lord-B——p of L——n.* [Williamsburg, 1759].

Clark, Elmer T., J. Manning Potts, and Jacob S. Payton, eds. *The Journal and Letters of Francis Asbury.* 3 vols. Nashville, 1958.

Coe, Richard E., ed. "Price's Priceless Penn." *Flintlock and Powderhorn: Magazine of the Sons of the Revolution* 1 (1976): 12–13.

Coke, Thomas. *Extracts of the Journals of the Rev. Dr. Coke's Five Visits to America.* London, 1793.

Colwell, Stephen. *New Themes for the Protestant Clergy.* 2d ed. rev. Philadelphia, 1852.

Conway, Moncure Daniel. *Omitted Chapters of History Disclosed in the Life and Papers of Edmund Randolph.* New York, 1888.

Crawshaw, M. Ethel, comp. "Letters from Virginia Quakers." *WMQ,* 2d ser., 6 (1926): 88–93.

[Dabney, Robert Lewis]. "Ecclesiastical Accumulations of Wealth." *Southern Review* 11 (1872): 417–37.

Davies, Samuel. *The Duties, Difficulties and Reward of the Faithful Minister: A Sermon Preached at the Installation of the Revd. Mr. John Todd, A.B. into the Pastoral Charge of the Presbyterian Congregation, in and about the upper Part of Hanover County in Virginia, November 12, 1752.* Glasgow, Scot., 1754.

———. *Sermons on Important Subjects.* New York, 1841.

———. *The State of Religion among the Protestant Dissenters; in a Letter to the Rev. Mr. Joseph Bellamy, of Bethlehem, in New England.* Boston, 1751.

Davis, John. *Travels of Four Years and a Half in the United States of America; during 1798, 1799, 1800, 1801, and 1802*. London, 1803; rept. New York, 1909.

A Declaration of Some of the Sufferings of the People of God Called Quakers. London, 1660.

Dew, Thomas R. "Baccalaureate Address." *SLM* 3 (1837): 401–6.

Dexter, Franklin Bowditch, ed. *The Literary Diary of Ezra Stiles* 3 vols. New York, 1901.

Douglas, David C., gen. ed. *English Historical Documents*. Vol. 8. *1660–1714*. Ed. Andrew Browning. London, 1953.

Dreisbach, Daniel L., ed. *Religion and Politics in the Early Republic: Jasper Adams and the Church-State Debate*. Lexington, KY, 1996.

Edwards, Morgan. "A History of the Baptists in the Province of Virginia." *VBR* 39 (2000): 1940–81.

Eleventh Annual Report of the Bible Society of Virginia, present April 6, 1824. Richmond, 1824.

Fleet, Elizabeth, ed. "Madison's 'Detached Memoranda.'" *WMQ*, 3d ser., 3 (1946): 534–68.

Foote, William Henry. *Sketches of Virginia, Historical and Biographical. First Series*. 1850. New ed. Richmond, 1966. *Second Series*. 2d ed. rev. Philadelphia, 1856.

Ford, Paul Leicester, ed. *The Works of Thomas Jefferson*. 12 vols. New York, 1905.

Fox, George. *A Journal or Historical Account of the Life, Travels, Sufferings, Christian Experiences and Labour of Love in the Work of the Ministry, of . . . George Fox*. 5th ed. 2 vols. Philadelphia, 1808.

Fristoe, William. *A Concise History of the Ketocton Baptist Association*. Staunton, 1808.

Gatewood, Joanne L. "Richmond during the Virginia Constitutional Convention of 1829–1830: An Extract from the Diary of Thomas Green, October 1, 1829 to January 31, 1830." *VMHB* 84 (1976): 287–332.

Gee, Henry, and William John Hardy, eds. *Documents Illustrative of English Church History*. London, 1914.

Giberne, Isaac William. *The Duty of Living Peaceably with all Men: Recommended in a Sermon Preached at Williamsburg, November 11, 1759, Before the Gen. Assembly of Virginia*. Williamsburg, 1759.

Gilmer, Thomas W. "An Address, Delivered before the Virginia Historical and Philosophical Society, at its late Annual Meeting, held in the Hall of Delegates, on the Evening of the 14th instant." *SLM* 3 (1837): 97–102.

Goode, John. *Recollections of a Lifetime by John Goode of Virginia*. New York, 1906.

Greene, L. F., ed. *Writings of the Late Elder John Leland*. New York, 1845; rept. 1969.

Grund, Francis J. *The Americans in Their Moral, Social and Political Relations*. Boston, 1837.

Gwatkin, Thomas. *A Letter to the Clergy of New York and New Jersey, Occasioned by An Address to the Episcopalians in Virginia*. Williamsburg, 1772.

[Harlow, Lawrence]. *The Richmond Alarm; A Plain and Familiar Discourse: Written in the Form of a Dialogue, Between a Father and his Son*. 2d ed. Pittsburgh, 1815.

Hawks, Francis L. *Contributions to the Ecclesiastical History of the United States of Amer-*

ica. Vol. 1. *A Narrative of Events Connected with the Rise and Progress of the Protestant Episcopal Church in Virginia*. App. *Journals of the Conventions of the Protestant Episcopal Church in Virginia from 1785 to 1835*. 2 vols. New York, 1836–39.

Henley, Samuel. *A Candid Refutation of the Heresy Imputed by Ro[bert] C. Nicholas Esquire to the Reverend S[amuel] Henley*. Williamsburg, 1774.

———. *The Distinct Claims of Government and Religion, Considered in a Sermon Preached before the Honourable House of Burgesses, at Williamsburg, in Virginia, March 1, 1772*. Cambridge, 1772.

Heron, Andrew. *Address to the Associate Congregations of Ebenezer and Timber Ridge*. Lexington, 1825.

Hill, William. *Autobiographical Sketches of Dr. William Hill . . . and Biographical Sketches of the Reverend Dr. Moses Hoge of Virginia*. Rept. Richmond, 1968.

———. *Ministerial Parity, or An Equality of Grade, Office, and Authority, among the Christian Clergy, Vindicated and Proved; in a Sermon, Delivered in Winchester, October 21st, 1819, at the Opening of the Synod of Virginia*. Winchester, 1819.

Hoge, Moses. *Sermons Selected from the Manuscripts of the late Moses Hoge, D.D.* Richmond, 1821.

Horne, Herman H. "Moral and Religious Instruction in the Public Schools." *VJE* 17 (1924): 269–71.

Howard, John. *An Address on Popular Education in Virginia, in Connection with the Proposed Changes in the Organic Law: Delivered July 13, 1850, at the annual commencement of the Richmond College in the First Baptist Church of the City*. Richmond, 1850.

Hunt, Gaillard, ed. *The Writings of James Madison*. 9 vols. New York, 1900–1910.

Hutchinson, William, et al., eds. *The Papers of James Madison*. 17 vols. Chicago, 1962–91.

Ireland, James. *The Life of the Rev. James Ireland, who was, for Many Years, Pastor of the Baptist Church at Buck Marsh, Waterlick and Happy Creek, in Frederick and Shenandoah Counties, Virginia*. Winchester, 1819.

James, Charles F. *Documentary History of the Struggle for Religious Liberty in Virginia*. Lynchburg, 1900.

Jarratt, Devereux. *The Life of the Reverend Devereux Jarratt, Rector of Bath Parish, Virginia, Written by Himself in a Series of Letters Addressed to the Rev. John Coleman*. Baltimore, 1806; rept. New York, 1969.

Jefferson, Thomas. *Notes on the State of Virginia*. Ed. William Peden. Rept. New York, 1982.

Jenyns, Soame. *View of the Internal Evidence of the Christian Religion*. London, 1776.

Johnson, Herbert A., et al., eds. *The Papers of John Marshall*. 12 vols. Chapel Hill, 1974–2006.

Johnson, Thomas Cary. *The Life and Letters of Robert Lewis Dabney*. Richmond, 1903.

Jones, Hugh. *The Present State of Virginia from Whence is Inferred a Short View of Maryland and North Carolina*. Ed. Richard L. Morton. Chapel Hill, 1956.

"Journal of Col. James Gordon, of Lancaster County, 1714–1767, from 1758 to 1763." *WMQ*, 1st ser., 11 (1902–3): 98–112, 195–205, 217–36; 12 (1903): 1–11.

A Journal of the Life of Thomas Story: Containing an Account of His Remarkable Con-

vincement of and Embracing the Principles of Truth, as Held by the People Called Quakers. Newcastle upon Tyne, UK, 1747.

Junkin, George. *Christianity the Patron of Literature and Science: An Address Delivered February 22, 1849, on the Occasion of the Author's Inauguration as President of Washington College, Virginia.* Philadelphia, 1849.

Koch, Adrienne, and William Peden, eds. *The Life and Selected Writings of Thomas Jefferson.* New York, 1944.

Larabee, Leonard Woods, ed. *Royal Instructions to British Colonial Governors, 1670–1776.* New York, 1935.

La Rochefoucauld-Liancourt, F.-A.-F., duc de. *Travels through the United States . . . 1795, 1796, and 1797 . . . .* Trans. Henry Neuman. 2 vols. London, 1799.

[Lee, Edmund Jennings]. *Selden and Others vs. the Overseers of the Poor of Loudoun County, and Others.* N.p., n.d. Copy in Church Pamphlets, VIII, VHS.

Leland, John. *A Storke at the Branch. Containing Remarks on Times and Things.* Hartford, CT, 1801.

"Letters of Patrick Henry, Sr., Samuel Davies, James Maury, Edwin Conway and George Trask." *WMQ,* 2d ser., I (1921): 261–81.

"Letters of Robert Pleasants, of Curles." *WMQ,* 2d ser., I (1921): 107–13.

"Letters of Roger Atkinson, 1769–1776." *VMHB* 15 (1908): 345–59.

Lipscomb, Andrew A., and Albert Ellery Bergh, eds. *The Writings of Thomas Jefferson.* 20 vols. Washington, DC, 1907.

Macfarland, William Hamilton. *Argument in Reply to the Rev. William S. Plumer, Before the Committee of courts of justice of Wm. H. Macfarland, esq., upon the petitions of the Baptists and Episcopalians, asking that the law may protect donations to pious uses.* Richmond, 1846.

[Madison, Bishop James]. *A Discourse Delivered at the Funeral of Mrs. Ann C. Semple, June 25, 1803.* Richmond, 1803.

———. *An Oration, in Commemoration of the Founders of William and Mary College, Delivered on the Anniversary of its Foundation, August 15, 1772.* Williamsburg, 1772.

———. *A Sermon Preached Before the Convention of the Protestant Episcopal Church in the State of Virginia, on the Twenty-Sixth of May, 1786.* Richmond, 1786.

Maury, Ann. *Memoirs of a Huguenot Family: Translated and Compiled from the Original Autobiography of the Rev. James Fontaine.* New York, 1872.

Maury, James. *To Christians of every Denomination among us, especially those of the Established Church, an Address enforcing an inquiry into the grounds of the pretensions of the preachers, called Anabaptists, ...* Annapolis, MD, 1771.

Maxwell, William. *Memoir of the Rev. John H. Rice, D.D., First Professor of Christian Theology in Union Theological Seminary, Virginia.* Philadelphia, 1835.

———. *An Oration Commemorative of the Late Rev. John Holt Rice, D.D. Spoken Before the Literary and Philosophical Society of Hampden Sydney College, at their Anniversary Meeting, on Thursday, the 27th of September, 1832.* Richmond, 1832.

Mays, David John, ed. *The Letters and Papers of Edmund Pendleton, 1734–1801.* 2 vols. Charlottesville, 1967.

McIlwaine, Richard. *Memories of Three Score Years and Ten.* New York, 1908.

McLoughlin, William G., ed. *The Diary of Isaac Backus.* 3 vols. Providence, RI, 1979.

Meade, William. *A Brief Review of the Episcopal Church in Virginia, From Its First Establishment to the Present Time; Being Part of an Address . . . to the Convention of the Church, in Fredericksburg, May 22, 1845.* Richmond, 1845.

Miller, Samuel. *Memoir of the Rev. John Rodgers, D.D.* New York, 1813.

Minor, John B. *Institutes of Common and Statute Law.* Vol. 1. *The Rights Which Relate to the Person.* 3d ed. Richmond, 1882.

Morgan, George. *Patrick Henry.* Philadelphia and London, 1929.

Muir, James. *Ten Sermons.* Alexandria, 1812.

Nicholson, Francis. "Correspondence." *VMHB* 7 (1900): 153–72.

Norwood, Frederick Abbott, ed. *The Methodist Discipline of 1798 Including the Annotations of Thomas Coke and Francis Asbury.* Rept. Rutland, VT, 1979.

Official Syllabus of Bible Study for High School Pupils: Course III. Bulletin State Board of Education. Supplement no. 2. Richmond: Correspondence School for Religious School Teachers Conducted by the Jewish Chautauqua Society. Philadelphia, 1914. Copy in Calisch Papers, Misc. box, Beth Ahabah Archives, Richmond.

Page, John. *[Poems by John Page and Others].* [Privately printed by John and Margaret Lowther Page, 1790]. Copy in WMC.

Pilcher, George William. ed. *The Reverend Samuel Davies Abroad: The Diary of a Journey to England and Scotland, 1753–55.* Urbana, IL, 1967.

Plumer, William Swan. *The Substance of an Argument against the Indiscriminate Incorporation of Churches and Religious Societies.* Baltimore, 1847.

Putnam, Martha A. *Early Quaker Records of Southeast Virginia.* Westminster, MD, 1996.

Randolph, Edmund. *History of Virginia.* Ed. Arthur H. Shaffer. Charlottesville, 1970.

Rice, John H. *Historical and Philosophical Considerations of Religion; addressed to James Madison, Esq. Late President of the United States.* Richmond, 1832.

———. *An Illustration of the Character and Conduct of the Presbyterian church in Virginia.* Richmond, 1816.

———. *A Sermon on the Duties of a Minister of the Gospel: Preached at the Opening of the Presbytery of Hanover, at Dee Ess Church; October 11, 1809.* Philadelphia, 1810.

Royall, Anne. *The Black Book. or a Continuation of Travels in the United States.* 3 vols. Washington, DC, 1828–29.

———. *Mrs. Royall's Southern Tour, or Second Series of the Black Book.* Washington, DC, 1830.

Ruffner, Henry. *Inaugural Address by Henry Ruffner, President of Washington College, Va. Delivered on the Twenty-Second of February 1837.* Lexington, 1837.

Ruffner, William Henry. *Africa's Redemption: A Discourse on African Colonization, in its Missionary Aspects, and in its Relation to Slavery and Abolition. Preached on Sabbath Morning, July 4th, 1852, in the Seventh Presbyterian Church, Penn Square, Philadelphia.* Philadelphia, 1852.

———. *Charity and the Clergy: Being a Review, by a Protestant Clergyman, of the "New*

Themes" Controversy; Together with Sundry Serious Reflections upon the Religious Press, Theological Seminaries, Ecclesiastical Ambition, Growth of Moderation, Prostitution of the Pulpit, and Gen. Decay of Christianity. Philadelphia, 1853.

[———]. "Christianity in the Public Schools." *EJV* 10 (1979): 449–52.

[———, ed.]. *Lectures on the Evidences of Christianity, Delivered at the University of Virginia, During the Session of 1850–1.* New York, 1852.

———. *The Public Free School System: Mr. Dabney answered by Mr. Ruffner.* Richmond, 1876.

[———]. "Remarks on Col. Allan's Hampton Address." *EJV* 9 (1878): 499–505.

———. *Virginia School Report: Second Annual Report of the Superintendent of Public Instruction. For the year ending August 31, 1872.* Richmond, 1872.

Rutland, Robert A., ed. *The Papers of George Mason, 1725–1792.* 3 vols. Chapel Hill, 1970.

Schopf, Johann David. *Travels in the Confederation* [1783–84]. Trans. and ed. Alfred J. Morrison. 2 vols. Philadelphia, 1911.

Semple, Robert B. *A History of the Rise and Progress of the Baptists in Virginia.* Rev. ed. Richmond, 1894.

Singleton, Arthur. *Letters from the South and West.* Boston, 1824.

Spencer, Gideon. [Printed letter concerning action of the General Assembly dated Richmond, 15 Jan. 1798]. [Richmond, 1798]. Copy at VHS.

[Swanwick, John]. *Considerations on an Act of the Legislature of Virginia, Entitled an Act for the Establishment of Religious Freedom.* Philadelphia, 1786.

Taylor, Robert J., Mary-Jo Kline, and Gregg L. Lint, eds. *Papers of John Adams.* 16 vols. to date. Cambridge, MA, 1977–.

Thrift, Minton. *Memoir of the Rev. Jesse Lee with Extracts from his Journals.* New York, 1823; rept. 1969.

Tucker, Henry St. George. *Commentaries on the Laws of Virginia, Comprising the Substance of a Course of Lectures Delivered to the Winchester Law School.* 2d ed. Winchester, 1836.

———. *The Opinion of Chancellor Tucker: Delivered at the April term of the Winchester Chancery Court, in the case of the vestry of St. James' Parish: against the overseers of Shelburne Parish, in the County of Loudoun.* Leesburg, 1830.

Tucker, St. George. *Blackstone's Commentaries, with Notes of Reference, to the Constitution and Laws, of the Federal Government of the United States, and of the State of Virginia.* 5 vols. Philadelphia, 1803.

Van Screeven, William J., Robert L. Scribner, and Brent Tarter, eds. *Revolutionary Virginia: The Road to Independence.* 7 vols. Charlottesville, 1973–83.

Weld, Isaac. *Travels through the States of North America, and the Provinces of Upper and Lower Canada, during the Years 1796, 1797, and 1798.* 4th ed. London, 1807.

White, William. *Memoirs of the Protestant Episcopal Church in the United States.* Philadelphia, 1820.

Wilmer, William H. *A Sermon, Delivered in the Monumental Church, in Richmond: before the Convention of the Protestant Episcopal Church, of the State of Virginia, and at the First Opening of the Monumental Church, on Wednesday, May 4, 1814.* Alexandria, 1814.

Wirt, William. *Letters of the British Spy.* 10th ed. New York, 1832.

———, et al. *The Old Bachelor.* Richmond, 1814.

COURT CASES

Abington School District v. Schempp, 374 U.S. 203 (1963).

Baptist Assn. v. Hart's Executors, 4 Wheat. 1 (1819).

Bradford v. Roberts, 175 U.S. 291 (1899).

Cantwell v. Connecticut, 310 U.S. 296 (1940).

Claughton v. Macnaughton, 2 Munford 513 (1811).

Engel v. Vitale, 370 U.S. (1962) at 421.

Everson v. Board of Education of the Township of Ewing, 330 U.S. 1, 18, 33 (1947).

Falwell v. Miller, 203 F. Supp. 2d 624 (W.D. Va. 2002).

Freeman v. Scheve, 65 Neb. 853, 91 N.W. 846 (1902).

Hallo's Executors v. Attorney Gen., 3 Leigh (1832).

Mason v. Muncaster, 22 U.S. 445 (1824).

McCollum v. Board of Education, 333 U.S. 203 (1948).

Reynolds v. United States, 98 U.S. 145 (1878).

Seaburn's Executor v. Seaburn et al., 15 Grattan (56 Va.) 423 (1859).

Selden and Others v. Overseers of the Poor of Loudoun County, 11 Leigh 132 (1840).

Terrett v. Taylor, 13 U.S. 43 (1815).

Turpin v. Lockett, 6 Call 113 (1804).

Wallace v. Jaffree, 472 U.S. 38, 107 (1985).

Young v. Pollock, 2 Munford 517 (1806).

Zorach v. Clausen, 343 U.S. 306 (1952).

NEWSPAPERS AND MAGAZINES

Atlanta Constitution, 1926.

Baltimore and Richmond Christian Advocate, 1904.

Central Presbyterian, 1904.

Christian Monitor, 1815–17.

Columbian Mirror and Alexandria Gazette, 1795–97.

Epitome of the Times, Norfolk, 1798–1800.

Methodist, Danville, 1924–25.

News Leader, Richmond, 1903–26.

Recorder, Richmond, 1802.

Religious Herald, Richmond, 1878–1926.

Richmond and Manchester Advertiser, 1795.

Richmond Dispatch, 1901.

Richmond Enquirer, 1804–12.

Richmond Evening Leader, 1896–1901.

Richmond Examiner, 1804, 1844.

Richmond News, 1900.

Richmond Times, 1916.

Richmond Whig and Public Advertiser, 1842–49.

Southern Literary Messenger, 1838–50.

Southern Review, 1972.

Times, Richmond, 1900.

Times-Dispatch, Richmond, 1904.

Union Seminary Magazine, 1900–1901.

Virginia Argus, 1797–1815.

Virginia Courier, Petersburg, 1896–1901.

Virginia Gazette (Purdie and Dixon), Williamsburg, 1766–74.

Virginia Gazette (Purdie), Williamsburg, 1775–78.

Virginia Gazette (Rind), Williamsburg, 1766–74.

Virginia Gazette, and General Advertiser, Richmond, 1790–1809.

Virginia Gazette, and Weekly Advertiser, Richmond, 1782–9?.

Virginia Gazette or the American Advertiser, Richmond, 1781–86.

Virginia Independent Chronicle, Richmond, 1787–89.

Virginia Journal and Alexandria Advertiser, 1784–89.

Virginia Religious Magazine, 1804–7.

Virginia School Journal. 1892–99.

Virginian, Lynchburg, 1822–29.

Watchman and Observer, Richmond, 1845–55.

Watchman of the South, Richmond, 1837–45.

SECONDARY SOURCES

Books

Adams, Francis. *The Free School System of the United States*. London, 1876.

After One Hundred Years, 1834–1934: Being the Story of Saint Joseph's Academy and Orphan Asylum Told in a Series of Sketches. Richmond, 1934.

Alexander, Archibald. *The Log College: Biographical Sketches of William Tennent and His Students, Together with an Account of the Revivals under their Ministries*. 1851; rept. London, 1968.

Alley, Reuben Edward. *A History of Baptists in Virginia*. Richmond, 1973.

Andrews, Dee E. *The Methodists and Revolutionary America, 1760–1800: The Shaping of an Evangelical Culture*. Princeton, NJ, 2000.

Athearn, Walter Scott. *Religious Education and American Democracy*. Boston and Chicago, 1917.

Audriot, Donna. *Population Abstract of the United States.* McLean, 1993.

Baker, Frank. *From Wesley to Asbury: Studies in Early American Methodism.* Durham, NC, 1976.

Baker, Meredith Henne. *The Richmond Theater Fire: Early America's First Great Disaster.* Baton Rouge, 2012.

Beeman, Richard R. *The Evolution of the Southern Backcountry: A Case Study of Lunenburg County, Virginia, 1746–1832.* Philadelphia, 1984.

———. *The Old Dominion and the New Nation, 1788–1801.* Lexington, KY, 1972.

Bell, Sadie. *The Church, the State, and Education in Virginia.* Philadelphia, 1930.

Benedict, David. *A Gen. History of the Baptist Denomination in America, and Other Parts of the World.* 2 vols. Boston, 1813.

Beneke, Chris. *Beyond Toleration: The Religious Origins of American Pluralism.* New York, 2006.

Bennett, A. L. *A Century of Methodism in Charlottesville, Virginia: A Brief Account* . . . . Charlottesville, 1934.

Berman, Myron. *Richmond's Jewry, 1769–1976: Sabbat in Shockoe* Charlottesville, 1979.

Billings, Warren M. *Sir William Berkeley and the Forging of Colonial Virginia.* Baton Rouge, 2004.

———. *Virginia's Viceroy: Their Majesties' Governor Gen.: Francis Howard, Baron Howard of Effingham.* Fairfax, 1991.

Boles, John B. *The Great Revival, 1787–1805.* Lexington, KY, 1972.

Bond, Edward L. *Damned Souls in a Tobacco Colony: Religion in Seventeenth Century Virginia.* Macon, GA, 2000.

Boorstin, Daniel J. *The Lost World of Thomas Jefferson.* Cambridge, MA, 1948.

Booty, John E. *Mission and Ministry: A History of the Virginia Theological Seminary.* Harrisburg, PA, 1995.

Borden, Morton. *Jews, Turks, and Infidels.* Chapel Hill, 1984.

Boylan, Anne M. *Sunday School: The Formation of an American Institution, 1790–1880.* New Haven, 1988.

Brant, Irving. *James Madison.* 6 vols. Indianapolis, 1941–61.

Brenaman, Jacob N. *A History of Virginia Conventions.* Richmond, 1902.

Bridenbaugh, Carl. *Mitre and Sceptre: Transatlantic Faiths, Ideas, Personalities, and Politics, 1689–1775.* London, 1962.

Brock, Peter. *Pioneers of the Peaceable Kingdom: The Quaker Peace Testimony from the Colonial Era to the First World War.* Princeton, NJ, 1968.

Bruce, Dickson D. *And They All Sang Hallelujah: Plain-Folk, Camp-Meeting Religion, 1800–1845.* Knoxville, TN, 1974.

Bruce, Philip Alexander. *History of the University of Virginia, 1819–1919.* 5 vols. New York, 1920–22.

Brugger, Robert J. *Beverley Tucker: Heart over Head in the Old South.* Baltimore, 1978.

Brunk, Harry Anthony. *History of Mennonites in Virginia, 1727–1900.* Staunton, 1959.

Brydon, George MacLaren. *Virginia's Mother Church and the Political Conditions Under Which She Grew.* 2 vols. Richmond, 1948–52.

Bryson, W. Hamilton, ed. *The Virginia Law Reporters before 1880*. Charlottesville, 1977.

Bucke, Emory Stevens, ed., *History of American Methodism*. 3 vols. New York, 1964.

Buckley, Thomas E. *"The Great Catastrophe of My Life": Divorce and the Old Dominion*. Chapel Hill, 2002.

———. *Separation of Church and State in Revolutionary Virginia, 1776–1787*. Charlottesville, 1977.

Burkitt, Lemuel, and Jesse Read. *A Concise History of the Kehukee Baptist Association From Its Original Rise to the Present Time*. Halifax, 1803.

Butler, Jon. *The Huguenots in America: A Refugee People in a New World Society*. Cambridge, MA, 1983.

Carwardine, Richard. *Evangelicals and Politics in Antebellum America*. New Haven, 1993.

Cash, Wilbur J. *The Mind of the South*. New York, 1941.

Chalmers, David Mark. *Hooded Americanism: The History of the Ku Klux Klan*. New York, 1981.

Cleaveland, George J., et al. *Up from Independence: The Episcopal Church in Virginia*. N.p., 1976.

Conser, Walter H., Jr. *Church and Confession: Conservative Theologians in Germany, England, and America, 1815–1866*. [Macon, GA], 1984.

Conway, Moncure Daniel. *Omitted Chapters of History Disclosed in the Life and Papers of Edmund Randolph*. New York, 1888.

Courtney, W. L. *The Literary Man's Bible*. Rev. ed. New York, 1908.

Cullen, Charles T. *St. George Tucker and Law in Virginia, 1772–1804*. New York, 1987.

Cunningham, Noble E., Jr. *In Pursuit of Reason: The Life of Thomas Jefferson*. Baton Rouge, 1987.

Dabney, Virginius. *Dry Messiah: The Life of Bishop Cannon*. New York, 1949.

Dain, Norman. *Disordered Minds: The First Century of Eastern State Hospital in Williamsburg, Virginia, 1766–1866*. Williamsburg, 1971.

Dashill, T. Grayson. *A Digest of the Proceedings in the Councils and Conventions of the Diocese of Virginia*. Richmond, 1883.

Davis, Derek H., ed. *The Oxford Handbook of Church and State in the United States*. New York, 2012.

Dawidoff, Robert. *The Education of John Randolph*. New York, 1979.

Dignan, Patrick J. *A History of the Legal Incorporation of Catholic Church Property in the United States, 1784–1932*. New York, 1935.

Dorr, Gregory Michael. *Segregation's Science: Eugenics and Society in Virginia*. Charlottesville, 2008.

Drakeman, Donald L. *Church, State, and Original Intent*. New York, 2010.

Dreisbach, Daniel L. *Thomas Jefferson and the Wall of Separation between Church and State*. New York, 2002.

Dunn, Susan. *Dominion of Memories*. New York, 2007.

Eckenrode, Hamilton James. *Separation of Church and State in Virginia: A Study in the Development of the Revolution*. Rept. New York, 1971.

Egerton, Douglas R. *Charles Fenton Mercer and the Trial of National Conservatism.* Jackson, MS, 1989.

Eisenberg, William Edward. *The Lutheran Church in Virginia, 1717–1962, Including an Account of the Lutheran Church in East Tennessee.* Roanoke, 1967.

Elson, Ruth Miller. *Guardians of Tradition: American Schoolbooks of the Nineteenth Century.* Lincoln, NE, 1964.

Fabian, Ann. *Card Sharps, Dream Books, and Bucket Shops: Gambling in Nineteenth Century America.* Ithaca, NY, 1990.

Fisher, George D. *History and Reminiscences of the Monumental Church, Richmond, Va., from 1814 to 1878.* Richmond, 1880.

Flippin, Percy Scott. *William Gooch, Successful Royal Governor of Virginia.* [Williamsburg, 1924].

Fogarty, Gerald P., S.J. *Commonwealth Catholicism: A History of the Catholic Church in Virginia.* Notre Dame, 2001.

Forrest, W. M. *Bible Classes for High School Pupils with Credit toward Graduation.* University of Virginia Record. Extension Series. Charlottesville, 1921.

Gaines, William H., Jr., *Biographical Register of Members, Virginia State Convention of 1861, First Session.* Richmond, 1969.

Gewehr, Wesley M. *The Great Awakening in Virginia, 1740–1790.* Durham, NC, 1930.

Gilreath, James, ed. *Thomas Jefferson and the Education of a Citizen.* Washington, DC, 1999.

Goldfield, David R. *Region, Race, and Cities: Interpreting the Urban South.* Baton Rouge, 1997.

Goodwin, William A. R. *History of the Theological Seminary in Virginia and Its Historical Background.* 2 vols. New York, 1923.

Gordon, Sarah Barringer. *The Spirit of the Law: Religious Voices and the Constitution in Modern America.* Cambridge, MA, 2010.

Gragg, Larry Dale. *Migration in Early America: The Virginia Quaker Experience.* Ann Arbor, 1980.

Green, Steven K. *The Bible, the School, and the Constitution: The Clash That Shaped Modern Church-State Doctrine.* Oxford, 2012.

———. *The Second Disestablishment: Church and State in Nineteenth-Century America.* Oxford, 2010.

Grell, Ole Peter, Jonathan I. Israel, and Nicholas Tyacke, eds. *From Persecution to Toleration: The Glorious Revolution and Religion in England.* Oxford, 1991.

Gunderson, Joan Rezner. *The Anglican Ministry in Virginia: A Study of a Social Class.* New York, 1989.

Hall, Virginius Cornick, Jr. *Portraits in the Collection of the Virginia Historical Society.* Charlottesville, 1981.

Hamburger, Philip. *Separation of Church and State.* Cambridge, MA, 2002.

Hanley, Mark Y. *Beyond a Christian Commonwealth: The Protestant Quarrel with the American Republic, 1830–1860.* Chapel Hill, 1994.

Hayden, Horace Edwin. *Virginia Genealogies.* Baltimore, 1973.

Hayes, Kevin J. *The Mind of a Patriot: Patrick Henry and the World of Ideas.* Charlottesville, 2008.

Healey, Robert M. *Jefferson on Religion in Public Education.* New Haven and London, 1962.

Heatwole, Cornelius J. *A History of Education in Virginia.* New York, 1916.

Heinemann, Ronald L. *Harry Byrd of Virginia.* Charlottesville, 1996.

Heinemann, Ronald L., John G. Kolp, Antony S. Parent Jr., and William G. Shade. *Old Dominion, New Commonwealth: A History of Virginia, 1607–2007.* Charlottesville, 2007.

Henry, William Wirt. *Patrick Henry: Life, Correspondence, and Speeches.* New York, 1891.

———. *The Presbyterian Church and Religious Liberty in Virginia.* Richmond, 1900.

Henshaw, J. P. K. *Memoir of the Life of the Rt. Rev. Richard Channing Moore, D.D., Bishop of the Protestant Episcopal Church in the Diocese of Virginia.* Philadelphia, 1843.

Hinshaw, William Wade. *Encyclopedia of American Quaker Genealogy.* Ann Arbor, 1936–50.

Hoge, Moses. *Portraiture of Four Pastors.* Richmond, 1892.

Hohner, Robert A. *Prohibition and Politics: The Life of Bishop James Cannon, Jr.* Columbia, SC, 1999.

Howard, A. E. Dick. *Commentaries on the Constitution of Virginia.* Charlottesville, 1974.

Howe, Daniel Walker. *What Hath God Wrought: The Transformation of America, 1815–1848.* New York, 2007.

Howison, Robert R. *History of Virginia: from its Discovery and Settlement by Europeans to the Present Time.* 2 vols. Richmond, 1848.

Isaac, Rhys. *Landon Carter's Uneasy Kingdom: Revolution and Rebellion on a Virginia Plantation.* Oxford, 2004.

———. *The Transformation of Virginia, 1740–1790.* Chapel Hill, 1982.

Johnson, Alvin W., and Frank H. Yost. *Separation of Church and State in the United States.* Rev. ed. Minneapolis, 1948.

Jordan, Daniel P. *Political Leadership in Jefferson's Virginia.* Charlottesville, 1983.

Jorgenson, Lloyd P. *The State and the Non-Public School, 1825–1925.* Columbia, MO, 1987.

Keiley, A[nthony] M. *Memoranda of the History of the Catholic Church, In Richmond, Va. Since the Revolution, Reported to the Fourth Annual Convention of the Catholic Benevolent Union of Virginia.* Norfolk, 1874.

Keve, Paul W. *The History of Corrections in Virginia.* Charlottesville, 1986.

Kilgore, Charles Franklin. *The James O'Kelly Schism in the Methodist Episcopal Church.* Mexico City, 1963.

Kimball, Gregg D. *Life and Labor in an Industrial City, 1865–1920.* Silver Spring, MD, 1991.

Kirby, James E., Russell E. Richey, and Kenneth E. Rowe. *The Methodists.* Westport, CT, 1996.

Kneebone, John, et al., eds. *Dictionary of Virginia Biography.* 3 vols. to date. Richmond, 1998–.

Knight, Edgar W., ed. *Documentary History of Education in the South before 1860.* 5 vols. Chapel Hill, 1953.

Kranish, Michael. *Flight from Monticello: Thomas Jefferson at War.* New York, 2010.

Lee, Edmund Jennings, ed. *Lee of Virginia: Biographical and Genealogical Sketches of the Descendants of Colonel Richard Lee.* Philadelphia, 1895.

Lemay, J. A. Leo, ed. *Essays in Early Virginia Literature Honoring Richard Beale Davis.* New York, 1977.

Levy, Andrew. *The First Emancipator: The Forgotten Story of Robert Carter, the Founding Father Who Freed His Slaves.* New York, 2005.

Little, Lewis Peyton. *Imprisoned Preachers and Religious Liberty in Virginia.* Lynchburg, 1938.

Lombardo, Paul A. *Three Generations, No Imbeciles: Eugenics, the Supreme Court, and Buck v. Bell.* Baltimore, 2008.

Loveland, Clara O. *The Critical Years: The Reconstitution of the Anglican Church in the United States of America, 1780–1789.* Greenwich, CT, 1956.

Lowe, Richard. *Republicans and Reconstruction in Virginia, 1856–1870.* Charlottesville, 1991.

Lower, Ann Rutherford. *Sheltering Arms Hospital: A Centennial History (1889–1989).* Richmond, 1989.

Lowry, Charles Wesley. *To Pray or Not to Pray! A Handbook for the Study of Recent Supreme Court Decisions and American Church-State Doctrine.* Washington, DC, 1968.

Maddex, Jack P., Jr. *The Virginia Conservatives, 1867–1879: A Study in Reconstruction Politics.* Chapel Hill, 1970.

Maddox, William Arthur. *The Free School Idea in Virginia before the Civil War: A Phase of Political and Social Evolution.* New York, 1918.

Malone, Dumas. *Jefferson and His Time.* 6 vols. Boston, 1948–81.

———. *The Public Life of Thomas Cooper, 1783–1839.* Columbia, SC, 1961.

Manarin, Louis H., and Clifford Dowdey. *The History of Henrico County.* Charlottesville, 1984.

Marsden, George M. *The Soul of the American University: From Protestant Establishment to Established Nonbelief.* New York, 1994.

Mays, David John. *Edmund Pendleton, 1721–1803: A Biography.* Cambridge, MA, 1952.

McDanel, Ralph Clipman. *The Virginia Constitutional Convention of 1901–1902.* Baltimore, 1928.

Meade, Robert Douthat. *Patrick Henry: Patriot in the Making.* Philadelphia, 1957.

Meade, William. *Old Churches, Ministers, and Families of Virginia.* 2 vols. Philadelphia, 1891.

Michaelsen, Robert. *Piety in the Public Schools.* London, 1970.

Miller, Howard. *The Revolutionary College: American Presbyterian Higher Education, 1707–1837.* New York, 1976.

Moger, Allen W. *Virginia: From Bourbonism to Byrd, 1870–1925.* Charlottesville, 1968.

Morton, Richard L. *Colonial Virginia.* 2 vols. Chapel Hill, 1960.

Murphy, Andrew W. *Conscience and Community: Revisiting Toleration and Religious Dissent in Early Modern England and America*. University Park, PA, 2001.

Najar, Monica. *Evangelizing the South: A Social History of Church and State in Early America*. New York, 2008.

Nelson, John K. *A Blessed Company: Parishes, Parsons, and Parishioners in Anglican Virginia, 1690–1776*. Chapel Hill, 2001.

Nelson, Margaret Virginia. *A Study of Judicial Review in Virginia, 1789–1928*. New York, 1947.

Nichols, J. Bruce. *The Uneasy Alliance: Religion, Refugee Work, and U.S. Foreign Policy*. New York, 1988.

Noll, Mark A. *American Evangelical Christianity: An Introduction*. Oxford, 2001.

———, ed. *Religion and American Politics: From the Colonial Period to the 1980s*. New York, 1990.

Noonan, John Thomas. *The Lustre of Our Country: The American Experience of Religious Freedom*. Berkeley, CA, 1998.

O'Donnell, W. C., Jr. *Creed and Curriculum*. New York, 1914.

Parker, Harold M., Jr. *The United Synod of the South: The Southern New School Presbyterian Church*. New York, 1988.

Peterson, Merrill D., and Robert C. Vaughan, eds. *The Virginia Statute for Religious Freedom: Its Evolution and Consequences in American History*. Cambridge, 1988.

Peyton, John Lewis. *History of Augusta County*. Bridgewater, 1953.

Pilcher, George William. *Samuel Davies: Apostle of Dissent in Colonial Virginia*. Knoxville, TN, 1971.

Pulley, Raymond H. *Old Virginia Restored: An Interpretation of the Progressive Impulse, 1870–1930*. Charlottesville, 1968.

Pulliam, David L. *The Constitutional Conventions of Virginia from the Foundation of the Commonwealth to the Present Time*. Richmond, 1901.

Puryear, B[ennett]. *The Public School in its Relations to the Negro. By Civis. Republished by Request. From the Southern Planter and Farmer*. Richmond, 1877.

Ragosta, John A. *Wellspring of Liberty: How Virginia's Religious Dissenters Helped Win the American Revolution and Secured Religious Liberty*. Oxford, 2010.

Reardon, John J. *Edmund Randolph: A Biography*. New York, 1974.

Rhoden, Nancy L. *Revolutionary Anglicanism: The Colonial Church of England Clergy during the American Revolution*. New York, 1999.

Risjord, Norman K. *Chesapeake Politics, 1781–1800*. New York, 1978.

Rugh, C. E. *Moral Training in the Public Schools*. Boston, 1907.

Rutland, Robert A. *The Presidency of James Madison*. Lawrence, KS, 1990.

Sarna, Jonathan D., and David G. Dalin, *Religion and State in the American Jewish Experience*. Notre Dame, 1997.

Scanlon, James Edward. *Randolph-Macon: A Southern History, 1825–1967*. Charlottesville, 1983.

Schneider, A. Gregory. *The Way of the Cross Leads Home: The Domestication of American Methodism*. Bloomington, IN, 1993.

Schweiger, Beth Barton. *The Gospel Working Up: Progress and the Pulpit in Nineteenth-Century Virginia*. New York, 2000.

Sekulow, Jay Alan. *Witnessing Their Faith: Religious Influences on Supreme Court Justices and Their Opinions*. Lanham, MD, 2006.

Seymour, Jack L. *From Sunday School to Church School: Continuities in Protestant Church Education in the United States, 1860–1929*. Washington, DC, 1982.

Shade, William G. *Democratizing the Old Dominion: Virginia and the Second Party System, 1824–1861*. Charlottesville, 1996.

Shain, Barry Alan. *The Myth of American Individualism: The Protestant Origins of American Political Thought*. Princeton, NJ, 1994.

Shalhope, Robert E. *John Taylor of Caroline: Pastoral Republican*. Columbia, SC, 1980.

Shepherd, Samuel C., Jr. *Avenues of Faith: Shaping the Urban Religious Culture of Richmond, Virginia, 1900–1929*. Tuscaloosa, AL, 2001.

Sherrill, Lewis Joseph. *Presbyterian Parochial Schools, 1846–1870*. New Haven, 1932.

Shockley, Martin Staples. *The Richmond Stage, 1784–1812*. Charlottesville, 1977.

Smillie, Dirk. *Falwell Inc.: Inside a Religious, Political, Educational, and Business Empire*. New York, 2008.

Spangler, Jewel L. *Virginians Reborn: Anglican Monopoly, Evangelical Dissent, and the Rise of the Baptists in the Late Eighteenth Century*. Charlottesville, 2008.

Sprague, William B. *Annals of the American Pulpit*. 9 vols. New York, 1857–69.

Stedman, Murray S., Jr. *Religion and Politics in America*. New York, 1964.

Sutton, Robert P. *Revolution to Secession: Constitution Making in the Old Dominion*. Charlottesville, 1989.

Taylor, James B. *Lives of Virginia Baptist Ministers*. New York, 1860.

———. *Virginia Baptist Ministers*. 5th ser., 1902–14, with Supplement. Lynchburg, 1915.

Taylor, William. *Secondary Education: The Proper Relation of Secondary Schools to the State System of Public Schools and to Denominational Control; the Work of Secondary Schools in the Past, and Their Future*. Richmond, 1881.

Thompson, Ernest Trice. *Presbyterians in the South*. 3 vols. Richmond, 1963–73.

Trinterud, Leonard J. *The Forming of an American Tradition: A Re-examination of Colonial Presbyterianism*. Philadelphia, 1949.

Tucker, George. *The Life of Thomas Jefferson, Third President of the United States*. 2 vols. Philadelphia, 1837.

Tyler, Lyon Gardiner, ed. *Men of Mark in Virginia*. 5 vols. Washington, DC, 1906–9.

Tyler-McGraw, Marie. *At the Falls: Richmond, Virginia, and Its People*. Chapel Hill, 1994.

Underwood, James Lowell. *The Constitution of South Carolina*. Vol. 3. *Church and State, Morality, and Free Expression*. Columbia, SC, 1992.

Weis, Frederick Lewis. *The Colonial Clergy of the Middle Colonies: New York, New Jersey, and Pennsylvania, 1628–1776*. Worcester, MA, 1978.

Westerhoff, John H. *McGuffey and His Readers: Piety, Morality, and Education in Nineteenth-Century America*. Nashville, 1978.

White, Blanche Sydnor. *A History of First Baptist Church, Richmond, 1780–2005*. Richmond, 2005.

White, Henry Alexander. *Southern Presbyterian Leaders*. New York, 1911.

Whitelaw, Ralph T. *Virginia's Eastern Shore: A History of Northampton and Accomack Counties*. Gloucester, MA, 1951.

Wigger, John H. *American Saint: Francis Asbury and the Methodists*. Oxford, 2009.

———. *Taking Heaven by Storm: Methodism and the Rise of Popular Christianity in America*. New York, 1998.

Witte, John, Jr. and Joel A. Nichols. *Religion and the American Constitutional Experiment: Essential Rights and Liberties*. 3d ed. Boulder, CO, 2011.

Wood, Gordon. *The Creation of the American Republic, 1776–1787*. Chapel Hill, 1969.

Wood, Irving, and Elihu Grant. *The Bible as Literature*. New York, 1914.

Worrall, Jay, Jr. *The Friendly Virginians: America's First Quakers*. Athens, GA, 1994.

Worsley, Lizzie, comp. *Old St. James Episcopal Church, Leesburg, Va., 1760–1897*. Leesburg, n.d.

Articles

Berman, Myron. "Rabbi Edward Nathan Calisch and the Debate over Zionism in Richmond, Virginia." *American Jewish Historical Quarterly* 62 (1973): 295–305.

Brown, Lawrence L. "Richard Channing Moore and the Revival of the Southern Church." *HMPEC* 35 (1966): 3–63.

Brydon, G. MacLaren. "A List of Clergy of the Protestant Episcopal Church Ordained after the American Revolution, Who Served in Virginia between 1785 and 1814, and a List of Virginia Parishes and Their Rectors for the Same Period." *WMQ*, 2d ser., 19 (1939): 397–434.

Bryson, W. Hamilton. "Robert Reid Howison." In *The Virginia Law Reporters before 1880*, ed. Bryson. Charlottesville, 1977.

Buckley, Thomas E. "Evangelicals Triumphant: The Baptists' Assault on the Virginia Glebes, 1786–1801." *WMQ*, 3d ser., 45 (1988): 33–69.

Butterfield, Lyman H. "Elder John Leland: Jeffersonian Itinerant." *American Antiquarian Society Proceedings* 62 (1952): 155–242.

Calisch, Edward N. "The Democracy of the Public Schools." *Virginia School Journal* 6 (1897):

———. "Hypocrisies: A Sermon for Eve of Atonement Day." In *Three Score and Twenty: Selected Addresses and Sermons*, 89–96. Richmond, 1945.

———. "What the American Jew Stands For." In *Three Score and Twenty: Selected Addresses and Sermons*, 69–74. Richmond, 1945.

Carroll, Kenneth L. "Quakers on the Eastern Shore of Virginia." *VMHB* 74 (1966): 170–89.

Christian, Joseph. "Hon. R. C. L. Moncure." *Virginia Law Journal* 6 (1883): 708–15.

Crowe, Charles. "Bishop James Madison and the Republic of Virtue." *JSH* 30 (1964): 58–70.

———. "The War of 'Pure Republicanism' against Federalism, 1794–1801: Bishop

James Madison on the American Political Scene." *West Virginia History* 24 (1962–63): 355–62.

Daniel, W. Harrison. "The Genesis of Richmond College, 1843–1860." *VMHB* 83 (1975): 131–49.

Dreisbach, Daniel L. "George Mason's Pursuit of Religious Liberty in Revolutionary Virginia." *VMHB* 108 (2000): 5–44.

———. "A New Perspective on Jefferson's Views on Church-State Relations: The Virginia Statute for Establishing Religious Freedom in Its Legislative Context." *American Journal of Legal History* 35 (Apr. 1991): 172–204.

Fox, Early Lee. "William Henry Ruffner and the Rise of the Public Free School System of Virginia." *John P. Branch Historical Papers of Randolph-Macon College* 3 (1910): 124–44.

Fraser, Walter J., Jr. "William Henry Ruffner and the Establishment of Virginia's Public School System, 1870–1874." *VMHB* 79 (1971): 259–79.

Gardner, Robert G. "Virginia Baptist Statistics, 1966–1790." *VBR* 21 (1982): 1020–38.

Godson, Susan H. "Bishop Richard Channing Moore and the Renewal of the Antebellum Episcopal Church of Virginia." *Va. Cavalcade* 32 (1983): 184–91.

Gohdes, Clarence. "Some Notes on the Unitarian Church in the Ante-bellum South: A Contribution to the History of Southern Liberalism." In *American Studies in Honor of William Kenneth Boyd*, ed. David Kelly Jackson, 327–66. 1940; rept. Freeport, NY, 1968.

Gundersen, Joan Rezner. "The Huguenot Church at Manakin in Virginia, 1700–1750." *Goochland County Historical Society Magazine* 23 (1991): 19–40.

———. "The Myth of the Independent Virginia Vestry." *HMPEC* 44 (1975): 133–41.

Hardwick, Kevin R. "Narratives of Villainy and Virtue: Governor Francis Nicholson and the Character of the Good Ruler in Early Virginia." *JSH* 72 (2006): 39–74.

Henriques, Peter R. "Major Lawrence Washington versus the Reverend Charles Green: A Case Study of the Squire and the Parson." *VMHB* 100 (1992): 233–64.

Henry, William Wirt. "The Presbyterian Church and Religious Liberty in Virginia." *Union Seminary Magazine* 12 (1900–1901): 16–31.

Hockman, Dan M. "'Hellish and Malicious Incendiaries': Commissary William Dawson and Dissent in Colonial Virginia, 1743–1752." *Anglican and Episcopal History* 59 (1990): 150–80.

Hofstra, Warren R. "'The Extension of His Majesties Dominions': The Virginia Backcountry and the Reconfiguration of Imperial Frontiers." *JAH* 84 (1998): 1281–1312.

Holmes, Henry W. "New Forces in Religious Education." *Harvard Theological Review* 3 (1910): 209–29.

Holt, Wythe W., Jr. "The Virginia Constitutional Convention of 1901–1902: A Reform Movement Which Lacked Substance." *VMHB* 76 (1968): 67–102.

Hughes, N. C., Jr. "The Methodist Christmas Conference: Baltimore, December 24, 1784–January 2, 1785." *Maryland Historical Magazine* 54 (1959): 272–92.

Humphries, W. R. "The Literary Study of the Bible in Michigan High Schools." *English Journal* 6 (1917): 209–20.

Isaac, Rhys. "Religion and Authority: Problems of the Anglican Establishment in Virginia in the Era of the Great Awakening and the Parsons' Cause." *WMQ*, 3d ser., 30 (1973): 3–36.

Kauper, Paul G., and Stephen C. Ellis. "Religious Corporations and the Law." *Michigan Law Review* 71 (1972–73): 1499–1574.

Kierner, Cynthia A. "'The Dark and Dense Cloud Perpetually Lowering over Us': Gender and the Decline of the Gentry in Postrevolutionary Virginia." *JER* 20 (2000): 185–217.

Kneebone, John T. "'It Must Be a Hoax': Protest, Cultural Pride, and Richmond's Columbus Statute." *Virginia Cavalcade* 42 (1992): 84–95.

Lamb, Brockenbrough. "Charles V. Meredith." *Proceedings of the Forty-First Annual Meeting. The Virginia State Bar Association . . . 1930*, 245–52. [Richmond, 1930].

Lumpkin, William L. "Early Virginia Baptist Church Covenants." *VBR* 16 (1977): 772–88.

Maier, Pauline. "The Revolutionary Origins of the American Corporation." *WMQ*, 3d ser., 50 (1993): 51–84.

Malone, Kathryn. "The Fate of Revolutionary Republicanism in Early National Virginia" *JER* 7 (1987): 27–51.

Mathews, Donald. "The Second Great Awakening as an Organizing Process, 1780–1830: An Hypothesis." *American Quarterly* 21 (1969): 23–43.

McLoughlin, William G. "Isaac Backus and the Separation of Church and State in America." *American Historical Review* 73 (1968): 1392–1413.

———. "The Role of Religion in the Revolution: Liberty of Conscience and Cultural Cohesion in the New Nation." In *Essays on the American Revolution*, ed. Stephen G. Kurtz and James H. Hutson, 230–53. Chapel Hill, 1973.

Mills, Frederick V., Sr. "The Colonial Anglican Episcopate: A Historiographical Review." *American Ecclesiastical Review* 61 (1992): 325–45.

Moore, R. Lawrence. "What Children Did Not Learn in School: The Intellectual Quickening of Young Americans in the Nineteenth Century." *Church History* 68 (Mar. 1999): 42–61.

Moorhouse, William M. "Alexander Campbell and the Virginia Constitutional Convention of 1829–1830." *Virginia Cavalcade* 24 (1975): 184–91.

Morgan, Bruce. "Stephen Colwell (1800–1871): Social Prophet before the Social Gospel." In *Sons of the Prophets: Leaders in Protestantism from Princeton Seminary*, ed. Hugh T. Kerr, 123–47. Princeton, NJ, 1963.

Mulder, Philip N. "Converting the New Light: Presbyterian Evangelicalism in Hanover, Virginia." *JPH* 75 (1997): 141–52.

Nord, David Paul. "The Evangelical Origins of Mass Media in America, 1815–1835." *Journalism Monographs* 88 (1984): 1–30.

Norwood, William. "Sketch of the Life and Character of Bishop Moore." *SLM* 8 (1842): 19–23.

Pilcher, George. "The Pamphlet War on the Proposed Virginia Anglican Episcopate, 1767–1775." *HMPEC* 30 (1961): 266–79.

———. "Virginia Newspapers and the Dispute over the Proposed Colonial Episcopate, 1771–1772." *Historian: A Journal of History* 23 (1960): 98–113.

Ragosta, John A. "Fighting for Freedom: Virginia Dissenters Struggle for Religious Liberty during the American Revolution." *VMBH* 113 (2008): 227–61.

Rainbolt, John Corbin. "The Struggle to Define 'Religious Liberty' in Maryland, 1776–1785." *Journal of Church and State* 17 (1975): 443–58.

Rankin, Hugh F. "The Gen. Court of Colonial Virginia: Its Jurisdiction and Personnel." *VMHB* 70 (1962): 142–53.

Scheiber, Harry N. "American Constitutional History and the New Legal History: Complementary Themes in Two Modes." *JAH* 68 (1981): 337–50.

Shockley, Martin Staples. "The Proprietors of Richmond's New Theatre of 1819." *WMQ*, 2d ser., 19 (1939): 302–8.

Smith, B[enjamin] M. "Merits and Defects of Common School Education in the United States." *EJV* 1 (1870): 318–29.

Smith, Elwyn A. "The Role of the South in the Presbyterian Schism of 1837–1838." *Church History* 29 (1960): 44–63.

Smylie, James H. "Francis Makemie: Tradition and Challenge." *JPH* 61 (1983): 197–209.

Spangler, Jewel L. "Becoming Baptists: Conversion in Colonial and Early National Virginia." *JSH* 67 (2001): 243–86.

Staples, Abram P. "William Gordon Robertson." In *Report of the Twenty-Second Annual Meeting of the Virginia State Bar Association*, ed. John B. Minor, 33 (1910): 100–109.

Steiner, Bruce Edward. "The Catholic Brents of Colonial Virginia: An Instance of Practical Toleration." *VMHB* 70 (1962): 387–409.

Stitt, Susan. "The Will of Stephen Charlton and Hungars Parish Glebe." *VMHB* 77 (1969): 259–63.

Sutton, Robert P. "Nostalgia, Pessimism, and Malaise: The Doomed Aristocrat in Late-Jeffersonian Virginia." *VMHB* 76 (1968): 41–55.

Sweeney, James R. "Rum, Romanism, and Virginia Democrats: The Party Leaders and the Campaign of 1928." *VMHB* 90 (1982): 403–31.

Swift, David E. "Thomas Jefferson, John Holt Rice, and Education in Virginia, 1815–1825." *JPH* 49 (1971): 32–58.

Sydnor, William, "David Griffith—Chaplain, Surgeon, Patriot." *HMPEC* 44 (1975): 247–56.

———. "Doctor Griffith of Virginia: Emergence of a Church Leader, March 1779–June 3, 1786." *HMPEC* 45 (1976): 5–24.

———. "Doctor Griffith of Virginia: The Breaking of a Church Leader, September 1786–August 3, 1789." *HMPEC* 45 (1976): 113–32.

Tate, Thad W. "The Coming of the Revolution in Virginia: Britain's Challenge to Virginia's Ruling Class, 1763–1776." *WMQ*, 3d ser., 19 (1962): 324–43.

Thomas, Arthur Dicken, Jr. "Reasonable Revivalism: Presbyterian Evangelization of Educated Virginians, 1787–1837." *JPH* 61 (1983): 316–34.

Tyler, Lyon G. "Major Edmund Chisman, Jr." *WMQ*, 1st ser., 1 (1892): 89–98.

Webb, Stephen Saunders. "The Strange Career of Francis Nicholson." *WMQ*, 3d ser., 23 (1966): 513–48.

Wright, C. "Piety, Morality, and the Commonwealth." *Crane Review* 9 (1967): 90–106.

Wyatt-Brown, Bertram. "The Antimission Movement in the Jacksonian South: A Study in Regional Folk Culture." *JSH* 36 (1970): 501–29.

DISSERTATIONS, THESES, AND UNPUBLISHED ESSAYS

Berman, Myron. "Edward Nathan Calisch, an American Rabbi in the South: His Views on the 'Promised Land.'" Paper read at the 70th annual meeting of the American Jewish Historical Society, Richmond, on May 5–7, 1972. Calisch Papers, box 1, Beth Ahabah Archives, Richmond.

Bidwell, Robert Leland. "The Morris Reading-Houses: A Study in Dissent." MA thesis: College of William and Mary, 1948.

Dresbeck, Sandra Ryan. "The Episcopalian Clergy in Maryland and Virginia, 1765–1805." PhD diss., Univ. of California, 1976.

Fraser, Walter J., Jr. "William Henry Ruffner: A Liberal in the Old and New South." PhD diss., Univ. of Tennessee, 1971.

Hellenbrand, Harold Leonard. "The Unfinished Revolution: Education and Community in the Thought of Thomas Jefferson." PhD diss., Stanford Univ., 1980.

Holmes, David Lynn. "William Meade and the Church of Virginia, 1789–1829." PhD diss., Princeton Univ., 1971.

Holt, Wythe W., Jr. "Virginia's Constitutional Convention of 1901–02." PhD diss., Univ. of Virginia, 1979.

Hopewell, John S. "An Outsider Looking In: John Garland Pollard and Machine Politics in Twentieth Century Virginia." PhD diss., Univ. of Virginia, 1976.

Lohrenz, Otto. "The Virginia Clergy and the American Revolution, 1773–1799." PhD diss., Univ. of Kansas, 1970.

Sutton, Robert P. "The Virginia Constitutional Convention of 1829–30: A Profile Analysis of Late Jeffersonian Virginia." PhD diss., Univ. of Virginia, 1967.

Waukechon, John Frank. "The Forgotten Evangelicals: Virginia Episcopalians, 1790–1876." PhD diss., Univ. of Texas at Austin, 2000.

Index

Italicized page numbers refer to illustrations.

Abingdon Academy, 178
Abington School District v. Schempp, 231, 256
Accomack County, 13–14, 58, 94, 169
Adams, John, 53, 62, 69, 112, 167, 171
Adams, John (mayor of Richmond), 180
Adams, Samuel, 244–45, 247
African Americans, 9, 87, 180–81, 200, 214; pastoral care of, 22, 30, 41, 114; as subject at Convention of 1901, 87, 114; emancipation of, as slaves, 180; percentage in Richmond in 1924 (table), 246
Ahavath Israel, denied incorporation, 137
Alexander, Rev. Archibald, 146, 148, 151, 198
Alexandria, 26, 27, 67, 105, 117, 123, 137, 145, 151; as site of the Episcopal Seminary, 155, 189
Allen, William, 204–5
Ambler, John, 100
American Protective Association, 235
American Revolution: Presbyterian support for, 69; Baptist support for, 71, 102
Anabaptists, 43, 47
Anglicanism, Anglicans. *See* Church of England in Virginia; Protestant Episcopal Church in U.S.; Protestant Episcopal Church in Virginia
anticlericalism, 35–37, 160, 173–75
Antrim Parish (Halifax Co.), glebe contest in, 100–101
Asbury, Bishop Francis, 74–76, 87, 150, 159
Asplund, John, *Register* of, 91
assessment for religion, 59, 65, 68, 76–77, 119–20, 122; support for, 69–70; opposition to, 70–72; defeat of, 79–82; Bishop Madison's position on, 120, 277n89
Atkinson, Archibald, 194

Atkinson, Roger, 38
Atkinson, William, 187
Avery, Benjamin, 24

Backus, Rev. Isaac, 91, 97, 109
Bacon, Nathaniel, 12
Baker, Rev. Elijah, 58
Baltimore, 73, 76, 112
Baltimore and Richmond Christian Advocate, 235
Bancroft, George, 2
Baptists, 1, 3, 8, 39–40, 143, 151, 157, 202; beliefs of, 12, 88; growth of, 39, 79, 87, 91, 102; persecution of, 40–44; and race, 41; petitions of, 46, 52, 60, 72, 79, 81–83, 177; supported by Patrick Henry, 47–48; support Jefferson's statute, 71–72, 81, 206; General Committee of, 72, 83, 85, 88–90, 92–94, 96, 102–6, 150; polity of, 89–90; disagree among themselves, 94, 237, 249; reasons for political success, 102–8; General Association of, 106, 133–34, 245, 250, 279n24; ask for incorporation, 131; support legislation of morality, 159; number in Virginia in 1906 (table), 209; oppose state funds for sectarian institutions, 223
—associations of, 39, 52, 72, 83, 88, 106–7, 139, 149–50, 157, 180, 222, 250; Kehukee, 39; Ketocton, 88; Dover, 89, 149–50, 157, 202, 204; —, asks state protection for religious services, 179; —, opposes state funding of sectarian institutions, 222; Roanoke, 94, 103; Goshen, 104; Old School, 139; Appomattox, 178
—varieties of: General Baptists, 14, 39; Separates, 26, 39, 88, 90; Regulars, 39, 88, 90, 278n20; Anti-mission (Old School)

Gabriel's revolt, 112

Gallego, Joseph, bequest voided by court of appeals, 129, 137

gambling, 108, 159, 161, 162, 177–78, 181; 1924 law against, 245, 248–49

Gardiner, Rev. Walter, 118

Gardner, Rev. Charles, 237

Garland, James, 194

George I, King, 33

German Reformed, 14, 28, 143

Giberne, Rev. Isaac William, 35–36, 268n14

Gilmer, Francis Walker, 185, 187

Glass, Carter, 219–20, 225, 229, 253

Glassell, Andrew, 41–42

Gooch, Gov. William, 16–17, 19–22, 33

Goode, John, 208, 213

Goode, William O., 194

Gordon, James, 31

Gordon, John, 156

Grace Street Baptist Church (Richmond), 212, 237

Graham, Rev. William, 171

Great Awakening, 4–5, 18, 39, 74. *See also* Second Great Awakening

Green, Rev. Charles, tithe list of, 26–27

Green, Steven, 5

Gregg, Rev. Jacob, 156

Griffith, Rev. David, 67, 72, 77–79, 81, 84–86, 117, 120, 124

Grigsby, Hugh Blair, 173

Grund, Francis, 176

Gwatkin, Rev. Thomas, 45–46

Hamburger, Philip, 5

Hampden-Sydney College, 69, 145–46, 151, 193, 198–99, 202, 204, 208; revivals at, 88–89; seeks state assistance, 105, 195

Hanley, Mark Y., 138

Hanover Presbytery, 29, 52, 55, 60, 69, 71, 83, 88, 105–6, 147, 159, 176

Harris, Elizabeth, 9

Hawthorne, Rev. James B., 235, 237

Hay, Rev. Alexander, 100

Hay, George, 120

Heath, James, 185

Henley, Rev. Samuel, 45–46

Henrico Parish, 67, 92, 162

Henry, John, 8, 37

Henry, Rev. Patrick, 7–8, 18–21, 23, 24, 37

Henry, Patrick, Jr., 8, 63, 67–68, 70, 212, 214; support for religious liberty, 37–39, 47–48, 53–54; links religion and virtue, 61–64, 65–66, 127; supports traditional Christianity, 65–66; and legislative prayers, 184

Henry, Sarah, 38

Henry, William Wirt, 222

Hill, Rev. William, 158

Hoge, Rev. Beverly Lacy, 240–41

Hoge, Rev. Moses Drury, 136, 145

Holloway, John, 17

Holmes (later Cocke), Louisa, 153

Hoover, Herbert, 254

Horne, Herman Harrell, 24

Horrocks, Rev. James, 44–45

horse racing, 159, 162, 177, 179, 181

Hosmer, Frederick Lucian, 250

House of Burgesses, 14, 23, 27, 30, 38, 43–44, 46, 48, 52–53

Howard, Francis, Baron Howard of Effingham, 11–12

Huguenots, 14

Hungars Parish glebe (Northampton Co.), 116, 117–18

infidelity, 109, 112, 127, 146–47, 166, 168, 192, 234

Ireland, Rev. James, 42

Isaac, Rhys, 5, 34, 38

Jackson, Rev. Thomas, 124

James II, King, 11–12

James, Rev. Charles Fenton, 222

Jarratt, Rev. Devereaux, 74–75, 109

Jay, John, 103

Jefferson, Thomas, ii, 1, 51, 54, 56–57, 62, 64, 157, 168, 171, 203, 206; drafts the statute, 1, 58; in Va. General Assembly, 56, 58; on religion, 60, 66, 148, 166; applauds the statute's passage, 82; silence on the glebe issue, 104; on clerical office-holding, 171–72, 181; lottery bill for, 178, 302n43; as rector of the University of Virginia, 190–92; on education, 206–7; and French infidelity, 234

Jenkins, Luther, 245

McCroskey, Elizabeth Bowdoin, 116–18, 125
McCroskey, Rev. Samuel Smith, 116–18, 120
McDaniel, Rev. George White, 240–45, 241, 247–54, 256
McDaniel, Martha Scarborough, 250
McDowell, James, 197–98
McGuffey, Rev. William Holmes, 193, 200
McIlwaine, Rev. Richard, 208–9, 219–20
McRoberts, Rev. Archibald, 74, 106
Mead, Rev. Stith, 159, 179
Mead, Thomas, 172
Meade, Bishop William, 34, 67, 107–8, 148, 151, 153, 162, 175, 179, 192; on church incorporation, 130, 134, 138
Mennonites, 14, 16, 28, 39, 52
Menzies, Rev. Adam, 31, 32
Mercer, Charles Fenton, 162, 163
Meredith, Charles, 225–26
Meredith, Samuel, 223
Methodist Episcopal Church: formation of, 72–76; doctrine and worship of, 73–74, 87–88, 153, 234; polity of, 74–75; growth of, 75, 87, 105, 125, 151, 166; rejects assessment and incorporation, 76–77, competition with Baptists, 90, 91, 105; division of, 105; and church property issue, 105–7; Virginia Conference of, 136, 150, 193, 245; moral issues of, 159, 163, 179, 245, 246; asks state protection for religious services, 179–80; colleges of, 197; number in Virginia in 1906 (table), 209; delegates in Constitutional Convention of 1901–2 (table), 210; number in Richmond in 1924 (table), 246. See also Bible: in the schools; camp meetings; Coke, Bishop Thomas; Early, Bishop John; Jarrett, Rev. Devereaux; Methodists; Wesley, Rev. John
Methodists, 2, 3, 105; banned in colony, 20; favor church incorporation at convention of 1901, 216, 219, 220; oppose state funding of sectarian institutions, 223; support for established church, 272n4
Minor, John Barbee, 183, 193, 201
missionaries, 44, 166; useful to government, 30
Moncure, Richard Cassius Lee, 137, 186
Monroe, James, 85, 169

Monumental Church (Richmond), 150–52, 154, 161, 165, 297n66
Moore, Bishop Richard Channing, 123–24, 130, 151–53, 154, 155, 158, 160–65, 188–89, 216
Moore, R. Walton, 216
morality: concern for, 44; linked to religion, 64–66, 69, 111, 119–20, 156, 158, 176, 235; laws urged for, 72, 177; Bible as a source of, 182, 192, 196, 239, 241; Jefferson and, 190; taught in common schools, 198, 204–5. See also dancing; gambling; horse racing; theaters
Morgantown, Baptist division in, 143
Morris, Samuel, 18, 20
Mount Carmel Baptist Church (Page Co.), trustees of, 143
Muir, Rev. James, 145

Nansemond County, Quakers in, 10–11, 15
Native Americans, missions to, 30
Nelson, John, 8
New Castle Presbytery, 18, 20
Newport News, 238
Newport Parish (Isle of Wight Co.), 15
News Leader (Richmond), 237
New York University, 248
Nicholas, Philip Norborne, 120
Nicholas, Robert Carter, 33, 46–48, 50–53, 56, 59, 122
Nicholson, Francis, 12–16
Noonan, John, 58
Norfolk, 73, 146, 153, 156, 189, 215, 221, 223–24, 227–28, 244, 246–48
Norris, Rev. Oliver, 151
North Carolina, 39, 75, 129, 131, 219, 234
Northumberland County, 17, 30–31

Odd Fellows, 137
O'Kelly, Rev. James, 105, 283n74
Old Bachelor, The (Wirt et al.), 153
overseers of the poor, 27, 100–101, 114, 117–19, 122–24, 127, 129

Page, John, 60, 77–80
Parliament, 11–12, 13, 16, 121, 182
Parsons, John May, 251